AUSTERITY

MARK BLYTH

AUSTERITY

THE HISTORY OF A DANGEROUS IDEA

OXFORD
UNIVERSITY PRESS

OXFORD
UNIVERSITY PRESS

Oxford University Press is a department of the University of Oxford.
It furthers the University's objective of excellence in research, scholarship,
and education by publishing worldwide.

Oxford   New York
Auckland   Cape Town   Dar es Salaam   Hong Kong   Karachi
Kuala Lumpur   Madrid   Melbourne   Mexico City   Nairobi
New Delhi   Shanghai   Taipei   Toronto

With offices in
Argentina   Austria   Brazil   Chile   Czech Republic   France   Greece
Guatemala   Hungary   Italy   Japan   Poland   Portugal   Singapore
South Korea   Switzerland   Thailand   Turkey   Ukraine   Vietnam

Oxford is a registered trademark of Oxford University Press in the UK and certain other
countries.

Published in the United States of America by
Oxford University Press
198 Madison Avenue, New York, NY 10016

© Oxford University Press 2013

First issued as an Oxford University Press paperback, 2015

Blyth, Mark, 1967-
Austerity : the history of a dangerous idea / Mark Blyth.
pages cm
Includes bibliographical references and index.
ISBN 978-0-19-982830-2 (cloth); 978-0-19-938944-5 (pbk)   1. Debts, Public.
2. Budget deficits.   3. Financial crises.   4. Economic policy.   5. Fiscal policy.
6. Economic development.   7. Income.   I. Title.
HJ8015.B59 2013
336–dc23
2012046882

9 8 7
Printed in the United States of America
on acid-free paper

For Jules

This book has cost you as many hours as it has cost me, possibly more. I really could not have written this without your love and support. Thank you.

CONTENTS

Part Three Conclusion

PREFACE: AUSTERITY, A PERSONAL HISTORY

This book has a rather unusual genesis. David McBride from Oxford University Press emailed me in July 2010 and asked me if I wanted to write a book about the turn to austerity in economic policy. I had been playing with a book idea called the "End of the Liberal World" for a while but really hadn't been getting all that far with it. Dave's offer seemed to be a ready-made alternative project. After all, someone had to write such a book, and since I had, as bankers say, "skin in the game" here, for reasons I shall elaborate below, I said yes. Shortly thereafter Geoffrey Kirkman, Associate Director of the Watson Institute for International Studies at Brown University, where I am a faculty fellow, wondered if there was anything that I would like to make into a short video. I said yes—I'd do something about this new book that I have agreed to write.

Both of these opportunities arrived shortly after the G20 issued its final communiqué at the end of its June 2010 meeting in Toronto. That G20 meeting marked the moment when the rediscovery of Keynesian economics that had informed state responses to the global financial crisis since 2009 gave way to an economically more orthodox, and austere, reading of events. The G20 communiqué called for an end to reflationary spending under the guise of something called "growth friendly fiscal consolidation," which is a fancy way of saying "austerity."

I remember thinking at the time "that's about as plausible as a unicorn with a bag of magic salt." So when I was afforded the opportunity to make a video, taking on this "austerity as a route to growth" nonsense seemed the way to go. The video can be seen at http://www.youtube.com/watch?v=FmsjGys-VqA.

Part of what academics do is generate ideas and teach. The other, perhaps more important part, is to play the role of "the Bu*l*hit Police." Our job is to look at the ideas and plans interested parties put forward to solve our collective problems and see whether or not they pass the sniff test. Austerity as a route to growth and as the correct response to the aftermath of a financial crisis does not pass the sniff test. The arguments given for why we all must be austere do not pass the sniff test. You will read the full version of why not in this book. The short version became the video. But in shooting the video, the producer Joe Posner forced me to distill what I wanted to say about this topic into five-and-a-half minutes. Once I did that, I went back to the book and wondered if I had anything else to say.

The opportunity to get into more detail and flesh out the argument, the academic rationale, was still there. Both the reasons given for why we all have to be austere (we have spent too much, etc.) and the logics expounded for the supposed positive effects of austerity as a policy—that cuts lead to growth—are, as we shall see, by and large dangerous nonsense. Yet they remain the governing ideas of the moment. By the time the book is published this may no longer be the case, but in the meantime, these ideas will have wrought tremendous damage.

Part of the reason for this is, as we shall see, ideological. But part of the reason these ideas are so powerful is very material. It has to do with how a "too big to fail" banking crisis in the United States became a "too big to bail" banking crisis in Europe, and how this drives us all down the road to austerity. We are, at best, still saving the banks that we started saving in 2008, especially in Europe. This book allowed me to work out why such bad ideas remain the governing ideas, for both ideological and material reasons. But going back to the book after doing the video made me remember another much more personal reason why I should write this book that has to do with the unfairness of austerity as a policy.

I was born in Dundee, Scotland, in 1967, the son of a butcher and a television rental agent (yes, back in the day, TVs were so expensive that most people rented them). My mother died when I was very young, and my care was given over to my paternal grandmother. I grew up in (relative) poverty, and there were times when I really did go to school with holes in my shoes. My upbringing was, in the original sense of the word, quite austere. Household income was a government check, namely, a state retirement pension, plus occasional handouts from my manual-worker father. I am a welfare kid. I am also proud of that fact.

Today I am a professor at an Ivy League university in the USA. Probabilistically speaking, I am as an extreme example of intragenerational social mobility as you can find anywhere. What made it possible for me to become the man I am today is the very thing now blamed for creating the crisis itself: the state, more specifically, the so-called runaway, bloated, paternalist, out-of-control, welfare state. This claim doesn't pass the sniff test. Because of the British welfare state, threadbare though it is in comparison to its more affluent European cousins, I was never hungry. My grandmother's pension plus free school meals took care of that. I never lacked shelter because of social housing. The schools I attended were free and actually acted as ladders of mobility for those randomly given the skills in the genetic lottery of life to climb them.

So what bothers me on a deep personal level is that if austerity is seen as the only way forward, then not only is it unfair to the current generation of "workers bailing bankers," but the next "me" may not happen.[1] The social mobility that societies such as the United Kingdom and the United States took for granted from the 1950s through the 1980s that made me, and others like me, possible, has effectively ground to a halt.[2] Youth unemployment across the developed world has reached, in many cases, record levels. Austerity policies have only worsened these problems. Cutting the welfare state in the name of producing more growth and opportunity is an offensive canard. The purpose of this book is to make us all remember that and thereby help to ensure that the future does not belong only to the already privileged few. Frankly, the world can use a few more welfare kids that become professors. It keeps the rest honest.

A word about the book itself. It's designed to be modular. If you want an overview of what's at stake in the fight over austerity, just read chapter 1. If you want to know why we all have to be austere and why a pile of stinky mortgages in the United States ended up blowing up the European economy, read chapters 2 and 3. If you want to know where the notion that austerity is a good idea comes from in terms of its intellectual lineage, read chapters 4 and 5. If you want to know why austerity is such a dangerous idea, apart from what's in chapters 2 and 3, read chapter 6. If you want one-stop shopping for why the world is in such a mess and you are being asked to pay for it—read the whole book.

I would now like to thank all the many folks who made this book come to its final overdue form. Special thanks go to Cornel Ban for his help with the East European cases and Oddny Helgadottir for her help with Iceland. For clarifying the US side of the story, many thanks to David Wyss, Beth Ann Bovino, Bruce Chadwick, and David Frenk. On the European side, special thanks go to Peter Hall, Andrew Baker, Bill Blain, Martin Malone, Simon Tilford, Daniel Davies, David Lewis Baker, Douglas Borthwick, Erik Jones, Matthias Matthijs, Josef Hien, Jonathan Hopkin, Kathleen McNamara, Nicolas Jabko, Jonathan Kirshner, Sheri Berman, Martin Edwards, Gerald McDermott, Brigitte Young, Mark Vail, Wade Jacoby, Abe Newman, Cornelia Woll, Colin Hay, Vivien Schmidt, Stefan Olafson, Bill Janeway, Romano Prodi, and Alfred Gussenbauer. For being my econo-nonsense detectors I owe Stephen Kinsella and Alex Gourevitch a special debt of thanks. Other folks who deserve a mention in this regard are Dirk Bezemer and John Quiggin. Chris Lydon helped me find my voice. Lorenzo Moretti helped me find my footnotes. Anthony Lopez helped me find what other folks had said already. Alex Harris found data like no one else can.

I want to thank the Watson Institute at Brown University for its help and support, and to express my gratitude to my colleagues at Brown University for providing such a supportive working environment. I want to thank the Institute for New Economic Thinking for actually enabling new economic thinking. Cheers to Joe Posner for producing the austerity video and to Robin Varghese for sending me things I would never have found. Intellectually, two rather contradic-

tory (in terms of each other) folks are important, one of whom—
Andrew Haldane— I have yet to meet, and Nassim Nicolas Taleb.
Thank you both for making me think harder about the world. Finally,
to David McBride at Oxford University Press for having the presence
of mind to ask, to push from time to time, and to leave me alone when
needed. But most of all, thanks for keeping the faith. To anyone I left
off this list, my apologies. As was once said about Dr. Leonard McCoy
by a Klingon prosecutor, it's most likely a combination of age plus
drink.

Mark Blyth
South Boston, Massachusetts
December 2012

A PRIMER ON AUSTERITY, DEBT, AND MORALITY PLAYS

Why Austerity?

On Friday, August 5, 2011, what used to be the fiscally unthinkable happened. The United States of America lost its triple A (AAA) credit rating when it was downgraded by the ratings agency Standard & Poor's (S&P's). This is a bit of a problem since the US dollar is the world's reserve currency, which means (basically) that the dollar is treated as the emergency store of value for the rest of the world; practically all tradable commodities, for example, are valued in relation to the dollar, and the dollar serves as the anchor of the world's monetary system. The following Monday, August 8, 2011, the Dow Jones Industrial Average (DJIA) lost 635 points, its sixth worst loss ever. At the same time, a continent away, the turmoil in the European bond market that began in Greece in 2009 now threatened to engulf Italy and Spain, undermining the European single currency while raising doubts about the solvency of the entire European banking system. Meanwhile, London, one of the world's great financial centers, was hit by riots that spread all over the city, and then the country.

The London riots quickly blew over, but then the Occupy movement began, first in Zuccotti Park in Manhattan, and then throughout the United States and out into the wider world. Its motivations were diffuse, but one stood out: concern over the income and wealth in-equalities generated over the past twenty years that access to easy credit had masked.[1] Winter, and police actions, emptied the Occupy encampments, but the problems that spawned those camps remain with us. Today, the European financial-cum-debt crisis rolls on from summit meeting to summit meeting, where German ideals of fiscal prudence clash with Spanish unemployment at 25 percent and a Greek state is slashing itself to insolvency and mass poverty while being given ever-more loans to do so. In the United States, those prob-lems take the form of sclerotic private-sector growth, persistent un-employment, a hollowing out of middle-class opportunities, and a gridlocked state. If we view each of these elements in isolation, it all looks rather chaotic. But look closer and you can see that these events are all intimately related. What they have in common is their sup-posed cure: austerity, the policy of cutting the state's budget to pro-mote growth.

Austerity is a form of voluntary deflation in which the economy adjusts through the reduction of wages, prices, and public spending to restore competitiveness, which is (supposedly) best achieved by cut-ting the state's budget, debts, and deficits. Doing so, its advocates believe, will inspire "business confidence" since the government will neither be "crowding-out" the market for investment by sucking up all the available capital through the issuance of debt, nor adding to the nation's already "too big" debt.

As pro-austerity advocate John Cochrane of the University of Chi-cago put it, "Every dollar of increased government spending must cor-respond to one less dollar of private spending. Jobs created by stimulus spending are offset by jobs lost from the decline in private spending. We can build roads instead of factories, but fiscal stimulus can't help us to build more of both."[2] There is just one slight problem with this rendition of events: it is completely and utterly wrong, and the policy of austerity is more often than not exactly the wrong thing to do pre-cisely because it produces the very outcomes you are trying to avoid.

Take the reason S&P's gave for downgrading the US credit rating. They claimed that, "the prolonged controversy over raising the statu-tory debt ceiling and the related fiscal policy debate...will remain a contentious and fitful process."[3] Yet the DJIA didn't fall off a cliff because of the downgrade. To see a downgrade on Friday followed by a DJIA collapse on a Monday is to confuse causation and correlation. Had the markets actually been concerned about the solvency of the US government, that concern would have been reflected in bond yields (the interest the United States has to pay to get someone to hold its debt) before and after the downgrade. Bond yields should have gone up after the downgrade as investors lost faith in US debt, and money should have flowed into the stock market as a refuge. Instead, yields and equities fell together because what sent the markets down was a broader concern over a slowing US economy: a lack of growth.

This is doubly odd since the cause of the anticipated slowdown, the debt-ceiling agreement of August 1, 2011, between Republicans and Democrats in the US Senate that sought $2.1 trillion in budget cuts over a decade (austerity), was supposed to calm the markets by giving them the budget cuts that they craved. Yet this renewed commitment to austerity instead signaled lower growth due to less public spending going forward in an already weak economy, and stock markets tanked on the news. As Oliver Blanchard, the International Monetary Fund's (IMF's) director of research, put it with a degree of understatement, "Financial investors are schizophrenic about fiscal consolidation and growth."[4] Today the US debt drama is about to repeat itself in the form of a so-called fiscal cliff that the United States will fall off when automatic spending cuts kick in in January 2013 if Congress cannot decide on what to cut. The schizophrenia Blanchard identified a year previously continues on this second iteration, with both sides simultaneously stressing the need for cuts while trying to avoid them.

Austerity policies were likewise supposed to provide stability to the Eurozone countries, not undermine them. Portugal, Ireland, Italy, Greece, and Spain (the PIIGS of Europe) have all implemented tough austerity packages since the financial crisis hit them in 2008. Greece's bloated public-sector debt, Spain's overleveraged private sector, Portugal's and Italy's illiquidity, and Ireland's insolvent banks ended up being bailed out by their respective states, blowing holes in their debts and deficits. The answer to their problems, as with the US debt-ceiling agreement, was supposed to be austerity. Cut the budget, reduce the debt, and growth will reappear as "confidence" returns.

So PIIGS cut their budgets and as their economies shrank, their debt loads got bigger not smaller, and unsurprisingly, their interest payments shot up. Portuguese net debt to GDP increased from 62 percent in 2006 to 108 percent in 2012, while the interest that pays for Portugal's ten-year bonds went from 4.5 percent in May 2009 to 14.7 percent in January 2012. Ireland's net debt-to-GDP ratio of 24.8 percent in 2007 rose to 106.4 percent in 2012, while its ten-year bonds went from 4 percent in 2007 to a peak of 14 percent in 2011. The poster child of the Eurozone crisis and austerity policy, Greece saw its debt to GDP rise from 106 percent in 2007 to 170 percent in 2012 despite successive rounds of austerity cuts and bondholders taking a 75 percent loss on their holdings in 2011. Greece's ten-year bond currently pays 13 percent, down from a high of 18.5 percent in November 2012.[5]

Austerity clearly is not working if "not working" means reducing the debt and promoting growth. Instead, in making these governments' bonds riskier (as seen in the interest rate charged), the policy has indirectly made big European banks that hold lots of them (mainly in Germany, France, and Holland) riskier in the process. This was recognized by global investors when pretty much all private-sector lending to the European banking sector disappeared in the summer and fall of 2011, the response to which has been emergency liquidity provision by the European Central Bank (ECB) in the form of the so-called long-term refinancing operation (LTRO), the ancilliary emergency liquidity assistance program (ELA), and of course, demands for more austerity.[6]

The United Kingdom was supposedly spared this drama by "preemptive tightening," that is, by adopting austerity first and then reaping the benefits of growth once confidence returns. Again, this approach hasn't turned out quite as planned. Despite the fact that the United Kingdom's bond yields are lower than many of its peers', this has less to do with pursuing austerity and more to do with the fact that it has its own central bank and currency. It can therefore credibly commit to backing its banking sector with unlimited cash in a way that countries inside the Euro Area cannot, while allowing the exchange rate to depreciate since it still has one.[7] UK growth certainly hasn't sprung back in response either, and neither has confidence. The British are in as bad shape as anyone else, despite their tightening, and the

United Kingdom's economic indictors are very much pointing the wrong way, showing again that austerity hurts rather than helps.

It's Not Really a Sovereign Debt Crisis

That austerity simply doesn't work is the first reason it's a dangerous idea. But it is also a dangerous idea because the way austerity is being represented by both politicians and the media—as the payback for something called the "sovereign debt crisis," supposedly brought on by states that apparently "spent too much"—is a quite fundamental misrepresentation of the facts. These problems, including the crisis in the bond markets, started with the banks and will end with the banks. The current mess is not a sovereign debt crisis generated by excessive spending for anyone except the Greeks. For everyone else, the problem is the banks that sovereigns have to take responsibility for, especially in the Eurozone. That we call it a "sovereign debt crisis" suggests a very interesting politics of "bait and switch" at play.

Before 2008 no one, save for a few fringe conservatives in the United States and elsewhere, were concerned with "excessive" national debts or deficits. Deficit hawks in the United States, for example, pretty much disappeared in embarrassment as, under the banner of fiscal conservativism, the Bush administration pushed both debts and deficits to new heights while inflation remained steady.[8] Even in places where fiscal prudence was the mantra, in the United Kingdom under Gordon Brown, or in Spain and Ireland when they were held up as economic models for their dynamic economies—really—deficits and debt did not garner much attention. Italian public-sector debt in 2002 was 105.7 percent of GDP and no one cared. In 2009, it was almost exactly the same figure and everyone cared.

What changed was of course the global financial crisis of 2007–2008 that rumbles along in a new form today. The cost of bailing, recapitalizing, and otherwise saving the global banking system has been, depending on, as we shall see later, how you count it, between 3 and 13 trillion dollars.[9] Most of that has ended up on the balance sheets of governments as they absorb the costs of the bust, which is why we mistakenly call this a sovereign debt crisis when in fact it is a transmuted and well-camouflaged banking crisis.

As we shall see in chapter 2, the US banking system, the origin of the global banking crisis, was deemed by the US government to be "too big to fail" and therefore wasn't allowed to fail when it got into trouble in 2007–2008. The price of not allowing it to fail was to turn the Federal Reserve into a "bad bank" (chock-full of bad assets that were swapped for cash to keep lending going) while the federal government blew a hole in its finances as it plugged the gaps caused by lost revenues from the crash with deficit spending and debt issuance. No good deed, as they say, goes unpunished. This much we know. What is less well known is how part two of this crisis is simply another variant of this story currently playing out in Europe.

The Greeks may well have lied about their debts and deficits, as is alleged, but as we shall see in chapter 3, the Greeks are the exception, not the rule. What actually happened in Europe was that over the decade of the introduction of the euro, very large core-country European banks bought lots of peripheral sovereign debt (which is now worth much less) and levered up (reduced their equity and increased their debt to make more profits) far more than their American cousins. Being levered up, in some cases forty to one or more, means that a turn of a few percentage points against their assets can leave them insolvent.[10] As a consequence, rather than being too big to fail, European banks, when you add their liabilities together, are "too big (for any one government) to bail," a phenomenon that the euro, as we shall see, only exacerbates.

France's biggest three banks, for example, have assets worth nearly two and a half times French GDP.[11] In contrast, the total value of the entire US banking sector is about 120 percent of GDP. The United States can print its way out of trouble because it has its own printing presses and the dollar is the global reserve asset. France cannot do this since the French state doesn't run its own printing press anymore and so can't bail its banks out directly. Neither can Spain nor anyone else. As a result, French government bond rates are going up, not because France can't pay for its welfare state, but because its banking system constitutes a too big to bail liability for the state.

Nonetheless, if one of these behemoth banks did fail it would have to be bailed out by its parent state. If that state is running a debt-to-GDP level of 40 percent, bailing is possible. If it is already running close to 90 percent, it is almost impossible for the state to take the liability onto its balance sheet without its bond yields going through the roof. This is, as we shall see over the next two chapters, why all of Europe needs to be austere, because each national state's balance sheet has to act as a shock absorber for the entire system. Having already bailed out the banks, we have to make sure that there is room on the public balance sheet to backstop them. That's why we have austerity. It's still all about saving the banks.

How this occurred is the subject of the next two chapters, but that it occurred is worth reminding ourselves now. This is a banking crisis first and a sovereign debt crisis second. That there is a crisis in sovereign debt markets, especially in Europe, is not in doubt. But that is an effect, not a cause. There was no orgy of government spending to get us there. There never was any general risk of the whole world turning into Greece. There is no risk of the United States ever going bust anytime soon. There is no crisis of sovereign debt caused by sovereigns' spending unless you take account of actual spending and continuing liabilities caused by the rupture of national banking systems. What begins as a banking crisis ends with a banking crisis, even if it goes through the states' accounts. But there is a politics of making it appear to be the states' fault such that those who made the bust don't have to pay for it. Austerity is not just the price of saving the banks. It's the price that the banks want someone else to pay.

Bill Gates, Two Truths about Debt, and a Zombie

But austerity intuitively makes sense, right? You can't spend your way to prosperity, especially when you are already in debt, can you? Austerity is intuitive, appealing, and handily summed up in the phrase *you cannot cure debt with more debt*. If you have too much debt, stop spending. This is quite true, as far as it goes. But thinking this way about austerity neither goes far enough nor asks the important distributional questions: who pays for the reduction in the debt, and what happens if we all try to pay back our debts at one time?

Economists tend to see questions of distribution as equivalent to Bill Gates walking into a bar. Once he enters, everyone in the bar is a millionaire because the average worth of everyone in the bar is pushed way up. This is at once statistically true and empirically meaningless; in reality, there are no millionaires in the bar, just one billionaire and a bunch of other folks who are each worth a few tens of thousands of dollars, or less. Austerity policies suffer from the same statistical and distributional delusion because the effects of austerity are felt differently across the income distribution. Those at the bottom of the income distribution lose more than those at the top for the simple reason that those at the top rely far less on government-produced services and can afford to lose more because they have more wealth to start with. So, although it is true that *you cannot cure debt with more debt*, if those being asked to pay the debt either cannot afford to do so or perceive their payments as being unfair and disproportionate, then austerity policies simply will not work. In a democracy, political sustainability trumps economic necessity every time.

There is, however, a second truth that completely undermines the first "too much debt, stop spending" story; that is, *we cannot all cut our way to growth at the same time*. It undoubtedly makes sense for any one state to reduce its debts. Greece, for example, is literally being driven to default by its ever-increasing debt; more debt, loans, and bailouts are not solving the problem. Yet what is true of the parts—it is good for Greece to reduce its debt—is not true of the sum of the parts. That is, if Greece cuts its debt while its trading partners—all the other states of Europe—are trying to do the same thing at the same time, it makes the recovery all the more difficult.

We tend to forget that someone has to spend for someone else to save; otherwise the saver would have no income from which to save. A debt, we must remember, is someone's asset and income stream, not just someone else's liability. Just as we cannot all hold liquid assets (cash), since that depends upon someone else being willing to hold less-liquid assets (stocks or houses), we cannot all cut our way to growth at the same time. For someone to benefit from a reduction in wages (becoming more cost-competitive), there must be someone else who is willing to spend money on what that person produces. John Maynard Keynes rightly referred to this as "the paradox of thrift": if we all save at once there is no consumption to stimulate investment.

As we shall see, if one starts from the premise that investment and growth flow from confidence, then one misses this point rather completely. What matters is a "fallacy of composition" problem, not a confidence problem, in which what is true about the whole is not true about the parts. This runs counter to common sense and much current economic policy, but it is vitally important that we appreciate this idea since it is the third reason austerity is a dangerous concept: *we cannot all be austere at once.* All that does is shrink the economy for everyone.[12]

A comparison of periods of inflation and deflation might help here. One of the odd things about periods of inflation is that they are practically the only time that people far up the income distribution express solidarity with the poor *en masse*. Whenever inflation rears its head, we hear that it "mainly hurts the poor" since their incomes are low and they are more affected by price rises.[13] This is at best half the story because inflation is perhaps better thought of as a class-specific tax. When "too much money" chases "too few goods"—an inflation—it benefits debtors over creditors since the greater the inflation, the less real income is needed to pay back the debt accrued. Since there are usually more debtors than creditors at any given time, and since creditors are by definition people with money to lend, democracy has, according to some, an inflationary bias. The politics of cutting inflation therefore take of the form of restoring the "real" value of money by pushing the inflation rate down through "independent" (from the rest of us) central banks. Creditors win, debtors lose. One can argue about the balance of benefits, but it's still a class-specific tax.

In contrast, deflation, what austerity demands, produces a much more pernicious politics, since any person's first move of self-protection (taking a pay cut to stay in a job, for example) is actually zero-sum against everyone else's move (since doing so lowers that person's consumption and shrinks demand for everyone else). It's that fallacy of composition again. There are no winners, only losers, and the more you try to win, the worse the outcomes, as the Eurozone periphery has been proving for the past several years.

This problem is especially pernicious under a policy of generalized austerity because if a country's private and public sectors are both paying back debt at the same time (deleveraging), then the only way that country can grow is by exporting more, preferably with a lower exchange rate, to a state that is still spending. But if everyone is trying the same strategy of not spending, as is happening in Europe today, it becomes self-defeating. The simple story of "too much debt, cut it now" becomes surprisingly complex as our own commonsense actions produce the very outcomes we are trying to avoid, and the more we try to cut, as Greece and Spain are proving to the world, the worse it gets. We cannot all cut our way to growth, just as we cannot all export without any concern for who is importing. This fallacy of composition problem rather completely undermines the idea of austerity as growth enhancing.

As we shall see in detail below, there have been a very few occasions when austerity has worked for states, but that has happened only when the fallacy of composition problem has been absent, when states larger than the one doing the cutting were importing, and massively so, to compensate for the effects of the cuts. Sadly, for the vast majority of countries, this is not the world we inhabit today. Moreover, under current conditions, even if the issue of political sustainability (who pays) can be addressed, the economic problem (everyone cutting at once) will undermine the policy.[14]

John Quiggin usefully terms economic ideas that will not die despite huge logical inconsistencies and massive empirical failures as "zombie economics." Austerity is a zombie economic idea because it has been disproven time and again, but it just keeps coming.[15] Partly because the commonsense notion that "more debt doesn't cure debt" remains seductive in its simplicity, and partly because it enables conservatives to try (once again) to run the detested welfare state out of town, it never seems to die.[16] In sum, austerity is a dangerous idea for three reasons: it doesn't work in practice, it relies on the poor paying for the mistakes of the rich, and it rests upon the absence of a rather large fallacy of composition that is all too present in the modern world.

So Does "All That Debt" Not Matter?

Actually, debt does matter. It's a problem, and those arguing for austerity out of more than just an innate hatred of the state and all its works are not tilting at windmills. While we may not be "drowning in debt," there are many folks out there who are concerned that we will do a bit more than just get our feet wet if we are not careful. Carmen Reinhardt and Kenneth Rogoff's much-cited paper, "Growth in a Time of Debt," argues that government debt above a critical threshold of 90 percent can become a substantial drag on the economy.[17] This claim is not without its critics, but notwithstanding those criticisms, the basic point can be rephrased as, why would any state want to carry and pay for such a debt load if it didn't have to?[18] Looking to the longer term, Simon Johnson and James Kwak argue that "America does face a long-term debt problem" that breeds a political climate of "hysteria, demagoguery and delusion," which over the long haul leads to cuts that most affect "the people who can afford it least."[19] The end result, assuming that the United States doesn't suffer an interest-rate shock in the short run, is that "the United States will look like the stereotypical Latin American country, with the super-rich living in private islands...a comfortable professional class...and a large, struggling lower class."[20] One could observe cynically that we are pretty much already there, but the point is once again well taken. Dealing with the debt now means, at least potentially, giving society more capacity to spend tomorrow.

Speaking of Latin America, some other analysts are a bit more worried. Menzie Chin and Jeffry Frieden, for example, argue that the US national debt is indeed a threat, but what really matters is the international debt and foreign borrowing that lies behind it. Looking at the international capital-flow cycle over time, they argue that America's position is not so different from that of Ireland, Spain, and even Argentina.[21] Other commentators, such as Paul Krugman, take a more relaxed view, arguing that large debts can be accommodated quite cheaply by running a balanced budget in a positive growth environment, so that real GDP grows faster than the debt, which shrinks the debt stock in real terms over time.[22]

We can, of course, raise issues with each position. To name but an obvious few: low growth could equally lead to more debt, so the solution would be to increase growth, not cut debt. Any savings that could be made through cuts now could simply be given away as yet another tax cut in the near future without any corresponding payoff to coming generations. A refusal by the United States to recycle foreign savings could be just as deleterious to the global economy as the excessive borrowing of foreign money, since the ability of the rest of the world to run a surplus against the United States, necessary because of its export-led growth models, would be compromised.[23] Finally, financial repression, what Krugman implicitly advocates, does have some costs as well as benefits.[24]

I do worry about the debt, but for different reasons. I worry because most discussions of government debt and what to do about it not only misunderstand and misrepresent cause and effect, they also take the form of a morality play between "good austerity" and "bad spending" that may lead us into a period of self-defeating budget cuts. First of all, let's establish something. If the United States ever gets to the point that it cannot roll over its debt, the supposed big fear, we can safely assume that all other sovereign debt alternatives are already dead. The United States prints the reserve asset (the dollar) that all other countries need to earn in order to conduct international trade. No other country gets to do this. Regardless of ratings agency downgrades, the US dollar is still the global reserve currency, and the fact that there are no credible alternatives (the Europeans are busy self-immolating their alternative, the euro) tilts the balance even more in favor of the United States. US debt is still the most attractive horse in the glue factory, period.

Second, we tend to forget that budget deficits (the increase in new debt accrued—the short-term worry that piles up and becomes "the Debt") follow the business cycle: they are cyclical, not secular. This is really important. It means that anyone saying "by 2025/2046/2087 US debt/deficit will be $N gazillion dollars"—and a lot of people are saying such things—is pulling a linear trend out of nonlinear data.[25] To see how silly this is, recall the great line by Clinton's (now Obama's) economic advisor Gene Sperling in 1999. Sperling predicted federal budget surpluses "as far as the eye can see." Those surpluses lasted two years. Building upon this linear nonsense, in its 2002 budget the Bush administration forecast a $1,958 billion *surplus* between 2002 and 2006.[26] The results, as we know, were quite at odds with the forecast.

Why, then, are we so worried about US government debt if it is still the best of all the bad options; the deficits that generate it are mainly cyclical; and, as we shall see later in the book, its level pales in comparison to the private debt carried by the citizens and banks of many other states? The answer is that we have turned the politics of debt into a morality play, one that has shifted the blame from the banks to the state. Austerity is the penance—the virtuous pain after the immoral party—except it is not going to be a diet of pain that we shall all share. Few of us were invited to the party, but we are all being asked to pay the bill.

The Distribution of Debt and Deleveraging

Austerity advocates argue that regardless of its actual origins, since the debt ended up on the state's "books," its "balance sheet of assets and liabilities," the state's balance sheet must be reduced or the increased debt will undermine growth.[27] The economic logic once again sounds plausible, but like Bill Gates walking into a bar and everyone becoming millionaires as a result (on average), it ignores the actual distribution of income and the critical issue of ability to pay. If state spending is cut, the effects of doing so are, quite simply, unfairly and unsustainably distributed. Personally, I am all in favor of "everyone tightening their belts"—as long as we are all wearing the same pants. But this is far from the case these days. Indeed, it is further from the case today than at any time since the 1920s.

As the Occupy movement highlighted in 2011, the wealth and income distributions of societies rocked by the financial crisis have become, over the past thirty years, extremely skewed. The bursting of the credit bubble has made this all too clear. In the United States, for example, the top 1 percent of the US income distribution now has a quarter of the country's income.[28] Or, to put it more dramatically, the richest 400 Americans own more assets than the bottom 150 million, while 46 million Americans, some 15 percent of the population, live in a family of four earning less than $22,314 per annum.[29]

As Robert Wade has argued:

> The highest-earning 1 per cent of Americans doubled their share of aggregate income (not including capital gains) from 8 per cent in 1980 to over 18 per cent in 2007. The top 0.1 per cent (about 150,000 taxpayers) quadrupled their share, from 2 per cent to 8 per cent. Including capital gains makes the

increase in inequality even sharper, with the top 1 per cent getting 23 per cent of all income by 2007. During the seven-year economic expansion of the Clinton administration, the top 1 per cent captured 45 per cent of the total growth in pre-tax income; while during the four-year expansion of the Bush administration the top 1 per cent captured 73 per cent.... This is not a misprint.[30]

If you reside in the middle or the bottom half of the income and wealth distribution, you rely on government services, both indirect (tax breaks and subsidies) and direct (transfers, public transport, public education, health care). These are the transfers across the income distribution that make the notion of a middle class possible. They don't just happen by accident. Politics makes them happen. Americans did not wake up one morning to find that God had given them a mortgage-interest tax deduction. Those further up the income distribution who have private alternatives (and more deductions) are obviously less reliant upon such services, but even they will eventually feel the consequence of cutting state spending as the impact of austerity ripples back up the income distribution in the form of lower growth, higher unemployment, withered infrastructure, and an even more skewed distribution of resources and life chances. In essence, democracy, and the redistributions it makes possible, is a form of asset insurance for the rich, and yet, through austerity, we find that those with the most assets are skipping on the insurance payments.

When government services are cut because of "profligate spending," it will absolutely not be people at the top end of the income distribution who will be expected to tighten their belts. Rather, it will be those who lie in the bottom 40 percent of the income distribution who haven't had a real wage increase since 1979.[31] These are the folks who actually rely upon government services and who have taken on a huge amount of debt (relative to their incomes) that will be "fiscally consolidated." This is why austerity is first and foremost a political problem of distribution, and not an economic problem of accountancy.

Austerity is, then, a dangerous idea because it ignores the externalities it generates, the impact of one person's choices on another person's choices, especially for societies with highly skewed income distributions. The decisions of those at the top on taxes, spending, and investment prior to 2008 created a giant liability in the form of a financial crisis and too big to fail and bail financial institutions that they expect everyone further down the income distribution to pay for. "We have spent too much" those at the top say, rather blithely ignoring the fact that this "spending" was the cost of saving their assets with the public purse.[32] Meanwhile, those at the bottom are being told to "tighten their belts" by people who are wearing massively larger pants and who show little interest in contributing to the cleanup.

In sum, when those at the bottom are expected to pay disproportionately for a problem created by those at the top, and when those at the top actively eschew any responsibility for that problem by blaming the state for their mistakes, not only will squeezing the bottom not produce enough revenue to fix things, it will produce an even more polarized and politicized society in which the conditions for a sustainable politics of dealing with more debt and less growth are undermined. Populism, nationalism, and calls for the return of "God and gold" in equal doses are what unequal austerity generates, and no one, not even those at the top, benefits. In such an unequal and austere world, those who start at the bottom of the income distribution will stay at the bottom, and without the possibility of progression, the "betterment of one's condition" as Adam Smith put it, the only possible movement is a violent one.[33] Despite what Mrs. Thatcher reportedly once said, not only is there something called society, we all live in it, rich and poor alike, for better and for worse.

The Book in Brief

Following this overview, chapter 2, "America: Too Big to Fail: Bankers, Bailouts, and Blaming the State," explains why the developed world's debt crisis is not due to profligate state spending, at least in any direct sense. Rather, we piece together how the debt increase was generated by the implosion of the US financial sector and how this impacted sovereigns from the United States to the Eurozone and beyond. To explain this I stress how the interaction of the repo (sale and repurchase) markets, complex instruments, tail risks, and faulty thinking combined to give us the problem of too big to fail. It takes us from the origins of the crisis in the run on the US repo market in September 2008 to the transmission of this US-based crisis to the Eurozone, noting along the way how a banking crisis was deftly, and most politically, turned into a public-sector crisis and how much it all cost.[34]

Chapter 3, "Europe: Too Big to Bail: The Politics of Permanent Austerity," analyzes how the private debt generated by the US banking sector was rechristened as the "sovereign debt crisis" of profligate European states. If chapter 2 places the origins of the debt in the United States, chapter 3 describes the bait and switch in Europe. We show how the world turned Keynesian for about twelve months, and examine why the Germans never really bought into it. We showcase British opportunism and American paralysis, and stress how the argument that austerity was necessary and that the crisis was the fault of state spending was constructed by an assortment of business leaders, bankers, and paradoxically, European politicians. This chapter fleshes out why the European fixation on austerity as the only possible way forward reflects not simply a strong ideological preference, but a structural liability that came to Europe through global and regional bank funding conduits. This liability, caused by a giant moral hazard trade among European banks prior to the introduction of the euro, was amplified further by the peculiar institutional design of the European model of "universal" banking, and the peculiarities of repo market transactions (again), to produce a banking system that is too big to bail. Austerity, plus endless public liquidity for the banking systems of Europe, is the only thing keeping macroeconomic and monetary mess afloat, and it's a time-limited fix.

Having examined where the crisis came from and why it constitutes the greatest bait and switch in human history in Part I (chapters 2 and 3), we can now engage Part 2, "Austerity's Twin Histories," in chapters 4, 5, and 6. The first history is austerity's intellectual history. The second history is how austerity has worked out in practice—its natural history. In chapter 4, "The Intellectual History of a Dangerous Idea, 1692–1942," we ask where austerity, as an idea, came from; why it appeared; and who popularized it? As we shall see, its intellectual history is both short and indirect. Austerity is not a well worked-out body of ideas and doctrine, an integral part of economic, or any other, theory. Rather, it is derivative of a wider set of beliefs about the appropriate role of the state in the economy that lie scattered around classical and contemporary economic theory.

We journey through the works of Locke, Smith, and Hume, noting how they construct what I call the "can't live with it, can't live without it, don't want to pay for it" problem of the state in liberal economic theory. We next discuss how economic liberalism splits in the early twentieth century between those who think we cannot (and should not) live with the state and those who think that capitalism cannot survive without it. British New Liberalism, the Austrian school of economics, British Treasury officials, Keynes's advance, and Schumpeter's retreat take us up to 1942, when the battle seems to have been won for those who hew to the "can't live without it" school of thought.

Chapter 5, "The Intellectual History of a Dangerous Idea, 1942–2012," continues this journey. We travel to Germany, the home of ordoliberalism, a set of ideas that was to prove unexpectedly important for the current crisis in Europe and which acted as a home for austere thinking during the long winter of Keynesianism. We touch upon the issue of timing and development as we visit the Austrian school's postwar redoubt of the United States to discuss its ideas about banks, booms, and busts. We then pass through Milton's monetarism and Virginia public choice on our way to chat to some time-inconsistent politicians in search of credibility. After this, we visit the IMF's monetary model and seek out Washington's consensus on how to get rich. Finally, we travel to Italy to find the modern home for the idea of why austerity is good for us, and then come back to Cambridge, the American one, to share the news that the state can't be trusted and that cuts lead to growth. This, then, is austerity's intellectual history.

Chapter 6, "Austerity's Natural History, 1914–2012," looks at austerity in practice. Noting that it's not until you get states that are big enough to cut that you really get debates about cutting the state down, we begin with the classical gold standard and how cuts were built into the script of its operation, with calamitous results. We examine six cases of austerity from the 1930s: the United States, Britain, Sweden, Germany, Japan, and France, and note how austerity in these cases mightily contributed to blowing up the world—literally—during the 1930s and 1940s. We next examine four cases from the 1980s: Denmark, Ireland, Australia, and Sweden, which are most commonly thought to prove that austerity is good for us after all. We then analyze the latest empirical studies on the relationship between austerity and growth, noting that far from supporting the idea of "expansionary austerity," it rather completely undermines it.

Finally, we examine the new hope for austerity champions, the cases of Romania, Estonia, Bulgaria, Latvia, and Lithuania—the REBLL alliance. These cases supposedly show that despite what the historical record and contemporary theory tell us, austerity does work. However, we find nothing of the kind. Austerity doesn't work for the REBLL alliance either, but the fact that we are still being told that it does shows us one thing: facts never disconfirm a good ideology, which is why austerity remains a very dangerous idea. A short conclusion summarizes the discussion, suggests why we should have perhaps let the banks fail after all, and suggests where we might be heading given the dead end that is austerity.

Part One

WHY WE ALL NEED TO BE AUSTERE

AMERICA: TOO BIG TO FAIL?

BANKERS, BAILOUTS, AND BLAMING THE STATE

Introduction

The Oscar-winning documentary *Inside Job* has many virtues. It gives a clear and understandable description of what happened in the financial crisis. It does a marvelous job of exposing the conflicts of interest endemic in the economics profession; for example, economists publishing "scientific" proof of the efficiency of markets and the positive role of finance while being paid lots of undeclared cash by the financial services industry for consultancy gigs that tell the industry what it wants to hear. The film is, however, less compelling as an explanation of why the crisis happened in the first place. It goes awry when it begins to focus on the moral failings of bankers. (Apparently, middle-aged men with too much money spend some of that money on prostitutes.) The filmmaker's point, I think, was to suggest that what underlay the crisis was the moral weakness of individuals. Given all that money, the story goes, morality went out the window.[1]

While this story satisfies some, the moral failings of individuals are irrelevant for understanding both why the financial crisis in the United States happened and why austerity is now perceived as the only possible response, especially in Europe. However, you could have replaced all the actual bankers of 2007 with completely different individuals, and they would have behaved the same way during the meltdown: that's what incentives do. What really matters is how seemingly unconnected and opaque parts of the global system of finance came together to produce a crisis that none of those parts could have produced on its own, and how that ended up being the state's, and by extension, your problem.

But how are we to adjudicate what is important and what is not important in reconstructing the US side of the crisis? After all, as Andrew Lo noted in a recent wickedly entitled essay called "Reading about the Financial Crisis: A 21-Book Review," the crisis is both overexplained and overdetermined.[2] The crisis is overexplained in that there are so many possible suspects who can be rounded up and accused of being "the cause" that authors can construct convincing narratives featuring almost any culprit from Fannie and Freddie to leverage ratios to income inequality—even though the meltdown obviously was a deeply nonlinear and multicausal process.[3] The crisis is overdetermined in that, being a nonlinear, multicausal process, many of these supposed causes could be ruled out and the crisis could still have occurred. For example, three excellent books on the crisis stress, respectively, increasing income inequality in the run-up to the crisis, the captured nature of bank regulation, and the political power of finance. Each book certainly captures an important aspect of the crisis.[4] But are these factors absolutely necessary to adequately explain it?

I hope to add to these accounts one simple thing: the idea that this crisis is first and foremost a private-sector crisis. In each episode we examine in this book, in the United States, the European Union, and Eastern Europe, we shall see that the crisis was generated by the private sector but is being paid for by the pubic sector, that is, by you and me. We can establish this by thinking counterfactually. One might ask the question, could we have had the crisis if the income distribution had been less skewed, if regulators had been more independent, and if finance had been less powerful? I believe we could. These were important factors—they turbocharged the problem—but they were not essential to it in and of themselves.

In what follows, I focus on four elements that I believe you cannot remove counterfactually and still explain the crisis. These are the bare essentials that made it possible, and they all lie firmly in the private sector. They are—and we shall unpack them in plain English as we go—the structure of collateral deals in US repo markets, the structure of mortgage-backed derivatives and their role in repo transactions, the role played by correlation and tail risk in amplifying these problems, and the damage done by a set of economic ideas that blinded actors—both bankers and regulators—to the risks building up in the system. Again, I stress that these are quintessentially private-sector phenomena. I do this so that I can ask one more question as a setup. If all the trouble was generated in the private sector, why do so many people blame the state for the crisis and see cuts to state spending as the way out of a private-sector mess? Answering that question is what concerns us in the rest of this chapter.

The Generator: Repo Markets and Bank Runs

The repo market is a part of what is called the "shadow banking" system: "shadow," since its activities support and often replicate those of the normal banks, and "banking" in that it provides financial services to both the normal (regulated) banks and the real economy. Take paychecks, for example. It would be hugely impractical for big businesses to truck in enormous amounts of cash every weekend to pay their employees out of retained earnings held at their local bank. So companies borrow and lend money to each other over very short periods at very low interest rates, typically swapping assets for cash and then repurchasing those assets the next day for a fee—hence "sale" and "repurchase"—or "repo." It is cheaper than borrowing from the local bank and doesn't involve fleets of armored trucks.

What happened in 2007 and 2008 was a bank run through this repo market.[5] A bank run occurs when all the depositors in a bank want their cash back at the same time and the bank doesn't have enough cash on hand to give it to them. When this happens, banks either borrow money to stay liquid and halt the panic or they go under. The repo market emerged in the 1980s when traditional banks lost market share because of a process called "disintermediation."[6] Banks, as intermediaries, traditionally sit in the middle of someone else's prospective business, connecting borrowers and lenders, for example, and charging fees for doing so. Before disintermediation, banks engaged in what was often called "3-6-3 banking": they would borrow at 3 percent, lend at 6 percent, and hit the golf course by 3 p.m. It was safe, steady, and dull. But as financial markets became more deregulated in the 1980s, large corporations began to use their own cash reserves, lending them to one another directly—they disintermediated—bypassing banks and squeezing bank profits. What further squeezed 3-6-3 banking was a parallel process called securitization.

The old 3-6-3 model presumed that the bank that issued a loan to a customer held the loan until it was paid off, with profits accruing from the interest payments it received. But what if these loan payments could be separated out and sold on to someone else? What if many such loans, mortgages for example, could be bundled together as a pool of mortgage payments and sold to investors as an income-generating contract called a mortgage-backed security? That way, the bank that issued the loan could borrow cheaper and make more loans because the risk of the loan not being paid back was no longer on its books, and the borrower would get better rates. It was win-win, as they say.

Collateral Damage: American Style

Although securitization was a threat to the traditional methods of banking, it was also an opportunity for the banks that got on board with the new model. They got to offset their risk by selling the loan on, and as a result they were able to borrow cheaper and lend more. What could be wrong with that? What was wrong was that the risks inherent in these loans never really disappeared: they just got pushed elsewhere. Indeed, the process of selling on loans inadvertently concentrated those risks in short-term repo markets. So, how did everyday mortgages end up in a repo market?

When you and I put our money in a bank, the Federal Deposit Insurance Corporation (FDIC) guarantees it against the failure of the bank: this default risk is covered. But there is no such insurance in the repo markets, so repo-market investors protect their cash by receiving collateral equivalent to the cash lent. If the borrower goes bust, the lender can still get the money back, so long as, and this is critical, the collateral doesn't lose value. What counts as high-quality collateral? Back in the early 2000s, it included such things as Treasury bills, of course. But increasingly, AAA-rated mortgage-debt securities began to be used as collateral, since T-bills were in short supply, which is how mortgages ended up in the repo markets.[7]

A decline in house prices in 2006 hit the value of these bundled mortgage securities. If you were using mortgage securities as collateral for loans in the repo market, you needed to find more collateral (which people were increasingly less willing to hold) or higher-quality collateral (alternative assets that were in short supply), or you would have to take a "haircut" (a discount) on what you would get back, all of which affected your bottom line. Now, if a big player in these markets, Bear Stearns or Lehman Brothers, for example, has problems "posting collateral" because the value of what it holds and can offer has fallen, it may be forced to reassure its investors by announcing publicly that there is no problem with the firm.

Unfortunately, doing so is deadly for a major financial firm. As Walter Bagehot noted over 100 years ago in his book *Lombard Street*, the moment a big bank has to say that its "money good," it isn't; or at least you can no longer assume that it is, so lending to the bank dries up: it gets hit with a "liquidity crunch." In the case of Bear Stearns, as house prices fell and mortgage defaults increased, the value of its investments fell, and its "collateral calls" (what the people it borrowed from would accept to continue lending to the company) rose. As a consequence, Bear Stearns' reputation fell and so did its capacity to borrow, which was a disaster given how much it was levered-up (how much debt it carried relative to its assets).

Leverage is how banks make such absurd sums of money. The Germans have a saying, "when you have two marks, spend one." In modern banking that becomes "when you have one dollar in the bank, lend thirty or forty or more." Leverage, the ratio of assets (loans and investments out in the world) relative to equity (reserve capital—the cushion you draw upon when things go wrong), rose precipitously throughout the 1980s and 1990s. If a major bank is running thirty times leverage, as was common in the run-up to the crisis, all it takes is a very small change in its asset values against its equity cushion to make it illiquid, if not close to insolvent. When securitized mortgages started to lose value in 2006, that very small decline became all too real, and the big banks that had funded themselves through the repo market (essentially borrowing overnight to loan for much longer periods with huge amounts of leverage on their balance sheets) saw their funding sources disappear. Liquidity, the very thing repo markets are supposed to provide, dried up, since no one was willing to lend to anyone else at normal rates. And because the banks were so levered up, they didn't need all their funding to dry up—just enough to make them almost instantly illiquid.

Liquidity, however, does not simply evaporate like the morning dew. It burns up in a "fire sale" as a process called "contagion" takes hold.[8] With everyone in the market knee-deep in mortgage securities and trying to raise money with the same devaluing collateral, they were trying to cash out what were essentially similar assets. And if they couldn't sell mortgages, they sold anything else they could to raise cash and cover their losses, even supposedly high-quality assets that had nothing to do with mortgages. Because the market could not absorb the volume of securities being dumped on the market all at once, asset dumping to raise cash created the very panic everyone had sought to avoid.[9] Prices plummeted, firms folded, and trust evaporated further.

Note here that this has nothing to do either with the state, which now gets the blame for the debt stemming from this crisis—a wonderful confusion of cause and effect—or with the individual moral failings of the bankers.[10] You can blame regulators for being lax or negligent and politicians for caving to banking interests all you like, but this was a quintessentially private-sector crisis, and it was precisely how you get a multi-billion-dollar financial panic out of a bunch of defaulting mortgages. But it was not yet sufficient to cause a global crisis. To get there, you have to understand how the structure of these mortgage securities combined with unbacked insurance policies called "credit default swaps" (CDSs) to produce a "correlation bomb" that spread the repo market crisis into the global banking system. Again, this had nothing to do with states and their supposedly profligate spending habits and everything to do with weaknesses internal to the private sector.

The Amplifier: Derivatives

It's hard to describe derivatives in the abstract. To say they are securities that derive their value from some other underlying financial asset, index, or referent, which is a typical definition, doesn't say all that much. They also tend to be known by their acronyms (CDO squared, synthetic ETF, and so on), which only increases their mystery. Derivatives are basically contracts, just like mortgage securities. They allow banks to do what banks have always done: link people together while acting as middlemen and charging a fee, but in ways that allow them to trade things that are not assets in any normal sense, such as movements in interest rates or currencies. Whereas an asset is property, or a claim on property or income, a derivative is a contract, a bet that pays out based on how a particular asset performs over a particular time period.[11] That is the key distinction. Derivatives come in multiple combinations of four main types: futures, forwards, options, and swaps.[12] The derivatives that concern us here are swaps,[13] specifically CDSs, and how these interacted with the mortgage securities that were being used as collateral in the repo market.

Key to understanding how derivatives amplified the repo market crisis is the idea of correlation between assets: when asset A goes up in price, asset B reliably goes down in price. These "negative correlations" allow investors to "hedge" their bets. A typical example is the relationship between the US dollar (USD) and the euro. When one goes up, the other (typically) goes down. The problem with relying upon correlations is that they sometimes break down, leaving you very exposed. CDSs were meant to help overcome this problem of correlation, but they ended up amplifying it.

Back in the mid-1990s when the stocks and shares that make up the world's equity markets were about to enter their dot-com–bubble phase, investors looked around for uncorrelated assets as hedges in case equities fell in value. They turned en masse to real estate to hedge their equity bets, and in the process pushed real-estate prices up by between 70 percent (in the United States) and 170 percent (in Ireland) over the next ten years. Real-estate assets were attractive because they were seen not only as uncorrelated to equities, but also as "uncorrelated within their class" and thus safe bets in their own right.[14]

"Uncorrelated within their class" means that if houses in Texas, for example, fall in value, there is no reason for that to impact house prices in Baltimore or apartment prices in Manhattan. So far, so good. But could you make it better? Mortgage-backed securities were already safe investments, but could that safety be maintained while enhancing returns? If you could figure this out, you could make a lot of money.

This was achieved by the technique of "tranching the security," which turned the simple mortgage-backed securities (the bucket of mortgage payments sold onto investors described earlier) into a contract called a "collateralized debt obligation" (CDO).[15] The technique combined the mortgage payments of many different bits of real estate, from many different places, in the same security, but it kept them separate by selling different parts of the security to different people via different "tranches" (or tiers). Basically, you take a bit of the east side of Manhattan and blend that with a bit of Arizona suburb and a bit of Baltimore waterfront, and you pay the holders of the different tranches (usually called *senior, mezzanine*, or *equity* tranches) different interest rates according to how risky a tranche they bought. People who wanted low risk and low return, for example, would hold the senior tranche. Those with greater risk appetite (and a desire for greater interest payments) would hold the mezzanine tranche. For those out for yield above all, the equity tranche was the prize.

The idea is that if these different real-estate markets are already uncorrelated, then cutting them up and recombining them should make them *super*uncorrelated. If the house in Baltimore defaults, the equity tranche holders are wiped out, but that loss is isolated from the holders of the loans on the condominiums and the Upper East Side penthouses. Safety combined with greater returns (at least for those holding the risk) led to an explosion of demand for these securities as US housing prices nearly doubled between 1997 and 2008. They were no longer a simple equity hedge. They became objects of investors' desire in their own right. But where things really got interesting was when these derivative securities were sold with an attached CDS.

A CDS is basically an insurance policy you can sell on.[16] It insures the purchaser of the CDS against the default of the bond upon which it is written. In return, the issuer of the CDS, the writer of the insurance policy, receives a regular income stream from the purchaser, just as an insurance company receives customers' insurance premiums. The difference is that insurance companies typically rely on such measures as actuarial tables to calculate the risks they are covering, and then work out how much cash they need to have on hand to cover people cashing in their policies, as they surely will. They also build up cash reserves to pay out on the policy claims that will inevitably be made against the firm.[17] But if the probability of default of a given entity (Lehman Brothers, for example) is considered to be extremely unlikely, and if you write a CDS contract on that entity, you won't think you have to keep very much capital at all in reserve to cover anticipated losses because no such losses are anticipated.

With a decade of house-price increases telling everyone that house prices only go up, and with these new mortgage derivatives seemingly eliminating a correlation problem that was deemed small to begin with and was now insurable with a CDS, you could almost begin to believe that you had what bankers call a "free option": an asset with zero downside and a potentially unlimited upside, and one that is rated AAA by the ratings agencies. The fact that many investment funds are legally required to hold a specific proportion of their assets as AAA securities pumped demand still further.[18]

By the mid-2000s the markets couldn't get enough of these securities, which was a problem because the banks and brokers writing these very profitable mortgages were running out of good borrowers to whom they could lend. The later batches of these securities were therefore increasingly made up of NINJA (no income, no job, no assets) mortgages collateralized by the eBay earnings or bar tips of the new mortgagers, or by purely fabricated income statements and robo-signed paperwork.[19] Because the new mortgages coming in were of such dubious quality, the issuers of these securities increasingly didn't want to hold any of this dubious risk on their own books and wanted them moved off-book.[20]

To get them off their books, CDO issuers set up a system in which their issuance and funding was moved to so-called special investment vehicles (SIVs).[21] These were separately created companies, isolated from the parent company's balance sheet, whose sole activity was to collect the income streams from these mortgages and CDS contracts and pay them out to the different investors holding them. By 2006, those investors included small Norwegian towns, US pension funds, and German regional banks. After all, with an attractive yield, bond insurance, a quasi-governmental AAA stamp of approval, and rising prices, what could go wrong?

Well, everything, really. When already tight credit markets froze in September 2008, prices for these securities collapsed. This further constricted credit, amplifying what had been going on with these securities in the repo market for months. With each bank holding similar assets and liabilities, and as each attempted to rid itself of these assets all at once, prices fell through the floor. But the real surprise, the amplifier, was that the design of these securities, rather than lessening correlation, actually boosted it.

Correlation and Liquidity

In principle, the different tranches of the CDO were isolated from each other. If they went bad, they went bad in reverse order, and it was thought that they couldn't all go bad since different people held different parts of the bond *and* the underlying markets were uncorrelated. Unfortunately, it turned out that the underlying markets were quite strongly correlated. Adding Manhattan to Arizona and Baltimore in a single security *made them correlated*. The sheer volume of cash invested in real estate created one big market in US real estate across the world that became increasingly correlated to equities, particularly to the equities of the banks that were trading real estate. When the income streams of the riskiest (junior) part of the bond dried up as NINJA mortgagers walked away from their debts, investors in the more-secure tranches took fright and dumped their assets as part of the general search for liquidity. What was uncorrelated in theory became extremely correlated in practice. Making matters worse were the CDS (insurance) contracts attached to the CDOs that would pay out if the security defaulted. If these insurance claims happened en masse, the insolvency of the entire system emerged as a distinct possibility. So, when the scope of CDS protection both written by and written on Lehman by firms such as AIG became apparent, not only did the markets take fright, the state for the first time began to see the problem as systemic rather than idiosyncratic, and too big to fail became a reality.

In sum, a web of mispriced risks, with the price set at zero, between the "normal" banking system and the shadow banking system was created through the unseen links between mortgage bonds and CDSs that amplified the grossly underestimated existing correlation between assets. A problem that began in the repo market in 2007 was no longer confined there. The crisis spread globally as investors sought the protection of liquidity but failed to find it. Just as one country's exports depends upon another country's imports, so one bank's liquidity depends upon another bank's willingness to be illiquid. And at that moment, no one wanted to be illiquid.

Note once again that this had nothing to do with the state (beyond the fact that states chose not to regulate derivatives markets—a cause only by omission) or individual morality. The behavior of the whole was not reducible to the sum of its parts. Rather than reducing correlation, these complex assets amplified an already ongoing liquidity crunch that had originated in the repo market months earlier. Too big to fail was the inevitable result of highly levered institutions discovering that all the liquidity in the world really could dry up all at once.

The First Blinder: Tail Risk

So, why didn't anyone see this coming? Queen Elizabeth asked the British economists assembled at the London School of Economics in 2009, who, like analysts everywhere, had failed to see the crisis coming. The answer lies in the way banks measure and manage risk, the third of our seemingly unrelated elements that together generated the crisis and that are quintessentially private-sector, not public-sector failings. Repo runs can start it, and derivatives can amplify it, but to be truly blindsided by a crisis of this magnitude you need to have a theory of risk that denies that catastrophic events can happen in the first place, and then leave it entirely to the self-interested private sector to manage that risk. Unfortunately, almost the entire global financial system worked with just such a theory of risk management.

The first and most basic risk-management technique in finance is called "portfolio diversification," which tries to ensure that your portfolio of assets is not overly exposed to any single source of risk, except by conscious choice. One way to diversify is to try not to buy the same assets as everyone else. Instead, buy different assets, preferably ones that are uncorrelated or even negatively correlated to other folks' assets.[22] The second technique is hedging. Rather than simply rely on passive correlations that are out there in the world to ensure your safety, such as the inverse relationship that typically prevails between the USD and the euro, banks can adopt particular strategies, or trade derivative instruments with specific characteristics, so that the gains from one set of exposures covers (hedges) any losses in another.[23]

In principle then, a combination of portfolio diversification and hedging—if appropriately executed in a given market environment—will at the very least keep your investments safe. Think the market will go down? Short sell one asset (profit from a stock price falling by borrowing the stock for a fee, selling it, and then buying it back when its cheaper), and take a long position (buy and hold) in an uncorrelated asset as cover. Want to benefit from the market going up? Use options (the right to buy or sell an asset at a predetermined price) to increase leverage (amplify the bet) while taking a short position as cover. But if this is all it takes to be safe, and to perhaps even make money, why did the banks not see the crisis coming? To answer that question, you need to turn to the trader-turned-philosopher Nassim Nicolas Taleb.

Taleb's Black Swans and Fat-Tailed Worlds

A common refrain when the crisis first hit was that no one *could* have seen it coming. It was the financial equivalent of the meteor that wiped out the dinosaurs. All the diversification and hedging strategies that were supposed to keep banks from blowing up were, as David Viniar, the chief financial officer of Goldman Sachs put it, blindsided by "25 standard deviation moves, several days in a row."[24] This is similar to the "ten sigma event" claim reportedly made by John Meriweather when his hedge fund, Long Term Capital Management (LTCM), blew up in 1998.[25]

What these sigmas refer to is the number of standard deviations from the mean of a probability distribution at which an outcome will, probabilistically speaking, occur, with each higher sigma (number) being increasingly less likely than the last. According to Mr. Viniar, what happened in 2008 was "comparable to winning the lottery 21 or

22 times in a row."[26] LTCM's ten sigma in 1998 was, likewise, an event that should have occurred roughly three times in the life of the universe. That these two events happened a mere nine years apart shows us that such claims are nonsense. It also tells us why Nassim Taleb has a huge problem with the idea of risk management and financial engineering.

Claims about sigmas typically refer to a "normal-distributed" probability distribution. The shape of the distribution is important. If the shape is "normal," it conforms to what is called a Gaussian distribution, the classic bell curve, where most of the action is in the middle of the distribution, and less action is likely to occur the further you go out into the tails (see figure 1.1).

To understand why this is important, imagine that we have sampled the height of 10,000 randomly selected adults. We find out that most people are between five and six feet tall, that far fewer people are either seven feet or three feet tall, and that no one in our sample is outside that range. Knowing this, we can figure out the probability of any one person of a given size being close to the mean of the distribution. Under a normal distribution, a one-sigma deviation means that there is a 68 percent chance that person is close to the mean height. Two

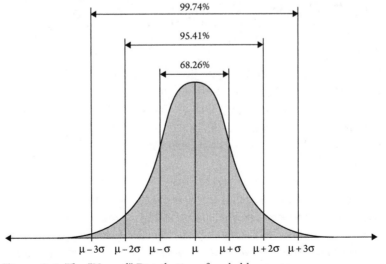

Figure 2.1 The "Normal" Distribution of probable events

sigmas translates into a 95 percent chance of being close to the mean, and so on, out into the (very) thin tails, where no one is ever eight feet tall. As the numbers get bigger, the probability of encountering some-one of such an extreme size gets exponentially smaller. The chance that someone will fall completely outside the sample becomes so un-likely that you can basically forget about it.

Change the variable from height to default probability, and you can see how such a way of thinking about the likelihood of future events could be of great use to banks as they tried to risk-adjust their portfolios and positions. The piece of technology that allowed banks to do this is known as Value at Risk (VaR) analysis, which is part of a larger class of mathematical models designed to help banks manage risk. What VaR does is generate a figure (a VaR number) for how much a firm can win or lose on an individual trade. By summing VaR numbers, one can estimate a firm's total exposure. Consider the following example.

What was the worst that could have happened to the US housing market in 2008? As in the height example, the answer depends on a data sample that calibrates the model. Prior to 2007, the worst down-turn firms had data on was the result of the mortgage defaults in Texas in the 1980s, when houses lost 40 percent of their value. Take this data as the parameter limit, or how far out the tail goes before the sigma becomes too large to be imaginable, and you will conclude, given the assumption of a normal distribution of events, that the probability that *all* the mortgages in your portfolio would lose more than 40 percent of their value at once is ridiculously small. So small, in fact, that you can ignore it. Indeed, the probability that all your mortgage bonds will go bad or that a very large bank will go bust is absurdly small, ten sigma or more, again, *so long as you think that the probability distribution you face is normally distributed.* Your VaR number, once calculated, would reflect this.

Nassim Taleb never bought into this line of thinking. He had been a critic of VaR models as far back as 1997, arguing that they systemat-ically underestimated the probability of high-impact, low-probability events. He argued that the thin tails of the Gaussian worked for height but not for finance, where the tails were "fat." The probabilities asso-ciated with fat tails do not get exponentially smaller, so outlier events are much more frequent than your model allows you to imagine. This is why ten-sigma events actually happen nine years apart.

Taleb's 2006 book *The Black Swan*, published before the crisis, turned these criticisms of VaR into a full-blown attack on the way banks and governments think about risk. Taleb essentially asked the question, what would happen if you ran into an eight-and-a-half-foot-tall person having sampled 10,000 people who were shorter? You might, given that we have never run into such a person, say with confidence that she doesn't exist. Meeting her would be a ten-sigma event. Taleb would bet against you, and you would lose, because in finance there is no way of knowing that you will not run into the equivalent of an eight-and-a-half foot-tall person.

Key here is the issue of observational experience. If you haven't been around for a third of the life of the universe (ten sigma), then how can you know what is possible over that time period? It's the assumed distribution that tells you what is possible, not your experience. To return to the height example, just because your model estimates that an eight-foot-tall person does not exist, it doesn't follow that she doesn't actually exist and that you will not run into her. In Taleb's example, all swans were white until Europeans went to Australia and found black swans. Their exhaustive, multiyear, multisite sample of all known swans had convinced Europeans that all swans were white—until they were not. Nothing in their prior sample, no matter how complete it was, could have told them that a black swan was coming. How, then, do you hedge against risks that are not in your sample? How can you know that which is unknowable until it happens? The answer is, basically, you can't, and if you think you can, you are setting yourself up for a fall.

Counting the Bullets

One way to think about the problem is to imagine playing a game of Russian roulette. Most people would prefer not to play this game when offered the option because the risk-reward ratio is too high, which is correct if we assume the classic "one bullet and six chambers in the gun" setup. But what if I have information you don't have, derived from a mathematical model called Brains at Risk (BaR), that tells me the gun has over a billion chambers and only one bullet, and that I can figure out where the bullet is by sampling (pulling the trigger millions of times)? Let's also say that each time I pull the trigger I receive $100. I click once and am $100 richer, so I click again. By lunchtime, I am a millionaire and have grown confident. In terms of estimating the risk that I face, each "click without a bang" is a piece of information about the probability distribution. As I sample (click) more, I grow more confident about the shape of the distribution. I think that I am generating a more accurate prediction of where the bullet is with each piece of information (click), right up until the moment when I blow my brains out. I have just run into a black swan: a low probability (given the sample and assumed distribution) and (very) high-impact event.

VaR and associated techniques sample the past to predict the future, and from this information we derive theories about the way the future should play out based on our expectations of the probability distribution rather than our actual experiences in the world. We also assume that more information is better than less information, regardless of how it's generated, and therefore believe that the more we sample, the more we converge upon the world "as it really is." But we do not actually do so. Rather, we are assuming far more stability than is warranted—simply because the gun hasn't gone off yet. As *The Black Swan* tells us, we get hit by events that our sample could not have warned us about right at our point of maximum certainty that such events will not happen.

What VaR and similar models make us forget is that we do not see the generators of reality (the number of chambers in the gun), only their outcomes (the clicks of the trigger), and as a consequence we massively underestimate the payoffs we face, most of which are decidedly negative. We think we see the generators, what causes things, but we do not. Instead, we have theories about what causes things and we act upon those theories, which activities, as the Russian roulette example shows, tend to end both abruptly and badly.

Let's apply the black swan idea to risk management in banks in 2008. Consider a data set comprising returns to the Western banking system. If you were to take a monthly time series average of financial sector profitability from June 1947 until June 2007, you could talk with some degree of accuracy about the mean rate of return, the "standard" deviation, and all the rest, until June 2007. But if you include returns from July 2007 through December 2008, you will have included an outlier so large that it will blow your earlier historical measures out of the water. Nothing in your VaR or other analyses can tell you that this event is coming. The risk is in the tail, not the middle of the distribution, and it's massive. Like the proverbial drunk looking for his keys only under the lamppost, we are drawn to see "normal" distributions in decidedly nonnormal worlds because that is where we find the light.

So, part of the reason no one saw the crisis coming lay within the very models that the banks used to see things coming. Such models see the future only as a normally distributed replication of the past. This makes big, random, game-changing events impossible to foresee, when in fact they are all too common. Such technologies give us, as Taleb says, the illusion of control. We thought that we were diversified and hedged. We thought that we were taking few risks, when they were in fact mounting exponentially, just below the surface, ready to blow up. This is why the events of 2007 and 2008 seemed to partici-pants to be ten and even twenty-five sigma, but what it really shows is that the models used were worse than inaccurate. As Andy Haldane of the Bank of England put it, "these models were both very precise and very wrong."[27] Add tail-risk-blind management techniques to a derivative-amplified and leverage-enhanced run on the repo market, and you end up with one heck of a multi-trillion-dollar mess. Not only did we not see it coming, we didn't see it coming because we didn't think it was possible in the first place.

Note once again how none of this has anything to do with the state's spending habits or individual morality. The causes are once again systemic and arise out of the interaction of the parts to produce an outcome that is irreducible to them. Why would people have such faith in a technology that hides risk rather than measures it? To answer that question, we need to address the deepest cause of the crisis—the other reason no one saw it coming: the theories of a generation of economic thinkers who only ever saw markets as good and the state as bad, which takes us back to economics as a morality tale, albeit of a different type.

The Second Blinder: The Political Power of Financial Ideas

We tend to think of economic theory as the instruction sheet for running the economy.[28] Like the instructions that come with an IKEA dining table, the theory says that the box marked "the economy" contains X items that fit together in Y order. Ignore the instruction sheet and your economic IKEA dining table will not come out too well. This view sees economic theory as what philosophers call a "correspondence theory" of the world. Whatever the instruction sheet (theory) says about the table (reality) is true about all tables (states of the world) regardless of where and when the information is applied. But what if economic theories are less than these perfect correspondences of the world? What if our knowledge of the economy becomes less relevant over time as the world changes while the theory stays the same? Our theory would then correspond less over time, becoming in the process a less reliable instruction sheet.

Economic theory, for better or worse, provides us with the blue-prints for the rules and institutions that we build to run the economy. For example, if you believe that VaR provides an adequate model of risk management, then you might argue that banks should be allowed to manage their own risks with their own models, as the so-called Basel II capital adequacy rules governing bank reserve capital require-ments, which were largely written by the banks themselves, argued, and governments dutifully implemented. Or, if you think that the number-one economic problem is always and everywhere inflation, you will probably champion independent central banks to tie the hands of so-called time-inconsistent politicians who, mistakenly, tend to lis-ten to the folks who elected them. But if those institutional blueprints are faulty or those rules are mistaken because the theory they are drawn from differs from how the world actually behaves, then our in-struction sheets may produce institutions that are much more fragile than we appreciate.

Finally, economic theories are also partial and rival insofar as dif-ferent economic ideas contain within them justifications for different distributions of resources. For example, as we shall see in chapter 4, both contemporary neoliberal and classical liberal economic theory focus on the microlevel supply-side of the economy; that is, on how saving leads to investment, which leads in turn to employment and to the wages that buy the products made by the workers themselves, which leads in turn to profits reinvested in the firm. No supply of investment, no demand and no consumption. Keynesian economics, in contrast, argues that consumption drives investment, not saving. For Keynesians it is the macro world of aggregates (income, consumption) and the demand-side of spending that matters. In a Keynesian world, consumers, not investors, are the heroes because consumers' demands determine what investors supply. No demand, no supply of investment. Given these "rival views of market society," as the economist Albert Hirschman once put it, who should get, for example, a tax cut? The Keynesian wants to give it to the poor so they will consume now to boost demand and consumption. Meanwhile, the neoliberal wants to give it to the rich to invest wisely. Different economic theories therefore empower, and disempower, different political and economic constituencies.

Economic theory is, then, both much more and much less than an instruction sheet. It is more because it is causally important in the world, and not just a correspondent reflection of it—it is, in the language of economics, endogenous to it. Different theories tell us which rules to pick, which policies to follow, and how to design institutions, providing different payoffs to different groups, in the process changing the world that the theories purport to map. But economic theory is also much less than an instruction sheet because of the partial nature of various theories and how incompletely they map onto the world they strive to describe. Indeed, if they turn out to be quite at odds with the world as it actually behaves, then liquidity, correlation, and tail risk are themselves ultimately derivative of this wider story of the failure of our ideas about how the economy works to act as adequate instruction sheets and institutional blueprints. They are the instruments through which we "see" the economy and the tools we use to act within the economy, which is the final reason we didn't see it coming. If VaR thinking made the crisis statistically impossible, our ideas about how markets work made it theoretically impossible, until it happened.[29]

Tearing up the Old Instruction Sheet

The way we think about financial markets today is a consequence of the revolution in macroeconomic theory that occurred in the 1970s, when the old way of thinking about the world, Keynesian macroeconomics, was seen, by the standards of the day, to fail a critical real-world test. By the 1960s, Keynesianism had, at least in the minds of policy makers, been reduced to a statistical relationship called the Phillips curve (see figure 2.2). The Phillips curve purported to show that the relationship between the rate of change in prices and wages over a long period was statistically stable: a given rate of inflation (wages/ prices) corresponded to a given level of employment. This implied that policy makers could "pick" a point on the curve that they liked (say, X percent inflation in a trade-off with Y percent unemployment) and get the economy to that point through active fiscal management. This was the instruction sheet of the day.

Rather than trading off inflation for employment, the economy of the mid-1970s seemed to trade in inflation with unemployment in a phenomenon called "stagflation," where wages/prices (inflation) and unemployment rose together. This dealt a serious blow to the credibility of Keynesian ideas because it seemed to show that unemploy-

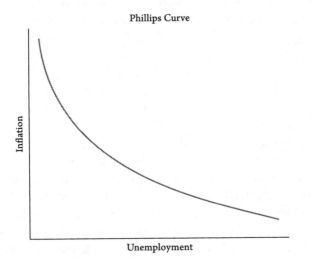

Figure 2.2 The Keynesian Phillips Curve

ment and inflation could coexist, which was extremely unlikely in Keynesian theory.[30] It also created an opportunity for then-marginalized economists who had never liked the Keynesian instruction sheet because of its distributional implications and because of its focus on aggregates rather than individuals to write a new one. In short, the world was seen to be at variance with the instruction sheet, so the instruction sheet had to be rewritten.

The new instruction sheet, which came to be known as "neoclassical," or more popularly, "neoliberal" economics, was quite technical, but basically it started from the premise that individuals were not the shortsighted, animal-sprit, driven businessmen lampooned by Keynes, but were instead supersmart processors of information.[31] The new approach distrusted anything bigger than the individual, insisting that accounts of the behavior of aggregates such as "financial markets" had to be based in prior accounts of the behavior of the individuals (investors, firms, funds) that made them up, and that any theory of the behavior of aggregates must be generated from the two main assumptions of this new neoclassical economics, that individuals are self-interested agents who maximize the pursuit of those interests, and that markets clear.[32]

According to this new view, the Keynesian instruction sheet must, in some sense, see individuals as being deluded all the time by government policy; otherwise, they would see the policy coming and anticipate it in their decisions, thus cancelling out its effects on real variables—so-called expectations or "Ricardian equivalence" effects. For example, if I know that the Democrats like to spend money, and that the money they like to spend is my taxes, I will change my spending decisions in advance of the Democrats coming to power to protect my money. Thus, if individuals do invest in being correct, as this new theory suggested, then chronically error-prone individuals would be eliminated from the market, which creates a world in which all the players in the market share the same true model of the economy. Consequently, government can't do much at all except screw things up by getting in the way. Left alone with common and accurate information, such individuals' expectations about possible future states of the economy will converge and promote a stable and self-enforcing equilibrium.

Given all this, while we can expect random individuals in markets to make mistakes, systematic mistakes by markets are *impossible* because the market is simply the reflection of individual optimal choices that together produce "the right price." Agents' expectations of the future, in new classical language, will be rational, not random, and the price given by the market under such conditions will be the "right" price that corresponds to the true value of the asset in question. Markets are efficient in the aggregate if their individual components are efficient, which they are, by definition. This world was indeed, to echo Dr. Pangloss, the best of all possible worlds.

As John Eatwell noted a long time ago, these ideas, formalized as the efficient markets hypothesis (EMH) and the rational expectations hypothesis (RATEX), are just as important politically as they are theoretically, for taken together they hold that free and integrated markets are not merely a good way to organize financial markets, *they are the only way*. Any other way is pathology. Indeed, you may have noticed in this account that the state, along with the business cycle, booms, slumps, unemployment, and financial regulation, is nowhere to be seen. To the extent that the state has a role, it devolves to "doing nothing" since doing something will only produce price distortions that will upset market efficiency.

Finance rather liked these ideas because they justified letting the financial system do whatever it liked, since apart from deliberate fraud and discounting the manipulation of informational asymmetries (where the bank knows more than you do, leading to insider trading), finance could, by definition, do no wrong. If you think markets work this way, the very notion of regulating finance becomes nonsense. Self-interested actors, whether individuals or financial firms, acting in an efficient market will make optimal trading decisions, and these outcomes will improve everyone's welfare. If you think markets work this way, then it follows that risk is calculable, sliceable, tradable, and best held by rational investors who know what they are buying. The only real policy problem becomes how to avoid moral hazard. That is, if individual institutions make bad bets and go bust, bailing them out simply encourages other firms to assume that they will be bailed out, too; so don't bail out anyone. In short, risk is individual and regulation is best left to the banks themselves (since they are the ones with "skin in the game," anything they get into is good for everyone), and so long as you don't start bailing them out, all will be fine. There is no public sector, only the private sector, and it is always in equilibrium.

Problems with the New Instruction Sheet

The problem with the new instruction sheet was that by seeing only equilibrium and efficiency arising out of the trading decisions of supersmart actors, it ignored the possibility of a crisis arising from any source apart from moral hazard or some large exogenous and usually state-induced political shock.[33] It simply could not imagine that the meshing of elements that were each intended to make the world safe, such as mortgage bonds, CDSs, and banks' risk models, could make the world astonishingly less safe.

The flaw in the logic was once again the expectation that the whole cannot be different from its component parts, that the denial of fallacies of composition haunts us once again.[34] The neoclassical insistence on grounding everything in the micro suggested that if you make the parts safe (individual banks armed with the right risk models), then you make the whole (banking system) safe. But it turned out that the whole was quite different from the sum of its parts because the interaction of the parts produced outcomes miles away from the expectations of the instruction sheet, a sheet that was quite wrong about the world in the first place.

The deep crisis was, then, a crisis of the ideas that had made these instruments and institutions possible. If you believed the new instruction sheet, shadow banks served the real banks by augmenting liquidity and assisting risk transfer. Derivatives made the system safe by making it possible for individuals to sell risk to those willing to buy it, who were presumed to be best suited to hold it by virtue of wanting to purchase it.[35] And the banks themselves, those with skin in the game, were assumed to be the best people to judge the risks they were taking using models they designed themselves, even if it turned out after the fact that the problem was precisely that the banks didn't have skin in the game since they were moving everything they could off book into SIVs.

The crisis, then, was much more than the stagflation that discredited Keynesianism, a crisis of ideas. It was a crisis of the instruction sheet of the past thirty years.[36] The claim that the prices at which financial assets traded represented the true economic fundamentals was, when the boom was exposed as a bubble, off by orders of magnitude. The rational expectations of sophisticated investors turned out to be shortsighted and bubble chasing, as irrational exuberance on the upside gave way to runaway pessimism on the downside, just as Keynes had warned about eighty years ago. Viewing moral hazard as the only policy problem led to the decision to let Lehman Brothers fail, which suddenly exposed the global banking system to the risk posed by unbacked CDS contracts.[37] Drawing risk-management procedures from these ideas produced the financial equivalent of flying a plane blindfolded because in promising a world devoid of tail risk, it actually set the world up to be smacked by those tails.

But most of all, what we couldn't see coming was something that the instruction sheet said was irrelevant, a form of risk that wasn't reducible to the sum of individual risks: *systemic risk*. Systemic risk is ever present as a residual: it's the risk you cannot diversify away. But it is also emergent from within and amplified by the interlinking of individual agents' decisions in a way that is not predictable from knowledge of those individual decisions. Systemic risk, the risk that cannot be foreseen, the bullet in the chamber of the gun, is what the different elements discussed here combined to produce. Systemic risk blew the efficient market down.

Again, and especially at this level, the crisis had nothing to do with either personal morality or state profligacy. The state had been written into irrelevance beyond providing courts, weights, measures, and defense goods. Just as it didn't start the run on the repo, amplify the crash, or cause risk blindness, so the state had nothing to do with the design of the new instruction sheet. Indeed, the new instruction sheet was designed to keep the state as far away from market processes as possible. Morality was present to be sure, but it was an upturned morality where the naked self-interest of financial market actors was taken to be the most positive virtue because its pursuit led to optimal outcomes despite moral intention. Smith's invisible hand had just given the public the finger. These new ideas were indeed a kind of morality play, but of a very odd type.

But what mattered fundamentally was the failure of a set of ideas that justified finance doing whatever it liked because whatever it did was by definition the most efficient thing that could be done. These ideas were supposed to be "the way the world works." So when it turned out that the world didn't work that way, it was hardly a surprise that the rest of the edifice based on them came crashing down. Not to put too fine a point on it, these ideas were battered by a single event that to date has cost, once lost output is included, as much as $13 trillion and, on average, a 40 percent to 50 percent increase in the debt of the states hit by the crisis.[38] That seems to be a very large price to pay to save something that was too big to fail and that wasn't meant to fail in the first place, especially when you and I are expected to pay for it.

Accounting for Finance: What It All Cost

Even the best official data on how much this crisis cost is incomplete because what one country calls recapitalization, another calls liquidity support. Some bailout measures, such as state guarantees of a bank's assets, may not have been cashed in, but were still at risk. The same applies to loans paid back by the banks after the crisis. In the US case, the IMF estimated that the amount of central-bank support pledged was initially 12.1 percent of 2009 GDP, which is around $1.75 trillion. However, when the Fed's actual support is added in (including foreign-exchange swap agreements with foreign central banks: that is, handing over as many dollars as needed in exchange for local currency to maintain dollar liquidity in a foreign banking system), the figure could be as high as $9 trillion.[39] The most recent accounting exercise undertaken by the Better Markets Institute of Washiungton, DC, places the total cost of the crisis in the US at nearly $13 trillion once GDP losses are fully incorporated.[40] In the case of the United Kingdom, the November 2009 IMF *Fiscal Monitor* footnotes the fact that the IMF's UK figures do not "include Treasury funds provided in support of central bank operations. These amount to . . . 12.8 percent [of GDP] in the United Kingdom."[41] Twelve and a half percent of UK GDP spent on bank recapitalization by the Bank of England, drawn from British Treasury funds, is not an insignificant thing to exclude from the balance sheet. But it does show quite clearly the costs of viewing the banking system as too big to fail.

Moreover, we must remember that these secondary costs have not gone back to the banks as a bill to be paid for the damage caused. Certainly, a lot of the bailout money has been paid back in different countries, but again, as IMF figures show, the net cost still far outweighs the sums recovered. By late 2010, nearly a trillion dollars remained unrecovered by the states that bailed out their banks. To get a true handle on how much this all cost, however, you would have to factor in the costs of output foregone because of the crisis and add this to these figures.

Lost output from 2008 through 2011 alone averages nearly 8 percent of GDP across the major economies. In some cases, such as Greece and Ireland, the losses are multiples steeper. But the drop in state tax revenues that comes with the crisis is perhaps even more significant because it compounds the loss in GDP. Both GDP loss and lost revenue end up being reflected in, first, the immediate budget deficit, and second, in the increase in government debt needed to plug the shortfall. As the so-called automatic stabilizers kick in, transfers such as unemployment benefits going up at the same time that revenues decrease, the public sector expands its budget as the private sector shrinks. Add to this the discretionary stimulus added by these countries to avoid even further collapses in GDP and revenue, and the net result is the most immediate mechanism for the transformation of bank debt into state debt.[42] Again, according to the IMF, of the near 40 percent average increase in debt across the OECD countries expected by 2015, half has been generated simply replacing lost revenues when tax receipts from the financial sector collapsed.[43] To put it bluntly, the state plugged a gap and stopped a financial collapse. It did not dig a fiscal ditch through profligate spending.

In the United Kingdom, in particular, this collapse in tax receipts was especially alarming since nearly 25 percent of British taxes came out of the financial sector. Little surprise then that Britain's debt ballooned. Of the rest of the increase in government debt, some 35 percent is the direct cost of bailing out the banks. Meanwhile, that antistate whipping boy for the growth in the debt, the fiscal stimulus, amounts to a mere 12 percent of the total.[44] So if you want to blame the stimulus for the debt, you are going to try to account for the missing 87.5 percent

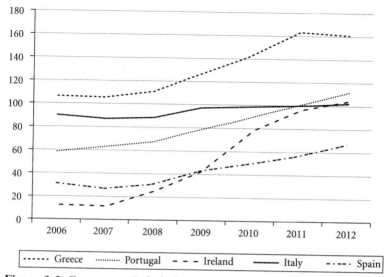

Figure 2.3 Government Debt before and after the Crisis 2006–2012
Source: OECD

of the effect. This is clearly seen in the increases in the debt-to-GDP ratios for the most affected states, the so-called European PIIGS, shown in figure 2.3, since 2006.

I hope this demonstrates that any narrative that locates wasteful spending by governments prior to the crisis in 2007 as the *cause* of the crisis is more than just simply wrong; it is disingenuous and partisan. In fact, average OECD debt before the crisis was going down, not up. What happened was that banks promised growth, delivered losses, passed the cost on to the state, and then the state got the blame for generating the debt, and the crisis, in the first place, which of course, must be paid for by expenditure cuts. The banks may have made the losses, but the citizenry will pay for them. This is a pattern we see repeatedly in the crisis.

Too Big to Fail?

A shorthand way of thinking about the decision to bail US banks rather than let them fail is to consider that there are 311 million people in the United States. Of these, 64 percent are aged 16 or over; about

158 million people work. Seventy-two percent of the working population live paycheck to paycheck, have few if any savings, and would have trouble raising $2000 on short notice.[45] There are, as far as we can tell, about 70 million handguns in the United States.[46] So what would happen if there was no money in the ATMs and no paychecks were being paid out? That was the fear. But what was the reality? Was the US financial system, comprising shadow banks, opaque instruments, bad risk models, and flawed blueprints, actually too big to fail? Giving a definitive answer is impossible because it would involve taking account of all the off-balance-sheet activities of the banks in question as well as their CDS exposures and other derivative positions. That is extremely difficult. However, looking only at balance-sheet assets, liabilities, and leverage ratios, one can clearly see why, after the failure of Lehman Brothers, the state blinked and shouted *too big to fail*.

By the third quarter of 2008, the height of the crisis, the top six US banks, Goldman Sachs, JP Morgan, Bank of America, Morgan Stanley, Citigroup, and Wells Fargo, had a collective asset-to-GDP ratio of 61.61 percent. They ran leverage ratios (assets/equity) as high as 27 to 1 (Morgan Stanley) and as low as 10 to 1 (Bank of America). Compare this to Lehman Brothers' footprint. Lehman was running 31 to 1 leverage on an asset base of $503.54 billion, which is equivalent to about 3.5 percent of US GDP.[47] If that wasn't enough to send the US government running to the tool shed to stop the contagion from spreading through the CDS and repo markets, the possibility of adding just over 60 percent of GDP to the bonfire, the collective total of the banks' asset footprints, would certainly focus the collective mind on the too big to fail problem.

So the banks were bailed out, and the costs, as we have seen, have been borne first by the state, and ultimately, by the taxpayer. Was it worth it? This is an even harder counterfactual to reason since "what could have happened" remains speculative. But if the whole system had melted down as was feared, the immediate cost could have been the sum of those bank assets, some 61 percent of GDP, which does not factor in the secondary costs in lost output, unemployment, and the damage that you can do with 70 million handguns.

The crisis started in America because this system had become too big to fail. Banking was transformed from its sleepy 3-6-3 origins. Disintermediation, securitization, and the rise of repo markets made funding cheaper and lending more plentiful but riskier. Those risks were supposed to be controlled by financial derivatives and risk-management tools, but instead these technologies seemed to amplify and spread, rather than reduce and control, the risk in the system. We were blinded to the possibility of crisis, as both the regulators and the regulated accepted the logic of efficient markets, rational expectations, Ricardian equivalence, and all the rest, as a description of the actual world rather than a stylized theory about the world. As a result, the opaque but highly interdependent parts of a complex system combined with overconfidence in our ability to manage risk to produce a bust that the state decided it had to shoulder. Maybe the $13 trillion cost to date was a price worth paying? Perhaps. But only if the costs had been shared according to both ability to pay and responsibility for the bust, but they were not.

As we shall see in the next chapter, what was a private-sector banking crisis was rechristened by political and financial elites as a crisis of the sovereign state in a matter of months. That this took hold as the dominant narrative for explaining the crisis in the Euro-zone countries seems at first glance rather odd. Europe usually sits to the left of the United States politically, but it was acting far to its right economically by mid-2010. The basic reason for this was the same one we saw in the United States. If you think the risk posed by hugely levered US banks that were too big to fail was terrifying, then consider the following: in November 2011 the Financial Stability Board, a coordinating body for national financial regulators, published a list of systemically important banks, in other words, the too big to fail list. Of the twenty-nine banks named, only eight were US banks; seventeen were European. The Europeans have managed to build a system that is *too big to bail*, which is the real reason why a bunch of putative lefties are squeezing the life out of their welfare states.

A final thought. Since the 2008 crisis, banks that file with the US Securities and Exchange Commission have awarded themselves $2.2

trillion in compensation.[48] I repeat—*since the crisis*. Austerity is a great policy for the banks because the people who are to pay for the mess are not the same ones who made it. Nowhere is this truer than in Europe. In fact, as we shall see next, it's the real reason we all need to be austere.

3

EUROPE—TOO BIG TO BAIL?

THE POLITICS OF PERMANENT AUSTERITY

Introduction

It is true that Europe, especially the countries that use the euro, is not in great fiscal health. But, as in the United States, it is not true that this came about through an orgy of public borrowing and spending. Only in the case of Greece is the profligacy story plausible. It simply doesn't apply to the other European states. Yet today, all we hear about is the profligacy of the Greek government and work-shy and uncompetitive Greek workers as the root cause of Europe's so-called sovereign debt crisis.[1] Again, I stress "so-called" because although the debt-to-GDP ratios of European states have grown substantially since the start of the crisis, from an average of 70 percent in 2008 to 90 percent at the end of 2012, this is the result of the financial crisis that began in the United States in 2007 hitting European shores in 2008 and pushing the European economy into recession.[2] Just as occurred in the United States, the private debt of highly leveraged financial institutions became the public debt of states for two reasons, one already familiar and one generated by the project of European monetary union itself.

The familiar cause was the freezing up in 2008 of the global banking system, which caused the European economy to contract. As states struggled to fill these fiscal holes, public debt once again took the place of private debt as states bailed out and recapitalized their banks (in some cases) at the same time as their automatic stabilizers kicked in to undergird their economies (tax receipts fell while transfers went up in all cases). Already debt-loaded sovereigns that hadn't looked risky before—for instance, Italy's debt-to-GDP ratio was over 100 percent in 2001 and no one seemed to mind—suddenly looked much riskier as their growth slowed and as a consequence their bond yields shot up.

The hidden cause was the role played by European banks in generating the sovereign debt crisis. In late 2008, it seemed that European banks had escaped the worst of the crisis. Apart from a few German banks and a Belgian bank here or there that got in over its head, what Europe had, said German politicians in particular, was a "crisis of Anglo-Saxon banking." As German finance minister Peer Steinbrück put it, the real cause of the financial crisis was "the irresponsible overemphasis on the 'laissez-faire' principle, namely giving market forces the most possible freedom from state regulation, in the Anglo-American financial system."[3] The European banking model, in contrast, was said to be much sounder because of its conservative practices, so there was no need for Europe to throw money at the problem as the United States and the United Kingdom had done. As German chancellor Angela Merkel put it in late 2008, "Cheap money in the US was a driver of this crisis. . . . I am deeply concerned . . . [with] reinforcing this trend . . . [and wonder] whether we could find ourselves back in five years facing the same crisis."[4] Once the immediate liquidity crunch of 2008 seemed to have passed, the crisis diagnosis preferred by Europe's dominant power was that the continent's problem was a crisis of state spending. The correct policy was therefore to cut the budgets of these profligate periphery states.

There is just one problem with this diagnosis: it is wrong. The ongoing Eurozone crisis really has very little to do with the fiscal profligacy of periphery sovereigns, only one of which, as noted, was meaningfully profligate. There is a crisis in European sovereign debt markets; of that there is no doubt. But treating it as a crisis brought about by debt-fueled consumption and profligate state spending is to confuse correlation (they happened at the same time) with causation (out-of-control spending caused the crisis).

Just as we saw in the US case, the crisis in Europe has almost nothing to do with states and everything to do with markets. It is a private-sector crisis that has once again become a state responsibility. It has almost nothing to do with too much state spending and almost everything to do with the incentives facing banks when the euro, a financial doomsday machine the Europeans built for themselves, was introduced. To understand why, let's start with the official story of the European crisis: how the crisis hit Europe, the ideological schism over spending, the discovery of the PIIGS and government debt, and the cry for austerity. Then we switch gears and examine why European politicians are knowingly saying some very silly things; that is, why they shy away from the real story of the crisis, and the real reason we all need to be austere.

The Crisis Hits Europe

Europe's largest economy, Germany, saw the first signs of trouble approaching in August 2007 when IKB, a Dusseldorf-based lender, had to be rescued after suffering losses on its US subprime investments. Following this incident, it seemed for a while that German banks had avoided the crisis, until the state had to step in and rescue the Hypo Real Estate bank in 2008 when its loans to Eastern European mortgagers dried up. This sounded the alarm that other, bigger German banks were still exposed to the East through their loans to Austrian banks, which in turn lent that cash, equivalent to over 70 percent of Austrian GDP, to Eastern European mortgagers whose currencies were now rapidly losing value.

In response, the German government announced a 500-billion-euro bank-bailout fund in late 2008. Germany got nervous again in 2009 when several *Landesbanken*, Germany's public-private regional development banks, which had, it turned out, also been investing in toxic US assets, got into trouble. But their losses, too, were easily dealt with. By the end of 2009, the German banking system was stable, if not healthy. What worried the Germans was how the global credit crunch would affect their exports—their growth machine—not exposure to US subprime mortgage bonds.

Those fears seemed justified when, in the fourth quarter of 2008, German exports contributed 8.1 percent of an overall 9.4 percent annualized decline in GDP.[5] By mid-2009, the Bundesbank was forecasting a 6 percent GDP contraction by the end of the year. Surprisingly robust demand in Asia, however, made up for declines in the Euro Area. German exports, however, rapidly rebounded. Industrial orders rose throughout 2009, and by August investor confidence had reached its highest point in three years.[6] Germany, it seemed, had dodged the financial bullets emanating from the United States. True, Germany had its own stimulus program in the form of the original cash-for-clunkers car program, a boost to family allowances, and, most significantly, subsidies to employers not to lay off workers. But unlike in the United States and the United Kingdom, there was no need to turn the money pumps on to fuel recovery. Little wonder then that the Germans looked on aghast as the United States and the United Kingdom seemed to do just that.

Twelve-Month Keynesians

One of the oddest aspects of the transmission of the financial crisis from the United States to Europe was the sudden embrace of Keynesian economics by, except for the European Central Bank (ECB) and the German government, almost everyone. Recalling the discussion of the political power of economic ideas in chapter 2, you may not think this is so odd. After all, if the financial crisis challenged in a very public way many of the core ideas of efficient markets, then replacing those ideas after the crisis shouldn't be such a surprise. But if you accept that economic ideas are more than instruction sheets: that they enshrine different distributions of wealth and power and are power resources for actors whose claims to authority and income depend upon their credibility, then the idea of giving them up, especially for the theory those actors had "defeated" a generation before, does seem a little odd. The crisis may have shaken neoliberal efficient-market ideas, but to replace them all with global Keynesian stimulus was another matter entirely. Yet that seems to have been just what happened—for about twelve months.

A major reason Keynesianism now became the policy du jour was that governing neoliberal ideas denied that such a crisis was possible in the first place. So when it happened, it was bound to open up room for ideas that said such events were inevitable if you let markets regulate themselves, which is the Keynesian point. It was hard to publicly defend the logic of self-correcting markets when they were so obviously not self-correcting. Indeed, such traditional standard bearers for the neoclassical cause as Eugene Fama, Edward Prescott, and Robert Barro who had previously enjoyed public prominence found themselves confined to the opinion pages of the *Wall Street Journal*. No one was buying "the price is always right/state bad and market good" story when prices had been shown to be wrong by a few orders of magnitude and the state was bailing out the market. Furthermore, neoclassical policy was entirely focused on avoiding one problem, inflation, and providing one outcome, stable prices. It seemed to have very little to say about a world in which deflation was now the worry, and price stabilization meant raising, not lowering, inflation expectations.

Helping such ideas along was the fact that, as Henry Farrell and John Quiggin put it, "There was a significant Keynesian party hidden in the academy," and it found unexpected allies.[7] Neoclassical economists and fellow travelers who were publicly reassessing their own beliefs during the crisis, such as Martin Feldstein and Richard Posner, joined prominent Keynesian economists such as Paul Krugman and Joseph Stiglitz in the campaign for stimulus, lending Keynesian ideas a new prestige. Even international economic institutions that were famous for forcing austerity on developing countries, such as the IMF, began to argue that monetary tools were not enough to solve the crisis and that an active and coordinated fiscal policy needed to be applied.[8] Parallel institutions that would shortly mount a counterattack against Keynesian policies and ideas, such as the ECB, largely kept out of the debate at this time, giving the Keynesians the stage. Finally, with the entire global payments system at stake and a "leave it to the market" policy that was untenable since the market was in triage, "governments quickly came to believe that monetary policy was insufficient on its own to help the real economy."[9]

The results were immediate and dramatic. Countries as diverse as Brazil, China, and the United States lined up to stimulate their economies and stymie the contraction of economic activity. China led with a whopping 13 percent of GDP; Spain promised 7 percent; and the United States committed around 5.5 percent of GDP. Even Germany stimulated to the tune of just under 3 percent of GDP. Whether this money was actually spent was another matter entirely, but that it was promised for its intended purpose was significant. As Keynes's biographer Lord Skidelsky put it in a book celebrating the 2009 rediscovery of Keynes, we had witnessed "the Return of the Master."[10] The only problem was that by the time the master returned, some very important folks had already left the building: the Germans, followed by the British and the Canadians. The global return of Keynes was to last only a year from start to finish.

The German Ideology

Why were the Germans determined to halt the return of the master? Three factors are often cited and each carries some weight. The first is Germany's collective historical neuralgia over the inflation of the 1920s, which inevitably leads German policy makers to the conclusion that "throwing money around" is never a good idea. While there is something to this, the reality is of course much more interesting.

German inflation in the 1920s was not the result of a policy of monetary stimulus by the German central bank and treasury trying to stave off a recession. First of all, inflation didn't just happen to Germany. Other Mittel-European countries, such as Austria, Hungary, and Poland, experienced hyperinflationary episodes at the same time, and none of these episodes was due to the enactment of Keynesian policies. Their common origins lay instead in the fact that World War I had been financed through debt rather than through taxes, which lowered postwar exchange rates and made imports more expensive, which in turn fostered inflation. The inflation pent-up from that earlier period ebbed and flowed for almost a decade.

Second, though the German hyperinflation was caused by government policy, it was intimately bound up with the desire of the German government to break the economic stranglehold of the war reparations that it owed to France under the Treaty of Versailles. France wanted Germany to pay off its war reparation in either gold-backed marks or foreign currencies. But for Germany to earn foreign currency when its own exchange rate was falling required more and more marks, further stoking inflation. The proverbial straw that broke the camel's back was the government's decision to continue to pay wages to German workers (in territory that France now occupied because of Germany's nonpayment of its Versailles treaty obligations in 1923) while the exchange rate was collapsing. The resulting hyperinflation had the convenient effect of wiping out large amounts of government debt and stymied its ability to make reparations payments to France. The hyperinflation also ended very abruptly with a currency reform in late 1923. That is, the government printed new money, and that ended the problem of the government printing money.[11] Today, this specter of hyperinflation is invoked by German and ECB policy makers whenever they want to either curtail criticism of austerity measures or go on the offensive against stimulus proposals. Yet, it seems an odd argument to make when the classic case of hyperinflation haunting the policy memory of Europe's most powerful country was singularly not caused by a deliberate monetary stimulus attempting to arrest an economic slump.[12]

A second, subtler, ideological argument that pushes in the same direction is that German policy makers are "ordoliberals" (literally, order liberals) rather than neoliberals. We will explore this topic more in chapter 4, but the basic insight is that the governing philosophy of German economic elites has never been the neoliberal mantra "markets good, state bad." Rather, the German ordoliberal tradition stresses the importance of state provision of the *Ramenbedingungen* (framework conditions) within which markets can operate. According to this view, states must provide adequate social safety nets and support extra-economic institutions to allow labor to adjust skills to match market needs, ensure that cartels do not develop, and limit unproductive speculation through taxation and other policy instruments. In short, regulation to make the market possible, rather than regulation to police its rough edges, becomes, along with strong budgetary discipline, the core of a *Sozialmarktwirtschaft* (social market economy), where the state regulates but doesn't stimulate or experiment, especially with the budget. *Ordnungspolitik,* a politics of order and stability, especially financial stability policed by a strong independent central bank, is the result.[13]

Third, nothing succeeds like success, and the German economy has been very successful with this instruction sheet. Despite its severe damage in World War II, Germany had become the largest and most powerful economy in Europe by the early 1960s.[14] Its strength was, and still is, based on the export of high-quality manufactures to the rest of the world. This not only made it rich, it enabled what was then West Germany to buy an entirely bankrupt country, East Germany, integrate it into its own economy, and then go on to reduce labor costs, regain competitiveness, brush off the recession following the financial crisis with a shrug, stabilize its banks, and return to export-led growth in 2009, while the rest of Europe fell off a financial cliff.

That the version of events preferred by the Germans themselves tends to underemphasize such factors as the patronage of the United States, especially insofar as the United States turned a blind eye to Germany's running an undervalued deutsche mark for the entire Cold War period, is beside the point.[15] German policy makers and voters believe the story. The policy lesson learned by the most powerful (and solvent) European state was that policy failures by governments, not financial markets, make crises. Consequently, the policy "success" of 2008—the return of the master and his stimulus measures—was seen by the Germans and their allies at the ECB as a policy disaster waiting to happen whose consequences would only become all too apparent in future inflation. Present debt increases were just the canary in the coalmine. Given this, the Germans were not about to sign on to any more stimulus efforts, regardless of pressure from the United States.

A Perverse Politics

It is worth remembering how perverse the politics of this was. When the crisis hit the United States in 2007 and 2008, it was a Republican administration with an ex-CEO of Goldman Sachs at its fiscal helm that invented the $700 billion Troubled Asset Relief Program (TARP) and engineered the bailout of the US financial system. Putatively Keynesian economists, such as Larry Summers, who were part of the Obama economic team in 2008, merely continued the work of their Republican predecessors. The new team may have been intellectually more attuned to a compensatory logic by virtue of being Democrats, but it was, we should remember, the Democratic administration of Bill Clinton that had balanced the US budget and "ended welfare as we know it." When the crisis hit, the United States may have been on the right ideologically, but it was very much on the left in terms of economic policy.

Europe, in contrast, was populated by left-leaning Social Democrats and center-right Christian Democrats who had spent the previous decade building a currency union that viewed monetary stability plus strict debt and deficit controls as the only policies worth bothering about. Thus, when the crisis hit, the European left (with the exception of the British under New Labour) and center-right argued and behaved in ways that we would normally expect from American Republicans: they championed financial stability, inflation control, and budget cutting as the way to get out of the crisis.

In the United Kingdom these perverse political dynamics played out in one country: Britain's prime minister, Gordon Brown, who as chancellor of the exchequer presided over the biggest boom and bust in British history while promising financial "prudence for a purpose," spent, lent, or otherwise guaranteed about 40 percent of British GDP to save the banks and even more to stimulate the economy. When the Brown government lost the election to Conservative David Cameron in May 2010, Cameron's party had spent the last two years trying to convince voters that it would not slash social spending and would actually be better than New Labour at providing public services. These were, as the Chinese proverb has it, interesting times. Given this odd mixture of political positions and ideological priors, spring 2010 produced the curious spectacle of the Americans arguing for global Keynesianism while the Germans, cheered on by the new British Conservative government under David Cameron, demanded regional austerity.

The Road to Toronto

During spring 2010, with the immediate danger of financial collapse abated and the new threat of sovereign contagion yet to fully emerge, a new ideological alignment began to take shape. For the previous year the United States, along with the British under the Labour Party's Gordon Brown, had increasingly questioned Germany's commitment to stimulating its economy. Germany was attacked for essentially free-riding on other countries' stimulus efforts, a charge it denied. In fairness, when one takes into account Germany's actual stimulus measures, such as its work-time subsidy and the impact of its bigger welfare state in a downturn, the Germans had more than a point in their favor. But they were not about to stimulate any further, especially since their exports were picking up again by mid-2009 and they did not, so it seemed at the time, have a banking crisis to deal with. The United States and the United Kingdom kept up the pressure on Germany in the run-up to the G20 meeting in Toronto in June 2010. Meanwhile, rather than simply continue to accept the continuing Keynesian counteroffensive, some of the neoliberal old guard, in both Europe and the United States, began to strike back in the public debate.

The *Financial Times* became a kind of bulletin board for elite economic opinion. Using the paper as a platform, former Federal Reserve chairman Alan Greenspan went from saying in October 2008 that the crisis had forced him to reconsider a "flaw" in his "ideology" of markets, and in February 2009 even admitting the desirability of bank nationalization, to, by June of that same year, defending austerity and worrying, in a very German manner, about future inflation.[16] Jeffrey Sachs opined that it was "time to plan for [the] post Keynesian era" since the stimulus was at best unnecessary and at worst harmful.[17] By mid-2010, the *Financial Times* was organizing an "austerity debate" that pitted increasingly on-the-defensive Keynesians against a coterie of conservatives and neoclassicals. Significantly, major German politicians began to join forces with principals at the ECB to send a common message. As ECB chief Jean Claude Trichet put it in a much-reported broadside in the *Financial Times*, "Stimulate no more—it is now time for all to tighten."[18] The campaign against the master was heating up.

A week before each full G20 meeting, the group's finance ministers get together to lay out the agenda. Their June 2010 meeting in Busan, South Korea, signaled that global Keynesianism was about to hit the buffers. The *Financial Times* had reported as recently as April 2010 that the G20 position on the crisis was that public spending "should be maintained until the recovery was firmly entrenched." By the time of the Busan meeting, the G20 finance ministers now thought that "recent events highlight the importance of sustainable public finances...growth friendly measures, to deliver fiscal sustainability." The United States objected to this shift in tone on the grounds that the "withdrawal of fiscal and monetary stimulus...need[s] to proceed in step with the strengthening of the public sector," but the tide had already started turning, even before the full G20 meeting in Toronto occurred.[19]

The ECB and the German government simultaneously cranked up the pressure on the American position in the run-up to the full meeting. Days before the G20 meeting, ECB chief Trichet explicitly rejected Keynesian demand-deficiency arguments, citing the need for "a budget policy...that we would call confidence building" that centered upon the reduction of debt. Two days later, the German finance minister Wolfgang Schäuble published an extended piece in the *Financial Times* in which he stressed the need for "expansionary fiscal consolidation." Invoking the specter of future inflation, he declared that "we [Germany]...are...more preoccupied with the implications of excessive deficits and the dangers of high inflation." As such, Germany would not respond to the crisis by "piling up public debt."[20] By the time of the Toronto meeting, the Canadians and the British had sided with the Germans, leaving the Americans isolated. The final communiqué of the Toronto meeting repeated the meme, authored by Trichet and amplified by Schäuble, of "growth friendly fiscal consolidation." Seen at the time as a fudge between the Keynesian and orthodox positions, what it actually signaled was the end of global Keynesianism.

Following on the heels of the G20 communiqué came the ECB's June 2010 *Monthly Bulletin*, which was an unabashed restatement of neoclassical economic ideas and a call for "growth friendly fiscal consolidation" going forward. In the *Bulletin*, "Ricardian consumers" with rational expectations who anticipated the effects of government policies years ahead went on display, alongside inflation-averse and confidence-sensitive investors appalled at the prospect of government "crowding out" investment, future inflation, and ever-larger government debts.[21] As Stephen Kinsella argues regarding the seemingly contradictory logic of expansionary fiscal consolidation, "Proponents of this theory argue that fiscal contraction, rather than leading to a decline in output...will result in higher output...[as] consumers and investors anticipate long run tax deductions because of cuts in expenditure [which will] offset...the contraction."[22] Given this version of rational expectations theory, the ECB could only conclude that austerity had to be the way forward because "the longer-run benefits of fiscal consolidation are largely undisputed."[23] Undisputed, that is, so long as the question is posed only in terms of this narrow rational-expectations model. Global Keynesianism was indeed on the way out. But German inflation phobia and ordoliberalism aside, why were the Europeans suddenly so sensitive to the problem of government debt and opposed to more stimulus spending? The answer brings us back to the PIIGS of Europe and their profligate ways.

The European PIIGS and the Discovery of Sovereign Debt: Greece

While the Germans were recovering and the Anglos were bailing, a quiet crisis was brewing on the periphery of Europe. Greece had long been the problem child of the European periphery. It came out of World War II and went straight into the bloodiest civil war in modern European history. When it ended, this already very poor country grew rapidly, but from a very low level, such that the unstable political order that emerged post war finally collapsed into a brutal military dictatorship in 1967. When Greece emerged from the dictatorship period and stabilized in the late 1970s, the European Economic Community (the EEC, as the EU was then known) provided it with much-needed external funding for infrastructure investment while its modern political party system took shape.

Greek politics in the 1980s and 1990s was dominated by the socialist Papandreou administrations that sought to increase personal income and public consumption, an understandable response to decades of instability, violence, and political polarization. These governments ran persistently expansionary policies that, given the country's low productivity growth, resulted in increasing debts and widening deficits. (In fact, Greece hasn't run a budget surplus in fifty years.) Debt to GDP passed 100 percent in 1994, hovered around 105 percent for a decade, and then shot up as a result of the financial crisis in 2008, reaching 165 percent of GDP in late 2011.[24]

What made this spending possible was that having adopted the euro, Greece and the other European periphery states (Portugal, Italy, Spain, and Ireland) were effectively endowed with Germany's credit rating on the assumption that the ECB would back all outstanding debt issued by member states since it was all in the "same" new euro currency. As such, the historically high borrowing costs of these countries fell. Greece's borrowing costs, for example, fell from 20 percent on a ten-year bond before the introduction of the euro to around 4 percent in 2005, and in the case of Greece in particular, more borrowing was the result.[25] Since Greece was able to borrow more easily, money became more plentiful locally, financing both consumption and investment. However, this also raised Greece's labor costs relative to its Euro Area neighbors; its competitiveness fell, widening its current account deficit—Greece was importing more than it was exporting with the extra cash.

Greece had some special structural problems that turned these vulnerabilities into accidents waiting to happen. First, leaving aside all the often-repeated stories of endemic corruption and dubious early retirements, of which there are many, Greece has a weak tax-collection capacity and an even weaker political will to enforce collection, so revenues have never balanced expenditures. Second, government spending was notoriously uncoordinated, with the result that in October 2009 the Greek government revealed that the reported fiscal deficit of 6.5 percent of GDP was in fact closer to 13 percent of GDP. Unsurprisingly, investors regarded this as the ringing of a rather loud alarm bell over the true state of Greek public finances. The low interest rates that Greek debt had enjoyed since adopting the euro via that borrowed German credit rating shot up, which made a difficult interest-payment environment very suddenly awful. Piling on the pressure, the ratings agencies took notice and downgraded Greek bonds from A to BBB−, which compounded the debt burden by lowering prices and further spiking yields. As a result, the economy began to contract such that outstanding debt increased as GDP collapsed.

In such situations bond market investors face a dilemma. If they believe that bonds are going to fall further in value, they should get rid of them as soon as possible.[26] But if they do dump the asset in question, they run the risk that everyone else holding these assets will do the same, with prices collapsing as a result. As we saw in chapter 2 with US mortgage securities, the risk of contagion looms large when the mass dumping of, in this case, Greek assets, leads to a collapse in their price. Anticipating this, people holding those assets want to dump them ahead of anyone else, which leads to the very fire sale everyone is trying to avoid. This in turn leads to the dumping of other (non-Greek) assets to cover their (Greek) losses, which then lowers the value of the unrelated assets, eventually leading to a fire sale of good assets as a whole. Given that Eurozone core banks were stuffed full of periphery bonds (they had, after all, lent the Greeks money by buying their bonds), any fire sale would end up costing a lot more than the value of the outstanding Greek debt, particularly if the debt fire spread to Portugal, Ireland, and—it was feared—maybe even Spain and Italy.

The ideal policy back in 2009 would have cost around 50 billion euros. It would have required either the ECB, or Germany as its major creditor, to buy the secondary-market Greek debt that was subject to near-term rollover risk, bury it somewhere deep in its balance sheet, and walk away. Why didn't they do so? One answer lies in German politics. There was a regional election coming up in Germany, and it was politically easier to blame the Greeks for being feckless than it was to explain to the German public that the ECB needed to bail them out for reasons of systemic risk. The other answer lies in the ECB statutes that forbid one country to bail out another for fear of generating moral hazard. Such bailouts are, except in exceptional circumstances (the treaty in question mentions natural disasters) not allowed. Remember, the ECB only has one problem, price inflation, and one tool, the rate of interest. As such, the ECB was completely unable, and the Germans were completely unwilling to take responsibility. As a consequence, investors began to price in the risk of contagion as increasingly likely, and the yields on all periphery bonds began to rise, which is why Portugal, Ireland, Spain, and Italy got lumped together with Greece. The PIIGS collective was born in the fires of contagion risk. Unfortunately, while the collective acronym is attractive, the problem is that Ireland, Spain, Portugal, and Italy are nothing like Greece.

Ireland and Spain: Property Bubble Trouble

Ireland and Spain are an odd pair to be lumped in with the Greeks. First of all, both have a better reputation for tax payments. But far more important were their fiscal and monetary positions back in 2007. Unlike Greece, both Ireland and Spain were "best in class" in terms of debts and deficits going into the crisis. In 2007 Ireland's net debt-to-GDP ratio was 12 percent, and Spain's was 26 percent. In contrast, Germany's debt sat at 50 percent of GDP.[27] Why, then, did Ireland and Spain have a crisis when Germany did not? The answer, as usual, begins and ends with the banks, in this case via real-estate lending. If Greece had dug itself a long-term fiscal hole that was covered over with low interest rates, then Ireland was unaware that the hole even existed and built houses right on top of it. Spain, as we shall see, is Ireland moved up a few orders of magnitude. Italy is Portugal moved up a few orders of magnitude. The song remains the same in both cases.

Ireland, like Germany, did well prior to the crisis. Ireland reduced its gross government debt-to-GNP ratio from 112 percent in 1986 to 25 percent in 2007, and its net debt to GDP in 2007 stood at a mere 12 percent.[28] It was able to do this by exporting to countries that were expanding and by up-skilling its workforce to take advantage of the influx of multinational corporations that were keen to use Ireland, with its English-speaking workforce and low corporate tax rates, as a gateway to a single-market Europe. Ireland's GNP rose significantly, as did wages, boosting both consumption and tax revenues. The growth of this so-called Celtic Tiger economy during the late 1990s encouraged more people to look to property as an investment, and in doing so Ireland generated a massive banking accident waiting to happen, without a Fannie, a Freddie, or anything like them being present.

Part of what stoked the bubble in Ireland had also affected Greece: the bond-buying activities of major European banks, which gave the periphery cheap money, combined with low interest rates set by the ECB that translated into zero, if not negative real rates, in Ireland and Spain from 2000 onward. "As a result [Irish] property prices soared by over 64 percent from 2002–2006."[29] To fund lending on such a massive scale, Irish banks increasingly turned to wholesale funding markets in the United States (the repo markets we learned about in chapter 2), essentially borrowing overnight to fund thirty-year mortgages. The three main Irish banks' combined asset footprint at the time of the crash was around 400 percent of GDP. One of those banks, Anglo-Irish, lent 67 billion euros to the nonfinancial sector (real estate) in 2007 alone.[30] Anglo-Irish was particularly dependent on short-term funding. When the interbank market froze following Lehman's collapse, the ability of the Irish banks to service their loans collapsed along with Irish property prices, taking the entire banking sector down with it.

Fearing financial Armageddon, the Irish government issued a blanket guarantee for the entire banking system's liabilities, and that 400 percent of assets as GDP on the private sector's balance sheet very suddenly became the Irish public's problem. The combined result of the property-bubble collapse and the banking system implosion was "the largest compound decline in GNP of any industrialized country over the 2007–2010 period."[31] Government debt increased by 320 percent to over 110 percent of GDP as the government spent some 70 billion euros to shore up the banking system. Meanwhile, unemployment rose to 14 percent by mid-2011, a figure that would have been higher had it not been for emigration.

Spain is a case of "the song remains the same," albeit translated and amplified through different banking institutions. Rather than having three big banks that dominate all domestic lending, as in the Irish case, Spain's largest banks are internationalized and are therefore somewhat hedged against domestic turbulence. In Spain the real problem, as became plain in the spring of 2012, lay in the regional savings banks: the *cajas de ahorros*.

To understand where Spain is today, you have to start from the fact that in 1979 Spain was the eighth-largest industrial economy in the world. Today, it has slipped to seventeenth place. In between, Spain effectively deindustrialized, becoming a banking, services, and tourism hub. The problem is that the income streams such a growth model relies on come primarily from outside the country: when such people stop spending and lending, you are in serious trouble. It's even more of a problem when what domestic growth you do have is debt-financed and based on little more than the swapping of houses.

As John Mauldin puts it, "Spain had the mother of all housing bubbles,"[32] which is true but also a little misleading since other countries had bigger bubbles. According to Bank of Spain data, while Spain's ten-year headlong rush into housing produced a 115 percent increase in house prices between 1997 and 2007, the United Kingdom's bubble was bigger still at 140 percent, and Ireland topped the list at 160 percent. Why Spain matters much more than Ireland, however, is that Spanish GDP is approximately seven times the size of Ireland's; Spain is the fourth-largest economy in the Eurozone and is responsible for almost 10 percent of Euro Area GDP. As such, the popping of the Spanish housing bubble was going to matter in more than just Spain.

In that sense Mauldin is quite correct. The scale of the Spanish property bubble was astonishing. Real estate had become so central to the Spanish economy that construction alone generated 14 percent of employment and 16 percent of GDP. Once related sectors were included, the figures jumped to nearly a quarter of GDP and of employment, respectively. Unsurprisingly, given this construction boom, credit expanded to meet demand. Indeed, loans to developers alone constituted nearly 50 percent of GDP by 2007.[33] When the bubble burst, unemployment shot up from 8 percent to 25 percent in three years, with youth unemployment reaching 52 percent in mid-2012. Domestic demand fell by 7 percent while GDP contracted 6.3 percent in the first quarter of 2009 alone.

Where Ireland differs from Spain—apart from the magnitude of the bust—lies in the peculiar institutions of Spanish banking. As mentioned earlier, with their international portfolios the big three Spanish banks are reasonably well hedged against domestic exposures. Where, then, did this volume of credit come from? The answer was the *cajas de ahorros,* the regional savings banks (think US credit unions), especially the conglomerate version, *Bankia,* that went bust in 2012. These institutions together made nearly 50 percent of all domestic banking-sector loans. The *cajas* matter because their loan books are opaque (think subprime); they are undercapitalized; and most importantly, they are stuffed full of assets that are not coming back any time soon, particularly because the assets in question were so mispriced to begin with. They are not coming back soon because the other side of the balance sheet for the *cajas'* loans is the phenomenal increase in private-sector debt in Spain. It grew at over 20 percent a year in the run-up to the crisis to over 200 percent of GDP, which is now held by a population which is one-quarter unemployed. Add to this the fact that Spanish mortgages are recourse loans, meaning that the bank can come after the debtor for the original loan—forever—and not for just the current value of the property, and mortgagers have every incentive to sit tight and not allow the market to clear, thus making the situation worse by inches. In the United States you can walk away from a mortgage and the house is the bank's problem. In Spain, when you walk away from the house, the mortgage debt is still your problem.

Take Ireland and Spain together and you do not have a story of profligate states, feckless workers, and all the rest. Certainly, the Spanish regional governments have a few white elephant projects that have worsened the situation, airports that have no traffic, massive opera houses with no customers, and the like; but these are symptoms, not causes. Indeed, in the Basque country, where there was more political control of the *cajas*, investment in property was not allowed to the same extent and the result was investment in manufacturing.[34] The underlying crisis is, once again, one of private, not public, finance.

What we have here is the same thing we saw in the United States, the United Kingdom, and, as we shall detail in a later chapter, Iceland—the implosion of privately funded housing bubbles—a quintessentially private-sector phenomenon that became a public-sector problem. The difference is that Ireland, by guaranteeing its banks' debts, explicitly and instantaneously transformed private debt into public debt that it is now hard pressed to pay off. Spain hasn't even managed to get a full accounting of its banking crisis, despite the biggest *cajas* conglomerate going bust in 2012.[35] But the fact that this is occurring in an economy seven times larger than Ireland's with more opaque banking institutions is more than enough to make bond market actors worry about the solvency of the sovereign standing behind those banks. A Greek default would be a risk on its own, but if it spread to Ireland and then Spain, all bets would be off.

Portugal and Italy: The Slow-Motion Growth Crisis

Portugal and Italy sit in the same relation as Spain and Ireland. Except that, rather than being tied together by a real-estate-cum-banking crisis, Portugal and Italy are united by a combination of low growth, old age, low productivity, and institutional sclerosis. What the PIIGS all have in common was how their adoption of the euro made the interest payments on their bonds fall as core banks came to prefer their debt to even lower-yielding German and French debt. Yet, despite all the cheap money this produced in the PIIGS, Portugal was in trouble long before the crisis of 2008.

Portugal's two main export industries, footwear and textiles, were clobbered by Asian and Eastern European competition in the 1990s. As a consequence, its trade deficits widened and its competitiveness fell while the services sector, much of which is nontradable, took up the slack. Young people increasingly went into education, temporarily lowering, at the public expense, the unemployment rate, without necessarily increasing skills. As *The Economist* magazine wryly noted, "The number of lawyers increased by forty-eight percent between 2000 and 2010."[36] Meanwhile, growth per person averaged 0.2 percent per year over the same period, while combined public and private debts reached over 240 percent of GDP by 2010.

Demography compounds these problems. Portugal is ranked 178th out of 230 countries in population growth and 195th in births. The median age of the country is forty, and 18 percent of the population is already over sixty-five years old. Before the crisis these things could be ignored because capital flows from the European core to the periphery masked the chronic lack of growth in these countries. But once those flows stopped in 2010 in a context of market worries about Greek and Irish indebtedness, what was not a problem before—long-term growth dynamics—suddenly became one. After all, if the underlying dynamics are not there to support growth, then no amount of austerity will reduce the debt accrued.

Italy is a giant version of Portugal while being in many ways the polar opposite of Spain. Italy has low private debt and massive public debt. Massive, in the sense that Italy has the third-largest bond market in the world. Let's think about that for a moment. A southern European country with the world's twenty-third-largest population and eleventh-largest economy has the world's third-largest bond market. How did that happen? Look only at Northern Italy, and you see one of the most developed industrial countries in the world, with competitive exports, price-inelastic products, and high incomes. Include the south of Italy, and you see a rather different world of agricultural producers and small, low-productivity firms.

What united these two very different versions of Italy was a political system that transferred resources from the North to pay for the South while not fully taxing its citizens to make up the shortfall because of the persistence of traditional class alignments in the South. As a consequence, persistent deficits, which turned into debts that were reduced by persistent devaluations of the exchange rate, made it possible. Adopting the euro ruled out such devaluations, but the collapse in interest rates that it engendered sustained the unsustainable a bit longer. In 2000, Italian net debt to GDP was 93 percent. In 2007, it was 87 percent. Today, it is 100 percent, as the crisis and austerity policies lower the Italian economy's already sclerotic growth rate of about 1.5 percent a year (for the past twenty-five years) while the debt owed gets bigger still and rates have shot up.[37]

As in the case of Portugal, what wasn't an issue in 2000 suddenly became one in 2010 when the markets noticed three things: Italy does indeed have the third-biggest bond market in the world; its growth rate is terrible, so its ability to pay back or even roll over its debt if interest rates go up is extremely constrained; and, its demographics are even worse than Portugal's. While Italy is ranked 158th out of 230 countries in population growth, a marginal improvement over Portugal, it is ranked 207th in births. The median age of the population is 43.5, and 20 percent of the country is already over sixty-five years old. Given that one of the few truly linear events in life is death (there are no 200-year-old people out there), over one-third of Italy's population will be over sixty-five by 2035. Meanwhile, the current incumbents are not exactly friendly to immigration as a way of getting out of this jam.

If Spain is Ireland writ large, then Italy is Portugal writ large. That these states can't grow out of the debt they have accumulated is true. That there is a sovereign bond crisis involving these states is also true. But are the PIIGS really in trouble because of a crisis of government spending? In the Italian case the reliance on deficits that became debts and on devaluations that were substituted by cheap capital flows and artificially low yields once the euro came in, suggests a slow-moving fiscal train wreck, where eventually markets woke up to the fact that thirty years from now there will be no one in Italy working to pay off the interest on those thirty-year bonds since they will be too busy paying for pensions. Moreover, markets no longer view what was sus-

tainable in 1999—running a debt-to-GDP ratio of over 100 percent—
as sustainable now given the contagion risk from the other PIIGS. The
perception of the risk has changed, rather than the underlying risks
themselves, which have always been there.

So, is the state complicit? Yes. Did the state cause these problems?
No. Not unless we are willing to say that in Italy the level of family
fertility is a fiscal responsibility and thus the state's problem. In the
Portuguese case, while demographics and low productivity play their
parts, Portuguese net debt to GDP in 2000 was 52 percent and in 2007,
66 percent, which is hardly evidence of a spending splurge. Rather, in
both cases, what was once seen as sustainable suddenly became seen
as unsustainable once the possibility of a contagion-led fire sale
through the European bond markets was factored into a slow-moving
growth crisis. As usual, it's the perception of risk that matters. And
again, just as we saw in the US case, there was no orgy of government
spending behind all this. Why, then, keep up the fiction that the bond
market crisis is a crisis of spendthrift governments?

Confusing Correlation and Causation: Austerity's Moment in the Sun

With yields spiking to unsustainable levels in Greece, Ireland, and
Portugal, each country received a bailout from the EU, ECB, and the
IMF, as well as bilateral loans, on the condition that it accept and
implement an austerity package to right its fiscal ship. Cut spending,
raise taxes—but cut spending more than you raise taxes—and all will
be well, the story went. In May 2010, Greece received a 110-billion-euro
loan in exchange for a 20 percent cut in public-sector pay, a 10 percent
pension cut, and tax increases,. The lenders, the so-called troika of the
ECB, the European Commission, and the IMF, forecast growth
returning by 2012. Instead, unemployment in Greece reached 21 percent in late 2011, and the economy continued to contract. In November 2010, Ireland needed a bailout and received 85 billion euros for a
26 percent cut in public spending. In March 2011, it was Portugal's
turn, and it received 78 billion euros in exchange for a similar packet
of reforms. However, given the contraction in all these economies and
the fear of contagion, yields on Portuguese ten-year debt reached 17

percent in early 2012, and their ten-year bonds were downgraded to BBB–, otherwise known as junk.

Far from being stabilized by the original package of loans and cuts, Greece continued to deteriorate and required a second bailout in July 2011. Another 110 billion euros of debt, which became 130 billion in October 2011, was added to the Greek balance sheet while another 20 percent wage cut was enforced, along with similar across-the-board reductions in public spending and more tax increases. Eventually, even private-sector bondholders had to take a haircut (a loss) on the value of Greek debt of about 75 percent, plus write-offs of about 100 billion euros. Despite these austerity binges, Greek debt is projected (if all things remain equal for the next eight years, which will never happen) to reach 120 percent of GDP by 2020. The IMF thinks 145 percent by 2020 is more likely. Just to keep things on track, democratically elected governments in Greece and Italy were deposed and replaced by unelected technocrats who promised to keep the reforms going.

It is worth noting the timing of events. Opposition to Keynesian policies intensified in spring 2010 just as the Greek crisis became newsworthy despite Greece's accounting for only 2.5 percent of total Eurozone GDP. In the United Kingdom, Germany, and the United States, politicians in favor of austerity zeroed in on the Greek crisis as a metaphor for the perils of Keynesianism. "Becoming Greece" became a scare story to justify cutting back at home.

George Osborne, Britain's new Conservative chancellor of the exchequer, made repeated comparisons to the fiscal situation of Greece and the United Kingdom as soon as he was elected, with "you can see in Greece an example of a country that didn't face up to its problems, and that is the fate that I want to avoid" being a typical example.[38] Ex-IMF chief economist Simon Johnson argued at about the same time that the United Kingdom and Greece were essentially similar.[39] Meanwhile, conservative historian Niall Ferguson likened Greece to the United States, with collapse just over the horizon.[40]

Congressional Republicans in the United States leaped upon such comments with glee, while media outlets picked up and amplified the story throughout the spring of 2010.[41] In Europe, the ECB repeatedly honed in on Greece as the future of all European states unless budgets were cut.[42] Austerity's moment in the sun had arrived courtesy of the Greeks. The offensive against Keynesianism at the global level was married to the discovery of the Greek debt crisis and amplified via the threat of contagion to establish fiscal austerity as the new policy du jour. But in doing so, cause and correlation were confused, quite deliberately, on a massive scale.

The Greatest Bait and Switch in Modern History

The result of all this opportunistic rebranding was the greatest bait-and-switch operation in modern history. What were essentially private-sector debt problems were rechristened as "the Debt" generated by "out-of-control" public spending. Yet, of all the PIIGS, only Greece was in any meaningful sense profligate. Italy may have been lax, but no one minded them having the third-largest bond market in the world until 2010, when contagion plus demographics gave pause to the holders of Italian debt. Portugal may have spent a fair amount on modernizing its infrastructure and built a few high-speed rail lines of dubious need, but it was hardly spending its way to oblivion. Ireland and Spain were quintessential private-sector-housing-cum-banking crises, governed by states more fiscally prudent than Germany, where the risks were socialized while the profits were privatized. In all cases, private-sector weaknesses ended up creating public-sector liabilities that European publics now have to pay for with austerity programs that make the situation worse rather than better. The fiscal crisis in all these countries was the *consequence* of the financial crisis washing up on their shores, *not its cause*. To say that it is the cause is to deliberately, and politically, confuse cause and effect.

We really should know better. Carmen Reinhart and Kenneth Rogoff, no friends of Keynesian policy, note that a banking crisis is followed by a sovereign debt crisis 80 percent of the time.[43] Reinhardt and Rogoff stop short of using the word "cause." However, as Moritz Schularick and Alan Taylor have shown, sovereign debt crises are almost always "credit booms gone bust."[44] They develop in the private sector and end up in the public sector. The causation is clear. Banking bubbles and busts *cause* sovereign debt crises. Period. To reverse causation and blame the sovereign for the bond market crisis, as policy makers in Europe have repeatedly done to enable a policy of austerity that isn't working, begs the question, why keep doing it?

While it is tempting to say that neither German politicians nor ECB bankers understand fallacies of composition and both are allergic to inflation, and leave it at that, there is a more satisfying answer, and it's the same one we saw in the US case: *what starts with the banks ends with the banks*. To really understand why Europe has been slashing itself to insolvency, we need to embed these very real ideological and political factors within an account of how the euro as a currency enabled the development of a system of banks that is *too big to bail*. If the US had banks that were too big to fail, Europe has a system of banks that are collectively too big to bail. That is, no sovereign can cover the risks generated by its own banks because the banks are too big and the sovereign doesn't have a printing press. In this world there can be no bailout big enough to save the system if it starts to fail. Consequently, the system cannot be allowed to fail, which is the real reason we must all be austere. In the United States we were afraid of the consequences of the banks failing. In Europe they are terrified of the same thing, and as we shall see, they are terrified for good reason.

To get there we encounter some very familiar themes: subprime mortgage special purpose vehicles (SPVs), repo market collateral problems, and banks chasing yield in a low-interest-rate environment, as well as some unfamiliar ones such as bank resolution regimes (who has the responsibility to bail or fail banks), moral hazard trades (too big to fail as a business model), and why national debt issued in a common currency is a really bad idea. Taken together they explain why we really all need to be austere: because once again we need to save the banks, from themselves. But this time around no politician, especially in Europe, is going to admit that is exactly what is being done, which is why the bait and switch is needed.

The EU and the Euro: A Bridge Too Far?

The European Union, as a political project, has been an astonishing success. Built quite literally upon the ashes of a continent destroyed twice by war in a little over thirty years, it has both kept the peace in Europe and spread prosperity throughout the continent. It took in the former dictatorships of Portugal, Spain, and Greece and turned them into stable democracies. Far from being a creature of the Cold War, its ambitions spread following the collapse of the Soviet Union. The tragedy of the Balkans in the 1990s aside, it has incorporated peoples from the Baltics to Romania into the European project while increasing trade, expanding the rule of law, and pushing the project of "an ever closer Union" further along. If only they hadn't tried to do this with money. While the European political project has been a resounding success, its monetary cousin, the euro, has been a bit of a disaster for everyone, except possibly the Germans.[45]

The project of bringing Europe even closer together through a common currency was supposed to work on two levels. First, economies that were not well integrated and that had different business cycles and little specialization according to their relative economic strengths would converge, becoming more similar and more efficient simply by using the same unit of account. That, at least, was the idea. Second, having different currencies meant different exchange rates, which had different consequences for states, people, and firms.[46] For people and firms, it was a pain to have to change currencies to travel or trade, and having to do so reduced both. At the state level the argument was that all the different exchange rates moving together generated currency volatility that was hard to hedge against, and it created incentives for weaker currencies to seek respite by devaluing against their stronger trading partners to improve their own competitiveness, which many European states did, repeatedly. The problem with devaluation as an adjustment policy is not only that it beggars thy neighbor; it also leads to import inflation in the countries that devalue. Italy became the poster child for these problems, having devalued the lira every year between 1980 and 1987, save 1984, thereby suffering much higher-than-average inflation than the rest of Europe while effectively reducing the average Italian's real wage through the inflationary back door.

Keeping up with the Germans

European leaders struggled with these inflation/devaluation/volatility problems throughout the past few decades, building successively more elaborate exchange-rate mechanisms to keep European currencies together. Currency arrangements called "snakes" were replaced by "snakes in tunnels" and then by formal "exchange rate mechanisms" that were all variants of keeping up with the Germans. The "German problem" in Europe used to be the problem of how to constrain the Germans to keep the peace. The "German problem" after 1970 became how to keep up with the Germans in terms of efficiency and productivity. One way, as above, was to serially devalue, but that was beginning to hurt. The other way was to tie your currency to the deutsche mark and thereby make your price and inflation rate the same as the Germans, which it turned out would also hurt, but in a different way.

The problem with keeping up with the Germans is that German industrial exports have the lowest price elasticities in the world.[47] In plain English, Germany makes really great stuff that everyone wants and will pay more for in comparison to all the alternatives. So when you tie your currency to the deutsche mark, you are making a one-way bet that your industry can be as competitive as the Germans in terms of quality and price. That would be difficult enough if the deutsche mark hadn't been undervalued for most of the postwar period and both German labor costs and inflation rates were lower than average, but unfortunately for everyone else, they were. That gave the German economy the advantage in producing less-than-great stuff too, thereby undercutting competitors in products lower down, as well as higher up the value-added chain.[48] Add to this contemporary German wages, which have seen real declines over the 2000s, and you have an economy that is extremely hard to keep up with. On the other side of this one-way bet were the financial markets. They looked at less dynamic economies, such as the United Kingdom and Italy, that were tying themselves to the deutsche mark and saw a way to make money.

The only way to maintain a currency peg is to either defend it with foreign exchange reserves or deflate your wages and prices to accommodate it. To defend a peg you need lots of foreign currency so that when your currency loses value (as it will if you are trying to keep up with the Germans), you can sell your foreign currency reserves and buy back your own currency to maintain the desired rate. But if the markets can figure out how much foreign currency you have in reserve, they can bet against you, force a devaluation of your currency, and pocket the difference between the peg and the new market value in a short sale.

George Soros (and a lot of other hedge funds) famously did this to the European Exchange Rate Mechanism in 1992, blowing the United Kingdom and Italy out of the system. Soros could do this because he knew that there was no way the United Kingdom or Italy could be as competitive as Germany without serious price deflation to increase cost competitiveness, and that there would be only so much deflation and unemployment these countries could take before they either ran out of foreign exchange reserves or lost the next election. Indeed, the European Exchange Rate Mechanism was sometimes referred to as the European "Eternal Recession Mechanism," such was its deflationary impact. In short, attempts to maintain an anti-inflationary currency peg fail because they are not credible on the following point: you cannot run a gold standard (where the only way to adjust is through internal deflation) in a democracy.[49]

Well, you can try, and the Europeans building the EU are nothing if not triers. Following the Exchange Rate Mechanism debacle, in a scene reminiscent of one in Monty Python's movie *The Holy Grail* in which the king tells his son that "they said you couldn't build a castle on a swamp, so I did it anyway, and it fell down, so I did it again, and it fell down, so I did it again, and it fell down," the Europeans decided to go one step further than pegging to the deutsche mark—they would all become German by sharing the same currency and the same monetary policy.

The euro, the successor to the Exchange Rate Mechanism, would become a one-time internal fix of all the different European currencies in exchange for a single external floating currency, with one important difference.[50] Rather than pegging and retaining national currencies and printing presses, after the fix the national currencies would be abolished and the printing presses would be handed over to the Germans to make sure that neither inflation nor devaluation of the currency would ever again be options. Instead, armed with a new independent central bank that had only one goal, to keep inflation around 2 percent, regardless of the output and employment costs, via control of interest rates, prices and wages would automatically adjust to the external balance. In other words, they built a gold standard in a democracy, again. Einstein is credited with the observation that doing the same thing over and over while expecting different results is the definition of madness. The European monetary project was a bit mad from the get-go. It has only recently revealed itself to be an exercise in insanity.

Why the Euro Became a Monetary Doomsday Device

At the time of its launch, many economists predicted that the euro would fail. Martin Feldstein noted that the countries adopting the euro did not constitute an "optimal currency area," where business cycles and the like would be strongly integrated such that efficiency gains could be realized.[51] Paul Krugman saw trouble in the decade of recession and unemployment necessitated by the convergence criteria of the Maastricht Treaty of 1992, the precondition for adoption of the euro, where budget deficits, debts, and inflation rates all had to be cut at the same time.[52] Both were correct, but what really caused problems was that instead of creating convergence, the introduction of the euro created a great divergence between European economies (see figure 3.1) in almost everything except their bond spreads and balance of payments.

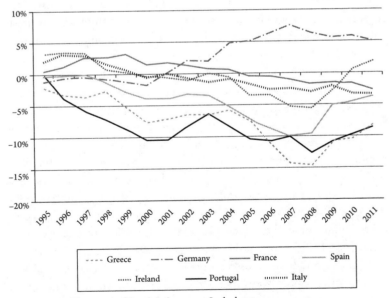

Figure 3.1 Eurozone Current Account Imbalances

Notice that before the introduction of the euro, France was the only country with a current account surplus. After its introduction, France held on until 2005 before moving into deficit. Germany moved into surplus in 2001, and the rest of the Eurozone moved further into deficit. There was a convergence of sorts. Everyone except Germany started to run deficits. To see why this happened, we need to turn to how such deficits were financed, which takes us into the realm of sovereign debt markets, and what the introduction of the euro did to the incentives of European banks (figure 3.2).

If a picture paints a thousand words, figure 3.2 paints a million. On the left-hand side, we see what the markets used to think of sovereign bonds before the euro was introduced. Greek ten-year bond yields started out at 25 percent, fell to 11 percent, and then came within fifty basis points (half a percent) of German bonds by 2001. Similarly, Italian bonds fell from a high of 13 percent in 1994 to becoming "almost German" in 2001 in terms of yields. Yet it is manifestly obvious that neither Greece nor Italy, nor Ireland, nor anyone else, actually became Germany, so why then did we see this convergence in yields? The popular answer is that the introduction of the ECB and its unending quest for anti-inflationary credibility signaled to bond buyers that both foreign exchange risk and inflation risk were now things of the past. The euro was basically an expanded deutsche mark, and everyone was now German.

Despite the fact that national bonds were still issued by the same national governments, banks and other financial players loaded up with them, assuming that the risks we saw on the left-hand side of figure 3.2 had all been magically sponged away by adoption of the euro. This flooded the periphery states with cheap money, completely swamping local wholesale funding markets, thereby making them vulnerable to the capital flight that was to render them illiquid in 2011, while pumping up, in the case of Spain in particular, private-sector indebtedness. While the Northern lenders lent to local banks, property developers, and the like, periphery consumers used this tsunami of cheap cash to buy German products, hence the current account imbalances noted earlier.

But why did these bond buyers believe that this new and untested institution, the ECB, would in fact guard the value of their bonds, that

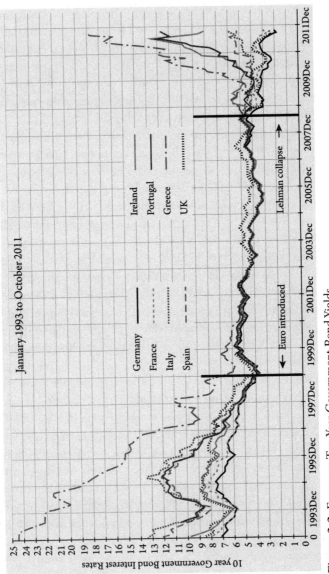

Figure 3.2 Eurozone Ten-Year Government Bond Yields

Source: European Central Bank Statistical Data Warehouse

national governments didn't matter any more, and that Greece was now Germany? The answer was, they didn't need to believe anything of the sort because arguably what they were doing was the mother of all moral hazard trades.

The Mother of All Moral Hazard Trades

If you were a European bank back in the late 1990s seeing sovereign bond yields falling, it might have bothered you since a source of risky profits was disappearing. On the other hand, if this new ECB gizmo really did get rid of exchange-rate risk for the sovereigns issuing the debt and take inflation off the table by housing in Frankfurt the only money press in Europe, then it really was a banker's dream—a free option—safe assets with a positive upside, just like those CDOs we saw in the United States. So you would be a fool not to load up on them, and European banks did exactly that. But as yields converged, you would have to buy more and more bonds to make any money. There was, however, a small but significant difference in yield between the bonds of Northern European sovereigns and those of the periphery after the yields converged. So, if you swapped out your low-yield German and Dutch debt and replaced it with as much PIIGS debt as you could find, and then turbocharged that by running operating leverage ratios as high as 40 to 1—higher than your US counterparts—you would have one heck of an institutionally guaranteed money machine. What makes this a moral hazard trade?

Imagine that you knew Greece was still Greece and Italy was still Italy and that the prices quoted in the markets represented the bond-buying activities of banks pushing down yields rather than an estimate of the risk of the bond itself. Why would you buy such securities if the yield did not reflect the risk? You might realize that if you bought enough of them—if you became really big—and those assets lost value, you would become a danger to your national banking system and would have to be bailed out by your sovereign. If you were not bailed out, given your exposures, cross-border linkages to other banks, and high leverage, you would pose a systemic risk to the whole European financial sector. As such, the more risk that you took onto your books, especially in the form of periphery sovereign debt, the more likely it was that your risk would be covered by the ECB, your national government, or both. This would be a moral hazard trade on a continental scale. The euro may have been a political project that provided the economic incentive for this kind of trade to take place. But it was private-sector actors who quite deliberately and voluntarily jumped at the opportunity.

Now, either because they really believed that the untested ECB had magically removed all risk from the system or saw the possibilities of a moral hazard trade, or both, major European banks took on as much periphery sovereign debt (and other periphery assets) as they could. Indeed, as we shall see below, these banks were incentivized by the European Commission to get their hands on as many periphery bonds as they could and use them as collateral in repo transactions, thereby upping the demand for them still further.[53] There was, however, one slight flaw in the plan. While bank lending and borrowing may be cross-border in the Eurozone, bank resolution and bailout responsibilities (notwithstanding the 2012 proposal for an EU banking union, which does little to fundamentally address these problems) are still national.[54] So, while any individual bank could play this moral hazard trade, if they all did it, all at once, then what was individually too big to fail became very quickly too big to bail as a whole. Once again, the dynamics of the system were different from those of the sum of the parts.

Dwarfing the King

To get an idea of the risks involved in this trade for the sovereigns, recall that if you take the combined assets of the top six US banks in the third quarter of 2008 and add them together, it comes to just over 61 percent of US GDP. Any one of these banks, on average, could then claim to impact about 10 percent of US GDP if it failed. Add the risk of contagion discussed earlier, and you have what the US authorities saw as a too big to fail problem. Now, do the same with European banks in the fourth quarter of 2008, which you must do on a national basis (the ratio of bank assets to national GDP) since there is at the time of writing, no EU-wide deposit-guarantee scheme, no EU-wide bailout mechanism for banks: it all falls on the national sovereign—and you get some seriously scary results.[55]

In 2008, the top three French banks had a combined asset foot-print of 316 percent of France's GDP. The top two German banks had assets equal to 114 percent of German GDP. In 2011, these figures were 245 percent and 117 percent, respectively. Deutsche Bank alone had an asset footprint of over 80 percent of German GDP and runs an opera-tional leverage of around 40 to 1.[56] This means a mere 3 percent turn against its assets impairs its whole balance sheet and potentially im-perils the German sovereign. One bank, ING in Holland, has an asset footprint that is 211 percent of its sovereign's GDP. The top four UK banks have a combined asset footprint of 394 percent of UK GDP. The top three Italian banks constitute a mere 115 percent of GDP, and yet Britain seems to get a free pass by the bond markets in comparison to Italy. The respective sovereign debts of these countries pale into insig-nificance.[57]

In the periphery states the situation is no better. Local banks weren't going to miss out on the same trade, so they bought their own sovereign debt by the truckload. According to a sample of Eurozone banks that underwent stress tests in July 2011, Greek banks hold 25 percent of Greek GDP in domestic bonds, and Spanish banks hold about 20 percent, and those bonds became increasingly national in terms of ownership through 2012.[58] Remember, these assets don't all have to go to zero to create a problem. You just have to impair enough to wipe out the bank's tier-one capital, which can be as little as 2 per-cent of its assets, especially when cross-border liabilities and conta-gion risks are factored in.[59]

In sum, in each country, and across the Eurozone as a whole, European banks have become too big to bail. No sovereign, even with its own printing press, can bail out a bank with exposures of this mag-nitude. If you have signed up to a currency arrangement whereby you gave yours away, you really are in trouble. As Simon Tilford and Philip Whyte put it bluntly, the Eurozone crisis is "a tale of excess bank le-verage and poor risk management in the core... [and] the epic misal-location of capital by excessively leveraged banks."[60]

From the start the euro was a banking crisis waiting to happen. One trigger for the crisis was Greece and the discovery that the PIIGS were pushing up yields, as detailed earlier. The other trigger was a series of events that happened, just as we saw in the United States in

2008, deep within the banking system itself and that centered upon the use of government bonds as repo collateral for funding banks. Once again, what is portrayed as a public-sector crisis is, at its core, an almost entirely private-sector (banking) problem.

Collateral Damage, European Style

So let's imagine that you are a big universal (retail and investment together) European bank and you have executed a giant moral hazard trade against EU sovereigns; or, you just really believe in the ECB's powers. To profit from this, you need to run very high levels of leverage. Where do you get the money to run such an operation? Generally speaking, banks can fund their activities in two ways, by increasing deposits and issuing equity, on the one hand, and by increasing debt, on the other. If equity is issued, the value of each share falls, so there is a limit at which equity issuance becomes self-defeating. Raising deposits, especially in an economy in which savings rates are falling, also has limits. Debt has no such limit.

So where could European banks find huge amounts of cheap debt to fund themselves? The repo markets we encountered in chapter 2 were one place, but this time they were located in London rather than New York.[61] US money-market funds that were looking for positive returns in a low-interest-rate world after 2008 was the other. After all, those conservative European banks were nowhere near as risky as those US banks, so why not buy lots of their short-term debt? The ECB will never let them fail, right?

As the 2000s progressed, those supposedly conservative European banks increasingly switched out of safe, local, deposit funding and loaded up on as much short-term internationally sourced debt as they could find. After all, it was much cheaper than getting your hands on granny's savings and paying her relatively high interest for the privilege. So much so that according to one study, by "September 2009, the United States hosted the branches of 161 foreign banks who collectively raised over $1 trillion dollars' worth of wholesale bank funding, of which $645 billion was channeled for use by their headquarters."[62] US banks at this time sourced about 50 percent of their funding from deposits, whereas for French and British banks the comparable figure was less than 25 percent.[63] By June 2011, $755 billion of the $1.66 trillion dollars in US money-market funds was held in the form of short-term European bank debt, with over $200 billion issued by French banks alone.[64] Just as in 2008, these banks were borrowing overnight to fund loans over much longer periods.

Besides being funded via short-term borrowing on US markets, it turned out that those conservative, risk-averse European banks hadn't missed the US mortgage crisis after all. In fact, over 70 percent of the SPVs set up to deal in US "asset backed commercial paper" (mortgages) we encountered in chapter 2 were set up by European banks.[65] The year 2008 may have been a crisis in the US mortgage markets, but it had European funders and channels, and most of those devalued assets remain stuck on the balance sheets of European banks domiciled in states with no printing presses. By 2010 then, just as the sovereign debt yields on the right-hand side of figure 3.2 began to really move apart, the ability of European banks to fund themselves through short-term US borrowing collapsed in a manner that was an almost perfect rerun of the United States in 2008.

Recall that in the United States in 2008, the collateral being posted for repo borrowing began to lose value. As such, the firms involved had to post more collateral to borrow the same amount of money, or they ran out of liquidity real fast, which is what happened to the US banking system. The same thing began to happen in Europe. While mortgage-backed securities, the collateral of choice for US borrowers in the US repo markets, were AAA-rated, for European borrowers in London the collateral of choice was AAA-rated European sovereign debt. Just as US borrowers needed a substitute for T-bills and turned to AAA mortgage bonds, so European borrowers had too-few nice, safe German bonds to pledge as collateral since the core banks were busy dumping them for periphery debt. So they began to pledge the periphery debt they had purchased en masse, which was, after all, rated almost the same, a policy that was turbocharged by a EC directive that "established that the bonds of Eurozone sovereigns would be treated equally in repo transactions" in order to build more liquid European markets. By 2008, PIIGS debt was collateralizing 25 percent of all European repo transactions.[66] You can begin to see the problem.

As investors fretted about European sovereigns, credit-ratings agencies started to downgrade those sovereigns, and their bonds went from AAA to BBB and worse. As such, you needed to pledge more and more of these sovereign bonds to get the same amount of cash in a repo. Unfortunately, with around 80 percent of all such repo agreements using European sovereign debt as collateral, when those bonds fell in value, the ability of European banks to fund themselves and keep their highly levered structures going began to evaporate.[67]

Banks with healthy assets might have been able to withstand this sudden loss of funding, but as well as US mortgages cluttering up their books, European banks were stuffed full of other rapidly devaluing periphery assets. The exposures were once again astonishing. By early 2010, Eurozone banks had a collective exposure to Spain of $727 billion, $402 billion to Ireland, and $206 billion to Greece.[68] French and German bank exposures to the PIIGS were estimated in 2010 to be nearly $1 trillion. French banks alone had some $493 billion in exposures to the PIIGS, which was equivalent to 20 percent of French GDP. Standard & Poor's estimated French exposures to be as high as 30 percent of GDP, all told.

Again, the vast majority of these exposures were private-sector exposures—property lending in Spain, and the like. The sovereign component of these figures was comparatively small. But what mattered was how levered these banks were and how important those sovereign bonds were for funding these banks. Once these bonds lost value, European banks increasingly found themselves shut out of US wholesale funding markets at the same time that US money markets began dumping their short-term debt. What happened in the United States in 2008, a general "liquidity crunch," gathered pace in Europe in 2010 and 2011. It was only averted by the LTROs of the ECB in late 2011 and early 2012. This unorthodox policy of quasi-quantitative easing offered only temporary respite. Paul De Grauwe called it "giving cheap money to trembling banks with all the problems this entails."[69] The results were that within two months of the first LTRO by the ECB, sovereign bond yields were rising again, and the banks those sovereigns were responsible for now had even more sovereign debt on their balance sheets—a fact not lost on investors now worrying about Spain and Italy. Another continent, another banking crisis, and yet all we heard about was profligate sovereigns spending too much—why?

You Can Run a Gold Standard in a Democracy (for a While)

The short answer is that with Europe's banks levered up beyond anything the US banks had managed, with asset footprints that were multiples of their sovereigns' GDPs and balance sheets that are both seriously impaired and seriously opaque, once again, the banks' problems become the states' problems. But unlike the US case (and the UK case), the states in question cannot even begin to solve those problems since they gave up their printing presses while letting their banks become too big to bail. Recognizing this, when France's AAA status was threatened in 2011, the bond markets were not worried about the ability of the French state to pay the pensions of retired teachers in Nancy. They were worried, quite reasonably, about its ability to deal with any of its big three banks (Societe Generale, BNP Paribas, and Credit Agricole) going bust, especially in an environment of unrelenting austerity. If states cannot inflate their way out of trouble (no printing press) or devalue to do the same (no sovereign currency), they can only default (which will blow up the banking system, so it's not an option), which leaves only internal deflation through prices and wages—austerity. This is the real reason we all have to be austere. Once again, it's all about saving the banks.

But You Cannot Tell the Truth about Why You Are Doing It

So, why, then, do European governments play the great bait and switch and then blame it all on sovereigns that have spent too much? Basically, it's because in a democracy you can hardly come clean about what you are doing and expect to survive. Imagine a major European politician trying to explain why a quarter of Spain needs to be unemployed, and why the whole of periphery Europe needs to sit in a permanent recession just to save a currency that has only existed for a decade. What would it sound like? I suspect that it would go something like this.

To: The Voting Public
From: Prime Minister of Eurozone Periphery X

My fellow citizens. We have been telling you for the past four years that the reason you are out of work and that the next decade will be miserable is that states have spent too much. So now we all need to be austere and return to something called "sustainable public finances." It is, however, time to tell the truth. The explosion of sovereign debt is a symptom, not a cause, of the crisis we find ourselves in today.

What actually happened was that the biggest banks in the core countries of Europe bought lots of sovereign debt from their periphery neighbors, the PIIGS. This flooded the PIIGS with cheap money to buy core country products, hence the current account imbalances in the Eurozone that we hear so much about and the consequent loss of competitiveness in these periphery economies. After all, why make a car to compete with BMW if the French will lend you the money to buy one? This was all going well until the markets panicked over Greece and figured out via our "kick the can down the road" responses that the institutions we designed to run the EU couldn't deal with any of this. The money greasing the wheels suddenly stopped, and our bond payments went through the roof.

The problem was that we had given up our money presses and independent exchange rates—our economic shock absorbers—to adopt the euro. Meanwhile, the European Central Bank, the institution that was supposed to stabilize the system, turned out to be a bit of fake central bank. It exercises no real lender-of-last-resort function. It exists to fight an inflation that died in 1923, regardless of actual economic conditions. Whereas the Fed and the Bank of England can accept whatever assets they want in exchange for however much cash they want to give out, the ECB is both constitutionally and intellectually limited in what it can accept. It cannot monetize or mutualize debt, it cannot bail out countries, it cannot lend directly to banks in sufficient quantity. It's really good at fighting inflation, but when there is a banking crisis, it's kind of useless. It's been developing new powers bit-by-

bit throughout the crisis to help us survive, but its capacities are still quite limited.

Now, add to this the fact that the European banking system as a whole is three times the size and nearly twice as levered up as the US banking system; accept that it is filled with crappy assets the ECB can't take off its books, and you can see we have a problem. We have had over twenty summits and countless more meetings, promised each other fiscal treaties and bailout mechanisms, and even replaced a democratically elected government or two to solve this crisis, and yet have not managed to do so. It's time to come clean about why we have not succeeded. The short answer is, we can't fix it. All we can do is kick the can down the road, which takes the form of you suffering a lost decade of growth and employment.

You see, the banks we bailed in 2008 caused us to take on a whole load of new sovereign debt to pay for their losses and ensure their solvency. But the banks never really recovered, and in 2010 and 2011 they began to run out of money. So the ECB had to act against its instincts and flood the banks with a billion euros of very cheap money, the LTROs (the long-term refinancing operations), when European banks were no longer able to borrow money in the United States. The money that the ECB gave the banks was used to buy some short-term government debt (to get our bond yields down a little), but most of it stayed at the ECB as catastrophe insurance rather than circulate into the real economy and help you get back to work. After all, we are in the middle of a recession that is being turbocharged by austerity policies. Who would borrow and invest in the midst of that mess? The entire economy is in recession, people are paying back debts, and no one is borrowing. This causes prices to fall, thus making the banks ever more impaired and the economy ever more sclerotic. There is literally nothing we can do about this. We need to keep the banks solvent or they collapse, and they are so big and interconnected that even one of them going down could blow up the whole system. As awful as austerity is, it's nothing compared to a general collapse of the financial system, really.

So we can't inflate and pass the cost on to savers, we can't devalue and pass the cost on to foreigners, and we can't default without killing ourselves, so we need to deflate, for as long as it takes to get the balance sheets of these banks into some kind of sustainable shape. This is why we can't let anyone out of the euro. If the Greeks, for example, left the euro we might be able to weather it, since most banks have managed to sell on their Greek assets. But you can't sell on Italy. There's too much of it. The contagion risk would destroy everyone's banks. So the only policy tool we have to stabilize the system is for everyone to deflate against Germany, which is a really hard thing to do even in the best of times. It's horrible, but there it is. Your unemployment will save the banks, and in the process save the sovereigns who cannot save the banks themselves, and thus save the euro. We, the political classes of Europe, would like to thank you for your sacrifice.

This is a speech that you will never hear because if it were given the politician making it would be putting a resume up on Monster.com ten minutes later. But it is the real reason we all need to be austere. When the banking system becomes too big to bail, the moral hazard trade that started it all becomes systemic "immoral hazard"—an extortion racket aided and abetted by the very politicians elected to serve our interests. When that trade takes place in a set of institutions that is incapable of resolving the crisis it faces, the result is permanent austerity.

Conclusion: The Euro's Hubris and Hayek's Nightmare

Jay Shambaugh sees the euro as caught in three interlocking crises, each of which worsens the others.[70] He sees the Euro Area's banking problem compounding the sovereign debt problem, which in turn (via austerity) hurts growth in the name of fostering competitiveness, which is undermined by deflation.[71] That about sums it up. But to his diagnosis and this one, which stresses the role of the banks first and foremost, one can add many more layers of misery. The LTRO money that was supposed to give the banks time to restructure and restart lending was used instead as catastrophe insurance. As periphery credit conditions worsened, capital flight from the periphery to the core (when Greek savers moved their accounts to German banks, for example), huge financial imbalances (like the trade imbalances in figure 3.1) appeared in the accounts of the so-called Target Two payments system of the Eurozone that threaten the German central bank with billions in foreign obligations to periphery central banks.[72] With no EU-wide fiscal authority, only a monetary one, there are no shock absorbers in the system of the type you would find in, for example, the United States. When a firm closes in Michigan and moves to Mississippi, capital flows out of one state and into another, but taxes raised in Connecticut smooth the adjustment through federal transfers. Labor is also much more mobile in the United States than in the EU, and America also lets its cities die, thus speeding adjustment. None of this happens in Europe. It turns out that cross-border borrowing in euros is, when bond markets reflect true risk premiums, just like borrowing in a foreign currency, with the result that banks increasingly want to match local loans with local assets.[73] Although there is no exchange-rate risk to cover, if your sovereign's yields go up and your parent economy deflates, then your ability to pay back your loans declines as if you were making payments in a depreciating currency.

I could go on listing the way that the euro emerges every day to be an ever more creative financial doomsday weapon. But what makes the situation in Europe terrible at its core aren't just these glaring holes in its institutional design or the immoral hazard posed by its banks. Rather, it's what might be termed the "epistemic hubris" behind the whole euro monetary project, which again comes down to the power of a set of economic ideas that blinds us to the effects of our institutional designs, just as it did in the US case.

No one knows the future, but we do know that it will have some shocks in store for us. We can imagine those shocks to be exogenous, and design mechanisms to compensate for them, such as well-conceived welfare states.[74] Or, we can view them as endogenous, always and everywhere the result of our own bad policy choices. If we take the latter view, and we do not know what the future may have in store, as well as take policy tools away from democratically elected politicians, we may want to try to make the future conform to our preferences. So, how would we do this?

Imagine the future as a space of unrealized possibilities. You can accept that uncertainty and roll with it, or you can try to make the future behave within certain specified parameters, narrowing the space of possible futures. The way you do that is with rules. So long as they are clearly stated and everyone follows them, then according to this logic, the future will unfold, as you would like to see it, in accord with the rules. This is ordoliberalism gone mad, as well as the logic behind the euro. From the Maastricht convergence criteria to the Stability and Growth Pact to the promised new fiscal treaty that will solve all the euro's problems once and for all (except that it will not), it's all about the rules. But those rules only ever apply to sovereigns. There was of course a worry that some states may not follow the rules, so more rules were put in place. But there was never much attention paid to the possibility that private actors, such as banks, would behave badly. Yet this is exactly what happened, and the EU is still blaming sovereigns, tying them down with new rules, and insisting that this will solve the problem. We can but think again about the old adage that drunks only look for their keys under the lamppost because that's where the light is.

Friedrich Hayek is often seen as the father of neoliberal economics.[75] It's not an unfair reading, and he was certainly no fan of the state. But what he really railed against was the epistemic arrogance of the planner who assumes that he can anticipate the future better than a local actor whose knowledge is much more fine grained. Although the Hayekian critique is usually applied to postwar Keynesian planners, today it is more germane to EU planners who think that by setting up rules they can make the future conform to the probability space that they want to see. As Paul De Grauwe put it beautifully, "This is like saying that if people follow the fire code regulations scrupulously there is no need for a fire brigade."[76]

By looking only at inflation rates, budget deficits, and state debts, EU planners failed to see the growth of a banking system that is too big to bail. The price of their hubris is the belief among European elites that only a decade or more of unremitting austerity will suffice to prop them up, perhaps at the ultimate cost of undermining of the European political project. This may be the true price of saving the banks. Not just the end of the euro, but the end of the European political project itself, which would be perhaps the ultimate tragedy for Europe.

Given what is at stake, we must wonder whether anyone ever really thought that austerity was a good idea, whether it was ever anything more than political cover for selfish interests. To do that, we must now attend to the first of austerity's twin histories, its intellectual pedigree. We then turn to its empirical history to examine where and when it has worked in practice. It is time we remembered why, setting current events aside for a moment, it is such a dangerous, but seductive, idea.

Part Two

AUSTERITY'S TWIN HISTORIES

INTRODUCTION TO CHAPTERS 4, 5, AND 6

AUSTERITY'S INTELLECTUAL AND NATURAL HISTORIES

TINA Is Not Enough

Having read the first part of this book, you might be wondering if any-one ever thought austerity was a good idea. Contemporary American politicians seem drawn to it because of a style of national politics that blames the public sector for anything bad that happens in the private sector. Like overindulgent parents who cannot believe that their progeny ever errs, American policy makers can only blame the state, and occasionally the banks, but never the market. To do so is somehow un-American—as if fealty to Wall Street is the same as honoring the Constitution. Meanwhile, European policy makers seem to be trapped in a room with a monetary doomsday device, an overlevered banking system on the brink, and a German instruction sheet for defusing the thing that makes the problem worse rather than better.

Yet, as we shall see, sometimes austerity can be the correct policy response. Unfortunately, it works only under a highly specific set of conditions that, sadly, do not happen to describe the world in which we live at the moment. Austerity fails miserably when these conditions are absent, and there is plenty of evidence to back this assertion up. Why, then, does the idea continue to "dominate the economic thought, both practical and theoretical, of the governing and academic classes of this generation, as it has for a hundred years past" as John Maynard Keynes put in 1936?[1] After all, it has been eighty years since Keynes wrote that line, and austerity's luster has yet to fade.

Two answers present themselves to us. The first is a variant of the line popularized by Mrs. Thatcher—"there is no alternative" (TINA). In light of the previous chapter, you might have the impression that this is exactly the case being made in this book. After all, it seems that when you have built a banking system that is too big to bail, and you have thrown away all your other policy tools (control of interest rates, exchange rates, etc.) in a fit of "Europeanness," there may not be much alternative to austerity, at least in Europe.

That is indeed how European policy elites see things, hence austerity; but that doesn't mean either that austerity will work or that there is no alternative. Europe is at the moment undertaking a giant austerity experiment and the results, as discussed, are predictably awful. If doing the same thing over and over again is still the definition of madness, then the madness is probably going to end badly, long before austerity ever pays off, which it cannot under current circumstances. So once again, why keep doing it? TINA is insufficient to explain austerity's enduring attraction in the face of contrary evidence. As we shall see in conclusion, there are always alternatives.

Austerity's Absent History and Conquered Past

In contrast to TINA's necessities, the answer built here looks once again to the power of economic ideas. I argued in chapter 2 that the most basic cause of the 2008 financial crisis was the acceptance by both regulators and practitioners in financial markets of a particular set of economic ideas as the instruction sheet of the day. Although there have been many economic instruction sheets produced over the past few centuries—mercantilism, communism, corporatism, just to name a few—we are interested here in the origins of liberalism, the most successful one of all, so we can trace austerity's origins and lineage. In particular, I want to draw attention to, in the manner of a paleontologist, an absence in the "fossil record" of liberal economic ideas.

The absence in question is austerity itself. For an idea so central to the governance of states and markets, austerity's intellectual history is both short and shallow. There is no well worked out "theory of austerity" in economic thought that extends back in time to some foundational statements that became more systematized and rigorous over time as there is, for example, with trade theory.[2] We have instead what David Colander has called a "sensibility" concerning the state, embedded in liberal economics from its inception, that produces "austerity" as the default answer to the question, what should we do when markets fail?[3]

Liberal economics grew up in reaction to the state. Not the state as we know it today—(usually) a representative democracy with large-scale spending ambitions—but the state personified by sovereigns: vicious, capricious, untrustworthy monarchs who would as soon steal your wealth as look at you. The state was therefore something to be avoided, minimized, bypassed, curtailed, and above all, not trusted. The market, in contrast, emerged in liberal thought as the intellectual and institutional antidote to the confiscatory politics of the king.[4] In such a world, if prices and merchants were set free, the wealth of nations (note, not "kingdoms") would multiply.

But from the start this liberal view of "the state versus the market" rested upon a misunderstanding: markets naturally appear when you remove the state from the equation. However, as Karl Polanyi noted at the end of World War II, there is nothing natural about markets.[5] Turning people into wage laborers, securing the private ownership of land, even inventing capital and preserving its monetary form are all deeply political projects that involve courts, regulation, enforcement, bureaucracy, and all the rest.[6] Indeed, gaining control of the state by the merchant class was a defining feature of early capitalism.[7] With the partial exceptions of the United Kingdom and the United States (the former because it was first to make the transition to capitalism and the latter because it was geographically isolated), from Germany in the 1870s to China today, states make markets as much as markets determine the fate of states.[8] Yet liberal economic thought remains largely oblivious to these facts. As a result, contemporary neoliberals who argue for austerity come at the issue with an antistatist neuralgia that produces "cut the state" as the default answer, regardless of the question asked or its appropriateness.

By the beginning of the twentieth century, "cut the state" was the only answer deemed acceptable by the governing classes of the capitalist world. But this answer took a severe knock in the 1930s, when, given the failure of austerity policies to promote recovery, states grew rather than shrank, as did the economy with which they were codeterminate, for the next thirty years. Yet the liberal neuralgia against the state never really went away, and the current crisis brought the same old arguments back full bore. As Albert Hirschman once observed, when the same arguments are repeated with almost no modification for over 300 years, regardless of any contrary facts impacting them, we should do well to hold them with suspicion.[9] In the spirit of Hirschman's suspicion, these chapters 4 and 5, drawing from austerity's intellectual history, offer an answer as to why it continues to dominate the minds of today's governing and academic classes. We then finish up our study of austerity with an examination, in chapter 6, of the key empirical cases of austerity in practice.

In chapter 4, we investigate the prehistory of austerity, first as an absence in early liberal economic thought, and then as a definite policy in early to mid-twentieth-century economic theory. Austerity was not a policy consistently argued *for* from the seventeenth century onward, since the conditions of its realization—big states that spend lots of cash that can be cut—do not arise until the twentieth century. Rather, austerity emerges over time as a derivative consequence of other shared beliefs—a sensibility—concerning the nature and role of the state in economic life that sit at the core of liberal economic thought.[10]

To make this case, chapter 4 examines the works of three critically important early liberal economic thinkers: John Locke, David Hume, and Adam Smith. We begin with Locke's arguments for the creation of private property and his derivative theory of the state. We move from Locke through the works of David Hume to Adam Smith, noting how Hume's ideas about money and merchants and Smith's about growth and taxes lead both of them to the view that government, and its debt, is deeply problematic. The relevance of these three early liberals for austerity thinking is a disposition they share that I term the *can't live with it, can't live without it, don't want to pay for it* problem of the state in liberal thought.

In setting markets up as the antidote to the state, liberals struggle to admit the necessity of states for the creation and preservation of markets. One strand of liberal thought consistently denies states anything more than a minimum role, which we see with Locke and Hume. The other strand admits the state's necessity, which we see in Smith, but worries about how to pay for it. The tension between these two viewpoints—can't live with it, can't live without it—generates a concern with how states should fund themselves, and it is this concern that creates the conditions for the emergence of austerity as a distinct economic doctrine when states become large enough budgetary entities in their own right to warrant cutting: that is, by the 1920s. When that happens, austerity appears in its own right as a distinct economic doctrine.

After briefly detailing some nineteenth- and early twentieth-century precursors, I examine the two key austerity doctrines formed in this period: "liquidationism"—sometimes called "the Banker's doctrine" in the United States—and the "Treasury view" in the United Kingdom. These ideas were, I argue, the original neoliberal ideas in that they drew on the classical liberalism of Locke, Hume, and Smith, and applied themselves anew to the policy issues of the day. I then discuss the responses that these ideas engendered, the most relevant of which are John Maynard Keynes's refutation of austerity policies and Joseph Schumpeter's strange abrogation of them.[11] By 1942, it seems that the die has been cast and austerity had been sent away to the retirement home for bad economic ideas. It turned out, however, to be a premature retirement.

Austerity's Contested Present

In chapter 5, we take the story forward. We begin by detailing the two places austerity found a home after Keynes's anti-austerity arguments seemed to have won the day: Germany—the home of ordoliberalism—and Austria, not the country, but Austria as a distinct school of economics. The former remained a peculiarly German way of organizing the economy until it became the design principle behind the euro project. The latter remained a fringe movement, at least until the 1980s, when the intellectual climate became more neoliberal in general. The Austrian school also formed a kind of American pied-à-terre for austerity arguments. Following our discussion of these two schools, we briefly survey the neoliberal shift of the 1980s, noting how these ideas enabled it. We then discuss how this neoliberal turn affected economic policy making in the global South, and how the IMF in particular came to see austerity, in the form of a set of ideas called "the Washington consensus," as developmental policy du jour during the 1980s and 1990s.

Austerity remained the policy for people in the developing world, however, at least until the current crisis. But even at that moment, ideas did not appear out of nowhere: they had precursors and promoters.[12] At the end of chapter 5, we turn our attention to a small group of economists based at Italian and American universities who during the 1980s and 1990s began developing the theory of "expansionary austerity" that finally gave austerity a serious theoretical underpinning. We examine these ideas, noting in particular their ordoliberal lineage and the critical challenges to them that have recently emerged.

Chapter 6 moves from the realm of theory to that of practice. Here we detail the crucial cases of austerity from the 1930s to the present. The analysis confirms that although a particular form of austerity that combines devaluations with large-scale labor agreements to cap wage growth does work occasionally to create expansions, these cases are vastly outnumbered by negative ones, and the conditions of those exapansions singularly do not apply to the world we happen to live in today. To that end, the first part of the chapter analyzes the cases that made us think for over thirty or more years that austerity is indeed a very dangerous idea. These are the attempts of the United States, Britain, Sweden, Germany, Japan, and France to right their fiscal ships in the 1920s and 1930s through austerity. We note how austerity in all these countries failed to produce recovery and how the expansionary policies that followed allowed them to recover.

The second part of the chapter turns to the positive cases of austerity from the 1980s that formed the core of the expansionary austerity claim—the idea that austerity, far from being dangerous—is positively virtuous. Here we examine the cases of Ireland, Denmark, and Australia, noting how even they are either less-than-perfect exemplars or were expansionary for reasons other than simple budget-cutting austerity. Finally, we turn our attention to the cases of the moment—the

REBLL alliance—Romania, Estonia, Bulgaria, Lithuania, and Latvia—the "new hope" for austerity advocates. I examine these cases in detail and argue that they carry neither positive examples nor transportable lessons for the rest of the developed world.

Milton Friedman once argued "only a crisis—actual or perceived—produces real change. When that crisis occurs, the actions that are taken depend on the ideas that are lying around."[13] The next three chapters explain why the idea of austerity has been "lying around" in various forms for the past four centuries. Its repetition, refinement, and continual redeployment do not improve it over time. But that doesn't stop liberals from finding it endlessly attractive and polishing it anew every time there is a crisis.

THE INTELLECTUAL HISTORY OF A
DANGEROUS IDEA, 1692—1942

Part One: Austerity's Classical Origins

John Locke: "Men Have Agreed to [an]
Unequal Possession of the Earth"

John Locke was one of England's most famous philosophers. Writing in the aftermath of the English civil wars of the seventeenth century, he was concerned with the appropriate foundation for civil government. Rather than some armchair exercise, Locke's writings were essential propaganda for the emerging merchant classes that were little-by-little taking power away from British aristocratic elites. He was a part of a movement that culminated in the Glorious Revolution of 1688, which disempowered the king and empowered, well, people like Locke.

Apart from philosophizing on the rights of citizens in a commonwealth and on the limits to the power of the kings who seek to rule them, Locke was an economic revolutionary. He grounded his notion of what constitutes legitimate rule in individual property rights, without which there can be no economic liberalism, no separation of the state from the market, and no capitalism as we know it today. Locke's vision is outlined in his *Second Treatise of Government* (1690). To create the separation of state and market he wanted, Locke had to make several moves: naturalize income and wealth inequality, legitimate the private ownership of land, explain the emergence of labor markets, and depoliticize the invention of the device called money that made all these things possible. At base, Locke's liberalism is an economic liberalism that pits the individual against the state. Austerity's intellectual history starts here.

John Locke Imagines the Market

Locke begins by wondering how it is possible for "God, who hath given the world to men in common" to allow the unequal, if not unlimited, accumulation of wealth.[1] The answer lies in Locke's conception of property. For Locke, property resides in us all, in our persons, but it is only important because it is alienable with our labor. That is, when we work on something, such as land, our laboring makes it our own. As Locke argued, "whatsoever then he removes out of the state [of] nature...[and] mixed his labor with...[he] thereby makes it his property."[2] Now, you might think that other folks at the time would object to someone taking possession of the common land this way. But Locke insists that, "the taking of this or that part [of land] does not depend on the express consent of all the commoners" because "there was still enough [for all] and as good left."[3]

Having dispatched the problem of distribution by assuming infinite abundance, Locke maintains that the only real argument against private property is the issue of spoilage, that more is taken than can be used, which God would not like.[4] Luckily then, time and habits have given us a device called money that allows us to get over the problem of spoilage because we can store money and swap it for consumables at any given time.[5] This also has the handy side effect of creating a labor market, since you can now get people to work for you on your property, and then, through the device of money, get them to alienate (give) the fruits of their labor to you as a free exchange. This allows Locke to conclude that "men have agreed to a disproportionate and unequal possession of the earth... by... voluntary consent [they have] found out a way how a man may fairly possess more land than he can fairly use the product of, by receiving... the overplus of gold and silver, which may be hoarded up without injury to anyone."[6]

In the context of a country racked by war, regicide, and rebellion, this view may seem rather bloodless: unlimited inequality in property naturalized by virtue of God's lack of foresight on the issue of spoilage. But it does allow Locke to explain as inevitable, and therefore good, the creation of markets in land, labor, and capital, which happened to be the very political project that people of his class were engaged in at that moment. His next step was to protect these new institutions of the market from this emergent capitalism's nemesis: the state.

John Locke Imagines the State

Locke's famous right to rebel against and deep suspicion of the government only makes sense in relation to the violation of the rights of private property he has just awarded himself. In Locke's world, the power of the legislature is "limited to the public good of the society," which is defined as freedom from the intervention of government into private affairs, especially concerning property, unless citizens consent to it.[7] As Locke put it regarding taxes, "to lay and levy taxes...without [the] consent of the people...invades the fundamental law of property."[8] Having done so, legislators "put themselves into a state of war with the people" such that it is the government, and not the people, that is "guilty of rebellion" and forfeits its right to govern.[9]

Remember that these arguments are being developed in seventeenth-century England, where public debt is the debt of kings, kings who invoke rights given by God to appropriate the property of others willy-nilly. That Locke deploys equally specious rationales for why he and his brethren in the commonwealth should have as much of the world as they want is beside the point. Rather, his point is to defend those gains from the state at all costs and to minimize the state's ability to extract further resources. It is this minimalist foundation for what the state can and should do, bequeathed by Locke, that later liberals built upon. Such a foundation has a hard time, by design, supporting any view of the state that extends beyond the protection of property. But even this narrow activity costs money, and this requires that the state raise it. Thus the liberal dilemma that generates austerity is born. *The state: can't live with it, can't live without it, don't want to pay for it.*

David Hume: "Public Credit Will Destroy the Nation"

Laying their intellectual bricks on Locke's narrow foundations are the twin giants of the Scottish enlightenment, Adam Smith and David Hume. Turning first to Hume, his contributions to political economy are legion.[10] The idea that a monetary stimulus can in the short run stimulate economic activity but in the long run must either show up as inflation or dissipate without effecting real variables forms the centerpiece of his essay "On Money." It is also the standard line in contemporary macroeconomic theory, where it is known as the long-run neutrality of money thesis. He is also credited with working out the details in Richard Cantillon's balance-of-trade ideas through his "price-specie-flow" mechanism, the mechanism that underlay the nineteenth-century gold standard.[11] We, however, are interested in Hume for his writings on "public credit"—what we call government debt.

Hume, like Locke, sees money as an instrument, as "nothing but the representation of labor and commodities . . . a method of rating or estimating them."[12] In Hume's version of events, however, money does not come into being to overcome the problem of spoilage/God's accountancy problems. Rather, money follows trade, which places Locke's merchant classes, and not the state, at the center of everything. For Hume, merchants are the catalyst for trade and the creators of wealth. They are, according to Hume, "one of the most useful races of men, who serve as agents between . . . parts of the state."[13] As a consequence, "it is necessary, and reasonable, that a considerable part of the commodities and labor [produced] should belong to the merchant, to whom, in great measure, they are owing."[14] While "lawyers and physicians beget no industry," only merchants can "encrease industry, and, by also increasing frugality, give a great command of that industry to particular members of society."[15] Those "particular members of society" would, of course, be Hume and those like him: the merchant classes.

What could threaten such a happy state of affairs in which the natural growth of trade is both caused and catalyzed by the merchant classes? That, of course, would be the state's demands for revenue, especially in the form of debt. Hume pulls no punches on the issue of government debt. It's a bad thing. Period. If the reasons he offers sound familiar today, it's because, as Hirschman warned us, the same arguments have been doing the rounds for the past few hundred years with little modification.

David Hume Despairs the Debt

Hume's basic problem with public debt is that it has no limit, at least until the interest rates on the debt become crushing. Plus, debt is easy to levy since its costs are hidden and intergenerational, which makes states love debt. As Hume put it, "it is very tempting to a minister to employ such an expedient, as it enables him to make a great figure during his administration, without overburdening the people with taxes.... The practice will, therefore...almost infallibly be abused, in every government."[16] Accordingly, government will issue debt at a rate that shall exceed the rate of interest that it could earn elsewhere, therefore finding ready buyers at the cost of diverting funds from industry. As a consequence, capital will become concentrated in debt securities that "banish gold and silver from the commerce of the state...and by that means render all provisions and labour dearer than otherwise they would be."[17]

When this issuance of debt eventually hits a ceiling, governments will need to sell more of it to foreigners, and that will result in foreigners possessing "a great share of our national funds [which will] render the pubic...tributary to them."[18] And if all this comes to pass, as it inevitably must according to Hume, liberty is undone. With taxes at their limits paying interest on the debt, there is no room to absorb any kind of financial shock. Consequently, even more debt will be issued, "a continual taxation of the annuitants," which results in a government that has "mortgaged all its revenues [and that will] sink into a state of languor, inactivity and impotence."[19]

If all this sounds familiar, it's because it is familiar. Hume's claims do not echo today's—today's claims are direct replicas of Hume's. For debt being politically easier than taxes, look no further than Northern European criticisms of the budget policies of Greece and Italy.[20] For government debt crowding out other investments, see the plethora of criticisms of the Obama stimulus.[21] For debt driving up prices and compromising the ability of the state to cushion further shocks, see the voluminous criticisms of quantitative easing and fears that a spike in US interest rates will cause exactly that.[22] For the fear of foreigners owning the United States, simply google "China owns USA." The search returns 25 million hits even though the statement is simply not true—foreigners hold less than one-third of outstanding US debt.[23]

Despite this broadside of familiar critiques, we must remember that Hume predicted the end of Great Britain due to excessive debt issuance just at the moment that Great Britain was about to dominate the world for a century. It's hard to be that wrong; and yet the arguments against debt, in essentially the same form, continue to be used today, three hundred years later. Facts, it seems, seldom triumph over a good liberal ideology, and when it comes to a good liberal ideology, you can't beat Adam Smith.

Adam Smith: "The Practice of Funding [Debt] Has Gradually Enfeebled Every State Which Has Adopted It"

Hume's contemporary, the even more famous Adam Smith,[24] was also troubled by the problem of public debt. The difference between Hume and Smith is that while Hume identifies the problem, he offers no solution, seeing the slide into insolvency and enfeeblement as unavoidable. Smith goes one step better. He identifies both the problem and the solution. To solve the problem of debt we should embrace the principal of austerity—otherwise known as the parsimony of the Scots.

Smith's economics are a bit like Shakespeare—often quoted, seldom read. From his notes on the division of labor in the eponymous pin factory to the "invisible hand" guiding selfish actions to common purposes, Smith's sound bites are well known. The details of what Smith said about the economy are far less well known and quite surprising. Smith brought together much of the scattered work of early economists on the nature of money, economic growth, the role of capital and labor, and a host of other issues, and then had the good sense to put it in one accessible place: *The Wealth of Nations.*[25] As Albert Hirschman observed, this book was no academic project. It was an argument for capitalism before its triumph, and a very successful argument, too.[26]

For our purposes here, we find in Smith a particular sensibility toward the state and its debt that brings us closer to the modern idea of austerity, but from a surprising angle: the importance of personal frugality and parsimony as the engine of capitalist growth. Undermine this sensibility, and capitalism itself falters. To fully understand what Smith had to say about debt and parsimony, we need to begin with what he said about banking, and go from there to savings, investment, growth, and, perhaps most surprisingly, the necessity of the state engendered by the problems of inequality and class politics and the problem of how to pay for it.[27]

Adam Smith's Productive Parsimony

For Smith, banking is all about having confidence in the banker. If customers have confidence in a banker's promissory notes (his paper money), he will then be able to lend out more in paper than he keeps in reserve in gold to cover his withdrawals.[28] Today, we call this "fractional reserve banking." Yet Smith, like Hume, sees money as being unable to affect real variables in the long run, so simply adding paper money to the economy will not lead to growth.[29] But if lots of trusted bankers produce more paper money than the economy can absorb, and crucially, if that paper is seen to be "as good as gold"—to use the phrase in its appropriate context—then the gold backing this paper in the bank vault will lack a role at home. Happily then, it can be sent abroad, thus allowing the home country to import more.[30]

Smith maintains that the imports this allows can be of two types: "goods...likely to be consumed by idle people who produce nothing" or goods that "may purchase an additional stock of materials...and employ...industrious people."[31] "So far as it is employed in the first way it promotes prodigality.... So far as it is employed in the second way, it promotes industry."[32] It is, then, the inherent frugality of the Scots—their parsimony—that appears to be the key to growth (industry). Why be parsimonious and buy investment goods rather than foreign wines? We do this, according to Smith, because of a sentiment that comes "with us from the womb, and never leave[s] us until we go into the grave"—a sentiment leads to economic growth.[33]

For Smith, the act of saving drives investment, not consumption. Why? Because the wealth of the nation is its total income. Take what is used for the reproduction of labor (wages) out of this income, and what is left is profit. Profits are then reinvested in the economy via merchants' savings, which are lent out to the productive members of society (other merchants) to invest. Today we call this supply-side economics. Investment both drives consumption and makes consumption possible—not the other way around. Because of this "the greater part of it [income] will naturally be destined for the employment of industry."[34] Underlying this worldview is a particularly Scottish psychology that is worth unpacking because it suggests why the idea of austerity has such *moral* force, even today.

For Smith, because saving leads to investment, there are no lags and leakages of income; neither hoarding nor uncertainty is possible. Consequently, debt has no role in his system while saving is both good and natural to us. As Smith puts it, "Parsimony, not industry, is the immediate cause of the increase of capital...whatever industry might acquire, if parsimony did not save and store up, the capital would never be the greater."[35] Frugality thus becomes virtue while prodigality becomes vice such that "if the prodigality of some was not compensated by the frugality of others, the conduct of every prodigal, by feeding the idle with the bread of the industrious...[would] impoverish the entire country."[36]

What saves us from poverty and the enfeeblement of the state is, then, this sentiment: that people are by nature parsimonious savers hardwired to invest. Smith's capitalism rests upon a psychological predisposition to save rather than spend. As Smith puts it rather hopefully, although "some men may increase their expense very considerably though their revenue does not increase at all, we may be assured that no class or order of men ever does so...because the principles of common prudence...always influence...the majority of every class."[37] Clearly, Smith did not envisage the twenty-first-century American mortgager or the European universal bank. But what did he see, and fear, was something that would upset this natural desire to save and invest: easy money, which is what credit markets (debt) offer. In short, by perverting the sensibility of saving into lending to the government, "great nations are...impoverished by...public prodigality and misconduct."[38] Once again, the market can do no wrong, so the fault must lie with the state.

Smith (Reluctantly) Brings the State Back In...

Smith fully acknowledges that the market cannot exist without the state. Indeed, an entire book of *The Wealth of Nations* details the necessity of the state supplying external defense, internal justice, and even the training and education of workers.[39] Most interestingly, he is disarmingly honest concerning the political effects of capitalism, noting that "wherever there is property there is great inequality," such that "the acquisition of valuable and extensive property...necessarily requires the establishment of civil government."[40] A civil government that, "in so far as it is instituted for the security of property, is in reality instituted for the defense of the rich against the poor, or of those who have some property against those who have none at all."[41] This acceptance places Smith a long way from Locke's voluntary contract among men and close once again to the liberal dilemma over the state: you can't live with it, and you can't live without it, but worst of all, you must pay for it, *and that's what undermines capitalism itself.*

Having admitted that he needs the state, Smith must now find a way to pay for it, which necessitates taxes. Smith's first principle of taxation is progressivity. That is, "the subjects of every state ought to contribute...in proportion to the revenue which they respectively enjoy under the protection of government."[42] This seems to imply that the rich should carry more of the tax burden since they enjoy more revenues protected by the state. However, Smith's examination of different forms of taxation leads him to downplay progressivity, recommending consumption taxes on luxuries—anything above bare essentials—as the best way to fund the state.[43] Yet consumption taxes are perhaps the most regressive form of tax. So, how does that sit with his idea of proportionality?

It sits well if you start with the observation that "the whole consumption of the inferior ranks of people...is in every country much greater...than that of the middling...and above...rank."[44] Therefore, taxing anything except luxuries "would fall altogether upon the superior ranks of people," which would diminish their parsimony, and thus lower growth.[45] But there is no way that a consumption tax on nonessentials will suffice to fund a state of the size envisaged by Smith. How, then, can goverment be funded? The answer is government debt, and Smith doesn't like that answer.

Smith's problem with debt is that states, unlike merchants, are not by nature savers. Indeed, to his regret, "the parsimony which leads to accumulation has become almost as rare in republican (merchant-run) as monarchical governments."[46] As a consequence, merchants are indirectly saddled with "enormous debts which at present oppress, and will in the long-run probably ruin, all the great states of Europe."[47] Similarly to Hume's claims, this ruin will occur because "great states" are states filled with merchants who have lots of cash they can lend to the government; and lend they will given the good terms they receive. This easy money undermines the incentive to save in both the merchant class and the state and undermines the state's incentive to tax, just as Hume suggested.[48] As a result, more debt is issued.[49] Eventually, this strategy hits a ceiling, and "taxes [are] then imposed for the sole purpose of paying the interest of the money borrowed on them."[50] When this comes to pass the entire merchant class might as well sell up and depart the country, leaving it bankrupt, since the only possible option left to the government is to default upon the debt it owes.[51]

What makes sovereign debt unbearable for Smith is not just the default that it inevitably leads to: he fears the distributional consequences of that default even more. To stave off the inevitable sovereign default, lenders will be paid in devalued coin.[52] Those lenders are of course "wealthy people, who stand more in relation as creditors rather than as debtors," and as a consequence of this inflationary financing, their fortunes, and hence their ability to invest via saving, will be destroyed. As a result "the idle and profuse debtor [will earn] at the expense of the frugal creditor ... transporting capital ... to those which are likely to ... destroy it."[53] In short, the easy money offered by purchasing government debt subverts parsimony, the engine of growth and progress. This is why government debt must be resisted and why austerity, in the form of parsimony, must be embraced.

Locke, Hume, and Smith: Producing Austerity by Default

Note that none of these theorists makes a direct argument for austerity, hence our focus on austerity's absence. Locke, Hume, and Smith are busy building and restraining states, states that are not yet spending enough to warrant a policy of expenditure cuts, but whose debts are deeply troubling nonetheless. We find austerity's genesis here in the pathological fear of government debt that sits at the heart of economic liberalism. Government debt perverts savers, distracts merchants, and ruins accumulated wealth.

Locke sets up liberalism to limit the state at all costs. Hume sees no real point to the state since merchants are the productive class to whom the money should flow. Smith sees a role for the state but then struggles to fund it. He wants to pay as few taxes as possible to support the state, but recognizes that without such support the capitalism that he favors cannot be politically sustained. Smith's parsimony (saving) not prodigality (consumption) drives everything, and yet government debt, a debt that *will* be issued, with taxes being insufficient and states being prodigal, undermines our natural propensity to save, thus threatening Smith's entire schema. Hume may have given us the economic rationales for limiting debt, so familiar that we find them repeated unmodified today. But it is Smith who turns debt into a morality play. He gives us the moral arguments against debt that still resonate today.

In fairness, it's not as if Smith and Hume were making all this up simply out of a desire to dodge taxes. Long before Locke's time, states piled up debt and went bust with monotonous regularity, impoverishing their lenders in the process.[54] In their own lifetimes both Hume and Smith saw examples of debt financing going awry. Smith lived though the trauma of the collapse of Ayr Bank, a debt-financed Scottish bank that threatened the solvency of Smith's main benefactor, the Earl of Buccleuch.[55] In his writings Hume reflected on the earlier attempt by John Law, another Scot, to discharge the national debt of France by issuing shares in a giant trading company that used the bank of France as its fiscal agent. By 1721, when the resulting bubble popped, France went bankrupt—again.[56]

But in terms of how we think about austerity today, Smith's moral critique of debt seems as familiar as Hume's economic one. Saving is a virtue, spending is a vice. Countries that save must be doing the right thing, while spenders must be storing up trouble. In the Eurocrisis, we see northern European savers juxtaposed with profligate southern Europeans, despite the fact that it is manifestly impossible to have overborrowing without overlending. Similarly, note how the claims of Western countries that their debt problems lie with Asian countries that save too much get little sympathy. Morality does not sit on the side of the prodigal.[57] Within the Eurozone, surplus countries have no problem running a permanent trade surplus but criticize others for running deficits, as if you can have one without the other.[58] Finally, Smith's concerns about saving versus debt and parsimony versus consumption find a ready echo in Chancellor Merkel's invocation of the values of a Swabian housewife as the cure to the troubles of Eurozone: saving, parsimony, and the avoidance of debt being the key to success.[59] Three hundred years later, and the song remains the same. Austerity as we know it today, as an active policy of budget cutting and deflation, may not be readily apparent in the history of early economic thought. But the conditions of its appearance—parsimony, frugality, morality, and a pathological fear of the consequences of government debt—lie deep within economic liberalism's fossil record from its very inception.

Part Two: Austerity Emerges

Growing Pains: Austerity Meets the Modern State

Nineteenth-century liberal economists built upon the foundations bequeathed by Locke, Hume, and Smith, and in doing so they both replicated and amplified the "can't live with it, can't live without it, don't want to pay for it" problem of the state that haunts economic liberalism. Later liberals, such as David Ricardo, sat firmly on the "can't live with it" side of the fence when it came to the state. Ricardo pioneered the study of aggregates (land, labor, and capital) as collective actors whose interests were zero-sum against each other. Ricardo imagined a highly competitive economy of small firms in which initially high profits accruing to those first to enter a market converged to a very low average rate of profit as more people joined in and technology was diffused throughout an industry. At this low point, capital and labor would exit the market, searching out new areas of profit, thus starting the investment cycle all over again.

There was no positive role for the state in Ricardo's vision. Indeed, the one thing that had to be avoided was any attempt by the state to cushion market adjustments, disruptive though such adjustments were. As Ricardo opined, even if "the condition of the laborers is most wretched," government should not try to compensate their lot.[60] Attempts to "amend the condition of the poor...instead of making the poor rich...make the rich poor."[61] As such, the proper role of the state is to teach the poor the "value of independence" rather than to alter the distributions of the market.[62] The state should police the frontiers of property, but it should not alter the distributions of that property. Ricardo's Lockean accent remains pronounced.

Yet the state was changing its role throughout the nineteenth century, despite Ricardo's admonishments. Those very nineteenth-century activities of nationalism and state building demanded a far more interventionist state than that envisaged even by Smith.[63] Furthermore, the very success of capitalism brought forth a variety of social movements that demanded political representation, economic compensation, and social protection, all of which cost money and threatened private property.[64] Struggling to deal with this new world as the ninetenth century progressed were economic liberals, such as John Stuart Mill, who sat on the opposite "can't live without it" side of the fence.

Mill's most famous philosophical treatise, *On Liberty,* tried to find a path between the encroaching claims of the masses and the protection of individual liberal rights, while his *Principles of Political Economy* demarcated ever more precisely the areas of legitimate state action, even in the area of government debt. That is, rather than repeat Hume's and Smith's "inevitable enfeeblement of the state through debt" thesis, Mill argued that so long as government borrowing did not compete for capital and thus drive up the rate of interest, debt issuance was acceptable, even if taxes would be preferable.[65] Once again, like Hume and Smith, we see how one side of liberalism rejects the state while the other side accepts a limited role for it.

One side of liberalism, as we saw with Locke and Hume, denies the state a role and then, in Smith, acknowledges its existence. Ricardo exemplified this tradition in which the market is set up as the opposite of the state. Mill's writings show us another side of nineteenth-century liberalism that adapts to the growth of the state and its demand for revenues. The tension between Ricardo and Mill over the role of the state was hardly unique. Rather, it was and remains endemic to economic liberalism. Its result was to drive liberal thought down two very different paths during the late nineteenth and early twentieth centuries. One path led to the New Liberalism, a primarily British movement that took liberalism beyond Ricardo and Mill in a more interventionist direction. The other path led to Austria, where liberalism took a more fundamentalist turn.

New and Neo Liberalisms

Britain's New Liberalism came into being when British Liberal Party elites essentially sided with Mill over Ricardo.[66] They sought to develop the role of the state as both the defender of capitalism and as a tool for social reform in an era of class conflict and incipient mass democracy. In short, if the primacy of private initiative and of liberal market institutions were to be maintained, then the poverty and inequality Ricardo regarded as natural and inevitable could no longer be tolerated. Moreover, the British New Liberals did not see this embrace of the state as a necessary evil, as a papering over the cracks to avoid revolution. Rather, the New Liberalism acknowledged the state's responsibility for the ongoing management and reform of capitalist institutions.

The long-term consequences of this transformation of British Liberalism were dramatic. Universal pensions, unemployment insurance, and the intensification of industrial regulation all followed in the early twentieth century. Twenty years later, the heirs to this movement were the great social and economic reformers of the 1930s and 1940s, such as T. H. Marshall, John Maynard Keynes, and William Beveridge. They in turn pushed the New Liberalism still further, laying the foundations for a comprehensive welfare state.

If the New Liberalism was what we might call "Mill's modification"—a pragmatic adaptation to the complexities of the modern economy, then Austrian economics was "Ricardo's rejection"—a fundamentalist reaction against the modern economy.[67] The Austrian economists believed that liberalism was best defended, not through more redistribution and state management, but through the complete withdrawal of the state from its role in the economy. To borrow a term that is commonplace today, the Austrians were the original "neo" liberals. I discuss the Austrian ideas more fully in chapter 5. In brief, the Austrians attacked the new, interventionist ideas on two fronts.

First, they challenged the New Liberal claim that the operations of the unadulterated free market endangered capitalism using the counterargument that the market had a long-run evolutionary structure that government intervention could neither change nor predict. As such, intervention is always and everywhere harmful. Moreover, because government interventions produce market distortions and malinvestments, they were the source of credit booms and busts. Markets were stable unless they were interfered with. Capitalism wasn't inherently unstable: government made it so. Second, Austrian economists never shed their fear of the Leviathan state, which they continued to see as the ultimate enemy of liberal values. Specifically, they charged that once governments were allowed to intervene, they would always use the printing presses to fund their activities. Where British New Liberals began to see recessions as ameliorable through more spending, the Austrians saw in recessions the necessary pain of austerity after the interventionist "party." In sum, while the New Liberals and their mid-twentieth-century heirs embraced the state and intervention, the Austrians, in particular, Friedrich Hayek, Ludwig von Mises, and Joseph Schumpeter, rejected these notions entirely.

John Maynard Keynes once noted that

> the ideas of economists and political philosophers, both when they are right and when they are wrong, are more powerful than is commonly understood. Indeed, the world is ruled by little else. Practical men, who believe themselves to be quite exempt from any intellectual influences, are usually the slaves of some defunct economist.[68]

Today's ideas about austerity are no exception to this rule. The midcentury heirs of New Liberalism and the Austrian School still define the basic terms of the austerity debate eighty years later. We now trace these ideas through the Great Depression and the interwar period using the works of Keynes and Schumpeter as our exemplars. In the next chapter we pick up from where austerity hid out during the long winter of Keynesianism and the rise of the postwar welfare state, which brings us back to the Austrians via a detour through Germany.

Austerity American Style: Liquidationism

Perhaps the most famous characterization of American austerity thinking comes from a line attributed to Herbert Hoover's treasury secretary Andrew Mellon in response to the crisis of the late 1920s and early 1930s: "Liquidate labor, liquidate stocks, liquidate the farmers, liquidate real estate."[69] The result would be that "rottenness [will be purged] out of the system.... People will... live a more moral life... and enterprising people will pick up the wrecks from less competent people."[70] Adam Smith, it seems, was alive and well on the Potomac. Yet, despite the moral invocations, the Hoover administration did not exactly cleave to Mellon's "liquidationist" line.

America by 1930 hardly looked like a pure laissez faire economy. The Sherman acts of 1912, which regulated monopolies and busted "trusts" were deeply interventionist, and Hoover, as president, urged a variety of interventions to alleviate unemployment.[71] Yet these interventions were, by their design, either voluntary agreements between business and the state that had little teeth, or they were regulations designed to make markets "more" perfect by increasing competition and reducing the size of firms. Thus, both sides of liberalism were present in America at this time: the one that adapted to the state and saw its utility, and the one that sought to limit it and increase the scope of the market.

Tending toward the latter view, American economists of this period did not see depressions as accidents amenable to treatment. They saw them as a part of the nature of capitalism itself: regular, cyclical, and expected occurrences. The basic model drew upon what was called "modern business cycle theory," which was cut from broadly similar cloth as the Austrian ideas described above.[72] A particularly clear expression of this theory can be found in publications of the 1923

President's Conference on Unemployment, which Hoover had created as commerce secretary under President Coolidge. The lead author of the report, Columbia University economist Wesley Mitchell, argued that "a period of depression produces after some time certain conditions which favor an increase of business activity...[that paradoxically] also cause the accumulation of stresses within the balanced system of business, stresses which ultimately undermine the conditions upon which prosperity rests."[73]

These "certain conditions" were elaborated upon a decade later in another authoritative volume, this time by a collection of Harvard economists.[74] In it Joseph Schumpeter, an Austrian émigré and follower of the work of other Austrian economists of the period, such as Hayek and Von Mises, argued that capitalism has at any given point a distinct "capital structure," that long-run evolutionary form alluded to earlier, which manifests itself as the particular mix of productive assets that investment has generated over a given cycle. When there are investment booms, as there inevitably are in capitalism, both "too much" and "too much of the wrong type" of capital is invested in the economy.[75] Coming off the crash of 1929, when the stock market blew up, and after an entire history of railroad investment booms and busts over the prior century, such a view made more than intuitive sense. What turned this intuitive sense into a theory, however, was the concept of growth that was drawn from it.

Echoing the role Hume and Smith accorded to merchants, Schumpeter put entrepreneurs at the center of his analysis of the Depression and what to do about it. For Schumpeter, entrepreneurs make investments, many of which go bad, but capitalism progresses because of these failures, not despite them. We need failures, or capitalism does not evolve. The process of liquidation, of failure, produces the raw material for the next round of innovation and investment. As such, intervention, whether inflationary or otherwise, would cause two problems. First, it would obstruct the necessary liquidation process, propping up firms with cheap money, only postponing the inevitable day of reckoning.[76] Second, it would disrupt the price signals that entrepreneurs rely upon so that they would not know in which sectors to invest. Investment would fall, despite the government intervention that was intended to increase it.

Liquidationism therefore argues *for* an inevitability—*the slump must happen*—and also *for* intervention's unintended consequences—if you get in the way of that inevitability *you will end up making it worse*. The consequence of this line of thinking is *austerity*—purging the system and cutting spending—which becomes the essence of recovery. Austerity may be painful, but it is unavoidable since undergoing such emetic periods is the essence of capitalism's process of investment and discovery. There was, therefore, no alternative.

The Hoover administration therefore actively sought not alternatives to austerity, but compliments and palliatives that took the form of voluntary policies to smooth the adjustment of labor and capital to new uses. Those policies were always conceived of as helping adjustment pro-cyclically rather than compensating for it countercyclically. For to do the latter would, Schumpeter warned, "lead to a collapse worse than the one it was called into remedy."[77]

This Austrian strain in American thinking about the inevitability of cycles, the centrality of the entrepreneur, and the importance of failure, coexisted with and was boosted by another line of American economic thought that stressed the need for a policy of "sound finance."[78] Favored by the banking community, these ideas reinforced the Austrian flank by insisting that business confidence, the key to supply-side growth, would only be restored if the government credibly signaled that it would allow the emetic process to unfold as it had to via austerity. While temporary relief of the symptoms of unemployment could be countenanced, the state's role in such moments devolved to balancing the budget, even raising taxes in a recession if this was deemed necessary, to restore the investor confidence. During 1931, the last year of his administration, Hoover did exactly this to signal resolve in the face of financial difficulties. The result was the worst depression in American history.

If these ideas sound familiar today, it's because, like the ideas of Hume and Smith, the same arguments are being recycled again, eighty years later. The idea that the current crisis was generated by the malinvestment of the past, particularly in real estate, is hardly an unreasonable point of view. That Fannie and Freddie caused a global crisis, the extension of that viewpoint, is not.[79] The notion that taxes should be raised to balance budgets in the middle of a recession is the policy orthodoxy of the IMF-EC-ECB troika in the Eurocrisis and US budget reformers such as the Simpson-Bowles Commission.[80] The need for "the return of business confidence" to start the recovery forms the centerpiece of contemporary British austerity policy, despite its yielding zero results to date. But then, as now, the Americans were far from alone in expounding such ideas. Indeed, back in the 1920s such ideas had a pronounced British accent.

Austerity with a British Accent: The Treasury View

Despite the expansion of the British state into the realm of pensions and insurance and regulation under the influence of New Liberal ideas in the first two decades of the twentieth century, the British response to the crisis of the 1920s and 1930s remained resolutely liberal and austere. The British version of austerity is commonly located in a British government white paper from 1929, "Memoranda on Certain Proposals Relating to Unemployment."[81] As usual, the reality is a bit more complex than that.

The so-called Treasury view expounded in this policy paper was really the latest iteration of the same classical liberal ideas we have encountered already. As the world's largest economy in the nineteenth century and the anchor of the gold standard, which facilitated international adjustments between surplus and deficit countries through movements in domestic money supplies tied to gold, the United Kingdom was a firm believer in free trade, free capital movements (very important for the City of London as a financial center), free labor (that is, no regulation thereof), and a limited liberal state.[82] Although that limited liberal state had been growing rapidly and acquiring new responsibilities during the prior two decades, it still accounted for only about 12 percent up until the eve of the First World War.[83]

More important was the mindset of Treasury officials that had yet to adapt to the reality of a bigger and more interventionist state. As Keynes's contemporary Joan Robinson put it, "For fifty years before 1914 the established economists...had all been preaching one doctrine...the doctrine of *laissez faire*...free trade and balanced budgets were all that was required.... These doctrines were still dominant in 1914."[84] By the mid-1920s, however, as the postwar slump had turned into a full-blown depression, and as these doctrines increasingly came under attack for worsening the situation, the Treasury view began to take form as a defense of the status quo. Its origins lie in the Treasury's response to proposals to alleviate unemployment through temporary public works programs. The logic developed and deployed was exactly the same "crowding out" argument we encountered in Hume and Smith, and the perils of easy money and debt were once again on full display.

The Treasury's argument, echoing Hume and Smith, was that to borrow money to finance spending, the government would have to offer better terms than those available elsewhere. This would have the effect of reducing overall investment by "crowding out" private capital while increasing the debt for what would offer only a temporary respite rather than a full-blown cure. As Conservative chancellor of the exchequer Stanley Baldwin put it in 1922, "Money taken for government purposes is money taken away from trade, and borrowing will thus tend to depress trade and increase unemployment."[85] Such views, however, were not limited to the Treasury. The mindset was so widely shared that no less a figure than John Maynard Keynes argued in 1924 that "public money which has been raised by borrowing, can do nothing of itself...and it may do actual harm if it diverts existing working capital from the production of goods."[86]

The British elite's rather monolithic view began to splinter in 1925 when Keynes criticized Churchill's decision to go back on the gold standard after an eleven-year hiatus.[87] Churchill put Britain back on at a high exchange rate, which, though it was good for the City of London and for foreigners holding sterling, was terrible for British exports. As a consequence, unemployment, already bad, shot up, and economic activity declined. Keynes had predicted that this would occur, and indeed it did, much to the chagrin of Churchill and the Treasury.

This conflict between Keynes and the Treasury, odd when one considers that Keynes was a Treasury advisor throughout this period, was exacerbated in 1929 when Keynes, with Hubert Henderson, produced the pamphlet "Can Lloyd George Do It?" in response to Liberal politician David Lloyd George's much-discussed proposals in a prior pamphlet called "We Can Conquer Unemployment." In his assessment of George's proposals, Keynes "first adumbrated the...relation of saving to investment."[88] That is, he argued that saving doesn't drive investment if "investment is free to fluctuate under the influence of expectations" such that income and employment adjust to the ex post level of saving.[89] As a consequence, government should "fill the gap/ prime the pump" by spending money that business is sitting on because of uncertainty about the future.

This view was extremely threatening to the Treasury since it implied that supply-side factors were insufficient to drive the economy to full employment. It required a response, which the Treasury duly provided in both the "Memoranda on Certain Proposals" and most publicly in Winston Churchill's 1929 budget speech in which he argued that "when the Government borrow[s] in the money market it becomes a new competitor with industry and engrosses to itself resources which would otherwise have been employed by private enterprise, and in the process raises the rent of money to all who have need of it."[90] This is as pure a statement of the notion that the government crowds out investment as one can find.

The "Memoranda on Certain Proposals" actually took this a step further, however, arguing that any such compensatory policy was doomed to failure, even if it could be funded. The Treasury now insisted that "increased government borrowing for public works would result in higher interest rates, if savings were to be attracted to gilt-edged stock so that the borrowing would not be inflationary, and that this would tend to divert money that would have otherwise gone to home industry, or to overseas investment."[91] Thus the threat of an interest-rate spike was here added to the original crowding out argument and the perversion of savings into unproductive debt securities.

But the Treasury wasn't just fighting Keynes and Lloyd George. It was also pandering to orthodox business opinion, which held that if public works are seen to be a waste of time by the business community, business would respond by shifting its money abroad, thus offsetting any effects of the spending.[92] Thus a Ricardian equivalence argument that rational investors anticipate and negate policy was joined to an investment-crowding-out/interest-rate-spike argument to corral the logic in favor of spending still further. Indeed, Keynes erstwhile collaborator Hubert Henderson, who also happened to be the secretary of the government's Economic Advisory Council, made exactly this argument in October 1930. Henderson then went on to invoke the general state of confidence as always and everywhere negatively impacted by government spending.[93] As Bill Janeway put it, "the constraining power of [austerity] ideas persisted: fear of loss of confidence still limited action by a government exempt from external financial and political challenge."[94]

The Treasury next added the argument that spending could not work because its stimulus effect would suck in imports. This would worsen the balance of trade, making British firms less competitive, and in the long run this would worsen rather than alleviate the slump.[95] Here again, we see echoes of Schumpeter's concern with limiting the liquidation process, without which there can be no improvement in the capital stock, and hence no recovery.[96] The state, once again, must remain limited in its ambitions and its actions.

But over time the side of economic liberalism that saw a more positive role for the state began to influence the Treasury view. By 1935, although the Treasury was still arguing that although "public works as a remedy for unemployment were quite futile," government nonetheless still had a role to play in maintaining "the impetus of recovery" in specific areas of the country via spending.[97] Indeed by 1937, the Treasury was willing to propose that a reserve fund of necessary public works be deliberately left not completed so that when a downturn worsened they could be released as a countercyclical measure.[98] But even here, concerns with inflation arising from debt-financed expenditure and the need to pay back the accumulated debt limited the appeal of such logics, even in the midst of a deep depression.[99] British austerity thinking, like its American cousin, proved remarkably immune to the economic facts of the day. It may have admitted the necessity of the state, but like Smith, it was in no mood to pay for the state's actions.

The End of 1930s-Style Anglo-American Austerity: Keynes and Schumpeter

The events of the 1930s are recounted in chapter 6 in the discussion of austerity's "natural history." Suffice to say here that despite states' adhering to these ideas for twenty years, from 1918 to 1938, such policies did nothing for recovery. Comparatively speaking, countries that abandoned the gold standard and that were able to concentrate on boosting domestically generated demand recovered further and faster than those that stayed on it and looked to austerity via deflation to right the ship.[100] The United States, for example, first experimented with alternative ideas concerning industrial concentration and cartelization as possible solutions to the slump during its 1934–1935 National Industrial Recovery Act (NIRA) period. Then, despite Franklin Roosevelt's being elected to balance the budget, the Roosevelt administration started to "prime the pump" under the auspices of the New Deal, and the economy began to recover.[101] A broadly similar shift occurred in Sweden.[102] Britain and France, in contrast, held on to austerity, and the Depression persisted in both countries until the start of World War II.[103]

Keynes's Anti-Austerity Arguments

During the 1940s, in the context of massive wartime spending, pro-spending, anti-austerity ideas rose to prominence and pro-austerity doctrines faded into the background. The most famous anti-austerity argument was Keynes's General Theory.[104] But Keynes's work was as much a consequence as a cause of the shift away from austerity. As Joan Robinson put it pithily, "Hitler had already found how to cure unemployment before Keynes had finished explaining why it occurred."[105] But these new ideas from Keynes and many others at about the same time were important precisely because, unlike the old instruction sheet, they explained not just the slump but normal times too, within one framework. Pro-austerity ideas could not credibly claim to do this after two decades of waiting for a recovery that was "just around the corner." After all, the liquidation process had run its course for an awfully long time, but it seemed, against Secretary Mellon's expectations, that there remained a shortage of more-competent people and cheap capital waiting—just around the corner—to pick things up again. Keynes's General Theory could explain where such folks were hiding and why they were doing so.

In brief, Keynes demonstrated a fallacy of composition that was present in both labor and investment markets, which Liberals had ignored and which led to resources being unemployed for extended periods of time. First, he showed that although any worker can accept a wage cut to price himself into employment, if all workers did this, it would in the aggregate lower consumption and prices, and thus increase the real wage (the wage-minus-price effects), leaving the worker who "adjusted" poorer and just as unemployed.[106] Second, he showed that under conditions of uncertainty about the future, it is irrational for any investor to invest rather than sit on cash, with the result that if investors look to each other for signals about what to do, they all sit on cash and no one will invest.[107] Thus we bring about, by our collective self-interested actions, the very depression we are individually trying to avoid. Smith's invisible hand may well have arthritis, and austerity may make it worse.

Keynes showed that decisions to save and invest were temporally separate, and that savings did not necessarily lead to investment. Saving could just as easily lead to hoarding and reduced consumption. The job of the state was, then, to alter the investors' investment expectations by raising prices so that profits could be made, thereby making it rational to begin hiring workers again and, by doing so, to get out of the slump. Rather than savings leading to investment, consumption via workers' paychecks ultimately drove investment. Today we call this demand-side economics.

These ideas were no mere addendum to the new liberal worldview. They were a transcendence of it to a more General Theory.[108] Instead of merchants' saving and driving growth through their parsimony, Keynes portrayed a world in which the investor class, the heroes of Smith and Hume, was really just the derivative supply-side tail of the demand-side dog, wagged by the consumption decisions of millions of average Joes. As Keynes put it, "Consumption—to repeat the obvious—is the sole end and object of economic activity."[109] Consumption drives investment through its effect on prices and thus is what drives investment expectations, not the other way around. Confidence is an effect of growth, not a cause.

But if this is the case, then not only is Smith's world overturned, austerity as a sentiment, as a morality, and as policy is overturned with it. The balance between state and market, the "can't live with it, can't live without it, don't want to pay for it" problem that generated austerity as the default policy to deal with recessions, has been resolved entirely in favor of the state. In this world spending, and with it debt, *especially by the government*, becomes good policy. Individual saving as a virtue, in contrast, falls to the paradox of thrift: if we all save (the very definition of austerity), we all fail together as the economy shrinks from want of demand. Austerity was, then, in the eyes of liberals, after Keynes sacrificed on the altar of fiscal profligacy. Yet after two decades of failure, austerity's arch defenders had little to say or show for all its virtue. Chief among those who were quieted was Joseph Schumpeter himself.

Schumpeter's Retreat

Twelve years after criticizing the Roosevelt administration's policies in *The Economics of the Recovery Program*, which gave Mellon's liquidationism a theory of growth, stressed the importance of entrepreneurs, and argued for austerity, Joseph Schumpeter cut an intellectually lonely figure. By 1946, the world had gone Keynes's way, not his. Schumpeter could, like many others, have jumped on the bandwagon, but for a true economic liberal, and a political conservative, that was never an option. He found "the stagnationist theory...as developed by the late Lord Keynes" to be "astounding" only for the fact that it has "not simply [been] laughed out of court."[110] What, then, was his response to these laughable ideas that seemed to explain the depression and what to do about it much better than his own set of austerity-inflected ideas?

Schumpeter's response to the Great Depression and the failure of austerity policies to cure it was his magisterial *Capitalism, Socialism and Democracy*, which appeared in 1942.[111] Schumpeter attributes the failure of austerity to two conjoined mechanisms: the substitution of the large conglomerate and the manager for the small firm and the entrepreneur and the collapse of the risk-taking culture that supported entrepreneurial activities. Despite the fact that it had been brewing for a decade before Schumpeter wrote his 1934 analysis, the Great Depression was supposed to be a regular cyclical dip that a good dose of austerity would correct by no later than 1935 or 1936. By 1942 Schumpeter hadn't changed his tune, or his mind: he had simply lengthened the time frame and added in a few harmonies.

Schumpeter's *Capitalism, Socialism and Democracy* argued that the Great Depression was neither great nor depressing. Rather, it was just a particularly marked transitional period of technological and organizational change that became hyperpoliticized, one of those "recurrent 'recessions' that are due to the disequilibrating impact of new products or methods."[112] We know this, he maintained, because capitalism, properly viewed, is a system in which constant change and adaptation is the name of the game. "Economic progress, in capitalist society, means turmoil."[113] Capitalism therefore cannot be judged over the short run. In fact, "we must judge its performance over time, as it unfolds through decades and even centuries."[114] By definition, then, compensating for turmoil, acting on the immediate short run, not only halts the process of creative destruction by entrepreneurs that lies at the heart of capitalism; doing so is guaranteed to produce more malinvestment that simply stores up trouble ahead since the job of austerity is left undone.

Capitalism, Socialism and Democracy appears, then, as a longer and more elaborate restatement of his earlier beliefs. Nothing has changed for Schumpeter, except everything around him. Indeed, rather than engaging Keynes and his ideas directly, *Capitalism, Socialism and Democracy* abrogates a robust defense of liberalism in favor of a lengthy discussion of Marx and a bureaucratic-cultural explanation as to why capitalism will inevitably be replaced by socialism. His argument is worth retelling since it shows the dead end that Anglo-American austerity thinking found itself in by the mid-1940s. Rather than engage, it retreated into moral commentary and "fin de siècle" certitudes.

Apart from normalizing turmoil, Schumpeter focused on changes in industrial structure of capitalist economies and the rise of very large firms to explain the failure of austerity to produce recovery. This is his long-run evolutionary story in which the locus of production and innovation has undergone a scale-shift, and as a result, the capitalism of small producers, entrepreneurs, and perfect competition "is not only impossible, but inferior" and on its way to being replaced.[115] Bureaucratization and institutional change are the prime movers in this story, driving economic evolution, taking innovation out of the hands of entrepreneurs and putting it in the hands of specialists and managers in large firms. Firms become giant bureaucratic entities that are slower to adapt to environmental shifts and that operate on much larger scales. They become, in short, more like, and more dependent upon, states. Oligopoly and interventionism go hand in hand.

More importantly for Schumpeter, this scale-shift takes a cultural toll. Whereas in the past "the rugged individualism of Galileo was the individualism of the rising capitalist class,"[116] today, technology and bureaucracy have together removed the possibilities for such individuals to thrive. As he laments, "the capitalist process rationalizes behavior and ideas and by doing so chases from our minds . . . metaphysical belief" such that "economic progress becomes depersonalized and automatized."[117] When large firms take over production it is not the entrepreneur's income that is replaced. After all, he gets shares in these new conglomerates. Rather, his social function is made redundant, "the stock exchange [being] a poor substitute for the holy grail."[118] This may lead to a material progress, to more consumption and all that Keynes thinks important, but it is for Schumpeter a morally empty future. It is also one that invites jealousy from the lower orders who, led on by classes of functionless left-leaning intellectuals who resent capitalism, have become accustomed to ever-rising standards of living and can no longer accept the dislocations of the market. Thus, the disorder of the previous decades is little more than the inability of the spoiled masses to accept necessary adjustments.[119]

As for those in the once proud investor class, they, too, now only care about consumption, thanks in part to these newly fashionable theories, with the result that both the bourgeois family unit and the ethic of saving, Smith's sentiment, disappear from the world. As Schumpeter put it, "The bourgeoisie worked primarily . . . to invest, and it was not . . . a standard of consumption so much as a standard of accumulation that the bourgeoisie struggled for and tried to defend against the government."[120] Thanks to the twin forces of bureaucracy and technology, the bourgeoisie has given up this struggle. "When all is said and done, it [the bourgeoisie] does not really care."[121] And when no one cares for capitalism, the result is socialism.

If Schumpeter reminds you of Ayn Rand's character John Galt, he should: he's cut from the same conservative cloth. And, as in Galt's long speech at the end of *Atlas Shrugged*, what starts as a robust defense of economic liberalism ends up being a weak retreat from it. With the Keynesian view ascendant, conservatives like Schumpeter had a choice: admit that they were wrong (or at least accommodate themselves to the new ideas that seemed to fit the facts better than the old ones) or find something else to talk about. Schumpeter chose the latter path, and so he spoke about the death of saving, the end of family virtue, and the triumph of bureaucracy. His own retreat was emblematic of the retreat of austerity as a serious intellectual argument among the economic mainstream of Anglo-American countries. Anti-austerity it seemed, had won the day. But the victory was not complete. Austerity survived in one part of the world immune to Lord Keynes: the German-speaking world. Austrian school economists continued to give austerity a globalized intellectual home, while German ordoliberals, as we shall shortly see, gave austerity a national base of operations.

THE INTELLECTUAL HISTORY OF A
DANGEROUS IDEA, 1942–2012

Part One: Austerity Finds a European Home—and an American Pied-à-Terre

Welcome to Germany: *Erst Sparen, Dann Kaufen!*

One[1] of Joseph Schumpeter's lasting contributions to economic thought was his concept of gales of "creative destruction" that sweep through the economy.[2] Torn asunder by the entrepreneurial utilization of technology, continual organizational innovation, and the rigors of competition, businesses rise and fall, driving the business cycle over time. It is, then, hard to imagine a less Schumpeterian economy than Germany's. Consider, for example, when some of Germany's flagship companies, which are still with us today, were founded: BASF (chemicals), 1865; Krups (appliances), 1846; ThyssenKrupp (metalworks), 1891 and 1811; Daimler/Mercedes Benz (automotive), 1901 and 1926; Siemens (engineering), 1847, to name but a few.

These firms have survived two world wars, occupation, partition, the Cold War, and reunification—let alone conglomeration and the ups and downs of the business cycle. Unlike in Schumpeter's world of entrepreneurs and competitive small firms, these companies in many cases started as large-scale concerns made possible by the complex state and banking linkages typical of late-industrializing states. These firms innovate incrementally, improving their dedicated product lines one step at a time using specialist engineers and scientists.[3] Most of them haven't seen an entrepreneur in a century. There has been plenty of creativity, but very little destruction—at least of firms—in Germany. Why then did Germany become the refuge for austerity arguments of the type typically associated with Austro-American thinkers such as Schumpeter? The answer lies in what a group of German economic thinkers called ordoliberals did to the idea of austerity, to the usual relationship between the state and the market in liberal thought, and in the process, to the postwar German economy. We touched upon ordoliberalism previously. Here, we flesh out its role as a redoubt for pro-austerity arguments during the long winter of the Keynesian era and as the basic design template for the contemporary European variant of austerity.

Taken on its own terms, ordoliberalism is a peculiar form of liberalism. It does not suffer from the "can't live with it, can't live without it, don't want to pay for it" problem that lies at the heart of Anglo-American liberalism. In the same way that Keynes solved the austerity problem for the New Liberals in Britain, ordoliberalism solved the problem of the state in Germany by transcending it, but in an entirely different manner. Ordoliberals see the role of the state as setting the framework conditions necessary for markets to operate effectively in the first instance. The state they are happy to live with is not, however, the macroeconomic manager focused on the demand side of the economy that emerged out of British New Liberalism. Rather, the ordoliberal state is a rule setter that enables competition and aids market adjustments through the development of specific economy-wide mechanisms and institutions.

Historically speaking, although there were many exponents of liberalism in the nineteenth-century German-speaking world, liberalism never became the dominant economic and social philosophy in Germany that it became in the Anglo-American world, for three reasons. First of all, German liberals had to contend with a conservative counternarrative of *Zivilisationskritik* that juxtaposed a deep German *Kultur* to a superficial Western (specifically English), liberal *Zivilisation*, stressing that Germany was of a different kind in such matters.[4] Second, liberalism's credibility as an economic doctrine was badly damaged in Germany by the huge stock market bust of 1873: the so-called founder's crisis (*Gründerkrise*). Third, following the founder's crisis, the German state became much more interventionist, which further crowded out liberalism's ideological appeal, allowing space for interventionist anti-liberal thinkers such as Friedrich List to flourish. Fast forward from the 1890s, and the relative novelty of liberalism in Germany after World War II plus the refashioned role for the state in the economy that it allowed, is what turned Germany into the postwar refuge, and later, the contemporary amplifier of austerity arguments in Europe.

The Importance of Being Late

Understanding Germany's historical relationship to both liberalism and austerity necessitates an engagement with the conditions under which states become capitalist. We tend to forget that Britain and the United States are the exception rather than the rule when it comes to the relationship between states and markets. The former had the advantage of turning capitalist without competitors, allowing a small and limited state to develop, while the latter was geographically isolated with a huge internal frontier to exploit.[5] The rest of the world, the *late* industrializers that came after these states, operated under vastly different and more competitive conditions. This matters because when you enter the world economy determines in no small part the type of state that you develop to engage with that economy, with the basic rule being the later the developer, the bigger, and the more interventionist, the state.

When we think about interventionist, late-industrializing states, we tend to think of the states of East Asia.[6] Yet, French experiments from the Place des Vosges to the Crédit Mobilier Bank notwithstanding, the original developmental state was Germany. Playing catch-up to the British in the latter half of the nineteenth century forced Germany (it came into being in 1871) to act as the broker, and in many cases as the insurance agent, among industrial, commercial, and agricultural interests.[7]

All late developers have a scale problem. To catch up with already industrialized states, the state in a late developer must underwrite the risk involved in investment because the scale of the capital required to industrialize after other states have done so outstrips the capacity of any individual entrepreneur to do so—hence the size, structure, and longevity of German firms. In playing this role, the German state, whether Wilhelmine, fascist, or democratic, has always accorded itself a more directive and coordinative role in the economy than is typical of liberal states. Critical throughout Germany's development has been the role of the state in suppressing consumption and increasing savings to provide adequate pools of capital for large-scale industrial investments, while also providing transfers to smooth, rather than block, such policies.[8] As such, the mantra of *Erst Sparen, Dann Kaufen* (first save, then go shopping) to save and invest before consuming—a parsimony that Smith would have applauded—formed the austere core of German economic thought long before the 1930s, when ordoliberalism appeared.

Ordoliberalism's Origins

Ordoliberalism took form under the aegis of Walter Eucken, Franz Böhm, and Hans Grossmann-Doerth, the founders of the Freiburg school of economics during the 1930s. Their bête noir was the private economic cartels rather than the state. The Freiburg liberals argued that Germany's basic economic problem in the 1920s was "the inability of the legal system to prevent the creation and misuse of *private* economic power."[9] Note that private, not public, power was the concern. The individual needed to be protected from the state, to be sure, but acknowledging that the state was not the only threat worth worrying about marked Frieburg's departure from the "can't live with it" version of Anglo-American liberalism. The Freiburg school's key contribution, however, was to go beyond this observation and focus attention on capitalism's structural form.

For Walter Eucken in particular, capitalism was not the haphazard assemblage of individuals envisioned by Smith. Rather, it was composed of two fundamentally incompatible structural orders that he termed the "transaction economy" and the "centrally administered economy."[10] Although these orders are incompatible in their essences, real economies necessarily combine elements of both, and that's where the problems start. Especially when parliaments get involved, elements of the administrative order can be captured by the most powerful members of the transactional order, hence the fear of cartels and private power. The optimal policy, therefore, is to make this combination of orders work such that the latter (the state) enables and enhances the conditions of operation of the former (the market).[11] As Eucken defined the role of the state in the economy: "First principle: the policy of the state should be focused on dissolving economic power groups or at limiting their functioning. [...] Second principle: The politico-economic activity of the state should focus on the regulation of the economy, not on the guidance of the economic process."[12] This was to be achieved, argued the Freiburgers, by paying attention to the "economic constitution," which is, according to Franz Böhm, the "comprehensive decision (Gesamtentscheidung) [of a society] concerning the nature (Art) and form of the process of socio-economic cooperation."[13] Or, in Eucken's less turgid prose, as the "general political decision as to how the economic life of the nation is to be structured."[14]

As legal theorist David Gerber notes, this notion "turned the core idea of classical liberalism...on its head by arguing that the effectiveness of the economy depended on its relationship to the political and legal systems."[15] Although early ordoliberal work during the Nazi period gave primacy to a strong state as the promoter of such an order, this view changed over time—and circumstance—to the position that economic policy should not be dictated by a strong state, especially one that could be captured.[16] Rather, the state needed to be strong enough only to provide an "order," an *Ordo,* and a consequent *Ordnungspolitik,* an "order-based policy," whereby the legal framework governing action both by firms and the state together forms the economic constitution critical, according to the Freiburgers, to any successful economy.[17] *Ordnungspolitik* therefore restrains both the state that practices it, and the private sector that grows within it, through the indirect regulation of the economic constitution.

This economic constitution was not simply something that could be set down on paper, however. Ordoliberals argued that the correct economic constitution cannot simply be deduced from theory and imposed by the state. It must be actively supported by members of the community to which it applies, and crucially, its implementation must be based upon a reciprocal duty of those members to act in the terms laid out in the constitution.[18] In short, everyone needs to follow the rules, and everyone doing so reconstitutes and legitimates those rules.[19]

To make this happen, the appropriate state policy was not to set the conditions of investment or to manipulate the level of prices via monetary stimulus, as the Keynesians argued. Instead, given its concern with limiting private power, competition policy, supported by the monetary policy of a politically independent central bank, formed the institutional core of the economic constitution. A dedicated monopoly office would ensure that the economy as a whole conformed to the meta-rules of competition, while an independent monetary authority would play the supporting role of keeping prices stable. Both institutions would be separate from and would not directly answer to the parliamentary state.

Competition, Not Consumption, Leads to Growth

By attacking concentration and cartels while keeping prices stable, ordoliberals hoped to generate growth by enhancing the competitiveness of German firms and the attractiveness of their products. The policy objective of these institutions was therefore the encouragement of "achievement competition" rather than "impediment competition," whereby the quality of products manufactured would create the demand for them, in a modern supply-side restatement of Say's law.[20] Under such institutional conditions the benefits of rapid growth would flow to all members of society.[21] As Christian Wartin put it, ordoliberals were of one mind that "unless a liberal constitutional state [was] prepared to see itself deteriorate into an interventionist state...the maintenance and enforcement of a competitive system must be regarded as one of its prime objectives."[22]

As we elaborate below, these new institutions and the underlying ideas that served as the blueprints for them were bolted, after a brief period of internal struggle among postwar Christian Democrats, to the existing Bismarkian patriarchal welfare state to form what Alfred Müller-Armack called "the social market economy," a "system of legal rules which can satisfy the general feeling of justice," which would tie citizens to the economic constitution as they realized its benefits.[23] As Ralf Ptak observed, despite their deep misgivings about the welfare compensation, ordoliberals keenly appreciated that the "stability and security [of] the working class was prerequisite to securing the market economy."[24] As a consequence, although the ordoliberals really did not want the economic constitution to be tied to a welfare state, circumstances and politics dictated otherwise: the market economy had to become social.

Building the Ordo

That ordoliberal arguments would become the local economic instruction sheet for economic policy in postwar Germany was almost overdetermined. First of all, the German population was exhausted and hungry while the country's capital stock was decimated. Fearing political instability, the postwar authorities needed growth, and like the population they governed, those authorities were suspicious of growth coming from "big-state" projects, whether from the left or the right. Second, the Freiburg school, which was not shy in hawking a growth project, emerged from the Nazi period unsullied and more or less intact. While some members were arrested and a few key players such as Wilhelm Röpke were driven into exile, the core of the school was in the right place at the right time, armed with what seemed to be, in the German context, new growth-friendly ideas. The ordoliberals also had powerful sponsors in the form of the leading newspaper of the day, *Franfurter Allgemeine Zeitung*, and the ear of the Allied occupation authorities, at least once the Allies moved out of the punitive phase of the occupation.[25]

Third, Germany's economic profile as a late developer has always been export-oriented manufacturing; so it was natural for Germany's postwar economic elites to focus on the reconstruction of export capacities and the recovery of export markets as a way to achieve the rapid growth they sought. Ordoliberals may have sought to preserve small- and middle-sized firms and feared cartels, but they had no problem with large firms per se, especially those that were able to produce export-led growth. But export-led growth requires a strict policy of cost competitiveness, which in turn requires wage control through the restriction of consumption and a strong anti-inflationary stance. This further strengthened the hand of the monetary authority over the fiscal authority, as controlling inflation became the monetary complement to ensuring competition.[26]

Fourth, the postwar political party system was a mess, and the center parties, particularly the Christian Democratic Union (CDU) were looking for a new set of ideas that spoke to their (predominantly) Catholic members' conceptions of their interests.[27] With its appeal to community, its distrust of *private* as well as public power, and its somewhat reluctant—but necessary given the conditions of the times—acceptance of welfare state redistribution through the family, ordoliberalism found both a willing audience and a launch vehicle in the CDU.

As Gerber argues, however, nothing succeeds like success, so when Ludwig Erhard, ordoliberal fellow traveler and de facto German economics minister during the occupation, freed prices by abolishing rationing and price controls in 1948 without it, initially at least, throwing the economy off a cliff, ordoliberal ideas gained prestige.[28] However, after the initial boom, the Korean crisis hit Germany hard, and the ordoliberals lacked a positive interventionist response. Concerned with rising unemployment, the Allies pressured the ordoliberals to consider active labor-market measures to deal with the rapidly rising numbers of people out of work. This allowed the Social Catholics within the Christian Democrats to push for a better integration of welfare policy and economic policy, which cemented the place of the welfare state in the ordo against ordoliberal impulses.[29]

This fusion gave institutional form to Alfred Müller-Armack's idea of the social market economy (*die Sozialmarktwirtschaft*). Under this banner, the CDU won every national election until 1966—a period that is referred to now as the "German economic miracle" (*das Wirtschaftswunder*), during which the purchasing power of wages increased 73 percent between 1950 and 1960. Meanwhile, inflation fell, increasing the real wage even further.[30] Indeed, despite the resettlement of 12 million displaced persons and the division of the country, unemployment in the 1950s averaged 8 percent and prices remained stable.[31]

Crowding out Keynes Locally

The success of the *Socialmarktwirtschaft* and the ordoliberal ideas that underpinned it was so complete that, as Christopher Allen reports, "Keynesianism was rarely given serious consideration as [a policy] option" by German economists, who, if they discussed Keynesianism at all, viewed it as inherently inflationary.[32] Consequently, when the German Social Democratic Party came to power in 1966 with a pro-Keynesian agenda in response to faltering growth rates, it found little receptivity to these ideas in either the bureaucracy or the academy. Locally, Keynes was "crowded out" in theory. Amplifying this exclusion, the monetary authority, "the fiercely independent Bundesbank... placed strict monetary limits on deficit financing," thus locally crowding out Keynesianism in practice.[33] This is hardly a surprise when one considers that the Freiburg ordoliberals had foreseen such a role for the monetary authority, arguing that "a strong central bank [would be] the guardian against any misuse of power by the political authorities."[34] In ordoliberal terms, spending equals misuse, and the central bank was specifically designed to prevent such misuse.

In sum, postwar Germany prospered with austerity-focused ideas of a particular type at its core. Germany both possesses and professes a liberalism that embraces the state and transforms it. In doing so, it does the same for austerity. The fact that *ordoliberalism, ordnungspolitik*, and the rest, are all about rules means precisely that good economic governance is not about spending. If the rules establish a framework within which prosperity is established through the enhancement of competition, then the supply side of saving and investment, rather than the demand side and consumption, still rules the day. Ordoliberalism may have modernized liberalism, but its economics in many ways remain as classical as Smith and Hume.

In the context of a late-developing, export-led economy that needs to force savings to catch up the British, this makes perfect sense: *Erst Sparen—Dann Kaufen*. But just as we saw in chapter 3, it rather spectacularly ignores the fact that for someone to be running an export surplus, someone else must be running a deficit. We cannot all run surpluses and save. Someone has to spend so that there is demand for these exports. Thus, a fallacy of composition of a different type rears its head again; and this is where the transfer of these austerity-based principles into the EU's constitutional framework and in Germany's policy response to the crisis, really shows up. If Germany's focus on rules, obligations, a strong monetary authority, a weak parliament, and no spending to compensate for busts sounds familiar, it should. It's the basic design of the EU. Germany's response to the crisis, and the crisis itself, both spring from the same ordoliberal instruction sheet.

Ordoliberal Europe

When the rest of Europe stagnated in the late 1970s, Germany suffered the least and recovered the quickest of all the major European states.[35] Its ability to withstand the inflationary pressures of the period became the model for other European states: first, through the abortive currency pegs to the deutsche mark of the 1980s and 1990s; second, through the incorporation of ordoliberal principles into the ECB constitution and the EU Commission's competition-focused policies; and third, through the rules-based approach to governing the Euro project. From the Maastricht convergence criteria to the Stability and Growth Pact to the proposed new fiscal treaty—it's all about the economic constitution—the rules, the ordo.[36]

For example, the centrality of competitiveness as the key to growth is a recurrent EU motif. Two decades of EC directives on increasing competition in every area, from telecommunications to power generation to collateralizing wholesale funding markets for banks, all bear the same ordoliberal imprint. Similarly, the consistent focus on the periphery states' loss of competitiveness and the need for deep wage and cost reductions therein, while the role of surplus countries in generating the crisis is utterly ignored, speaks to a deeply ordoliberal understanding of economic management. Savers, after all, cannot be sinners. Similarly, the most recent German innovation of a constitutional debt brake (*Schuldenbremse*) for all EU countries regardless of their business cycles or structural positions, coupled with a new rules-based fiscal treaty as the solution to the crisis, is simply an ever-tighter ordo by another name.

If states have broken the rules, the only possible policy is a diet of strict austerity to bring them back into conformity with the rules, plus automatic sanctions for those who cannot stay within the rules. There are no fallacies of composition, only good and bad policies. And since states, from an ordoliberal viewpoint, cannot be relied upon to provide the necessary austerity because they are prone to capture, we must have rules and an independent monetary authority to ensure that states conform to the ordo imperative; hence, the ECB. Then, and only then, will growth return. In the case of Greece and Italy in 2011, if that meant deposing a few democratically elected governments, then so be it.

The most remarkable thing about this ordoliberalization of Europe is how it replicates the same error often attributed to the Anglo-American economies: the insistence that all developing states follow their liberal instruction sheets to get rich, the so-called Washington Consensus approach to development that we shall discuss shortly. The basic objection made by late-developing states, such as the countries of East Asia, to the Washington Consensus/Anglo-American idea "liberalize and then growth follows" was twofold. First, this understanding mistakes the outcomes of growth, stable public finances, low inflation, cost competitiveness, and so on, for the causes of growth. Second, the liberal path to growth only makes sense if you are an early developer, since you have no competitors—*pace* the United Kingdom in the eighteenth century and the United States in the nineteenth century.[37] Yet in the contemporary world, development is almost always state led.

Germany was in many ways the first country to prove this very point during the catch-up with Britain. But then, like the United States and the United Kingdom, Germany forgot her uniqueness, in terms of both timing and context and in terms of how building the export-led ordo that made Germany rich was only possible precisely because other countries were *not* doing the same at the same time.[38] Now Germany and the EC want everyone else in Europe to be more German: another fallacy of composition that cannot work. As Martin Wolf put it beautifully, "Is everybody supposed to run current account surpluses? If so, with whom—Martians? And if everybody does indeed try to run a savings surplus, what else can be the outcome but a permanent global depression?"[39] Germany was able to take the lead in Europe because German ideas have been at the heart of the EU and the euro since its inception. This is also why the Germans were able so successfully to turn the debate about the crisis their way—they were the only people who really believed what they were saying. Whereas the Americans were Keynesians by default, the Germans were ordoliberals by design. In monetary matters above all, *credere* (belief) matters.

In sum, Germany gave austerity a new lease on life through the social market economy and its postwar economic miracle. *Erst sparen, dann kaufen* leaves no room for the profligate except austerity, and it allows no room for compensation apart from policies that speed the adjustment of the market. The imprint of these ideas on EU institutions is not in doubt. There is no place for Keynes and compensation in an economic union in which competition produces growth through the production of competitive products and the running of surpluses, not the shallow demand of the money press. In such a world, the slump, not the boom, is the right time for austerity.

All of which brings us to the role played by ordoliberal's cousins, the Austrian economists, in pushing austerity arguments forward. If the influence of ordoliberalism has been felt primarily in Europe, then the influence of Austrian ideas lies in the United States. Austrian ideas have long had an American pied-à-terre, as we saw in Schumpeter's diagnoses of the 1930s.[40] They came back into vogue in the current crisis because they seemed to have been onto something that few Keynesians (except Hyman Minsky) had paid much attention to, and in doing so they gave us another set of reasons to be austere.

Austerity's American Pied-à-Terre: The Austrian School

In the late nineteenth century, Austrian economics emerged in the Austro-Hungarian Empire from the debate over the role the state might play in fostering economic development following Germany's state-led growth spurt. The key figure here was Carl Menger, one of the first of the so-called marginalist economists, who saw economic value as a question of subjective utility and relative prices, rather than as a function of costs of production. More important for our purposes, he was also dead against the state being involved in helping capitalism along the way. Megner started a "methodological debate" (*Methodenstreit*) with members of Germany's Historical school of economics over these matters that led the Germans to label Menger and his followers "the Austrian school." An academic generation later, Menger's students contested the increasing interventionism of the liberal state from these particularly Austrian premises.

For these theorists—Ludwig Von Mises and Friedrich Hayek being the most prominent, along with Joseph Schumpeter as the Austrian émigré voice in the United States—the free market has a long-run evolutionary structure that government intervention can only harm. Siding firmly with the "can't live without it" school, the Austrian school rejected the state as having any positive or necessary role in the economy. They also rejected the increasing mathematization of economics that was underway at that time. Seeing the economy as evolutionary, disequilibrial, and driven by entrepreneurs acting in uncertainty, they preferred historical analysis to differential calculus. Given these choices, the Austrians found themselves increasingly out of step with the tenor of the times.

For example, during the 1920s, Mises and Hayek became embroiled in the so-called socialist calculation debates of the period, seeking to prove the impossibility of central planning. Mises argued that planning was literally impossible, a line that was hard to defend as anything other than ideological. The more he stuck to his guns, the more he found himself ignored by other economists. Meanwhile Hayek, having received a second wind when the like-minded Lionel Robins got him a job at the London School of Economics in 1931, found himself in trouble the moment he set foot in Britain. As Joan Robinson recalled, Hayek gave a talk at Cambridge shortly after he arrived at which R. F. Kahn asked, "If I went out tomorrow and bought a new overcoat, that would increase unemployment?" "Yes," said Hayek, "but . . . it would take a very long mathematical argument to explain why."[41] By 1944, Hayek found himself similarly ignored, in semiretirement, writing on the dangers of socialism in his epic *The Road to Serfdom*. Hayek's earlier *Prices and Production*, his *Meisterwerk* on business cycle theory, like Schumpeter's 1939 *Business Cycles*, arrived dead at the presses.

First ignored and then defeated in Europe, Austrian ideas survived in America, where their popularity has ebbed and flowed for nearly a century. Although battered and beaten-down by the Keynesian revolution after World War II, Austrian ideas never quite disappeared from the American scene. They staged something of a comeback in the 1970s when Hayek was awarded the Nobel Prize in economics and served as a popular justification for Reagan's supply-side policies, but they disappeared again until the current crisis brought them back to the fore. Why this reappearance? The answer lies in what they said about banks.

The Austrian Guide to Boom and Bust

Despite Keynes's *General Theory* being subtitled "of Employment, Interest and Money," postwar economics never put all that much thought into money. There was a view that gained prominence in the 1970s—monetarism—that thought about money a great deal, and we will examine that view shortly for different purposes. But for most economists from the 1930s on, money was seen in pretty much the same way that Hume saw it 200 years before, as short-run stimulative, long-run neutral, and/or potentially inflationary.[42] Money, it is sometimes said, "changes neither preferences nor possibilities." Money in the form of credit, therefore, is simply one person's nonspending transferred to another person to use for an interest payment plus the return of the principal. Put more simply, one person's debt is another person's income. It's simply a redistribution of existing assets and nothing to get excited about. The credit system simply replicates the fundamentals upon which the economy is based.

This view made it perfectly possible for mainstream economists in the 2000s to talk about "the elimination of the business cycle" while living in a period of "Great Moderation," where the volatility of the past had been tamed by good central bank policies.[43] And then, of course, the world blew up, right in the middle of this supposed Great Moderation, just as the Austrians would have predicted. And while everyone seemed to know that the explosion had something to do with asset bubbles and banks, at the start of the crisis few had a convincing story about how the banks had caused it. This is where the Austrians came back in. Their writings from the 1930s seemed to describe the 2008 financial crisis perfectly. Its aftermath, and what to do about it, was to prove another matter entirely.

The Hayek/Mises Model of Credit Crunches and Collapses

Writing in the 1920s, Hayek and Mises drew attention to the rather obvious fact that banks make money from the extension of credit. And while each bank may wish to be prudential, each has an incentive to expand credit beyond its base (at that time, gold) reserves to stay in business against more aggressive banks and/or capture market share. Moreover, banks are encouraged to do so by the presence of a central bank that backstops the financial system with liquidity. Both these forces produce an expansion of credit beyond what "real" savings would allow and lower the interest rate on loans.

Such an extension of credit signals to entrepreneurs that the real cost of capital has fallen, and that as a consequence, they can now undertake projects, financed through this cheap credit, that hitherto would not have been profitable. Even if entrepreneurs suspect that this is an artificial stimulus, no one likes to watch competitors take market share, so they take the money regardless. In the aggregate this leads to an expansion of borrowing and a weakening of the desire to save. Astute, thrifty, and prudent in free-market conditions, entrepreneurs become reckless, debt-juggling dupes once the banks start handing out oodles of cheap money.

Suitably incentivized, entrepreneurs hire more people and buy more materials, which pushes up prices and wages. This produces a classic short-run monetary stimulus effect that begins to show up in rising prices, particularly asset prices, which encourages still more borrowing. The underlying economy, however, has not changed. There is simply more money chasing fewer goods: an inflation. Realizing their error, banks now stand to make losses, so they do everything they can to not realize those losses. They extend more credit, lower interest rates further, and generally kick the can down the road.

This is, from an Austrian point of view, exactly the wrong thing to do since it pumps up the credit bubble still further while diverting capital away from what the market would have better allocated in the absence of all this cheap credit. This policy really gets inflation going, and as a result the real value of money falls; so all this malinvestment must generate an even greater return, or everyone's balance sheet collapses. Knowing this, and in the context of an ever-increasing inflation, banks start to raise interest rates at the same time their ability to generate new credit shrinks. Meanwhile, demand for credit to keep the bubble inflated accelerates.[44] Eventually, the public figures out that all this asset growth is really just a monetary inflation and not a rise in real asset values, and the bubble pops, the panic begins, assets are dumped, balance sheets implode, and the economy craters.

This is where austerity comes in. As Mises puts it, once the "flight into real values" begins, people realize that "the crisis and the ensuing period of depression are the culmination of the period of unjustified investment brought about by the extension of credit."[45] Therefore, the "economy must adapt itself to these losses [so]...the thing to do...is curtail consumption."[46] Savings that have been squandered need to be rebuilt, which means less consumption. Banks must realize their losses to begin the process of recovery, which means austerity. The last thing we should do is to bail out either banks or consumers. After all, what started because of an intervention into the market, the lowering of rates via the expansion of credit beyond that which "real savings" would produce, cannot be dealt with by more of the same.

The (Supposed) Idiocy of Intervention

Indeed, the very worst thing that can happen is for the government to get involved. By flooding the market with liquidity, keeping the rate of interest low when credit is scarce, or attempting to stimulate the economy to smooth out the cycle, government intervention simply prolongs the recession. Moreover, intervention produces a further pathology that is perhaps even more dangerous: it creates, according to Mises, a capital strike among investors.

When there is a financial bust, there are (mainly) four ways to adjust: inflate, deflate, devalue, or default.[47] Deflation, cutting wages and prices so that the economy can adjust to real values is, according to the Austrian school, the right thing to do, but governments don't like this because it causes unemployment and instability. So, putting default to one side since that tends to create instability, too, governments prefer devaluation, if they have their own exchange rate, or inflation, or both, as the way to pass the costs on to creditors (the few) to pay for the mistakes of debtors (the many).

According to the Austrians, then, we should not be surprised to find lots of companies sitting on very large piles of cash in the middle of a recession. Per contra what stimulators would tell you about this behavior being a response to uncertainty about the future or a lack of demand, what's really behind it is the perfectly rational belief that given half a chance the government will inflate or devalue its way out of trouble on the backs of the investor class. Companies may be sitting on piles of cash and not investing, but the recession is not, as Keynes would have you believe, the capitalists' fault. Rather, investors are quite reasonably covering the risk of backdoor expropriation by the state through inflation or devaluation. The fear of the state taking away your property—the original liberal nightmare—rears its head once more. Instead, "public opinion is perfectly right to see the crisis...as a consequence of the policy of the banks."[48] Consequently, the sum of the Austrian view is that we should let the banks fail and then restart the system.

Later Austrian theorists added to this basic framework. Some, such as Gottfried Harberler, stressed the role of trade unions in setting wages, thereby forcing the central bank to increase credit through the commercial banking system to realize labor's excessive wage demands.[49] Murray Rothbard, in turn, stressed the role of central banks as the ultimate credit pump qua extortion racket played by the banking system on the public.[50] But the basic model remains the same. It's all about the banks producing cycles of boom and bust that are always made worse by the government getting involved either through central-bank-based monetary policy or through simulative fiscal policy. Austerity is the correct and only possible response to a slump. Everything else is folly.

America's Austrian Accent: The Pros and Cons of Being Austrian

It is hardly surprising that these arguments resonated in America after the crisis. They have, after all, a submerged prior history in the United States stretching back to the 1920s via Schumpeter. Indeed, as a description of what went wrong in 2007–2008, these ideas seem to fit the facts rather well. Banks, the dangers of debt, excessive leverage, asset inflation, a collapse of savings: it's all there. The "don't bail them out" message taps into a strong current of populist American opinion.[51] Meanwhile, the "don't intervene/let it run its course" message found strong support in the right wing of the Republican Party and among elements of the financial community that were not too big to fail, particularly hedge funds.[52] Why, then, apart from few key high-profile figures such as Glenn Beck, Peter Schiff, Ron Paul, and (the younger) Alan Greenspan, is it difficult to find mainstream economists, even in America, who publicly accept the Austrian theory of the business cycle? To see why, we need to look at the assets and liabilities side of the Austrian explanatory balance sheet.

On the asset (theory) side, we find the action of central banks in producing asset bubbles with prolonged policies of too-cheap money and the epistemic hubris of managing the Great Moderation blowing up in the faces of the same central bankers who declared that they had tamed the cycle, which is not an unreasonable description of the 2000s. The broad sweep of an asset bubble's inflation and deflation is well described by the basic Austrian model. The notion that debt is not simply redistributionary (my income is your debt) because leverage matters and that the payoff to debt financing is asymmetric, especially on the downside, is also a telling and important contribution. The problems start when we move to the liabilities (policy) side.

First, being the last redoubt of the "can't live with it" liberals, Austrians bemoan austerity but see no alternative to it. "Do nothing" and let the economy "self-heal" are their main policy proposals. A version of this is currently being tried in the Eurozone, and as we saw there, the healing is not going so well. We should also remember that we have been here before. These same ideas were offered as explanations and implemented as policies in many countries in the 1920s and 1930s, and as we shall see in chapter 6, they didn't work then either. As Keynes demonstrated, there is no reason for an economy to "naturally" return to a full-employment equilibrium after a shock. It can settle into a state far from full employment for a very long time.[53] The Austrian explanation of sustained unemployment after a bust—the inability of the economy to self-heal as it should—is that trade unions are holding up the market-clearing wage. But in the United States, for example, where unions cover less than one in eight workers, such an explanation is simply not credible.[54] Moreover, Germany and Sweden, countries with much higher unemployment rates through the business cycle, also have far higher unionization rates.

Second, if the only policy on offer is to get the government out of economic affairs completely, then its not clear how one does it short of engaging in a kind of "year zero" purge of the modern economy and polity. Similarly, the notion of relying on "real savings" rather than "artificial credit" would require the abolition of fractional reserve banking—where the bank lends out multiples of its reserves—and therefore an end to, for example, securitization, car loans, education loans, mortgages, and so on. It's hard to see this as either welfare improving or politically sustainable in any meaningful sense.

Third, you don't have to be a Keynesian to acknowledge that economies do not necessarily self-heal. One of America's Great Depression–era monetary economists, Irving Fisher, analyzed how, much to his dismay, depressions do not in fact "right themselves" owing to a phenomenon called *debt deflation*.[55] Simply put, as the economy deflates, debts increase as incomes shrink, making it harder to pay off debt the more the economy craters. This, in turn, causes consumption to shrink, which in the aggregate pulls the economy down further and makes the debt to be paid back all the greater. Fourth, just as it does not follow that governments should always intervene to stave off market adjustments, as the "Greenspan put" and Ireland's bank rescue showed only too well, to argue that there should never be intervention presumes knowledge of the system—it will return to full employment if left alone—that Austrians themselves say is impossible to attain. The Austrian counterfactual, that in the absence of interventions market allocation will be optimal, can never be satisfied. After all, if entrepreneurs are duped by short-term interest-rate cuts, there is no reason to assume that their choices would necessarily be any better than those of the state doing the duping when it comes to choosing how to allocate capital in the first instance.[56]

Fifth, one doesn't have to accept a John Galt anti-inflationary capital strike thesis to explain why companies are currently sitting on tons of cash. Simply put, it is irrational to invest during a recession—you don't know if you will get your money back no matter how cheap the cash. Finally, asset inflation was as much a symptom of the crisis as it was a cause. The more fundamental causes, as argued in chapter 2, were the interaction of excessive balance-sheet leverage, the fragility of the shadow banking system (the repo markets), and the structure of complex derivatives, all of which are premier examples of financial entrepreneurship. Apparently, and per contra Schumpeter, not all entrepreneurship and innovation is good.

In sum, while the Austrian theory is very insightful in some areas, especially in covering the broad story of the credit cycle and the dangers of excessive debt, the Austrian policy proposal that follows from this analysis—"maximum austerity as quickly as possible"—makes little sense given what we know about how actual economies perform when they go through busts. Far from encouraging "self-healing," nonintervention and noncompensation can produce the politics of permanent austerity, as Europe is finding out. Politically attractive to some, especially to antistatist conservatives, such ideas resonate in theory, but they detonate in practice.

By way of summing up so far, Germany provided a postwar home for austerity arguments in the form of ordoliberalism, the instruction sheet for how to run a late-developer, high-savings, high-technology, export-driven economy. It's a great instruction sheet—so long as you are indeed the late-developing, high-savings, high-technology, and export-driven economy in question. If you are not, as the periphery of the Eurozone is finding out, then it's a one-way ticket to permanent austerity. The Austrian school provided an American pied-à-terre to a set of related and even more austere liberal arguments. Whereas the ordoliberals transcended the "can't live with it, can't live without it" problem by turning the state into the framework for the economy, the Austrians invite us to abolish the state once and for all as the only way to save ourselves from boom and bust cycles.[57]

Both ordoliberal and Austrian liberal ideas shot to prominence in the crisis, but the crisis itself did not produce these ideas as some kind of automatic, obvious, and uniquely appropriate response. The first part of chapter 3 noted the near-term politics behind this shift in ideas. What we will do next is examine the long-term enablers of these ideas that explain their current receptivity. Understanding this tranche of austerity's intellectual history takes us on a tour from the general neoliberal turn in economics in the 1970s and 1980s, through the policies of the IMF in the 1990s, to the work of mainstream pro-austerity economists in the 2000s.

Part Two: Austerity's Enablers

Crowding out Keynes Globally: Monetarism, Public Choice, and the Dangers of Democracy

Despite their finding German homes and American pied-à-terres, appreciating why these decidedly local ideas were able to spring to global prominence in the current crisis requires an engagement with what I term *austerity's enablers*: broader ideological and institutional shifts that bit-by-bit brought austerity back to the status of economic common sense after it had been relegated so decisively to the status of old-time religion. We encountered some of these ideas in chapter 2 when we detailed the rise of ideas about efficient markets and of investors with rational expectations—and we noted how the crisis punctured belief in these ideas. But these ideas did not sit alone in the financial markets. They were part of a much broader intellectual shift in economics and economic policy worldwide that was part and parcel of the tearing up of the Keynesian instruction sheet in the 1970s. It is the rise of these neoliberal ideas that enabled the return of austerity as the commonsense thing to do in a slump. Remove these ideas from the intellectual fossil record and it is impossible to jump from the battered and isolated state pro-austerity ideas found themselves in by the 1960s to their modern instantiations.[58]

Critical here were the ideas of so-called monetarist and public choice economists. What united these ideas and made them politically powerful was their joint production of the state as the inflationary pump rather than the economic shock absorber. By painting the state in this way, they made the state "doing more" a dangerous idea. In short, classical liberals produced austerity by default, Austrians and ordoliberals produced austerity by design, and latter-day neoliberals produced austerity by exclusion: by definition, any other policy would fail. Taken together, they made it possible for austerity to become, once again, last idea standing.

Neoliberalism: Milton's Monetarism

Monetarism is a set of ideas developed in the 1960s and 1970s, most notably by Milton Friedman in the United States and by Patrick Minford in the United Kingdom.[59] Monetarism's basic claims are twofold, with the first clearing the ground for the second's more substantive argument about the pathologies of the state. First, the Great Depression was caused by shortsighted Federal Reserve policy that led to a decline in the money supply. Contra Keynesianism, it was not caused by underconsumption or by a decline in the level of money income.[60] This claim called into question the causal relationship between money and income seen by Keynesians. Second, and more important for enabling austerity arguments a generation later, is Freidman arguing that attempts by the government to stimulate the economy to full employment, which it would be tempted to do if it got that causal relationship backwards, can only show up as inflation.

As we saw in our discussion of the fall of the Keynesian instruction sheet in chapter 2, Friedman's argument was that if the government expanded the money supply to increase employment, employers would initially expand output in response to rising prices. Unemployment would decline, which would in turn boost wages. So far, so Keynesian. This cannot last, however, because Friedman, and this is crucial, assumed that *unemployment was voluntary and was not due to a deficiency of demand*. People choose labor or leisure at the prevailing wage. There is no demand-deficient unemployment in Milton's world. In other words, the 25 percent of Spaniards who are presently without work simply don't (by Milton's presumption) want to work at the prevailing wage and are on vacation.

Unemployment, then, only falls because of spending in the short term, as more workers are drawn back to work at the apparently higher wage, trading off leisure against labor. But because it is workers' money wages that have increased, not their real wages (the money wage minus the effects of higher prices), nothing has really changed for them. Wages have gone up, and so have prices: it's a wash. Realizing this, these newly employed workers, being voluntarily employed, either force up wages to compensate for the rise in prices, which their employers then pass off as price increases—inflation—or they withdraw their labor, bringing employment down to what Friedman called its "natural rate." Regardless, the higher inflation generated by this process eats away at their standard of living. Once labor-market equilibrium is reestablished at this "natural rate" of unemployment, expectations will again adjust to the new, higher, underlying rate of inflation, and it can only continue to rise. With inflation rising and unemployment not improving, Keynesianism, according to monetarists, eventually eats itself.

Friedman's monetarism pushed hard against one of the key ideas of the postwar economic instruction sheet—the Phillips curve—that we also discussed in chapter 2.[61] Crucial was his idea that there is a natural rate of unemployment, an evolutionary throwback to classical ideas about labor markets clearing at the equilibrium wage, with the amount of employment generated being a function of structural supply-side factors plus the degree of trade-union militancy. As Michael Bleaney once observed, accepting Milton's monetarism ensures that "ideas concerning a lack of effective demand have disappeared out the window... we are back in a completely classical world where... full employment follows automatically."[62]

Indeed, monetarism was in many ways simply a restatement of the quantity theory of money that goes all the way back to David Hume. Its power lay in how it provided liberals with an alternative way of thinking about the macroeconomy to that offered by Keynes, one that put money front and center. In doing so, monetarist ideas not only reduced the appeal of the Keynesian instruction sheet, especially in the context of the inflationary 1970s, they helped enable austerity arguments some forty years later. By giving us a new set of reasons why state intervention to compensate economic downturns can only end up producing inflation, monetarism helped naturalize Austrian and ordoliberal ideas, pulling them off the fringe and into mainstream acceptance.

When combined with the ideas of rational expectations and efficient markets that we encountered in chapter 3, monetarism paved the way for the modern understanding of austerity by making markets always efficient and the state always pathological. But what really held the door ajar and allowed these ideas to come flooding back was a parallel set of arguments that sought to overturn, not only misguided state policies, but the role of the state in the economy itself. All of which brings us back to a more familiar "can't live with it" form of liberalism.

Neoliberalism: Democracy Is a Problem

Public choice theory emerged at about the same time monetarism did as a full-blown critique of the state in the economy. Rather than simply reassert how the state would eat itself, such economists as George Stigler, William Niskanen, and James Buchannan brought the tools of microeconomics to bear on the analysis of politics and policy to show how the state would eat the economy too.

Their point of entry was to assume that agents inside the state behaved no differently from agents elsewhere: they maximized their incomes subject to their constraints. Rather than seeing politicians as neutrally steering the economy according to the vagaries of the business cycle with an eye to the public betterment, public choice theorists discerned a political business cycle, wherein state spending was matched to the electoral calendar to produce booms and slumps that were the cost of elected officials seeking to maximize votes. This argument combined with monetarism to produce a new—or *neo*—liberal interpretation of appropriate economic policy.

The logic was both simple and universal. Given Friedman's notion of the natural unemployment rate, politicians cannot simply pick the point on the Phillips curve that suits their preferences for levels of employment and inflation and trade them off in a stable way. Rather, as detailed earlier, once the state intervenes to stop a slump, expectations adapt, and the economy shifts to a new, higher rate of inflation that leaves unemployment unchanged over the long run. So far, so Freidmanite. Now for the Virginian twist.[63]

Unable to sustain this inflation politically, the government has to deflate to bring unemployment down to the natural rate. Unfortunately, this does not wring inflation out of the system since expectations have adapted to the new, higher rate of inflation. Meanwhile, unemployment has gone up, and as a new election approaches politicians must once again reflate to ensure their reelection. The result is a boom and bust cycle that produces ever-higher inflation. In other words, it is elections that determine the content of economic policy making, and not the other way around.

Inflation is then the inevitable outcome of democratic governments trying to interfere in the economy. Just as market agents maximize income, so political actors maximize votes: inflation is the inevitable result. Unlike the *invisible hand* that promotes the public welfare by giving free reign to individuals' *income* maximization, the *visible hand* that maximizes *votes* brings nothing but chaos to the social order and inflation to the economy. As public choice theorists James Buchanan and Richard Wagner argue, government-induced "inflation destroys expectations and creates uncertainty; it increases the sense of felt injustice and causes alienation. It prompts behavioral responses, which reflect a generalized shortening of time horizons. 'Enjoy, enjoy!'... becomes a rational response... where the plans made yesterday seem to have been made in folly."[64]

Similarly, Milton Friedman opined that because of government-induced inflation, "[p]rudent behavior becomes reckless and 'reckless' behavior becomes 'prudent.' The society is polarized; one group is set against another. Political unrest increases. The capacity of any government to govern is reduced at the same time that the pressure for strong action grows."[65] Given these pathologies that are endemic to democracy, what must be done to save the liberal economy from the destructive forces of democracy? Banning democracy would be effective but might be unpopular. A second-best solution would be to have an institution that would effectively override such inflationary decision making. Luckily, such an institution already existed thanks to those ordoliberals, or neoliberals would have had to invent one: the independent central bank.

Central Bank Independence Is the Solution

During the Keynesian era, central banks almost everywhere were *dependent* creatures. That is, central banks were the financing agent for the national treasury: they cut the checks that the politicians said needed to be cut. As noted earlier, the one exception was Germany's Bundesbank with its singular goal of stabilizing the price level, which was only made possible by its unique late-developer profile and equally unique ordoliberal instruction sheet. Everywhere else, banks were politically dependent even if they were nominally independent, as in the United States Federal Reserve's dual mandate to fight inflation and unemployment, and that, according to neoliberals, was exactly the problem.

The telling contribution here came from two economists associated with the Real Business Cycle school, Edward Prescott and Finn Kydland.[66] They pointed out that even if we don't assume that politicians are instrumentalist to the core, caring not a fig for the country as a whole, and assume instead the best of intentions, a "time inconsistency" problem sits at the heart of democratic decision making. Time inconsistency is familiar to any smoker who wants to quit: "really, just one more, and then I will stop." Politicians are time inconsistent insofar as they may sincerely promise to, for example, tackle the debt or lower inflation, but when a shock happens to the economy and/or an election looms, other priorities get in the way, and they renege on their promises; hence, inflation. Politicians are also heavily incentivized to focus on short-term measures, for the same reasons.

But if politicians cannot, in the language that this literature spawned, "credibly commit" to a given policy, both voters and market agents will discount government policies and attempt to offset their effects, which will lead to greater economic instability and uncertainty. Kydland and Prescott argued that the key to solving this problem was for the central bank to be made independent from politicians and, in the manner of the Bundesbank, to be mandated to pay attention only to price stability. Critical here were a set of institutional reforms designed to shield the central bank from public scrutiny and central bankers from public recall or redress, while ensuring that these bankers are more conservative than the median voter to further protect the institution from populist demands.

Such reforms would ensure that government attempts to spend against the cycle would not happen in the first instance because the politicians in question would know that the central bank has credibly committed to holding the line on prices by being both institutionally protected and politically conservative.[67] Thus the bank can "credibly commit" in a way that the politicians cannot. As a consequence, policy making should be delegated away from democratically elected politi-

cians to independent conservative central bankers who will dish out
the bad medicine when required because their jobs do not depend
upon pleasing constituents—except, perhaps, their constituents in the
financial sector who benefit from ultralow inflation—but that's another story.[68]

Austerity and Neoliberalism: Opening up the Policy Space

The acceptance of these ideas by a generation of policy makers, politicians, and economists as the common sense of the day considerably
narrowed the space for any type of "spend against the cycle" compensation arguments—Keynesian or otherwise—long before the current
crisis. Conversely, these arguments widened the policy space for austerity's comeback considerably. After all, why compensate when we
know that compensation only causes inflation? Why expect a stimulus
to work when we know that it only ever promotes inflation and when
politicians only enact a stimulus to get reelected?

What would have once been, without these ideas, simply the
old-fashioned musings of cynical policy makers and their ancient economic advisors was now given a firm, and very liberal, theoretical
foundation. Their evidentiary basis, however, was another matter entirely.[69] The fact that these theories rest upon incredibly narrow oper-
ational premises and have scant evidence going for them is beside the
point. That they are highly effective policy rhetorics that only narrow
the menu of choice for governments is what matters.[70]

Nonetheless, these "neo" neoliberal ideas revolutionized economic
policy making in the developed world in the 1970s and 1980s, so much
so that by the 1990s central bank independence, for example, had
spread like a rash over the face of the planet, most notably throughout
all of Europe, with the drive to the euro and the founding of the ECB
marking its high point.[71] When the ECB was unleashed on Europe in
1999, it was arguably the most independent central bank around,
charged with only one goal: fight inflation, even in the middle of a
deflation, a task it has been succeeding in rather well up to this
point.

Monetarism, as a specific policy of targeting the money supply to
fight inflation, foundered on the rocks of defining what money in the

modern world actually is back in the 1980s. But its legacy of assuming a natural rate of unemployment has been critical in sustaining arguments against spending and compensation. After all, why spend to get past the natural rate when that will only ever produce more inflation? If unemployment is "structural," and not due to a lack of demand, then spending will not have any effect on it, so we should not try.[72] The fact that the "natural rate" jumps around far too much across countries and time periods to be reduced to structural factors or unionization rates has done nothing to discredit it.[73]

Similarly, the notion that unemployment is voluntary is, in the context of the current self-inflicted wound in Europe, downright offensive. Real workers must pay bills and feed families from jobs that have fixed hours and fixed wage rates. The idea that workers "trade off" labor against leisure by figuring out the real wage rate and then slacking off or going on an indefinite unpaid leave is the type of thinking that leads us to see the Great Depression as a giant, unexpected, and astonishingly long unpaid vacation for millions of people: original, yes; helpful, no.

Public choice theory, like any universal gizmo, has not only helped revolutionize the institutional relationship between voters, politicians, and bankers in democratic societies, it has become, as Daniel Dennett said about evolution in *Darwin's Dangerous Idea*, the "universal acid" that eats away everything it touches by turning everything into a principal-agent/rent-seeking problem.[74] Think that countries in a currency union might actually come to each other's aid out of a sense of solidarity? Don't be so naïve. Moral hazard is ever present. Worried that you can't tell what the future may hold? Don't worry. Properly defined rules will make the future conform to your preferred vision. Terrified that profligate governments will not reform their economies when you compensate for their unemployment through transfers? You are right. They will not do so, they will "hide and rent seek" off your taxpayers; so their governments should be replaced with ones that you can trust. Welcome to Europe.

The moral hazard logic embedded at the core of public choice arguments covers, and infects, all possible circumstances. Yet in doing so, it mistakes the mechanisms that generate trust—diffuse reciprocity, norms of mutual aid, and so on—for naïve weaknesses that can only be eliminated by more rules and stronger sanctions: exactly the things that eliminate the possibility of trust. While social capital does not trump moral hazard per se, when policy makers view all mutual interactions as agency problems, where one party will inevitably take advantage of another, the only solutions imaginable are the elimination of institutional ambiguity, the tightening of rules, and the writing of superficially complete contracts—which looks a lot like current Eurozone reforms. The problem is that what economists call moral hazard is what normal people call trust. You cannot eliminate the former without destroying the capacity for generating the latter. Without some degree of rule ambiguity and norms of reciprocity, trust cannot emerge. The EU's political project was built on trust, not the elimination of moral hazard. That's why it worked. Its monetary project is based on opposite principles. Yet at the end of the day, how can you run an economy, especially a pan-European monetary economy, without trust as its basis? While the German word for debt has the same root as the German word for guilt, *schuld,* the Italian word for belief forms the English root for the word credit, *credere.* At their base, money, trust, guilt, and faith are all norms, not rules. Smith's self-interest and ordoliberal rules can only get us so far.

Seen from this vantage, democracy is similarly not an end in itself, since it is little more than an inflation-causing pathology from which only rules, not discretion, can save us. Replacing a government or two in the Eurozone is simply, then, what needs to be done. The question of the legitimacy of such policies or of how the presumed preference for low inflation over all other goals becomes the preference of all society, especially when those enforcing that preference as policy don't want to ask the voters, remains conspicuous by its absence.[75]

Together these arguments crowded out Keynesianism in the developed world and enabled the return of pro-austerity arguments during the crisis. For the developing world, however, a version of neoliberalism that put austerity front and center became *policy du jour* courtesy of a policy consensus born in Washington years before it was tried in the developed world. It was the Global South where the policies unleashed upon the periphery of Europe, and which stand ready to strip the American welfare state, were first road tested. Once again, their failure did nothing to eclipse their popularity.

Austerity's Foreign Road Test: Washington's Consensus and the IMF's Monetary Model

The Washington Consensus was a list of ten "must do" policies authored by development economist John Williamson in 1989. The full list was fiscal discipline, reordering public expenditure priorities, tax reform, liberalizing interest rates, (maintaining) a competitive exchange rate, liberalizing trade and foreign direct investment (FDI), privatization, and deregulation. They were intended to capture "the extent to which the old ideas of development economics...were being swept aside."[76]

Those old ideas, from the 1960s and 1970s, were the work of old-school Latin American developmental economists who championed industrial policy and other state-led industrialization projects. By the late 1980s, they were very much out of fashion, having foundered on the rocks of the Latin American debt crisis of the 1980s. Williamson's new policy ideas were, in contrast, drawn from "ideas that had *long been accepted as appropriate* within the OECD."[77] As such, the failed old ideas that accepted a positive role for the state in economic development were juxtaposed with the new antistatist neoliberal ideas of the already successful, developed North.

Williamson has claimed, on repeated occasions, that he did not intend his list of policies to constitute "a general acceptance of neoliberalism."[78] But his list nonetheless captured the essential features of what we now call austerity policies rather well. Moreover, taking exchange rate and FDI policies off the list, it's hard to see how this set of policies, drawn up in 1989 at the "end of history" moment, was reflective of the actual practices of OECD states in this period. For example, France, Italy, and all of Scandinavia, to name but a few OECD states, did not pursue such policies to any significant degree before 1999, let alone 1989. Outside the OECD the more successful developing states such as Korea, Taiwan, and latterly China, practiced these policies even less.[79] Individual states may exhibit a few of these policies, with the United States and the United Kingdom once again at the forefront in generalizing their policies as universal, but the notion that they constituted an empirically settled consensus on "what the rich folks do" was taking it a bit far.

Regardless, those who were willing to take Williamson's ideas whole cloth and road test them around the world were the Washington-based institutions of international development, specifically the IMF and the World Bank. Formulated for and in Latin America during a period of chronic inflation following the debt crisis of the prior decade, these ideas quickly became the instruction sheet applied to any developing or transitioning (from communism) economy in the 1990s.

Reinventing the Bretton Woods Institutions

These Bretton Woods institutions (so named because they were set up in the aftermath of the 1944 Bretton Woods conference that reshaped the world economy after World War II) were, by the early 1980s, having a tough time of it.[80] The IMF, in particular, had lost its original role and was struggling to find a new mission. The IMF was originally designed to provide offsetting finance to states facing exchange-rate shocks under the fixed-exchange-rate system that governed the world's money from the 1940s until the 1970s—the Bretton Woods system that pegged the dollar to gold and everyone else's currency to the dollar. Once the United States shut down gold convertibility in 1971, Bretton Woods fell apart, and the world's major currencies began to float against each other. The IMF, literally, had nothing to do.

But large bureaucratic entities do not cease to exist the moment their mission is either accomplished or disappears. As the March of Dimes shows us so well, they invent new missions.[81] In the case of the IMF, they became the provider of "firm-surveillance" of member states' policies to increase global transparency, at least for the developed world. In the case of the developing world, however, the IMF became the financial police force behind the implementation of what were termed "structural adjustment programs": also known as the Washington Consensus checklist applied in practice.[82]

As Dani Rodrik notes, IMF policy in this period, aided and abetted by the World Bank, devolved to a mantra of "stabilize, privative, and liberalize" as "codified in John Williamson's well-known Washington Consensus."[83] The result was a series of one-size-fits-all policies that were applied from Azerbaijan to Zambia whose objective was to "minimize fiscal deficits, minimize inflation, minimize tariffs, maximize privatization, maximize liberalization of finance."[84] It was, in other words, "expansionary fiscal austerity" in a developmental form, and the results were, by and large, terrible.

As Rodrik demonstrates, a decade into these adjustments the majority of "adjusted" countries had not yet returned to where they started from in terms of lost GDP—lost through the implementation of these policies. Successes were few, far between, and subject to frequent reversals. Latin America's economic record was actually much better during the 2000s, a period when the pace of reforms slowed down considerably, and in some countries halted or was even reversed. As a recent survey of the results of IMF and World Bank reforms in Latin America shows, after the crises of the 1990s, the region's reform index was basically flat in the 2000s.[85] What seemed to be generated instead of growth were large financial crises, as capital accounts were opened up and controls on inflows were abolished—a uniquely IMF addition to the Washington Consensus checklist—and banking systems were liberalized.[86] For Latin America in particular, the 1990s compounded the losses of the debt crisis decade of the 1980s.[87] Far from creating growth, these policies shrank the economies that pursued them, just as we see happening in Europe today.[88] In fact, it's hardly a stretch to see EU policy in the European periphery as little more than a localized set of structural adjustment policies implemented with just as much success as one would expect given past results.

The IMF's Hidden "Treasury View"

Interestingly, what made the IMF so receptive to these ideas, apart from the changing intellectual climate of economic concepts and the tenor of 1990s graduate training in economics, was the then forty-year-old monetary model that the IMF used to examine the effects of its policies, the so-called Polak model.[89] When the IMF was formed in the late 1940s to help countries with balance-of-payments problems through short-term financing of their deficits, the IMF needed to figure out how changes in a country's exports and imports, bank credit, and foreign reserves interact over time such that the offsetting financing given to states (IMF loans) would provide the maximum bang for the proverbial buck. The result was the Polak model, the underlying assumptions of which tended to the austere rather than the reflationary.

As the model's author Jacques Polak put it, what the IMF sought to do was to distinguish between "credit to the private sector (usually to be encouraged) and credit to the government sector (usually to be discouraged)" because the "balance of payments problems that brought countries to seek the assistance of the IMF were typically due to bursts of excessive domestic expansion [that] *could usually be cured by the introduction of financial restraint.*"[90] The reason for such an austere policy was that "excessive expansion" causes both the current account and fiscal deficits to rise, which will "crowd out investment by the private sector."[91]

In short, deep beneath the IMF's Keynesian surface in the 1940s a set of classical liberal assumptions was built into a model of the behavior of states that would not have been out of place in the British Treasury of the 1920s.[92] The Polak model, a mainstay of IMF practice, primed the IMF to accept the conclusions of the Washington Consensus long before Washington Consensus ideas became the austere instruction sheet of the 1990s. That the liberal contradictions at the heart of postwar Keynesianism came into their first flowering at the IMF was not surprising. After all, the top management of this organization was from its inception dominated by people who hailed from central banks, treasuries, and ministries of finance—the institutions in which the "can't live with it, don't want to pay for it" form of liberalism was most likely to survive.[93]

Given all this, you might think that the limited success of "austerity in the Global South" would encourage a rethink of these policies. In one quarter, it did. The IMF's sister institution the World Bank produced a report in 2005 that pretty much acknowledged the near total failure of the Washington Consensus checklist of reforms.[94] But the IMF, echoing the classical liberal tradition, produced an evaluation the same year that argued the opposite. Indeed, according to the IMF report, the only thing that failed was, as ever, countries' implementation of the reforms, which left the content of the reforms both unquestioned and untouched.

What Karl Polanyi once said about the failed ideas of an earlier era also rings true in this instance: by the standards of the IMF, the Washington Consensus' "spectacular failure… did not destroy its authority at all. Indeed, its partial eclipse may have even strengthened its hold since it enabled its defenders to argue that the incomplete application of its principles was the reason for every and any difficulty laid to its charge."[95] Once again, when it comes to austerity, mere facts seldom get in the way of a good ideology. And a good ideology, in the absence of supporting facts, can always supply a few good models to generate those facts when needed. All of which brings us finally to the folks Paul Krugman calls the modern "Austerians" and their theory of expansionary fiscal contraction, the zenith of modern austerity thinking. Setting Africa and Latin America back a decade by trying to cut your way to growth was just the overture. Now we get to the symphony.

Part Three: Austerity Enabled

There Is a Free *Pranzo* if You Skip Your *Cena*: The Italian Origins of Expansionary Austerity

One of the most famous lines attributed (incorrectly) to Milton Friedman is "there is no such thing as a free lunch." In other words, growth is always costly in some respect, which is generally true. But an offshoot of the public choice literature developed in the late 1980s and early 1990s sought to indirectly challenge that truism by demonstrating that a free lunch of sorts is possible if the government forgoes dinner. That is, you can cut your way to growth while reducing your debt. At the same time, then, that the IMF was proving that such expansionary cuts do not actually work in practice by implementing Washington Consensus economics throughout the developing world, a whole new literature began to spring up proving that, despite such evidence, expansionary cuts do work, at least in theory, and at least in the developed (OECD) world.

The lineage of this new work goes further back and comes from another direction, however, beginning with the efforts of the midcentury Italian economist Luigi Einaudi. Einaudi was the founder of a school of public finance economics at the Bocconi University of Milan that produced an economics that was a hybrid of German ordoliberal ideas and what would later be called public choice economics.[96] Einaudi was a contributor to *The Economist* magazine during the 1920s, a prominent academic economist in his own right, the first postwar governor of the Bank of Italy, and president of the Italian Republic from 1948 to 1955. Einaudi's economics are the last link in the fossil record of economic ideas that explain why we came to think, once again, that we can all cut our way to growth at the same time.[97]

Einaudi sought to develop a *"liberalismo economico*—the economic order adequate to the liberal vision" that would augment man's natural drive to work, save, and compete.[98] State actions that produced inflation, especially misguided Keynesian efforts, blunted these natural drives and should be avoided at all costs. Again, like the German ordoliberals, Einaudi wanted a strong state only to the extent that it expanded the boundaries of the market, facilitated competition by prohibiting monopolies, and created "the legal and political milieu in which men can organize, invent and produce."[99] In other words—he, too, wanted an ordo. Einaudi was, however, much more than ordoliberalism in Italy, sotto voce. He was also much more than an economic theorist. He was, given his postwar institutional positions, a powerful advocate for European unity, especially through the mechanisms of single markets and single currencies.

As far back as the 1940s Einaudi had argued, in definite ordoliberal terms, for a European monetary union. This future "European Federation," as he called it, would be built around a large single market that would make it much more difficult for firms to form monopolies or create impediments to competition. He argued that this single market should have a single currency that should be policed by an independent central bank on the grounds that this would make fiscal activism, and hence inflation, impossible. As Einaudi put it somewhat awkwardly, "if the European Federation takes away the possibility to face public works by groaning the press of the banknotes from member states, and forces them to cover these expenditures with the taxes and with voluntary loans, it will have finished great work."[100] Just to make sure of this desired fiscal incapacity, Einaudi also argued for constitutional rules banning fiscal deficits, more than sixty years before Merkel argued for the same.

Einaudi's intellectual legacy, and why he really matters to us today, lies not just in his ideas on Europe, even if they gave the drive toward European union an ordoliberal push from the Italian side of the border. Rather, Einaudi and his ideas matter because of the school of economics that he founded at the Bocconi University of Milan, which produced two generations of economists reared in these ordoliberal views. The modern argument for austerity was developed primarily by these second-generation Bocconi graduates, who went on to become some of the most influential members of the global economics profession, especially Alberto Alesina, Franceso Silvia Ardagna, Guido Tabellini, and Roberto Perotti. The importance of Alesina and his collaborators' work in defining and defending the modern policy case for austerity cannot be overestimated. It is through their efforts that Einaudi's legacy lives on in the form of an Italian ordoliberalism that, like Hume and Smith, has a deep distrust of the state and its management of debt as its core.[101] It is this intergenerational legacy that has decisively shaped the final form of contemporary austerity arguments.

Democracy, It Turns Out, Produces Debt as well as Inflation

During the late 1980s and early 1990s the public choice literature coming out of Europe, particularly from Einaudi's Bocconi School, began to focus on the role of the state in producing, and being constrained by, its budget deficits and debts. These early pieces were vital in opening the door for subsequent literature that would be used during the crisis to make the case for expansionary austerity.

The first significant paper in this line of work was Alberto Alesina and Guido Tabellini's "A Positive Theory of Fiscal Deficits and Government Debt in a Democracy."[102] Anticipating what would later be known as the "starve the beast" theory of public spending, Alesina and Tabellini modeled the strategic use of debt by governments for partisan ends.[103] Departing from earlier public choice accounts that sought to show how democracy produced inflation, their analysis attempted to show how "a deficit bias in democracies" occurs because of alternating partisan control of the government.[104] As such, governments now stood accused of producing higher than necessary debt.

Alesina and Tabellini's basic idea was that if competing parties agreed to the same levels, but different compositions, of public expenditure, then if the incumbent party is likely to lose the next election, it should rationally create a deficit. This allows the incumbent party to provide more of its preferred public goods while it is still in charge, effectively leaving the bill, in the form of more debt, to the successor party. It also has the convenient effect of tying the next government's hands. But the next time around the affected party will do the same thing, with the end result that the overall stock of debt balloons is due to this democratic alternation of parties.

A related paper by Torsten Persson and Lars E. O. Svensson took this analysis a stage further by asking a similar question, namely, "will the current government run fiscal deficits when it knows that its successor's choice of public spending will be influenced by the level of public debt that the successor inherits?"[105] The answer is, of course, yes—why wouldn't they? Given politicians' time-inconsistent preferences, "the (level of the) public debt is the state variable that gives the current government an instrument to control the future government."[106] The short version of this complementary story is that conservatives should collect less in taxes and leave more debt so that any liberal government coming to power will be constrained. The result is still a second-best level of expenditure from a conservative point of view, but it is at least better than what those spendthrift liberals would do left to their own devices.[107]

These pieces were significant because they made the level of government debt an outcome of electoral competition, not the economic cycle. Once again, the liberal tradition in which the state cannot be trusted with the economy rears its head. Whether debt levels were actually driven by such mechanisms was an open question. As Persson and Svensson admitted, "Finding clear empirical evidence in support of this theory will...not be easy."[108] So, the question was left open as research shifted to a new terrain—away from governments producing "bads" such as inflation and debt—to producing "goods" such as growth, which is achieved by, given their penchant for creating inflation and debt, cutting the government.

Cutting Your Way to Prosperity—Again

The locus classicus for expansionary fiscal consolidation is Francesco Giavazzi and Marco Pagano's "Can Severe Fiscal Contractions be Expansionary? Tales of Two Small European Countries."[109] The answer to that question is, once again, yes. This piece has an interesting ordoliberal slant to it insofar as it draws inspiration from an idea plucked from the German Council of Economic Advisors Report from the summer of 1981: cutting spending can increase growth by improving expectations.[110] Giavazzi and Pagano picked up this idea and ran with it.

Giavazzi and Pagano built upon a piece by Hellwig and Neumann, who argued that Germany in the early 1980s demonstrated such an expectations effect. Specifically, if "the indirect effect . . . [on] expectations of the measures taken are understood to be part of a credible . . . program of consolidation, designed to permanently reduce the share of government in GDP . . . [and thus] taxation in the future," then the shift in expectations will bring forth an expansion greater than the contraction caused by budget cuts. Inspired by this "German view," Giavazzi and Pagano went looking for similar cases and found two: Denmark and Ireland.[111] While most Western European countries went through a punishing recession in the early 1980s, Denmark and Ireland, a bit later in the decade, cut spending and their economies expanded, Ireland being "the most prominent example of an expansionary cut in public spending."[112]

Denmark expanded for four years after substantial budget cuts in 1982. In Ireland "a similar outcome occurred during the 1987–1989 stabilization."[113] Why, then, do these cases "so sharply contradict the Keynesian prediction about the effects of a fiscal contraction?"[114] Giavazzi and Pagano conjectured that "in both cases, cuts in spending and tax increases were accompanied by a shift in the balance of political power, and by complementary monetary and exchange rate policies; after an initial devaluation, both countries pegged . . . to the German mark, inducing a sharp monetary deflation, and liberalized capital flows."[115]

This did not, however, sound very expectations related. New policies and developments external to the budget brought about a major fall in interest rates that increased income (a wealth effect—less debt to pay back) more than the contraction in spending hurt the economy. To get over this problem, Giavazzi and Pagano teased out econometrically the part of the postcontraction boom that can't be attributed to the wealth effect. They found that in Denmark, "the unexplained component of the boom is related to cuts in public spending... as a signal of lower taxes further in the future."[116] In Ireland, this did not seem to occur because of the constrained state of credit markets—it was mainly a wealth effect. Nonetheless, Giavazzi and Pagano found it "tempting" (their word) to say that, "the German view" (the expectations channel) "may have something to say... for the... Irish stabilization."[117] This in turn allowed them to argue that "there are cases in which the German view has a serious claim to empirical relevance."[118] To be precise, that is one positive case, and one other that they were "tempted" to include as positive based on a large forecast error in their econometric estimate. It's worth recalling that during this decade, over a dozen OECD countries cut spending and none of them grew as a result.

Amplifying Austerity: The Bocconi Boys on Spending and Taxes

Building upon this opening Alberto Alesina returned with an important paper written with Roberto Perotti in 1995 that sought to expand the set of positive fiscal adjustments well beyond Denmark and Ireland and to explain why the negative cases of cutting outweigh the positive cases.[119] After all, unless this is cleared up, cutting might hurt more than it helps. This paper took the Giavazzi and Pagano's framework and amplified its scope and claims dramatically.

Alesina and Perotti questioned which types of policies gave the best bang for the buck when budgetary consolidation is the only game in town: tax increases (revenue increases) or spending cuts (program reductions). They found that "successful adjustments (a minority of the total) rely mostly on cuts in transfer programs and in government wages and employment."[120] Examining twenty OECD countries over thirty-two years, they looked for "successful adjustments," where a very tight fiscal stance (cuts) led to "the gross debt/GDP ratio" three years out being "at least five percentage points of GDP lower" than when the consolidation began.[121] They found that of "14 successful adjustments and 38 unsuccessful ones...in successful adjustments almost all the action comes from expenditure cuts."[122] Because of this, "any serious fiscal adjustment...cannot avoid dealing with cuts in the welfare state."[123]

However, politicians need not fear making these cuts because, according to these econometric results, states that cut "grow one percent faster than the G7 countries" while "business investment as a share of GDP rises by a full 1% point" and competitiveness improves.[124] Tax increases, in comparison, cause the failing cases of adjustment. When done correctly, on the expenditure side "the good news is that major fiscal adjustments do not cause major recessions."[125] Moving beyond the cases of Denmark and Ireland, and dealing with the negative cases in a way that reinforced the message that cuts lead to growth, Alesina and his collaborators were laying the groundwork among neoliberal economists for expansionary austerity to be seen as "the new normal" rather than the policy exception.

Keynes, it seems, had it all backwards. Cuts produce growth and a reduction of debt. Spending produces inflation and more debt. David Ricardo would have been pleased. Liberalism hadn't been quite so antistatist since the early nineteenth century. And there was more to come. If Giavazzi and Pagano gave us the original locus classicus of this literature, that locus was moved to a new location a decade later by Alesina and Silvia Ardanga in their 1998 paper "Tales of Fiscal Adjustment."[126]

TINA Returns

"Tales of Fiscal Adjustment" brings together the claims made in this body of research and distills them into a few simple policy lessons. As Alesina and Ardanga put it, "Three ingredients seem to be important for a successful, long-lasting expansionary fiscal adjustment. It must combine spending cuts in transfers, welfare programs and the government wage bill, some form of...wage moderation, and a devaluation immediately before the fiscal tightening."[127] Raising taxes in a recession, as noted already, is said to simply make things worse. As such, a new form of TINA returns—*there is no alternative to cuts.*

The same expectation-based mechanisms as before are on display in this later paper but are more fully specified. Thus, in the absence of any significant liquidity-constraint, "when spending cuts are perceived as permanent, consumers anticipate a reduction in the tax burden and a permanent increase in their lifetime disposable income." This leads them to spend and invest more today because they perceive that "previously expected large tax increases will not be necessary in the future," which is especially true at higher rates of taxation.[128] When such policies are followed in periods of "fiscal stress," the results are better because the signal that the cuts will be permanent is more credible. So, not only should we cut, we should cut when it hurts, in the slump, not the boom, and we should cut decisively.[129]

This time, however, to make the set of cases bigger, what constitutes a significant expansionary adjustment is now defined as a 2 percent improvement in the cyclically adjusted primary balance over two years.[130] This yields a universe of fifty-one cases, nineteen of which are successful, and twenty-three of which are expansionary. The results of the econometrics confirm these claims. You get more bang for the buck when you cut in a slump, almost all contractionary expansions are the result of expenditure cuts, and now "successful adjustments experience a 'spectacular' investment boom during and after" the cuts.[131] Doing the opposite, running a loose (expansionary) fiscal policy, leads to the opposite results.

To hone in on the particulars of these successful cases and fine-tune the policy lessons, Alesina and Ardanga select ten cases of fiscal adjustment: Ireland (twice), Australia, Belgium, Denmark, Canada, Netherlands, Sweden, Greece, and Italy (twice, but one is discounted). All occur during the mid-1980s through the mid-1990s. The results are remarkable, in part for their modesty. Of the ten cases (a limited number drawn from a distinct period to keep the sample manageable) only "two cases appear unambiguously expansionary: Ireland 1987–9 and Australia."[132] Denmark, per contra Giavazzi and Pagano, now appears to be "mixed." Notably, "Canada, Netherlands, Sweden, Ireland and Greece show no sign of an expansionary fiscal advantage."[133] Belgium is "somewhat unclear," while in Italy it was too soon to tell.[134] In short, of the ten cases examined in detail, only two support the thesis advanced so powerfully on the basis of the earlier econometric tests: cuts lead to growth if and only if they are on the expenditure side.

To their credit, Alesina and Ardanga fully admit that the case for expectations having their purported powerful effect is "weak," while acknowledging that devaluations, wage agreements, and several factors other than expectations matter.[135] Yet despite these acknowledged limitations, when the crisis hit, "Tales of Fiscal Adjustment" was seen by anti-Keynesians as the appropriate instruction sheet on how to stop the twelve-month Keynesians discussed in chapter 3 from dominating policy during the bust, and it worked. But what clinched the case in policy circles, especially in Europe, was an update to "Tales" by the same authors written in 2009, especially a version of it Alesina delivered to the ECOFIN (Economic and Financial Affairs Council of the European Council of Ministers) meeting in Madrid in April 2010.[136] This was to be, as Bloomberg noted, "Alesina's Hour."[137]

Nailing Keynes's Coffin Shut

Alesina and Arganda's "Large Changes in Fiscal Policy: Taxes versus Spending" updates and expands "Tales of Fiscal Adjustment."[138] As noted in the introduction to chapters 4, 5, and 6, Milton Friedman, always handy for a quote, once noted that the (real?) function of economists was "to develop alternatives to existing policies, to keep them alive and available until the politically impossible becomes politically inevitable," which usually happens in moments of crisis.[139] Alesina had been keeping these ideas alive for just such an occasion. Just as the Eurozone crisis was really beginning to heat up, "Large Changes" looked not only at consolidation and growth but also, given the shock the financial crisis had delivered to the real economy, at what policies best promote fiscal stimulus. You can guess the answer already, but the real focus of the paper remained the expansionary effect of cuts.

Alesina and Ardanga begin by noting that the ballooning of debts and deficits across the OECD is due in large part to the "bailout[s] of various types in the financial sector." However, about this they "have nothing to say."[140] What they do have to say is that regardless of how we got into this mess, the only way out is through cutting the state. As before, they argue that "spending cuts are more effective than tax increases in stabilizing the debt and avoiding downturns."[141] And despite acknowledging in the prior paper that the evidence for such expectations-driven expansions was "weak," they deploy this explanation here again in full force and with no caveats about its actual explanatory power.

Consumers with rational expectations are seen to calculate their lifetime consumption function based on the credibility of the signal to cut spending sent by the government, and they accurately incorporate these estimates into their private spending decisions. In this version of events, interest-rate changes that create wealth effects are now no longer exogenous to expectations, but are part of the same mechanism by which credible cutting leads to bond-yield-premium reductions, and hence cheaper loans, which consumers rationally anticipate as coming in the future, and so they spend now.[142] Indeed, expectations now impact the labor market directly, as cuts in government employment lowers wages, which leads not to recession as the Keynesians warn, but to "higher profits, investment, and [greater] competitiveness."[143] Expectations are now everything. They dictate outcomes, and they are always improved when the government does less, even in a slump. They are the final nail in Keynes's coffin because they make the most contractionary of circumstances expansionary. In such a world, the slump is the perfect place to cut while spending is always and everywhere the wrong policy.

To make this new case for expectations-driven expansions, Alesina and Ardanga examine twenty-one OECD countries from 1970 to 2007 and select 107 episodes of positive and negative adjustment to make their case. Twenty-six of those episodes qualify as expansionary fiscal adjustments, occurring across nine countries. That is, debts are lower three years out and growth is higher than the seventy-fifth percentile of the average of the set of the observations.[144] This time around, as we saw in the section on the effects of expectations, the results of the econometrics again lack the caveats of their prior piece.

Cuts lead to expansion and "have far superior effects on growth than those based on increases in tax revenues."[145] This time around Alesina and Ardanga even smuggle a quasi-Laffer curve into the piece, whereby cutting spending (rather than taxes) leads to more tax revenues, whereas "they [taxes] go down quite significantly in expansionary adjustments."[146] Most significantly, successful adjustments see welfare transfers fall, while unsuccessful adjustments see them rise. As such, the welfare state has to go because "it is very difficult if not impossible to fix public finances when in trouble without solving the question of automatic increases in entitlements."[147] And in complete contrast to what Keynesians believe, government spending lowers growth, since "a one percentage point higher increase in the current spending to GDP ratio is associated with a 0.75 percentage point lower growth."[148]

Eleven years later and the ambiguity, nuance, and qualification that characterized "Tales" has disappeared. Rather than two positive cases, we now have twenty-six "episodes." Rather than "weak" expectations effects, everything is reduced to and works through expectations. And rather than these ideas just "lying around," as Milton suggested, they were actively thrust into the middle of the European policy debate as ammunition for German policy makers and their allies at the ECB during their counterattack on those unexpectedly Keynesian Anglo-Americans, as we detailed in chapter 3.

One year later, in April 2010, Alesina presented a simplified version of this paper at the ECOFIN meeting in Madrid. He began by noting that, unlike previous high-debt occasions, such as the aftermath of World War II, growth is not going to make the Eurozone's pile of debt disappear. Rather, there is no alternative (TINA) to fiscal adjustment. Happily, "many even sharp reductions of budget deficits have been accompanied and immediately followed by sustained growth rather than recessions even in the very short run," so long as the policy has been credible, which means decisive and large.[149] Once again, expectations of a better future create a better present while falling bond yields create more wealth, again due to expectations effects.[150] In terms of actual policy, taxes should not be raised and entitlements should be cut.[151] This much is drawn from the previous paper. Key here is what is added.

Drawing on separate work on the composition of governments and policy making, Alesina assures the assembled finance ministers that if they go in this direction and start to cut budgets in the middle of a recession, not only will it make things better, it will not cost them their jobs. In fact, the public will reward them for their boldness since cutting the welfare state is neither unfair nor avoidable. Cutting is fair since "the rhetoric about the immense social cost of fiscal adjustment is blown out of proportion and is often used strategically by certain groups, not necessarily the most disadvantaged, to protect themselves."[152] And it's unavoidable because the welfare state and its transfers are too big not to touch and are precisely what need to be cut to make growth return and reduce the debt.[153] Remember, increasing taxes or spending more has the opposite effect.

As Anis Chowdhury has shown, Alesina's analysis was cited in the ECOFIN final communiqué and deployed in the rhetoric of Jean Claude Trichet, then president of the ECB; in the UK Treasury's 2010 emergency budget; and in the discussions of the US Council of Economic Advisors in 2010. And, as noted in chapter 3, it was written more or less word for word into the June 2010 ECB *Monthly Bulletin*, which cited both of Alesina's papers and drew directly on Giavazzi and Pagano and related works to make its case for cuts.[154]

Welcome to Austerity: *Kein Kaufen, Nur Sparen!*

This, then, is the essence of modern austerity thinking. This is how it emerged. These are the personalities and the politics involved in its production. These are its core claims. It has been astonishingly influential and serves as the contemporary instruction sheet for economic reform in the European Union, and regardless of Obama's 2012 victory, we can most probably expect to see it deployed in the United States too. The only remaining question we need to ask is, does it work? The answer, as we shall see next, is certainly not in the big cases of the past in the 1920s and 1930s, not at all in Europe at the moment, and only very occasionally and under very specialized conditions elsewhere.

Crucially, those conditions have practically nothing to do with expectation mechanisms or cutting the welfare state. Deploying austerity in less than those ideal conditions has helped propel Spain and Greece to the brink of economic and political collapse and impoverished millions of people throughout the rest of Southern Europe. This is not "blown out of proportion rhetoric." It is a fact. Austerity's continuing application may well result in the eventual breakup of the Eurozone and have political repercussions that the weak institutions of the EU are unlikely to withstand. The cases cited as its successes, the justification for following this policy are, as we shall see, like positive cases of structural adjustment: few, far between, and quite possibly wrong.

Austerity works in the same way that Keynes maintained classical economics works, as a "limiting point of the possible positions of equilibrium."[155] That is, one special case out of billions of possible cases. He continued, "The characteristics of the special case assumed...happen not to be those of the economic society in which we actually live, with the result that its teaching is misleading and disastrous if we attempt to apply it to the facts of experience."[156] Once again, what we learned in the 1930s has been forgotten. That forgetting is perhaps the strongest reason why austerity remains such a dangerous idea. To see what we forgot, we now turn to austerity's natural history.

AUSTERITY'S NATURAL HISTORY, 1914—2012

Introduction: History Lessons, the 1980s, and the REBLL Alliance

Now that we have examined austerity in theory, our purpose of this final chapter is to examine austerity in practice. But if austerity's intellectual history has been relatively short—you can't really argue all that much about state spending until states actually start spending in large amounts—its natural history has been even shorter. During the eighteenth and nineteenth centuries, economies went through boom and bust cycles and states, particularly those on the gold standard, did not try to compensate. Because those processes unfolded when classical liberal states were in charge, there was nothing to cut, and no democratic imperative to which policy makers had to respond. Laissez faire was the policy of the Belle Époque because *La Belle*, by and large, was not all that democratic. It's not until the early twentieth century, as detailed in chapters 4 and 5, that we encounter states that are both big enough to cut, and democratic enough to cause problems for austerity policy.

We therefore survey austerity's natural history along three avenues. First, we examine the cases that used to make us think austerity was a very dangerous idea: the United States, the United Kingdom, Sweden,

Germany, Japan, and France on and off the gold standard during the 1920s and 1930s. These are the cases where austerity as policy reached its limits and either broke down or broke the society it was being imposed upon. The natural histories of these episodes demonstrate quite clearly that economies do not "self-heal" once "the bust" has run its course. Austerity was tried, and tried again—its application was not wanting—and it simply didn't work. In fact, its repeated application made things worse, not better, and it was only when states stopped pursuing austerity that they began to recover.[1] We examine why this was the case and spell out the lessons that period holds for austerity policy, especially in the Eurozone, today.

The second part of the chapter has two targets. The first section hones in on the positive cases highlighted by Alesina, Giavazzi, and others as examples of successful expansionary austerity because they form the countercase to the lessons learned from the 1930s: Denmark, Ireland, Australia and Sweden. I then juxtapose the experiences of these countries to the current state of the Eurozone to stress that even if these cases are granted positive status, which as we shall see is dubious at best, the conditions that made these cases possible are simply absent in Europe at the moment, especially the PIIGS. This makes the argument for expansionary austerity, at best, possible as a very special case, but wholly inappropriate as the general case.

The second and final section, to play-off *Star Wars* for a moment, analyzes the "new hope" for austerity champions: Romania, Estonia, Bulgaria, Latvia, and Lithuania (REBLL). The REBLL countries have been most recently held up by the IMF and the EU as proof that austerity is possible and that they can serve as a useful model for others— namely, Western and Southern Europe—to emulate. Actually, they prove neither point. The REBLL's conditions of action and their unique economic and political structures make the lessons of these cases even less transportable to the rest of the world than those of Western Europe in the 1980s. The countries of the REBLL alliance have indeed managed, in some cases, to maintain their exchange rates through the crisis—by choosing to suffer massive deflation, migration, and unemployment—and they have indeed bounced back. But we must ask if the candle was worth the game? The answer is no. Austerity's natural history contains some positive cases to be sure, even if they are massively outnumbered by negative cases. They do not, how-ever, contain many positive or transportable *lessons*, which makes them, to complete the Star Wars analogy, even more like the REBLL alliance: you can indeed, against all the odds, blow up the Debt Star—but only in very specific circumstances and only at enormous cost to those involved.

Part One: Why We Thought Austerity a Dangerous Idea

The Allure of Shiny Things: The Gold Standard and Austerity

Today, many seemingly sensible people on both sides of the Atlantic, but particularly in the United States, seem to think that the solution to any and all economic problems lies in returning to something called the gold standard.[2] This is odd because apart from being a heavy, shiny rock, gold has no particular noteworthy features—besides being a major contributory cause of the two worst economic depressions in world history: the 1870s and the 1930s. I can only assume that the folks peddling the return of gold as a good idea are ignorant of the actual history of the gold standard. Working on that assumption, and to en-able us to understand why austerity in the 1920s and 1930s lasted so long, did so much damage, and why its history matters for the Euro-zone today, it is worth revisiting the workings of the gold standard.[3]

The gold standard was built during the nineteenth century because of a problem endemic to international trade. Namely, how do you know that when you hand over your goods (an export) to someone far away, that the money in which they will pay you back (as payment for their import) is not just a pile of worthless paper—the so-called fiat money problem?[4] The answer is, you don't know, and so international trade was historically limited by the extent to which trust could be maintained, or hostages, literally, could be exchanged.

The gold standard solved this problem of trust by eliminating the need for it. The solution was to tie the notional value of different na-tional currencies to gold at a fixed rate, gold being a conventional store of value that both is internationally exchangeable and cannot (easily) be altered by governments.[5] X units of currency Y therefore could be exchanged everywhere for Z units of gold. And if all countries "pegged" their currencies to gold in this way, it facilitated trade by solving the fiat money/trust problem.

Since each country is pegged to gold at a fixed rate, when you earn foreign currency through trade, you can, in principle, take it back to the issuing country's central bank and ask for the gold that backs it. Because the paper you now hold is convertible for gold at a fixed rate, the paper will be exactly equal in value to gold. So long as this promise of convertibility is maintained, you don't have to worry about the value of the paper you are holding.[6] If, however, a country on gold decides to run the printing presses to pay for imports in excess of their gold reserves, then that excess currency will show up in the countries exporting to these *inflationistas*.

No longer trusting the pegged rate, the receiving country could return these notes to the issuing country for exchange, where the re-patriated currency would be in excess of the available gold. Their reserves, sometimes called their "gold cover," would be insufficient to cope with demand. This would call everyone's attention to the fact that the issuing country is inflating its currency—issuing more than can be backed by gold at the fixed rate. This would cause people to lose confidence in that currency and dump it en masse, ending convertibility, and wrecking the offending economy in the process. Being on gold therefore gave holders of a foreign currency a "credible" signal that the money was "sound," so long as convertibility was maintained.

But that wasn't the half of it. The gold standard also worked as a mechanism of adjustment for international trade by bringing states' exports and imports into balance through the inflation and deflation of domestic prices and wages. For example, if a country on gold exported more than it imported, it would, in effect, be importing gold from the recipient countries. This would add to its own domestic money supply, enabling the issuance of more domestic currency. It would also raise wages and prices as the economy boomed but It would also make its exports less competitive and its imports cheaper. Over time, this coun-try's trade surplus would turn into a trade deficit, with more imports than exports. Gold would move out of the country to pay for these increased imports. Domestic prices and wages would fall as the money supply (tied to gold) shrank, but the country's competitiveness would improve (cheaper exports), and the trade balance would right itself as exports picked up and imports fell.

With everyone on the gold standard being open to trade and financial flows, the promise of convertibility combined with the flexibility of prices and wages to act as the mechanism of adjustment to ensure that the global economy produced a balance between imports and exports in one country and a balance across the system of countries as a whole. This is how the gold standard created the conditions for the growth of trade across the world, free from government interference and the danger of inflation. It was self-regulating, automatic, and impersonal—which was precisely the problem the moment ordinary people got involved.

You don't have to be a public choice theorist to see that you can only really run a system like this, where domestic wages and prices do most of the adjusting to external prices, if you are *not* a democracy. While widgets, potatoes, steel, and pneumatic pumps care not one jot about their supply price, labor most certainly does care, especially when that price (wages) goes down. By making the mechanism of adjustment the random inflation and deflation of prices and wages, a great deal of uncertainty, and unemployment, was created in these economies. It also created conditions where the domestic monetary authorities, to maintain that all important gold cover, would pursue austerity policies such as cutting spending and raising interest rates to shrink deficits, keep gold at home, and defend the currency. It was hardly surprising, then, that it was under the gold standard that labor across the world, both industrial and agricultural, started to join together in unions, political parties, and social movements to demand protection from the vagaries of the market and the policies of their own governments.[7]

Making this worse apart from the effect of austerity policies, the global supply of gold puts a ceiling on growth. If trade demand increases faster than the money supply, and the money supply is limited by the gold supply, interest rates will rise and the economy will slump in response. The gold standard had, then, an inbuilt contractionary bias. It could solve the problem of inflation, but only at the price of creating deflation. Deflation is a particularly pernicious problem because in a deflation everyone's first best guess about what to do to protect themselves—for example, workers taking a pay cut to price themselves into a job—has the aggregate effect of cutting consumption, which shrinks the economy and makes everyone's unemployment all the more likely. States with large trade or budget deficits going into a recession fare especially badly in such situations because it becomes almost impossible to grow out of the problem as recession and deflation compound each other. Taking on more loans and more debt to gain temporary relief will not help in the long run because you cannot grow out of it.

Two Lessons from the Gold Standard for the Eurozone

If you think this sounds a lot like the Eurozone at the moment, you would not be wrong. Swap the "convertibility into gold" for "the integrity of the euro," and it's the same system. The basic problem of running a gold standard and the Eurozone are one and the same. As was noted in chapter 5, there are (mainly) four ways to get out of a financial crisis—inflate, deflate, devalue, and default.[8] In both the gold standard and the Eurozone, states can neither inflate nor devalue because the system in both cases was designed to remove exactly these options on the grounds that you can't trust politicians with the printing press. That leaves default—which you want to avoid—and deflation (austerity) as the only remaining way to adjust in both cases.[9]

Being on the gold standard promised creditors that the convertibility of the currency would be maintained via austerity: wages would downwardly adjust to the prices set by the international economy. Unfortunately, once politicians had to answer through the ballot box to the mass publics that bear the costs of this adjustment, the credibility of the claim that "no amount of austerity was too much" became less believable, and less supportable, over time. As Barry Eichengreen put it, once democracy became the norm in the 1920s "when employment and balance of payments goals clashed, it was no longer clear which would dominate."[10]

By the time the euro arrived, democracy plus fifty years of the welfare state as a shock absorber had become even more of a constraint on such policies. Yet the euro demands deflation and austerity today, as it remains the Eurozone's primary mechanism of adjustment.

There may be no convertibility into gold under the euro, but the credibility of the claim to be able to pay back government debt performs the same function, providing an external constraint to policy as gold did eighty years ago. Indeed, the euro arguably provides even more of a constraint than the gold standard in one respect. Whereas states on gold can always "get off gold"—there is no need to print a new currency when doing so—the "once and for all bargain" that was the euro made states dump their old currency for good. There is nothing to go back to, which adds an extra layer of bondage to what is effectively a gold standard without gold.

There are then two key lessons for the Eurozone from the gold standard era. Repeated attempts to get back on gold and stay on it in round after round of austerity in the 1920s made the already unbearable simply impossible, and the system fell apart in the early 1930s. States that stayed on gold and kept trying to cut their way to growth after 1930 fared far worse than those that abandoned it and reflated internally.[11] The first lesson of austerity from the 1920s and 1930s follows: *austerity simply doesn't work, no matter how many times you do it.* Recognizing this leads us to the gold standard's second lesson for the Eurozone: *you can't run a gold standard in a democracy.* Eventually, it will fall apart because there are only so many rounds of austerity people will vote for before the system breaks down.

These are the two key lessons that the Eurozone forgot in the crisis. It's also what it needs to re-learn if it hopes to survive. To see why this is so, we investigate the dysfunctions of the gold standard as a system in the 1920s and 1930s, and then drop down to the level of individual states to examine how six countries adapted to, or broke free from, its binds and constraints.

Austerity and the Global Economy in the 1920s and 1930s

The United States emerged from World War I stronger than ever. The main combatants—France, Germany, and Britain—returned much weaker. The European states sought a return to the gold standard as a way to restore the prosperity of the old era. There were just two issues about how to do this. First was whether to reestablish parity at pre-war levels, which would require significant austerity to get domestic prices down to where they needed to be, or to aim for new lower parities that would better reflect the actual conditions of these war-battered economies. The second issue was intimately related: how to cope with demands from these newly democratized populations for compensatory policies that would make this adjustment all the more difficult. These countries, and several more, opted for the hard road, and it would take years of grinding austerity to get them back on gold. Germany returned to gold in 1924, Britain in 1925, and France in 1926. Once they got there, as we shall see, things only got worse.

Compounding these difficulties was the issue of war debts and reparations. France and the United Kingdom owed hundreds of millions of dollars to the United States. Germany was ordered to pay the Allied powers billions of Goldmarks in reparations under the notorious Treaty of Versailles. The problem was that Germany didn't want to pay; the Americans and the French wanted the Germans to pay; and the British sat in the middle realizing that asking the Germans to pay so much was impossible but lacked the power to do anything about it.[12]

Luckily, since the US economy was doing rather well in the immediate postwar period, a solution of sorts presented itself. The United States had capital to export and it did exactly that, sending gold and short-term capital (dollar loans) to Europe, betting on a rapid German recovery. So long as US capital flowed to Europe, Germany could grow (or at least borrow) enough to pay its debts to France and the United Kingdom, which in turn used the same money to pay back its debts to the United States, so long as the United States sent it back to Germany to keep the whole system of payments going. As Fred Block put it with justified irony, "The American contribution to…the problem was to lend Germany huge sums of capital, which were then used to finance reparations payments."[13] If you think this sounds a little like continually giving the European periphery loans that those countries can never hope to pay back because of their already high debt burdens, again, you would not be completely wrong.

The whole system stayed afloat, after the German hyperinflation of 1923, for about four years, until United States capital exports slowed down as a result of the Wall Street boom of 1928 and the subsequent crash of 1929.[14] Alarmed by the booming stock market, the US Federal Reserve raised interest rates in 1928 to cool domestic demand. This had the effect of reversing the flow of capital to Europe as US capital came home to take advantage of these higher interest rates, which unexpectedly further stoked the stock market boom.[15] After all, why put your money in Germany when you can make 15 percent buying shares in an investment trust and 7 percent in a bank deposit in the USA? The resulting capital flight placed enormous pressure on the German economy, which responded with ever-stricter austerity policies, especially, as we shall see, under Chancellor Brüning in 1930–1931. Deprived of external liquidity—all the money had gone back to the United States—bank runs in Austria and Germany were met with ever-tighter austerity policies in exchange for more loans (that failed to materialize) to stave off the inevitable default. Eventually, and tragically, as loans dried up tariffs rose, currencies were devalued, and the postwar recession became the Great Depression.

Beyond this overview of why austerity failed on a macro level, what is of most interest to us here is how different countries' austerity policies fared on a micro level during this crisis. The critical point to note is that while there are a few positive instances of austerity leading to expansion among the legion of failures in this period, just as there were in the 1980s and 1990s, these episodes took place just after World War I, when the states in question, Germany and the United States foremost among them, were off the gold standard. As such, they could adjust their domestic costs by letting their exchange rate slide rather than through the forced internal deflation of domestic wages and prices. They were also implementing austerity at the height of the postwar boom.[16]

Once gold was restored, the game changed and the application of any and all austerity policies simply made things worse—in some cases, as we shall see, with deadly results. The parallel to the Eurozone as a gold standard without gold (you can't devalue, inflate, or default there either) is both obvious and vitally important. That is, if none of these countries managed to make austerity work when they were on the classical gold standard and were far more authoritarian, why would we expect anything different to occur today in the Eurozone—or even America—when they are far more democratic?

Austerity as Policy in the USA: 1921–1937

Rather than a slump after World War I, the United States experienced a boom as pent-up demand and massively expanded money supplies erupted from within war-shocked economies around the world. The boom was, however, short-lived, and in the continental European economies it was accompanied by significant inflation and, in some cases, a hard landing. No slump followed in the United States, however, for an unexpected reason—floating exchange rates in Europe (most countries were off gold) allowed countries to deflate externally instead of through domestic prices—and so recovery followed rapid disinflation.[17] The Roaring Twenties began with a bump in Europe but not the United States, precisely because the Americans were not on gold.

The early warning lights for the United States were blinking, however, in the form of falling agricultural prices and an increasingly volatile banking sector. Unemployment slowly rose throughout the 1920s, making its reduction a political priority for both the Harding and Hoover administrations. As noted in chapter 4, Hoover, first as secretary of commerce under Harding and then as president, sought both limited public works and voluntary cooperative solutions to the unemployment problem. Neither policy had much impact on the recessions of 1924 and 1926. Indeed, given that the federal expenditures in 1929 were only "about 2.5 percent of gross national product" this was hardly surprising.[18] Such policies also seemed increasingly redundant by 1929. Because of the stock-market boom, unemployment had fallen to a postwar low.

Even though the state had limited its ambitions to balancing the budget and ensuring convertibility, because of the unexpected bursting of the stock market bubble, Hoover spent $1.5 billion on public works when he became president in 1929. By 1931, overall federal spending was up by a third from its 1929 level.[19] Given how small state expenditures remained relative to GDP, however, the now-accelerating decline in private spending meant that tax "receipts dwindled by 50 percent and expenditure rose by almost 60 percent."[20] At this juncture Hoover saw austerity as the only way, and the right way, to restore "business confidence" and balance the budget.

Hoover's contractionary policies were given a further negative boost by Britain's decision to abandon the gold standard in 1931. Confidence in the dollar fell as investors thought that the United States would follow Britain off gold. Capital began to flow out of the United States, interest rates rose, and bank failures soared.[21] It was in these circumstances that Hoover authorized a tax increase, thereby producing a massive recession in the name of maintaining "sound finance." In December 1931, Hoover raised taxes by $900 million to eliminate the deficit. As Hoover put it in classic austerity-speak, "We cannot squander ourselves into prosperity."[22] The price of this parsimony was to throw the US economy into depression. By 1932 unemployment had reached 23 percent of the labor force, up from 8 percent in 1930.[23]

The long and winding reflationary road that the Roosevelt administration took through the depression years, from the quasi-cartel arrangements of the National Industrial Recovery Act and the Agricultural Adjustment Act through the Social Security Act and the Wagner Act's focus on maintaining consumption, is not of direct interest here.[24] Rather, we need only note two things. First, when the United States abandoned the gold standard in 1933 it created immediate room via devaluation for the reflation of the economy. Given the relatively large size of the US domestic economy, increasing domestic demand was bound to have a significant effect. Second, as a consequence, the net effect of Roosevelt's policies was to increase government spending and debt while bringing unemployment down to 17 percent by 1936. No good deed goes unpunished, of course, and this turnaround in the economy by late 1936 created demands for a return to balanced budgets, sound finance, and America's second round of austerity in 1937.

Since recovery seemed under way, the lip service that Roosevelt had been paying to the notion of balancing the budget became a policy issue, and after the 1936 election his treasury secretary Henry Morgenthau sought a return to orthodoxy. This led to a round of monetary tightening, which came on the heels of a fiscal contraction that was a result of new social security taxes kicking in. This increased unemployment, causing a short but sharp recession in 1937 and into 1938. This recession, a perfect natural experiment in austerity policy since the contraction was deliberate, expenditure focused, and happened in an upswing, failed miserably and shifted the balance of power from budget balancers to advocates of spending.[25]

By October 1937, austerity as a way forward was finally and firmly repudiated in one of Roosevelt's radio fireside chats. Blaming the depression on the failure of purchasing power, Roosevelt advocated a new round of expenditures totaling $3.5 billion, concluding, "Let us unanimously recognize...that the federal debt, whether it be twenty-five billions or forty billions can only be paid if the nation obtains a vastly increased citizen income."[26] America did not recover fully until massive wartime spending reduced unemployment to 1.2 percent in 1944. For our purposes here, we need only note that the US economy got worse each time austerity was applied—first in 1931 and again in 1937.

Defending Sterling and the Treasury View: British Austerity 1921–1939

Britain, as noted in chapter 4, returned to the gold standard in 1925 after five years of austerity policies designed to wring inflation out of the system. The objective was to deflate prices to their pre-war levels, restore the pre-war parity of Sterling, and to act once again as the anchor of the gold standard system.[27] Britain was, however, much diminished, financially speaking, so trying to restore pre-war parity was always going to be painful. It was, nonetheless, from the point of view of the Treasury and the City of London at least, essential.

As the lynchpin of the gold standard and the largest foreign investor of the nineteenth century, Britain had major offshore liabilities in the form of foreign holdings of sterling-denominated assets. Returning to gold at a lower than pre-war parity would quite literally devalue those assets. This would have led to a serious run on the pound as investors tried to dump sterling en masse, just as the gold standard intended, which would have resulted in massive losses for the City. So when Churchill put Britain back on gold in 1925, the domestic economy was quite deliberately going to be squeezed so that the value of sterling and, not coincidentally, the profits of finance, would be maintained.

Britain stayed on the gold standard thereafter, pursuing, as we saw previously, austere policies under the watchful eyes of the Treasury, which refused virtually all efforts and initiatives to reflate the economy. Unemployment rose from 10.4 percent in 1929 to 22.1 percent in early 1932 as a result of the combined effect of the Treasury's austerity policies and the contractionary effect of being on gold, which demanded, of course, ever-more austerity.[28]

What kept Britain afloat at this juncture, financially speaking, were precisely those "invisible" earnings on the capital account from sterling assets abroad that made up for the curtailment of exports and the reduction in domestic consumption wrought by austerity. The choice to save sterling was, then, not simply the City against everyone else. Banking was making a buck because sterling was not devalued, and that was (almost) balancing the books. Unfortunately, the sudden stop in capital flows from the United States in 1929 and the deleterious effects this had on Germany, Austria, and the other central European countries brought this happy state of affairs to an end. Britain now needed to import capital to cover its deficit, which was hard to do since it was all flowing to the United States instead.

Britain's aggressive use of interest rates to compete with the United States for capital, with unemployment at 22 percent nationally, coming on the heels of a general strike in 1926 and much social agitation thereafter, was no easy option.[29] Indeed, sustaining such high levels of unemployment had boosted unemployment transfers and worsened the deficit. This made any effort by the British state to borrow its way out of trouble ever more treacherous since doing so required further rounds of austerity policies to reduce the deficits that prior rounds of austerity had caused, so that Britain could be eligible for more loans to reduce the deficit. By 1931, Britain's austerity policies had become self-defeating.

The minority Labour government, in charge since 1929, was devoid of alternative economic ideas and went along with austerity policies sufficient to worsen the economy but insufficient to right the deficit. When the Labour government fell over how deep to cut, it was replaced by the National (coalition) Government. It enacted sufficient spending cuts and tax increases to convince J. P. Morgan and Company to lend Britain $200 million. But the loan was too little and too late to make a difference. With official reserves almost depleted (no gold cover) and unemployment at record levels after a decade of austerity policies, this final round of austerity forced Britain off the gold standard in September 1931.

Although recovery in some parts of the economy was swift due to the effects of the resulting devaluation, with national unemployment falling to 15.5 percent by 1935, outside London the recovery was much weaker and unemployment remained much higher, while "real output in 1938 was barely above the level in 1918."[30] Despite the austerity, and just as we see in the Eurozone today, Britain's debt increased rather than decreased throughout this period. Debt went from 170 percent of GDP in 1930 to 190 percent of GDP in 1933.[31] The currency depreciation that getting off gold facilitated helped restore exports, but with the Treasury view of the economy still dominant, Britain continued to stagnate with endemic high unemployment until rearmament, the crudest form of stimulus, created the conditions for recovery. Inflation, the great fear of the rentier class, never appeared. Never once did austerity help.

Abandoning Austerity: Swedish Lessons 1921–1938

The early postwar period was a difficult time for small export-dependent countries such as Sweden. As Erik Lundberg notes, "The strong deflation, the big decline in production (25 percent in the volume of industrial output), and the tremendous rise in unemployment were generally considered to be the natural and unavoidable consequences of the post-war boom of 1918–20."[32] Nothing was done to cushion these blows and austerity was allowed to run its course. Real wages fell by 30 to 35 percent from fall 1920 to summer 1922, and contrary to liberal expectations, unemployment got worse rather than better.[33] Like the British Labour party, the governing Swedish Social Democrats (SAP), lacking any other ideas about what to do, saw no alternative but to continue with austerity, accepting the recommendations of leading Swedish economists such as Gustav Cassel, who argued that "deflation, unemployment, falling prices and wages…were required" to cure the depression.[34]

Persisting with austerity, Sweden returned to the gold standard in 1924, a year ahead of the British, despite the further deflationary effect it had on the economy. GDP fell by approximately one-third and unemployment rose by one-third as a result.[35] Being back on gold combined with an almost continuous contractionary fiscal stance in the latter half of the 1920s to produce unemployment of the order of 12 percent by the late 1920s, notwithstanding an export boom. Despite (or perhaps because of) this huge deflation, industrial unrest spiked, with five million working days lost in 1928 alone. When the combined forces of American capital flight, the central European liquidity crunch, and the British leaving the gold standard hit the Swedish economy in 1931, unemployment rose to nearly 25 percent in 1932. Austerity had helped Sweden produce an export surplus in the 1920s at the price of 12 percent unemployment. By the 1930s continuing austerity had produced the greatest slump in Swedish history and doubled that unemployment rate. What changed at this juncture was the instruction sheet, which began to evolve from the mid-1920s onward, from austerity and gold toward a more expansionary fiscal policy and a more accommodating monetary policy.

Reelected in 1932, the SAP eschewed austerity this time around in favor of policies that would give "the state...a totally different role than it had before in order to stabilize employment on a high level."[36] The new SAP government proposed ninety-three million Swedish crowns in spending on public works. Crucially, however, rather than focus exclusively on policies that benefit labor alone, the government took the stability of the price level as the coequal policy goal alongside full employment, all the while resisting trade protectionism despite the collapse of the gold standard.[37]

In 1933, the government resolved to ensure that business got on board by giving them a commitment to balance budgets over the whole cycle rather than over a given financial year. By 1936, this commitment spawned an economic commission that advocated the creation of a budget-balancing fund that would use accumulated surpluses to reduce government deficits.[38] Countercyclical fiscal policy had arrived. Meanwhile taxation was structured in such a way that it stimulated investment.[39] These reforms were in turn coupled to a policy of centralizing labor market institutions and promoting the increasing concentration of business to ensure trust and cooperation over wages among labor market partners.[40]

Taken together, these initiatives facilitated an expansionary policy that worked through the supply side of the economy as well as the demand side, while taking the price-stability concerns of business seriously. As Swedish economist Rudolph Meidner said of economic policy in this period, the objective was to "maintain the market economy, to counter short-sighted fluctuations through anti-cyclical policies, and to neutralize its negative effects through fiscal policies. The rallying cry was full employment, economic growth, [a] fair division of national income, and social security."[41]

The surprising thing was that it worked. Farmers, business, and labor all came together with the state in an encompassing coalition that allowed the costs and benefits of adjustments to be equally shared.[42] Swedish austerity ended when it came off gold and actively changed its mind about how to run an economy. When Germany, Sweden's major trading partner, did the same and began to grow rapidly after adopting a very different kind of expansionary policy after 1933, external demand really picked up and austerity in Sweden disappeared for the next fifty years.

Austerity as Policy and Party Ideology: Germany 1923–1933

The hyperinflation that still scars the contemporary German psyche so deeply was not, as noted in chapter 3, promoted by some kind of misguided Keynesian stimulus. Rather, it was the German government's deliberate policy, designed to make the payment of reparations, especially after the French occupation of the Ruhr, all but impossible. In that regard, it was quite successful. Knowing that the reward for putting their fiscal house in order would be giving the French even more money meant that Germany decided to pull the fiscal house down.[43] As Albrecht Ritschl put it succinctly, "Inflation proved to be a formidable weapon against reparations creditors, at least in the short run. It helped insulate Germany from the international slump of 1920/21, improving her export position and fueling internal demand. . . . It also exploited Germany's remaining foreign creditors, largely neutral countries, by depreciating the paper mark reserves they had accumulated during the stabilization period. . . . Above all, it paralyzed the financial system that would have been needed to organize an orderly transfer of reparations."[44]

The domestic consequences of this policy, the mechanisms through which resistance became hyperinflation, were that the exchange rate plummeted and producers began to calculate "prices with reference to the exchange rate . . . [from which] it was a short step to transacting in foreign currency" and de facto abandoning the mark.[45] In such an environment, where holders of marks are effectively dumping the currency, the deficit worsens. This requires the central bank to either raise interest rates to attract capital or to monetize the problem, that is, run the printing presses. Given that the inflationary genie was being deliberately pulled out of the bottle, monetization won.[46] *Passive resistance plus devaluation plus deficit monetization equals hyperinflation.* It certainly wasn't about providing a compensatory fiscal stimulus. Let's put that notion to rest.

Moreover, while the hyperinflations are seen these days as an uncontrollable phenomenon, this one at least was not only deliberately provoked, it ended rather quickly with the introduction of the rentenmark, which was tied to, of all things, real estate assets. The new stable reichsmark succeeded it within a year. The next four years saw the German economy perform rather well, so long as US capital flows kept flowing. When those flows turned off in 1929, the German government abandoned the countercyclical policies it had pioneered in the 1920s, especially when its unemployment insurance scheme generated a large deficit, and reached for the austerity levers.[47] The Reichsbank raised interest rates to encourage capital inflows, but the flows failed to arrive given the general shortage of liquidity in Europe following the Fed's interest rate hike.[48] The only thing that happened was that the economy tanked further. Official reserves fell precipitously, and so did the gold cover.[49]

In politics, the Social Democratic Party (SPD) abandoned the governing coalition that had been in power since 1928, and in response Center Party leader Heinrich Brüning was appointed chancellor in March 1930. Lacking parliamentary support, Brüning implemented austerity policies by decree to right the financial ship, which in the main took the form of extremely large budget cuts. Despite being out of the coalition, Brüning's policies undermined support for the Social Democrats still further since they saw no alternative to austerity and continued to passively support them. The National Socialists unsurprisingly picked up support in the 1930 election on the back of this cross-party austerity policy, winning 18.3 percent of the vote and becoming the second-largest party in the process. They were, after all, the only party actively arguing against austerity. Indeed, perhaps the oddest thing about the entire German experience with austerity in the 1930s was how it was ruthlessly implemented by the left and so quickly abandoned by the right.

As Sheri Berman brilliantly illuminates, the German Social Democrats of this period (the SPD) were intellectually Marxist but programmatically Ricardian: classical liberals in socialist clothing. Marx's economics were, apart from his view of the rate of profit and the possibility of a general failure of demand, as much Ricardo's as they were his own, especially as they were interpreted by the leading "theologians" of the German Social Democrats. Upon such a view, when the economy was in a slump, there was literally nothing to be done except let the system melt down until socialism magically appeared.

In fact, for the SPD, good economic policy meant being more orthodox than the liberals they argued against. As SPD member and one time vice president of the Reichstag Wilhelm Dittmann put it in a speech to the SPD faithful, "We want the current situation [the crisis] to develop further, and can only follow in the general direction that these tendencies show us."[50] In response to this structuralist fatalism, the German trade unions began to agitate for an alternative "full-fledged Keynesian type assault on the depression" in direct opposition to SPD policies.[51] This reflationary policy took form under the aegis of the so-called WTB plan (named after the formulators' initials), which the unions pressed hard upon the SPD and the government. Brüning ignored the plan and pressed on with austerity. But the SPD hierarchy set out to destroy it since it offended their faith.

The SPD's main economic theorist Rudolph Hilferding argued that not only was the WTB plan un-Marxist, it "threatened the very foundations of our program."[52] As Berman put it, the SPD, as good Marxists, still saw letting the business cycle run its course as the only possible policy. Like the Austrians that they opposed in every other way, the SPD thought that intervention would simply delay the inevitable and make matters even worse. This was hard-core austerity thinking, except it came from the heart of the putatively democratic left. As Union leader Fritz Naphtali, who sided against the WTB plan, argued, "The crisis, with all of its changes and shifts of purchasing power, is a means of correction which must necessarily be accepted."[53]

The Nazis, unburdened by such structuralist nonsense, were able to take these ideas and make them their own. The centerpiece of their July 1932 election propaganda, the *Wirstchaftliches Sofortprogramm* (the immediate economic program) laid out an alternative to austerity that looked an awful lot like the WTB plan. The pamphlet's first three points could not have been more anti-austerity: first, "unemployment causes poverty, employment creates prosperity"; second, "capital does not create jobs, jobs create capital"; and third, "unemployment benefits burden the economy but job creation simulates the economy."[54] Also, the program argued, Germany should get off the gold standard as quickly as possible. The July 1932 elections saw the SPD vote collapse; the Nazis received 37.3 percent of the vote. That they polled lower in the subsequent November elections proved irrelevant. The Nazis still came to power through the ballot box. In 1933, they took 43.9 percent of the total vote.

In 1932, unemployment accounted for 30 percent of the workforce. By 1936, full employment was restored. However, because of the Nazis' repression of labor, real wages did not increase, and unlike Sweden, practically all the improvement was due to the fiscal stimulus of armaments. As Adam Tooze has shown, the much-touted work-creation programs of the Nazis were a propaganda sideshow. What really made the economy boom was the drive toward total war.[55] As Keynes noted with regret in 1940, "It is, it seems, politically impossible for a capitalist democracy to organize expenditure on the scale necessary to make the grand experiment which would prove my case—except in war conditions."[56] Nonetheless, once the Nazis ended austerity and abandoned gold (even if they did this more through exchange controls than through devaluation), growth returned. That this turn against austerity took a particularly murderous direction in Germany does not invalidate the basic point that austerity didn't work. In fact, the point that really needs to be recognized is that repeated rounds of austerity policy, plus the ideological intransigence of the Social Democrats, helped to bring Hitler to power far more than any memory of inflation a decade earlier.

By 1933 the lesson should have been clear. *You can't run a gold standard in a democracy.* Eventually people will vote against it. They did so in Sweden and they did so in Germany. Austerity gave interwar Europe both social democracy and genocidal fascism. Yet, like the gift that keeps on giving, in Asia austerity was about to bequeath us a new and virulent form of imperialism.

"From Those Wonderful Folks That Brought You Pearl Harbor": Japanese Austerity and Military Expansion 1921–1937

It took Japan thirteen years to get back on gold after abandoning it in 1917,[57] but it wasn't for want of trying. If there were an award for the country that tried hardest to be austere, Japan would win it at a canter. Japan emerged from World War I on the side of the Allies with almost no wartime damage (save for some losses in Siberia in 1918). Underneath the façade, however, lay a fragile banking system and a great deal of pent-up inflation. Being off the gold standard allowed a devaluation of the exchange rate, but being heavily import dependent meant that a policy of devaluation could only go so far without stoking inflation through imports. As such, austerity in the form of high interest rates was applied more thoroughly than in our other cases, turning the postwar rally in securities and commodities markets into the Black Monday bust of March 1920.[58] After Black Monday economic growth vanished as deflation took hold and successive rounds of austerity made it worse. As Yuji Kuronuma calculated, "the real rate of economic growth was −2.7% in 1922, −4.6% in 1923 and −2.9% in 1925."[59]

Despite being in a near permanent slump, Japanese banking elites and the Bank of Japan sought a swift return to the gold standard. But arrayed against them were a variety of domestically focused farming, labor, and business interests. This necessitated extensive public debates in the academy, policy circles, and the mass media over what was called "the 'kin kaikin' [repeal of the gold embargo] controversy."[60] Complicating this picture, the two dominant political parties, the Seiyukai and the Kenseikai, both wanted to go back on gold, but disagreed about the conditions under which that should happen.[61]

In 1928, financial elites and those sections of the government pressing for an immediate return to gold enlisted the help of the major newspapers of the day to convince the public to return to gold. Typical was a series of editorials in *Osaka Mainichi* from the summer of 1928 through the spring of 1929. For example, when France went back on gold in June 1928, *Osaka Mainichi* argued that "France realized the repeal of the gold embargo: Japan should Shame Itself." The same editorial asked rhetorically, "Why shouldn't we repent ourselves of being left behind if we think our nation is a civilized and first-rate one?"[62] In July 1928 the public was told that to rejoin gold "people must endure a pain of surgical operation...Shrink first in order to extend."[63] Later that summer, an editorial noted that although a return to gold would be painful "it is a hopeful pain. Eventually it would restore us."[64]

Having prepared the austere ground in this way, the final push to get Japan back on gold came from Junnosuke Inoue, the finance minister of the new Hamaguchi cabinet that was formed in 1929. Inoue was tasked with conducting a propaganda campaign that would clinch the case for gold. Thirteen million pamphlets, dozens of radio broadcasts, and many more newspaper editorials were unleashed on the public.[65] And it worked. As Koichi Hamada and Ashai Noguchi report, "The motto 'repeal the gold embargo' became fashionable."[66] Inoue himself authored several short books on the subject, each of which was a triumph of austerity thinking. As Inoue put it, "We cannot avoid fiscal tightening and liquidation at least once in the process," and so "the surest way is to go straight towards the repeal of the gold embargo...since we cannot avoid some pain...and sacrifice anyway."[67] Inoue traveled the length and breadth of the country arguing his case, asking the people to be prepared for the tightening of the already austere economic environment.[68]

Inoue got his wish and Japan rejoined the gold standard in January 1930, right at the point that the rest of the world's economy was contracting. The result was the *Showa Depression*, the greatest peacetime collapse in economic activity in Japan's history. Japan's growth rate fell to −9.7 percent in 1930 and −9.5 percent in 1931, while the Yen rose approximately 7 percent against the dollar.[69] Demand in the United States and elsewhere for Japanese manufactures fell as the Yen appreciation and the general collapse strangled trade. Average Japanese household income fell like a stone from ¥1,326 in 1929 to ¥650 in 1931.[70] You might think that such a performance might signal a rethink of policy—but Japanese financial elites were having none of it.

The state had kept public spending in check throughout the 1920s, rising from only ¥1.2 to ¥1.4 billion over the course of the decade. The folks taking the brunt of this shrinkage in real terms were the military, who saw their spending cut from 47.8 percent to 28.4 percent of the budget over the same period.[71] Amplifying Inoue's austerity crusade, his party's 1930 election slogan was "economy, disarmament, purification of politics, reform of China policy and removal of the gold embargo."[72] The military were none too pleased. Inoue pressed on regardless.

Interest rates were raised "into the teeth of the depression" and government spending was cut by almost twenty percent from an already low level.[73] By the time the London Naval Treaty, which condemned the Japanese navy to permanent inferiority status, was ratified in October 1930, the military had had enough. Prime Minister Hamaguchi was shot by a supporter of the military in November 1930 and died of his wounds the following year. Unperturbed, the finance ministry pressed on. In early 1931 they tried to cut another ¥28 million from the army and navy budgets. In October 1931 a plot by the army to overthrow the government was uncovered. The two facts were related. Civil-military tensions reached a head. The government blinked first and resigned in December 1931.

The new government couldn't have been more different. The opposition Seiyukai party, now in power, appointed Takahashi Korekiyo as finance minister. Takahashi left the gold standard as quickly as possible and then cut the discount rate on commercial bills (the de facto lowest interest rate) from 6.57 percent in early 1932 to 3.65 percent in July 1934.[74] He drastically increased the money supply and instituted capital controls to stop its flight. He instructed the Bank of Japan to underwrite long-term government bond issues.[75] Government spending increased by an initial 34 percent, and by the end of 1932 it totaled an extra 10 percent of GDP.[76] Prices rose, debt burdens fell, and the Japanese economy rocketed out of the depression, growing 4 percent a year in real terms each year between 1932 and 1936. When one considers that the rest of the world was deflating at that moment, and one also remembers that Japan was, and still is, an export led and import dependent economy, the result was all the more remarkable.

Inoue, however, was still campaigning for a return to the gold standard when he was assassinated in 1932. Later that year, a leading bank director and Takahashi's prime minister were also assassinated. Austerity was racking up quite a body count. A decade of austerity had convinced the Japanese military that they were "at war with the entire civilian political elite."[77] Even Takahashi, the architect of recovery, was first excluded from cabinet by the military when he began to argue that since the economy had recovered (by late 1934), it was time cool the spending and worry about inflation. Two years later, Takahashi was murdered, along with several other political figures, in another abortive coup in February 1936. His replacement at the finance ministry was a cipher for the military who turned on the money pumps full bore. When war was finally declared on China in 1937, finance in Japan, along with any financial prudence, died.

Austerity not only didn't work in Japan. It created the worst depression in Japanese history, provoked an assassination campaign against bankers, and empowered "the wonderful folks that brought you Pearl Harbor." Now, if you think this enough to demonstrate why austerity is a dangerous idea, just wait until you see what happened in France around the same time.

Defending the Franc—But Not France: French Austerity Policies 1919–1939

Despite being on the victorious side in the First World War, France, among all the Allied powers, suffered the most wartime destruction of persons, property, and wealth. So much so that getting the Germans to pay for all the damage constituted a significant part of forward budgetary planning. That the Germans did not want to pay and, after the hyperinflation, basically didn't pay, was to prove a significant problem for the French economy going forward.

The boom-slump-stabilization pattern that characterized the world economy in the early 1920s hit France in a peculiar way. By relying on German reparations to supply a large portion of their budget, when payments were not forthcoming, the resulting budget deficits had to be met with higher interest rates to attract capital. In such a situation a reasonable policy would have been to raise taxes, which is precisely where democracy and taxes came together to produce inflation.[78]

France was a deeply divided society in which the political right sought to raise excise and consumption taxes on everyone else, while the political left wanted to tax only the right's income and wealth.[79] Protecting the right, whenever it looked like the left might win an election, the Bank of France refused to roll over Treasury bills, that is, the short term debt instruments funding the government, thereby "forcing the authorities to print money."[80] By 1924, after several rounds of stoking inflation this way, the right came to power and as expected raised taxes on the left's constituents. The left won the next election that same year but was unable to shift the burden back. As a result, deficits ballooned. Eventually, the left government resigned and in 1926 a rightist government under Raymond Poincaré raised enough taxes to close the shortfall. In reply to this balancing of the budget and reduction in inflation, investors bought francs. This enabled France to go back on the gold standard in 1926 since their reserves were rebuilt. Between 1926 and 1930 the economy stabilized and gold in-flows increased, augmented by high interest rates, such that the newspaper *Le Figaro* proclaimed France should "rejoice in our timid yet prosperous economy as opposed to the presumptuousness and decadent economy of the Anglo-Saxon races."

Such hubristic nationalist nonsense was of course the perfect moment for the combined effects of US-bound capital flight, the Wall Street Crash, and the central European liquidity crunch to slam into the French economy at great speed. The result was that gross national product fell 7 percent and industrial production fell 13 percent by 1932.[81] The desire to stay on gold when everyone else was leaving meant that France could only deflate as everyone else reflated.

What saved France to some extent was that the depression fell mainly on capital expenditures and investment rather than consumption.[82] But even in France, there was only so much deflation a democracy could take. Reflation was needed, but reflating on the gold standard was simply going to produce capital flight, especially if the monetary authority decided not to play ball. For reflation to work, you needed supportive policies by the Bank of France, which was exactly what the Bank of France was not about to supply.

As Jonathan Kirshner has detailed, the Bank of France was a powerful and thoroughly undemocratic institution that confused its own interests with the national interest. Although it was the fiscal agent for the French Treasury, it was also a private institution with 40,000 shareholders whose 200 largest shareholders, often called "the 200 families," determined both personnel and policy.[83] They paid the governor's (large) salary in return for the usual diet of gold, cuts, and budget balance, all of which benefited the rentier class at the expense of everyone else.[84] With the political right already on board, the de facto policy of the Bank of France was to paralyze the political left. Continual austerity was the result.

From 1932 to 1936 government spending was cut by 20 percent, industrial production fell nearly a quarter, the real exchange rate rose, and the money supply collapsed.[85] Any attempt to compensate led to capital flight, which the Bank actively supported as a way of disciplining the government. The Bank planted stories in the press discrediting fiscal experiments elsewhere, insisted on budget cuts as the only way forward, and generally vetoed any policies that the democratically elected government promoted that did not meet with its approval.[86]

A critical instance of this was the Flandin government's experiment with reflation in 1934–1935 when France was still on gold. The Bank of France vetoed these policies even though Flandin was a conservative. They made no effort to stop the outflow of gold his meager spending promoted, which eventually resulted in Flandin's resignation.[87] Pierre Laval, whose policy of "super-deflation" followed Flandin, produced no less than 549 decrees, most of which were cuts to the budget. The economy plummeted further despite the Bank of France increasingly underwriting short-term debt instruments to buy Laval breathing space, something they never did for the left.[88]

The situation only came to a head when the public began to riot. Laval was forced out in January 1936 and a left-wing cross-party alliance called the Popular Front took over. Austerity had been tried, had failed, was tried again in Laval's superdeflation, and it had failed again. The Popular Front wanted to follow countries that were breaking with orthodoxy. The problem was of course the Bank of France. The Popular

Front increased wages, reduced working time, and reformed the structure of the Bank of France so that the Regents did not control the governing council.[89] This was all very laudable, but it simply led to another round of capital flight, interest-rate increases, and more deflation. Reflationary policy, in the absence of effective capital controls, means that capital flight wins, especially when it is aided and abetted by the central bank. When the leader of the popular front Léon Blum suggested capital controls to make reflation and greater spending possible, he was forced out by the increasing capital flight that the Bank of France once again did nothing to forestall.

Even when France eventually abandoned gold in September 1936, little improved. To mix metaphors, while devaluation can create room to move, spending must pick up the slack. So when the monetary authority acts as a de facto veto on all policies except austerity, devaluation simply increases the import bill and deepens the slump. Most states in this period that left gold behind rebounded through devaluation *plus spending*, even if it was through rearmament. Yet the Bank of France continually vetoed budget increases that would have allowed the French military to modernize, and even mobilize, to meet the German threat.[90] As a result, French defense spending between 1934 and 1938 was one-tenth that of Germany.[91] French central bankers chafed at the already "ruinous level of military spending" and called for defense cuts as late as 1940.[92] Even the suggestion of preemptive mobilization promoted capital flight, which the Bank of France, once again, did nothing to halt.[93] As one scholar put it tellingly, by 1936 Hitler knew one thing. The franc would be defended at all costs. As for France, that was another matter entirely.[94]

Austerity's Dangerous Lessons

The interwar period taught us some valuable lessons about why austerity does not work and why its application is a dangerous idea. Building an entire international monetary order with an inherent deflationary bias that can't work in a democracy is bad idea, number one. Number two, Einstein was right. If doing the same thing over and over again while expecting different results is the definition of madness, then repeated rounds of austerity in country after country was madness.

No good came of it. Apart from a few short-term expansions in the early 1920s when countries were not on gold, not only did the application of austerity not work, it made the depression deeper, longer, and, arguably, laid the foundations for the war that would engulf the world in the 1940s.

The United States' "liquidationist" doctrine continued after the Wall Street crash, turning a series of bank failures and a relatively minor budget deficit into a full-blown financial crisis and depression that abated only when austerity was ended. The British heroically restored their pre-war parity and almost instantly generated a million unemployed and a slump that persisted until the end of the 1930s. The Swedes initially, and quite classically, cut to make things better, but then began to experiment with reflationary policies earlier, and to a more significant degree than anyone else, except the Japanese. Germany's hyperinflation in 1923 had little to do with the austerity policies that followed or their ultimate outcome: the rise of genocidal fascism. Rather, as capital flight hit Germany in the late 1920s, austerity was applied to keep the country on gold, which had the effect of throwing the economy off the proverbial cliff. The majority party in the Reichstag, the Social Democrats, was, perversely, even more orthodox than its liberal opponents. The result was a cross-party austerity that held the doors of power open, and the Nazis walked right through them.

Japan underwent several rounds of deliberate deflation to get back on gold that proved utterly futile. In the process they annoyed their own military so much that it began to assassinate key members of the financial elite and forced a reflation of the economy far greater than the Swedes or the Germans ever managed. Finally, France remained on the gold standard longer than anyone else and ended up, arguably, suffering the most. They ceased to exist as an independent nation. French financial elites were so afraid of inflation, and were so determined to maintain the value of the franc, that they paralyzed the French military's ability to mobilize against Hitler. Austerity didn't just fail—it helped blow up the world. That's the definition of a very dangerous idea.

So why did we forget these lessons? As we saw in chapter 5, thirty years of neoliberal ideas chipping away at our perceptions of the 1930s was certainly a part of it. This new economic instruction sheet not only denied such an interpretation of possible events. As we saw previously, it even proposed that the opposite was true—that austerity leads to growth, and that the slump, not the boom, is the time to cut. But were they right? We now return to the cases of expansionary austerity examined earlier to see if they really do force us to change our minds about austerity. From there we turn to some REBLLs and their recent assault on the Debt Star.

Part Two: The New Cases for Austerity: Expansionary Fiscal Contraction in the 1980s Meets the REBLL Alliance

Revisiting (and Revising) Expansionary Austerity

Just to refresh our memories about why austerity is good, despite all of the above, the key findings of the literature on expansionary fiscal contractions were as follows. The original Giavazzi and Pagano paper from 1990 highlighted Denmark's expansionary contraction in the period 1982–1986, claiming a political regime shift to the right, plus devaluation, plus a peg to the deutsche mark promoted growth.[95] They were also "tempted" to say that the same applied to Ireland.[96] Five years later Alesina and Perotti found fourteen successful adjustments in twenty countries over thirty-two years, with positive shifts in investors' expectations, cuts on the expenditure side, and devaluations doing the work.[97] These cases were more thoroughly examined in their article "Tales of Fiscal Adjustment," in which the twenty-three positive episodes discerned in the data were narrowed down to ten case studies, of which, the authors concluded, "two cases appear unambiguously expansionary: Ireland 1987–9 and Australia."[98] Denmark, Giavazzi and Pagano's best case now appeared to be a "mixed" result. Alesina and Ardagna's main point was that "regardless of the initial level of debt, a large fiscal adjustment that is expenditure based and accompanied by wage moderation and devaluation is expansionary."[99] The 2009 update of this paper found nine examples of expansionary fiscal adjustments, and in every case "successful fiscal adjustments are completely based upon spending cuts accompanied by modest tax cuts."[100] The key channel for expansionary austerity to work, across all the cases, is the rational expectations of consumers.

Throughout this body of work Ireland's adjustment in the late-1980s is repeatedly cited as the best example of this thesis, with Australia, and then less frequently Denmark and Sweden playing supporting roles. These are the cases that are supposed to show us that the lessons drawn from the 1920s and 1930s are no longer applicable. They set out to demonstrate that the slump is the right time to cut, that we should cut on the spending side, and decisively. Because the state can positively effect expectations of future income by decisively cutting, austerity can be expansionary. If these cases do in fact make good on these claims, then perhaps we have sound reason to forget the lessons of the prior period. So, do they live up to their billing as "proving" the case for austerity?

The answer is no, but to get there you have to work for it. This literature is extremely uneven and highly technical. Different scholars use measures and statistical tests; debates over the relevant merits of each metric and measure occupy more journal space than the actual cases themselves; and widely divergent interpretations of the same cases characterize the literature. Nonetheless, the broad contours of the debate seem to be that the case studies don't hold water on the microlevel once country experts get their hands on them, while on the macrolevel, the case *for* expansionary fiscal consolidation has been increasingly challenged—by scholars from inside the academy, from inside the IMF, and even from within the Bocconi school itself. To get a handle on this plethora of literature, we focus on primary and secondary work on the most common case studies in the literature and the most recent large-n (statistical) studies.

Expectations, Expansion, and Austerity in the 1980s Cases

We begin with Denmark, Giavazzi and Pagano's best case, but one that Alesina and Ardanga chose to label as "mixed." Alesina and Ardanga note that the size of the adjustment in Denmark was large, around 10 percent of GDP, and was "divided about equally between spending cuts and tax increases."[101] They argue that centralized wage-bargaining institutions held the line on wage growth while the currency was pegged rather than devalued. This led to a disinflation rather than a devaluation, which nonetheless led to falling unit labor costs. Alesina and Ardanga do note, however, that after the initial successful consolidation, growth fell dramatically in 1988–1989 while unemployment rose, the main cause of which was the end of centralized wage bargaining—thus for them the case is "mixed." Similarly, Roberto Perotti, in a separate piece, notes that after the successful consolidation, "growth ground to a halt and consumption declined for three years."[102]

Ulf Bergman and Martin Hutchinson's reevaluation of the Danish consolidation of 1982–1986 broadly supports Alesina and Ardagna's interpretation, but these authors more forcefully stress the expectations channel as the primary mechanism that explains positive adjustment. Their study of Denmark also notes the large turnaround in the budget and the strong growth exhibited from 1984–1986. They do not, however, acknowledge the very large slump the economy fell into immediately after the consolidation. Given this, the ability to lend credence to the expectations story must be tempered. If expectations were altered when a major "regime shift" was signaled in 1982–1986, as these authors maintain, why then did those same expectations end up producing a slump in 1988?[103]

To explain this slump and keep the expectations channel as the main avenue for adjustment would mean either that the regime shift was not credible after all, which would make it hard to explain the original expansion via expectations, or the authors would have to explain why consumers and investors' expectations changed due to some exogenous factor that overpowered them, which they do not. Much remains unclear, and so the case for the expectations channel, what Paul Krugman calls "the confidence fairy," is weakened despite this attempt to demonstrate its importance. In fact, later work by the IMF does not see Denmark as an example of "fiscal consolidation motivated by a desire to reduce the budget deficit" because the economy was overheating when the consolidation was undertaken. That is, the cuts were taken in a boom, not a slump.[104]

The one country that routinely appears in the list of positive cases of expansionary austerity is Ireland in the late 1980s. Going back to the discussion in "Tales," Alesina and Ardanga narrate Ireland's experience from 1987–1989 as follows. When Irish debt to GDP reached 116 percent in 1986, a right-wing government came to power that cut transfers, the government wage bill, and taxes. Devaluation and negotiated wage moderation reduced unit labor costs by 12 to 15 percent. Growth rates and foreign investment both soared.[105] Key to all this, as before, was the large expenditure-based cut plus wage moderation and devaluation.[106]

Stephen Kinsella offers a rather different version of events in his recent study of Ireland's twin experiments with austerity: in the late 1980s and today in the aftermath of the banking crisis of 2008.[107] Kinsella emphasizes that Ireland did have an expansion following a consolidation, as the literature claims, but notes that correlation is not causation in this case. Instead, he notes another correlation; that Ireland's consolidation "coincided with a period of growth in the international economy, with the presence of fiscal transfers from the European Union, the opening up of the single market and a well-timed devaluation in August 1986."[108] An earlier paper by John Considine and James Duffy makes a similar point, namely, that it's the boom in British imports—the so-called Lawson boom—that combined with the 1986 devaluation to make the difference.[109] This is backed up by a piece by Roberto Perotti, who argues that in the Irish case "the concomitant depreciation of Sterling and the expansion in the UK...boosted Irish exports."[110]

Kinsella also notes that the adjustment was considerably eased by an income tax amnesty that raised the equivalent of 2 percent of GDP.[111] The part that stands out in Kinsella's account is, however, something completely absent in other retellings of these events. That is, "the average industrial wage rose by over 14 percent in the period 1986–1989 [which] boosted government revenue and increased...private consumption."[112] As Kinsella concludes, this makes the whole Irish experience look more like a "proto-Keynesian story, where a laggard country converges rapidly to OECD averages" during a global upswing, than any case of contraction altering the long-term tax-and-spend expectations of Irish consumers.[113] Once again, the much-lauded expectations channel of adjustment, the main claim to fame for the expansionary austerity school, is at best overpowered by other factors, if not wholly absent, in the Irish case.[114] Meanwhile, what's really doing the work, pay increases and global upswings, are similarly absent in the standard expectations model. It is almost as if we were talking about two quite different Irelands.

If Denmark and Ireland don't really make the case for expansionary austerity and the all-important expectations effect, what about the Australian case? Actually, Australia problematizes the case for expectations-augmented austerity still further. John Quiggin has examined Alesina and Ardagna's "Tale" of Australian adjustment and declared it to be little more than "shoddy scholarship" that gets basic facts about the case entirely wrong.[115] On Quiggin's account, and contrary to Alesina and Ardagna's telling of the tale, neither cuts in unemployment benefits nor capital taxes actually occurred in the Australian case, so their effect in altering expectations must be declared null and void. After all, if they didn't happen they can't have an effect. Similarly, the role accorded to wage bargaining by Alesina and Ardagna was, by Quiggin's estimation "absolutely opposite to the story told here," which actually featured "a major expansion in the role of government" rather than any contraction.[116] Most interestingly in this case, Alesina and Ardagna do to Australia what Bergman and Hutchinson do to Denmark—they omit the fact that "almost immediately after their story ends, Australia entered the worst recession in its postwar history."[117] Given Quiggin's demolition of the Australian case, we are forced to conclude that yet another often-cited positive case of expansionary austerity seems to collapse the moment any weight of historical evidence is placed upon it. Most significantly, the expectations mechanism, the key claim in all the literature, is again nowhere to be seen in the final analysis.

Finally, Sweden occasionally pops up as an example of expansionary contraction, and a 1995 paper by Giavazzi and Pagano sets up Sweden in 1990–1994 as the showcase for the role of expectations, so it's worth dwelling a little on this case.[118] Giavazzi and Pagano examine a period of economic stress for Sweden where, against most of this literature, the budget expanded rather than contracted, and consumption stayed flat rather than expanded. Why then examine this counter-case? The point is to show the reciprocal of the normal expansionary austerity claim and strengthen it by doing so. That is, tax cuts in a slump can work through the expectations channel to signal to consumers that *bad times are ahead*—the reason they got the tax cut—and so they should *not* increase consumption despite the increase in available cash and the ongoing slump.[119] It is the same expectations mechanism, but this time rational consumers are seeing through the bad policies of a spendthrift government rather than reacting positively to the cuts of a credibly austere one. The case potentially strengthens the claims for the expectations effect by extending its empirical reach. Not only do cuts in spending lead to expansions in consumption (positive expectations), expansions of spending can lead to cuts in consumption (bad expectations).

Giavazzi and Pagano begin by noting that Swedish debt grew from 24.9 percent of GDP in 1990 to 67.8 percent in 1994. Acknowledging that Sweden went through a steep recession at this time, they nonetheless press the claim that "over half of the budgetary deterioration cannot be attributed to the recession."[120] Explaining this variance are "discretionary policy actions" such as tax cuts and bank bailouts that depressed private consumption by signaling bad times ahead.[121] Specifically, what drove this drop in consumption in this period, despite a compensatory stimulus in the form of a tax cut, was a "fear of a sovereign default by the Swedish government [that increased] significantly by the end of 1992."[122]

The author's evidence for this claim is a spread between a Swedish thirty-year bond and a World Bank issued note of the same currency and duration that rose "100 basis points in 1993," plus a series of OECD simulations that suggested Swedish debt might not be stabilized until 1999.[123] Because of the immanent fear of default that this generated, Swedish consumption fell 13 percentage points between 1989 and 1994 "as public debt started to sky-rocket."[124] These terrifying developments, working through their rational expectations, would have "led Swedish consumers to reduce their estimate of permanent disposable income...their consumption...and their estimates of the future earnings of productive assets."[125] "This downward revision in permanent disposable income may [then] have been triggered by the government's fiscal laxitude...which...has led Sweden to accumulate public debt at a breakneck rate."[126]

To recap Giavazzi and Pagano's main claims, the Swedish government ran up public debt to 67.8 percent of GDP during a massive recession, but most of it was its own choice. This was enough to create a bond spread of 1 percent (100 basis points = 1 percent = nothing to get worried about) over an equivalent World Bank note issue. This supposedly upset Swedish consumers (who apparently spend their time watching bond spreads) so much that despite being in the middle of a recession, rational expectations and Ricardian equivalence kicked in through the expectations channel to make sure that when free money from the state arrived in the form of a tax cut, it had no effect on consumption. Consumers rationally discounted the stimulus as a sign of terrible times ahead and offset the expansion via their long-sighted expectations.

Anyone who knows the political economy of Sweden, especially in this period, would note a rather large omission from this paper's version of events—the triple meltdown of real estate markets, stock markets, and the exchange rate that happened to Sweden between 1989 and 1993. Sweden had just popped a bubble in its real estate and stock markets that developed after deregulatory moves by the government in 1987 massively expanded the supply of private credit, but you would never know that from this paper. As Peter Englund tells it, in 1989 alone "the construction and real estate stock price index fell by 25 percent...[and] by the end of 1990 the real estate index had fallen 52 percent."[127] On top of this massive deflation, which had huge knock-on effects in the labor market, Sweden was hit by the deflationary effects of a currency crisis in the ERM mechanism that combined with the real estate bust to reduce GDP growth by −5.1 percent between 1991 and 1993. Then, and only then, did interest rates really skyrocket.[128] No one cared one jot about the national debt at this point.

In such a situation, however, consumers who have taken on a fair amount of debt in the expectation of capital gains in stocks and real estate, and who suddenly find themselves underwater, might not spend all that much—even if they receive a tax cut. To explain this, there is no need to invoke the specter of Swedish consumers watching unlikely bond spreads while fretting about the national debt of one of the most solvent countries in the world. This is hyperbolic neoliberal fantasy looking for a set of supporting econometrics. Simply paying back debt when the economy is tanking, a classic "Balance Sheet Recession" a la Richard Koo, would suffice to explain what's going on.[129] That consumption didn't rise is not a surprise unless you frame the problem in this absurdly counterintuitive way. That it stayed constant is the evidence for a common or garden stimulus effect—it didn't fall despite the bust. It should have fallen further, but didn't, because the tax cuts worked.[130]

In sum, none of the commonly referred to cases in this literature support the contentions made about them, especially the role of expectations in producing expansions by cutting. This is perhaps why later work in this tradition has by and large eschewed case studies and gone back to large-scale statistical analyses. But even here, the results have proven controversial if not damning for the expansionary austerity case. Specifically, recent work has, to a very large extent, gone against the findings of the 2009 Alesina and Ardagna paper that proved so influential in the crisis, "Large Changes in Fiscal Policy." Given this, it is perhaps no longer appropriate to talk of this moment being "Alesina's hour," especially at, of all places, the IMF.

Debunking the "Austerity Myth"

Alesina and Ardagna's 2009 paper has been dissected, augmented, tested, refuted, and generally hauled over the coals. The main results of these exercises further weaken the case for expansionary austerity. Arjun Jayadev and Mike Konczal undertook the first major critical examination of the 2009 paper's data and key claims.[131] They note several oddities in the paper. First, that of the twenty-six expansionary episodes identified in the data "in virtually none did the country . . . reduce the deficit when the economy was in a slump and . . . increase growth rates while reducing the debt-to-GDP ratio."[132] This is especially odd when compared to another finding, namely, that across these episodes "examples of successful consolidation were, on average, growing steadily the year before the year of adjustment."[133] In other words, and per contra one of the main claims made in the literature, it turns out that no state that tried this actually tried it during a slump.

Following on from this piece, the team of researchers at the IMF that put together the *World Economic Outlook* set out to test the entire notion of expansionary austerity from the ground up using new measures and new data.[134] Their main findings strongly contradicted those of the expansionary austerity camp. Specifically, they found that the main concept used to assess whether a contraction was expansionary or not—the cyclically adjusted budget surplus—biased the original analyses to find positive cases and discount negative ones.[135] When an alternative measure was employed to test for expansionary contractions they found that fiscal contractions were indeed contractions. There was no offsetting gain.[136] There may be gains to be made later in reducing debt from lower interest payments, but that is an entirely different, and altogether more orthodox, claim.[137]

Furthermore, and especially relevant to the situation of the Eurozone and the United States today, they find that while it is true that cuts in spending contract the economy less than tax increases, this occurs not because of expectations but because of the ability of the central bank to offset the contraction with an interest-rate cut. Given that interest rates are at or are near zero, no such effect will be forthcoming at the moment—there is only hurt to look forward to from such policies.[138] Finally, even a devaluation, which is always an important component of expansionary adjustments, will not suffice to promote growth. "Because not all countries can increase net exports at the same time, this finding implies that fiscal contraction is likely to be more painful when many countries adjust at the same time."[139]

Echoing the earlier study by Jayadev and Konczal, after US Republicans picked up on Alesina's work, the US Congressional Research Service (CRS) did its own study of expansionary austerity, adjudicating between the IMF's and Alesina and Ardagna's versions of events.[140] The CRS also found that "successful fiscal adjustments...occurred when the economy was at or near potential output."[141] As such, the applicability of this policy to economies that are nowhere near potential output is questionable at best.[142]

By the middle of 2011, empirical and theoretical support for expansionary austerity was slipping away. Even current members of the Bocconi School began to defect. Especially significant here was a piece by Roberto Perotti.[143] Although he is critical of the new methodology employed by the IMF to question the case for expansionary austerity, Perotti nonetheless argues that almost all the time cutting your way to growth doesn't work, at least in the short run.

Perotti concentrates on something that Alesina's work has actually always admitted, but perhaps never stressed sufficiently, namely, that it is the overall policy mix that matters. Wage bargaining institutions, the ability to devalue, export-led growth from demand generated elsewhere—these things matter a great deal. In fact, they matter much more than expectations. They also happen to be found in large welfare states like Sweden and Denmark and precious few other places. But if this is so, then there is nothing new or surprising to note. Contractionary policies cause fiscal contractions unless they are supported by external demand, devaluations, and cooperative domestic labor organizations, and even then, it's best to go into the consolidation from a position of high growth. Not only does Perotti's paper "cast[s] doubt on the confidence explanation," it observes tellingly that at the moment "an export boom is also obviously not available to the world as a whole" to support such policies.[144] In the context of a Europe where austerity was being tried, tested, and tried again without positive gain, even members of the Bocconi School were finding it hard to defend the indefensible.

Two IMF papers that appeared in July 2011 and July 2012 effectively brought Alesina's hour to a close. The first paper by Jamie Guajardo et al. built upon the IMF paper from October 2010 that employed different methods and data, and again, they find similar disconfirming results. Confirming earlier work, they report that while it is true that raising taxes hurts more than cutting spending, this has nothing to do with expectations and everything to do with accommodative monetary policy. Moreover, finding contractionary effects from contractions are the unsurprising norm.[145] Basing their work upon a wider set of simulations, they are bolder in their conclusion, however, noting that their "estimation results...provide little support for the expansionary austerity hypothesis."[146]

It is the July 2012 paper that really kicks the argument into touch, however. Nicoletta Battini et al.'s "Successful Austerity in the United States, Europe and Japan"—an examination of the big cases that matter—pretty much pulls any remaining theoretical and empirical supports out from under the expansionary austerity case.[147] Taking aim straight at the confidence channel, they argue that "while it is plausible to conjecture that confidence effects have been at play in our sample of consolidations, during downturns they do not seem to have *ever been strong enough to make the consolidations expansionary.*"[148] They then, one by one, point by point, directly refute virtually all the core claims of the expansionary austerity thesis.

They argue, inter alia, that consolidating in a downturn is twice as risky as doing it in an upturn; that smooth and gradual consolidations always work better than strong and abrupt ones; that frontloaded contractions are more contractionary and worsen the debt-to-GDP load, and that cutting taxes is less contractionary than cutting transfers, especially when it's done gradually.[149] The conclusion of the paper is especially damning and is therefore worth quoting at length.

> [W]ithdrawing fiscal stimuli too quickly in economies where output is already contracting can prolong their recessions without generating the expected fiscal saving. This is particularly true if the consolidation is centered around cuts to public expenditure...and if the size of the consolidation is large.... From a policy perspective this is especially relevant for periods of positive, though low growth...frontloading consolidations during a recession seems to aggravate the costs of fiscal adjustment...[and] greatly delay the reduction in the debt-to-GDP ratio—which, in turn, can exacerbate market sentiment in a sovereign at times of low confidence, defying fiscal austerity efforts altogether. Again this is even truer in the case of consolidations based prominently on cuts to public spending.

If you are thinking of the effect of repeated rounds of austerity in the Eurozone, you would not be wrong here either. Indeed, the IMF's October 2012 World Economic Outlook concluded that the negative fiscal multipliers in the Eurozone had been massively underestimated such that the effect of cuts was amplified through the economy by as much as one-and-a-half times.[150] This might go some way toward explaining quite why Southern Europe's expansionary consolidations have been anything but expansionary. Alesina's hour ended the moment the IMF remembered that austerity, when applied to real economies and the lives of real people, is still a very dangerous idea.

But even if the IMF has lost faith in austerity, it does not mean that its champions will not try to find other examples where it has supposedly worked. Too many reputations and too much sunk political capital are at stake for mere facts to get in the way of this ideology. It is in this regard that we turn to the new hope for austerity champions—the REBLL alliance of Romania, Estonia, Bulgaria, Latvia, and Lithuania. These countries have supposedly demonstrated, in the real world, never mind in the econometric world, that austerity works. As such, the Greeks, the Spanish, and everyone else simply aren't trying hard enough. But is this really case? What can we really learn from the efforts of the REBLLs? And why did they decide to go for austerity in such a gung-ho manner in the first place? Turning our attention to that question in particular leads to a very different view of the REBLLs and their austerity policies, as well as their potential role-model qualities.

The REBLL Alliance and the Debt Star: Adventures in the Science Fiction of Austerity

A July 9, 2012, cartoon in *The Economist* shows two men on a beach. One is a blond, beaming, Baltic man flexing his biceps. Crouched next to him, under a sign that says "South," is a swarthy, mean-looking man holding a beggar's cup. It's not a ridiculous picture of how policy elites in Europe and elsewhere saw the morality tale playing out between the Baltic countries and Southern Europe in the summer of 2012: guts versus surrender, work versus sloth, real austerity versus fake austerity. Beginning in 2008 Estonia, Latvia, and Lithuania voluntarily embraced an extraordinarily deep fiscal adjustment, keeping their currencies pegged to the euro while internal prices and wages collapsed. Romania and Bulgaria joined them in this exercise in 2009. By 2011, they had all returned to growth levels higher than the rest of Europe, especially Southern Europe (see figure 6.1). Maybe austerity did work after all? Again, if a picture paints a thousand words, this one takes your breath away.

Starved for good news on the austerity front, the troika of the IMF, ECB, and EC responded to the Latvian government's call to join them in a celebration of the success of Baltic States.[151] After the party in

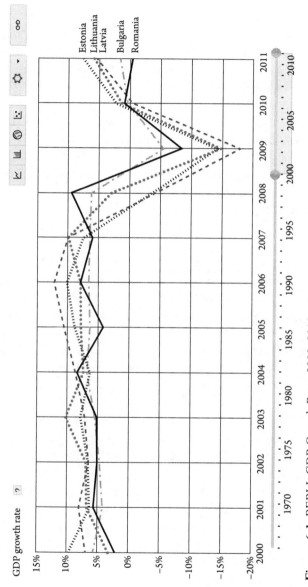

Figure 6.1 REBLL GDP Growth Rates 2000–2011

Source: Data from World Bank; last updated September 6, 2012.

Riga, an ECB board member read straight from the expansionary austerity script:

> Undertaking the necessary austerity measures at an early
> stage...allowed the Baltics to benefit from positive confidence
> effects...allowed Latvia to return to the financial markets well
> ahead of schedule...allowed growth to bounce back after exceptionally severe output contractions.... The concept of "expansionary contraction" has been used and criticized in the
> ongoing debate about growth and austerity. The Baltic experience provides an indication that this need not be an oxymoron:
> even if fiscal consolidation weighs on the growth prospects in
> the short term, it has sizeable positive effects in the medium to
> long term.[152]

Praise came from other prominent sources. For IMF director general Christine Lagarde, Latvia was an "inspiration" for Southern Europe.[153] Olivier Blanchard, IMF chief economist and austerity skeptic, noted that the Latvians "can take pain."[154] Even Hillary Clinton praised Latvia, saying that austerity will ensure a "stable, prosperous future."[155] But, the Latvians were not alone. The Romanians and the Bulgarians received praise from the austerity camp later that summer, thus joining the Baltic States' austerity alliance.[156]

Despite these states constituting an astonishing example of massive fiscal retrenchment and demonstrating a robust bounce back in growth, the REBLLs do not in fact provide much evidence for the expansionary austerity thesis. To see why, we need to understand that the economies the REBLLs built for themselves after communism were accidents waiting to happen. This is why they had to be so austere in the first place—the accident happened and it cost them a fortune. It's an accident we have already seen in this book: yet another banking crisis that ended up on states' balance sheets. No one does this sort of thing for fun—not even Balto-libertarians. We need to understand why the REBLLs were compelled to undertake such extreme measures before we can understand why their experiences prove neither the expansionary austerity thesis nor provide much in the way of portable and practical lessons for the rest of the world.

The REBLL Growth Model

By the eve of the 2008 crisis, the REBLLs had developed a unique growth model based on massive foreign investment, even more massive foreign borrowing, and economic institutions that could only be described as open to money coming in and people going out. The problem with this growth model was that it was extremely vulnerable to external shocks due to its high degree of dependence on transnational capital flows, its tendency to develop large current account deficits, and its chronically weak export performance.

They ended up this way because the post-communist period of the 1990s was one of extensive deindustrialization in the REBLLs. This prompted the migration of between 10 percent and 30 percent of the most active part of their labor force to Western Europe. These losses compounded an already weak capacity to develop infrastructure, which in turn led to the concentration of investment in real estate and finance rather than manufacturing. As a consequence, exports were never a strong foreign currency earner, which meant a shortage of foreign exchange to cover imports.[157] This led to increasing dependence on foreign capital inflows and remittances from all that expatriate labor to provide for the financing of these large deficits. Yet despite such problems these economies grew rapidly because by the 2000s there was plenty of credit at the local bank to finance consumption. There was just one problem—the local banks were not local—and neither was their financing.

Encouraged by the prospect of EU membership for the REBLLs, which made these countries appear to be undervalued assets that would appreciate simply by adopting the euro, Austrian, French, German, Swedish, and even Greek banks went on a shopping spree to buy Eastern European banks in the early 2000s. REBLL banking sectors became between 80 percent and nearly 100 percent foreign owned in short order.[158] These banks made little contribution to industrial investment, in part because there wasn't much industry in some of those states in which one could invest, so they provided instead plenty of consumer credit to cash-strapped REBLL citizens and real estate speculators. Given the spread between the home banks' funding costs and the rates they could loan at locally, this was a good deal for all concerned. This also encouraged local actors to load up on foreign currency loans, thereby building time bombs into their balance sheets set to explode the minute exchange rates moved against them.[159]

This transnational credit pump created a phenomenal construction bubble that made the Spanish and Irish property experiences look tame by comparison. Spain and Ireland managed a paltry 6 and 8 percent annual growth in construction expenditures, respectively, in the 2000s. Romania was the laggard with 11 percent yearly increases. Bulgaria busted the curve with a near 20-percent-a-year increase.[160] Therefore, while REBLL states busily cut their debt even before the crisis, their citizens and firms increased it exponentially in the form of nonproductive assets, on the back of weak exports and current account deficits, using foreign sourced cheap credit. All that was needed to make this whole system explode was a detonator—and the foreign banks provided that too.

Yet Another Banking Crisis

The 2008 crisis hit the REBLLs as a combination of a current account crisis—exports slumped as financing for imports dried up and deficits, already large, exploded—and the bursting of real estate bubbles once the foreign banks that owned their financial sectors tried to cover their losses in the credit crunch. As we discussed back in chapter 2, when a bank makes a loss in one part of its portfolio, it looks to liquidate assets elsewhere in the portfolio to cover those losses.[161] The REBLLs were the very definition of "elsewhere in the portfolio." Worried about the solvency of their home-base operations in the aftermath of the Lehman crisis, the parent banks of these REBLL banks let it be known to the REBLL governments that they were considering pulling out of their countries to supply much-needed liquidity to their core (home) operations.[162] Given the extremely open and market-friendly economic institutions of the REBLLs, these states had no way to keep capital at home. As such, they rather suddenly discovered that the Western banks didn't just own their banks—they owned their money supplies too. Fear set in, the money started to flow out, demand abroad constricted, their construction bubbles popped, and the REBLL economies collapsed (table 6.1).

Table 6.1 REBLL GDP and Consumption Growth in 2009

Country	Change in GDP	Change in Consumption
Romania	−6	−10.1
Estonia	−14	−15.6
Bulgaria	−5.5	−7.6
Latvia	−7	−22.6
Lithuania	−14	1–17.5

Source: Eurostat

At this point, the EU and the IMF intervened and orchestrated a massive bailout of the Central and Eastern European financial systems—in other words, of the Western banks' wholly owned foreign subsidiaries—just at the point when current accounts in these states were exploding. In Vienna in 2009, and long before any Greek or Irish bailout, an agreement was signed between the Western banks, the troika (EU-IMF-EC), and Romania, Hungary, and Latvia that committed Western European banks to keeping their funds in their Eastern European banks *if these governments committed to austerity to stabilize local banks' balance sheets.*[162] The Vienna agreement prevented the liquidity crunch from spreading to the rest of the REBLLs, so long as the same balance-sheet guarantee (austerity) was applied elsewhere—and it was. Once again, it was all about saving the banks, and the bill for doing so, in the form of austerity, high interest rates, unemployment, and the rest, was dumped once again on the public-sector balance sheet of the states concerned. As early as 2009, then, while the United States and Western Europe were rediscovering Keynes, the REBLLs were enforcing local austerity packages to save core EU country banks. If you think that you have heard this story already, it's because you have. It's an earlier form of what is going on in the Eurozone with the periphery states' sovereign debt and the core banks' exposures.

Given this bust and deflationary bailout, the size of consolidation following the collapse was massive: 17 percent of GDP in Latvia, 13 percent in Lithuania, and 9 percent in Estonia, with half of it enforced in the first year, and most of it, per Alesina's recommendations, on the expenditure side.[163] Double-digit public-sector wage cuts became the norm across the REBLLs despite the IMF's then managing director Dominique Strauss Kahn protesting that, at least in the case of Romania, the government should have taxed the wealthy instead.[164] Expenditure cuts of such magnitude wreaked havoc in health, education, and social protection.[165] Taxes were increased, but only on regressive value added taxes (VAT) and labor taxes. Massive tax evasion predictably followed, which simply worsened the overall fiscal situation.

Let's stop for a moment and take this in. A set of patently unsustainable and unstable economies financed by foreign credit bubbles blew up, quite predictably, the minute there was a shock to these economies. These countries are now supposed to be the role models for the rest of the world to follow? Spain is in bad shape, certainly, but is it really supposed to hollow out its economy entirely and live off more foreign borrowed money? Is Italy supposed to abandon its competitive export sector and sell off its banks? That would be what "following the example of the REBLLs" actually means. In fact, these so-called "models" are little more than the worst features of Ireland, Spain, and Greece combined, with no compensatory airbags, a sideline in divide-and-rule ethnic politics, and a libertarian instruction sheet. The REBLLs may have bounced back, but why would anyone want to copy policies that led to such an unstable and inequitable growth model in the first place? What lessons, then, are we to take from the REBLL alliance if becoming more like them is surely not one of them?

Life Lessons from the REBLL Alliance

First, to the question, do the REBLL cases actually prove that expansionary austerity works? The answer is most certainly no. While it is almost true that austerity eventually, and after huge welfare losses, put the REBLLs on an upward growth trajectory—almost true because Latvia started growing again when austerity ended in 2010—it is also clear that austerity after the crash did nothing to prevent the deepening of the economic crisis that necessitated it. Nor did the bounce back in growth have anything to do with the positive shock to expectations so central to the expansionary austerity claim. Take Latvia, for example, since it hosted the party celebrating its success. Close to 4 percent of Latvians left the country between 2008 and 2011.[166] In 2009, 79 percent of Latvians surveyed classified the economic situation in their country as "bad." By 2011, when the Latvian growth rate was the highest in the EU, 91 percent of Latvians surveyed perceived the economic situation to be "bad," and 58 percent said the worst was yet to come.[167] The best we can say in this supposed best case is that, while expectations may follow growth with a lag, they certainly do not drive it.

Second, the much-lauded catch-up is limited, fragile, and likely to be reversed. None of the REBLLs will have closed by 2013 the output gap that they opened up in 2009. Even after several more years of high growth, the REBLL states, especially the Baltic States, will remain years away from recovering the loss of output that austerity engendered. They are still poorer than they started despite all their efforts. Even at the rather optimistic growth rates estimated by the IMF, it will take Latvia until 2015 to get back to precrisis output levels.[168] In fact, according to the EC, REBLL growth is likely to be too sluggish over the next several years to sustain the recovery. According to EC estimates, the REBLLS will see their growth rates fall after 2012 to a much more modest 2 percent a year.[169] These levels will still likely be higher than in the core Eurozone countries, but the task facing the REBLLs is much harder given the scale of their losses and the unresolved fragility of their growth models.

Given this, the REBLL bounce back is simply not big enough to reverse the huge rise in unemployment in these countries any time soon. Again, taking austerity poster child Latvia as our example, IMF projections have Latvian unemployment remaining in double-digit territory until 2017, and that's with rosy growth forecasts.[170] This is no different from the situation in the PIIGS. If we add those who work part time or gave up searching for work, we get peak unemployment/ underemployment of 30 percent in 2010 and 21 percent in the third quarter of 2011. If we add emigration to the figure, we end up with an unemployment/underemployment rate of 29 percent at the peak of the Latvian recovery.[171]

Third, austerity did not work the way it was supposed to in two critical areas: on private-sector wages and on government debts and deficits. Private-sector wage cuts did not happen on the scale needed to allow the increase in cost competitiveness that the deflation engineered to be effective.[172] Unit labor costs were downwardly sticky during austerity programs despite massive public-sector cuts. This means only wage increases in Western Europe would make REBLL relative wages fall to more competitive levels, and that is hardly likely to happen in Western Europe in the middle of an austerity-induced double-dip recession. Similarly, REBLL austerity packages did not cut budget deficits as abruptly as the theory said they should. Latvia, Lithuania, and Romania ran much higher budget deficits at the peak of their austerity programs in 2009–2010 than did either Greece or Spain.

Austerity is also supposed to reduce debt. In fact, that's the whole point of it. Yet it didn't do it in the REBLLs and it didn't do it in the PIIGS. While all of the REBLLs had extremely low levels of debt—below 20 percent of GDP—going into the crisis, and had the advantage post-Vienna agreement of a sovereign bond market structure populated by patient (local or troika-tied foreign) investors who relieved bond market pressures, today they all have, with the exception of Estonia, more debt now than when they started, in some cases dramatically so.[173] By comparison, imagine what would have happened if already high Greek or Italian debt levels were multiplied by four, as was Latvia's debt when it rocketed from 10.7 percent of GDP in 2007 to 42 percent in 2012. Indeed, the REBLLs will be saddled with much higher debt levels for a long time because of their austerity. Far from blowing up the Debt Star, they have built themselves a bigger one. The candle in all of this, once again, is simply not worth the game.

Fourth, and most critical in terms of exporting this "success" elsewhere, the external demand that caused the REBLLs to bounce back cannot be used to bring back the PIIGS or anyone else. While Bulgaria and Romania have relied on domestic demand and linkages to the German auto sector as the main driver of the economy, exports make about half of the Baltic States' GDP. Since it is precisely domestic demand that suffers the most when austerity is implemented, this leaves exports as the main engine of growth. While all the REBLLs, but especially the Baltic States, have seen significant increases in exports, this provides little hope for anyone else since the REBLLs' main trading partners are countries that have by and large avoided recession since 2008, such as Germany, or recovered very quickly, such as Sweden, Finland, and Russia. Finnish growth isn't going to do much for Italy and Spain.

The Baltic States are a quick commute away from the economies of Scandinavia, to whom they offer wage arbitrage and a deregulated, culturally proximate, low-tax business environment. Spain can't do that. It's too far away and, crucially, it's too big to replicate the same trick. While Romania and Bulgaria are medium-sized, middle-income states, the Baltic states are tiny. The average Baltic state is about the same size as a New York City outer borough. They can survive in the cracks of the world economy in a way that large economies cannot. Can you imagine what would happen to political stability if 4 percent of Southern Europe's labor market left their respective countries in a three-year period? Where would they all go to find work? Lithuania?

Finally, the politics of austerity that made cuts of this magnitude possible in the REBLLs cannot be replicated in the Southern periphery, nor should we wish that it could be. A rather divisive ethnic politics was the card played by the REBLL governments in some of the Baltic States to isolate and marginalize opposition to austerity. Where that card was not played, in Romania and Bulgaria, citizen protest was strong enough to slow down the austerity drive, and most recently, defeat it at the ballot box in Romania in December 2012. Again, to take the example of Latvia, the biggest political party opposed to austerity was the party associated with ethnic Russians, which made the divide-and-conquer politics needed to isolate them, given Latvia's history with Russia, much easier.[174] Playing nationalism to force budget cuts is not a policy that ends well, as we know from the experience of the 1930s.[175] Perhaps then, once again, those old lessons from the 1930s stand up to scrutiny much better than the new lessons we are encouraged to learn from the REBLLs.

In sum, the REBLL alliance does not prove the case for expansionary austerity any more than interwar Japan proves the case for sensible Keynesianism. The political and economic structures of these states are neither transportable nor stable. Their policies prove nothing about expectations or the sustainability of consolidations. Their recoveries and economies are inherently fragile and are based upon sources of demand that cannot be replicated elsewhere. They are in more debt than when they started. Far from being a model, they are a reminder of the futility and costs of austerity.

When world leaders keen to legitimize the damage that they have already done to the lives of millions of their fellow citizens reach for examples such as these to vindicate their actions, applauding these countries for creating misery, it shows us one thing above all. Austerity remains an ideology immune to facts and basic empirical refutation. This is why it remains, despite any and all evidence we can muster against it, a very dangerous idea.

Part Three

CONCLUSION

THE END OF BANKING, NEW TALES, AND A TAXING TIME AHEAD

A Conjecture in Lieu of a Conclusion

This book has examined the case for austerity as both a sensible economic policy and as a coherent set of economic ideas, and it has found austerity to be lacking in both respects. Austerity doesn't work. Period. Insofar as the fossil record contains a few cases of what look like "expansionary fiscal consolidations," as we saw in chapter 6, these cases are either driven by factors other than what the austerity proponents maintain, or those proponents simply get the case wrong. Expectations leading to confidence fairies really are a fairy story. The few positive cases we can find are easily explained by currency devaluations and accommodative pacts with trade unions. In general, the deployment of austerity as economic policy has been as effective in us bringing peace, prosperity, and crucially, a sustained reduction of debt, as the Mongol Golden Horde was in furthering the development of Olympic dressage. It has instead brought us class politics, riots, political instability, more rather than less debt, assassinations, and war. It has never once "done what it says on the tin."

As a set of ideas, what begins as an absence in the history of liberal economic thought becomes a schizophrenia over the role of the state in the economy—the "can't live with it, can't live without it, don't want to pay for it problem"—which in turn becomes a neuralgia regarding the state in general. Expelled from the corpus of reasonable ideas after the Great Depression, austerity waited for its chance, was enabled by other supporting intellectual developments during its long hibernation in the institutions of Germany and in the minds of Austrian and Italian economists in the United States, and reappeared full-blown in the 1990s and 2000s.

Austerity has been applied with exceptional vigor during the ongoing European financial crisis, and it has produced exactly the same failures one would expect if its previous intellectual and natural histories had been investigated. The costs of this epistemic arrogance and ideological insistence have been, and continue to be, horrendous.[1] If European economic policy makers, like medical doctors, had to swear "to do no harm," they would all be banned from "practicing" economics. If austerity becomes the policy mantra of the United States anytime soon, despite all the evidence to date, we can expect it to be equally destructive there, too, and remember, we Americans are more heavily armed.

But the desire to apply austerity is not just ideological, although it is that. There are also good material reasons for the continuing application of austerity, especially in Europe—that is, clearing space on the balance sheet of sovereigns in case one of the region's too big to bail banks goes bust. What began as a banking crisis in the United States continues as one in Europe. The euro has turbocharged this problem by effectively turning the twenty-first-century European economy into a classical gold standard. The results are once more predictably awful. How did we get into this mess again?

In one sense—and leaving behind the Mother of All Moral Hazard Trades that was the generator of the European side of the crisis—the trigger for all of this was a classic case of good intentions gone bad. While the US financial system was, as we saw in chapter 2, an accident waiting to happen, what brought us down the particular path we find ourselves stuck on now was the decision to bail out the banks, starting with the US TARP program, in 2008.

I gave an analogy for why governments, especially the US government, did this earlier in the book: 150-odd million workers, 72 percent living paycheck to paycheck, 70 million handguns, no cash in the

ATMs. It still focuses the mind. Personally, back in 2008 I thought bailing out the banks was the right thing to do. I thought "there was no alternative." But as with all TINA logics, there are always alternatives. When we consider now the costs of this decision, I am no longer so sure it was the right thing to do.

To the immediate costs of the crisis discussed in chapter 2 one must add the devastation and waste caused by years of austerity policies that have cost far more than any simple bank run, no matter how big. Perhaps we should have let the banks fail. Yes, systemic risk says otherwise. But if the alternative produces nothing but a decade or more of austerity, then we really need to rethink whether the costs of systemic risk going bad are any worse than the austerity we have already, and continue to, put ourselves through.

Bailing led to debt. Debt led to crisis. Crisis led to austerity. Perhaps we could have avoided this sequence—as this book has shown, there were moments of choice. There was nothing inevitable about austerity—even if its root cause is a too big to bail banking system stuck inside a modern gold standard/monetary doomsday device that seems to have limited the options to "add central bank liquidity, squeeze the budget, and pray." But could we have done otherwise? I want to use the rest of this chapter to explore whether, like austerity itself, the game of bailing has been worth the candle of keeping the banks alive.

Part of what follows is a conjecture—the business model of investment banking may be dying. If so, all the money we spent and have lost in recession was wasted on a system that may be in terminal decline anyway. Another part is a new tale of fiscal adjustment in two small countries: Iceland and Ireland. One let its banks fail and is now doing really quite well, especially when compared to Eurozone Europe. The other bailed them out and has condemned itself to a generation of misery because of it.

The final part of this concluding chapter turns to the question of how this all ends. The discussion of the cases of austerity from the 1920s, especially the French case, shows us that austerity is generated in part by the inability of societies, as Barry Eichengreen first proposed, to agree on an equitable distribution of the tax burden.[2] There is a strong parallel to be drawn between France in the 1920s and the condition of the crisis-shocked countries today. The alternative to cut is to tax. Given this, there are two other ways out of the crisis in addition to the usual choices of inflation, devaluation, endless austerity (deflation), and default. The financial community will welcome neither of these two options, but it is not as if the other options on the table are great for them either. Those alternative choices are, first, what is known as financial repression, and second, a renewed effort to seriously collect taxes on a global scale. These efforts to get us out of this mess may not be popular, but one, or both, is coming.

The End of Banking

The story of the crisis reconstructed in chapters 2 and 3 can, and perhaps should, be seen in a bigger context. At the end of the Bretton Woods era, when the United States finally went off gold in 1971, states around the world had to adjust to what Eric Helleiner has called "the reemergence of global finance."[3] Floating exchange rates, deregulation, disintermediation, and the rest, which made finance the most profitable sector of the American and British economies by the 2000s, was the new order of things. But what was it all really based upon? After all, finance is most properly thought of as a part of the information system of the economy: linking borrowers and lenders while sitting in the middle collecting a fee. It's not an industry in the traditional sense, and it certainly should not have been producing 40 percent of corporate profits in the United States on the eve of the crisis—so why was it able to do just that?

Global finance made so much hay, not through efficient markets but by riding up and down three interlinked giant global asset bubbles using huge amounts of leverage. The first bubble began in US equities in 1987 and ran, with a dip in the dot-com era, until 2007. It was the longest equity bull market in history, and it spread out from the United States to boost stock markets all over the world. The smart cash that was being made in those equity markets looked around for a hedge and found real estate, which began its own global bubble phase in 1997 and ran until the crisis hit in 2006. The final bubble occurred in commodities, which rose sharply in 2005 and 2006, long before anyone had heard the words "quantitative easing," and which burst quickly since these were comparatively tiny markets, too small to sustain such volumes of liquidity all hunting either safety or yield. The popping of these interlinked bubbles combined with losses in the subprime sector of the mortgage derivatives market to trigger the current crisis. A picture again is useful. In figure 7.1 we see these three asset bubbles (Dow Jones Stocks, S&P's Case-Schiller Index of Housing, and gold/oil prices) scaled against time.

We can clearly see the bust beginning in housing in 2006 hitting stocks and then commodities. What we see since then are stocks rising due to central bank liquidity programs providing asset insurance for purchases of underwater equities. Commodities have also rallied as investors increasingly piled into them in an effort to find positive yield in a zero interest-rate environment. Real estate has yet to recover.

Now, take away liquidity support and the hunt for yield and there's a problem going forward. You can only generate bubbles of this magnitude if there are assets that are either undervalued, or are at least

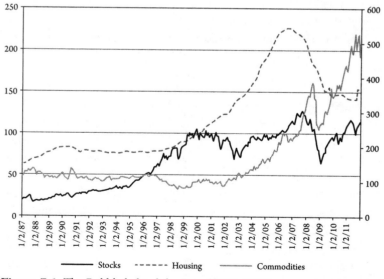

Figure 7.1 The Bubble behind the Bust (1987–2011)

perceived to be undervalued, and that can serve as fuel for the bubble. US equities had been flat for a generation back in the early 1980s. US housing was cheap and patterns of demand were changing. Commodities used to be a niche market. Finance changed all that, pumping and dumping these asset classes and taking profits along the way for twenty-five years. It was a great run while it lasted, but now, after the bust, could it be over?

Sovereigns are stretched, and eventually liquidity support and zero rates will come to an end on what will be a much weaker underlying economy. Equities will decline in value, commodities too, as global demand weakens, and housing, outside a few markets, is not going to be increasing in value at 7 to 10 percent a year anytime soon. But deprived of fuel for the asset cycle, all those wonderful paper assets that can be based off these booms—commodity ETFs, interest rate swaps, CDOs and CDSs—to name but a few—will cease to be the great money machine that they have been to date. Having pumped and dumped every asset class on the planet, finance may have exhausted its own growth model. The banks' business model for the past twenty-five years may be dying. If so, saving it in the bust is merely, and most expensively, prolonging the agony. Anticipating John Quiggin's *Zombie Economics*, we may have endured austerity to bring back the nearly dead.

Is there any evidence for this bold conjecture? A bit. Banks everywhere are delevering, which will reduce lending, hitting growth and thus the volume of business that they conduct. Bank equity prices and market capitalization have fallen drastically over the past two years. Revenues by asset class are falling. Underwriting has shrunk and trading is not what it used to be.[4] Fixed costs are increasing while bonuses are shrinking and the sector as a whole is getting smaller.[5] Meanwhile, what growth there is seems to be on the retail rather than the investment banking side.[6] But retail depends more directly on the real economy, which is shrinking because of austerity. In sum, we may have impoverished a few million people to save an industry of dubious social utility that is now on its last legs. This is a discomfiting thought that strongly suggests that we really should not have bailed them after all. And there's another reason for thinking this way, independent of this: it's called Dublin.

Tales of Fiscal Adjustment Redux: Ireland, Iceland, and the Alternatives to Austerity

The joke doing the rounds at the beginning of the crisis, before Ireland blew up, was, what's the difference between Iceland and Ireland? The answer was, one letter and six months. The joke, it turned out, was a prophecy. Ireland was discussed in chapter 3, and it was noted then that between 1994 and 2007 Irish GDP grew much more rapidly than in the 1980s and 1990s. During this boom period, when cheap money was abundant in global markets, Ireland's banking sector also grew rapidly, and on the back of the credit bubble grew a housing bubble. When the bubble popped in 2008, the Irish government issued a blanket guarantee to its banks and soon after gave five and a half billion euros to three banks: Anglo Irish bank, Allied Irish Bank, and Bank of Ireland.[7] Unfortunately, since the assets of these banks were little more than dead real-estate loans, this was just throwing good money after bad. It kept the banks going, however, until January 2009 anyway, when Anglo-Irish was nationalized—at the same time that 2 billion euros in savings were chopped off the public budget. Realizing that such ad hoc measures were not enough to stop the complete collapse of the economy, the government set up a bad bank, the National Asset Management Agency (NAMA), to take the toxic assets off the banks' books.

The end result of all this activity was a full guarantee of the assets of the entire banking system: a total bailout. NAMA bought the assets at above book value with taxpayer money, sold shares of NAMA back to the banks, and they, in turn, used these shares as collateral to get liquidity from the ECB. In short, creative accounting and a helpful government enabled the banks to walk away scot-free from the carnage they had caused. Ireland was now shut out of international markets and placed at the mercy of the IMF-ECB-EC troika. Since then, over 70 billion euros have been injected into its banking system—divided by a population of some 4.5 million. Some 47 billion euros disappeared into Anglo-Irish alone, never to be seen again.[8] The "assets" the taxpayer purchased via NAMA are not coming back anytime soon. The cost of bailing out the banks amounts to 45 percent of GDP, and that figure does not include the cost of the NAMA program, which is over 70 billion euros.[9] Under the troika Ireland has endured round after round of austerity. Because of this Ireland is often held up as a role model for austerity, implying that things are getting better and that austerity is working. As ex-ECB head Jean Claude Trichet put it in 2010, "Greece has a role model and that role model is Ireland."[10] But if one looks at the economic consequences of the bust and the bailout, it's hard to see the recovery.

The salaries of public-sector workers have been cut by close to 20 percent while regressive taxes and user fees have been increased.[11] Welfare and social spending have been sharply reduced.[12] In 2007, GDP contracted by −2.97 percent, by −6.99 percent in 2008, and −0.43 percent in 2010. Low growth returned in 2011, but at the very moderate level of 0.71 percent. Even this moderate growth, however, is suspect.

Low corporate tax rates made Ireland a popular site for multinational corporations to establish headquarters and declare their profits, which played an important role in the country's boom.[13] Google, Apple, Microsoft, and Facebook have set up headquarters in Ireland, but most of them have very few employees in the country. These firms pay a corporate tax rate of 12.5 percent in Ireland, which is just over a third of the 35 percent they would pay in the United States.[14] Because of this dynamic, Irish GDP is inflated by global firms booking huge revenues through Ireland for tax purposes. When one looks at Irish GNP, which takes out such revenues, growth declined by 2.5 percent in 2011.

This anomaly also explains the high rate of exports from Ireland, which went from 80 percent of GDP in 2007 to 101 percent of GDP in 2010, which is also held up as evidence of the boom after the bust.[15] The revenue of multinationals operating out of Ireland is booked as an export of Irish services—even if there is no real economic activity going on. Given this, exports of services have grown five times faster than the export of goods.[16]

However, as Martin Malone of Mint Partners put it bluntly, "The entire increase from 2007–2012 in Ireland's service exports is almost complete fluff...they are overstated by Euro 30 billion, which as a measure versus GNP comes to almost 25 percent of the total."[17] This overstatement of export-led recovery explains why unemployment has risen steadily, from 4.5 percent in 2007 to 14.8 percent by in mid-2012, even as emigration has risen notably, from 46,300 in 2007 to 80,600 in

2011 despite this supposed boom. Irish debt to GDP was 32 percent in 2007. Today it stands at 108.2 percent *after three years of austerity*. Indeed, if the cost of NAMA is added to the national accounts, its Ireland's debt-to-GDP-ratio would rival that of Greece. Ireland bailed its banks, and then banked on an export-led recovery without a devaluation that was based upon phantom exports that create very few jobs and that are only made possible by tax dodging. Apparently this is Greece's role model.

Dublin is not a happy place to be these days, nor is it likely to be for the next several years. The Irish government, which has implemented 24 billion euros in cuts since 2008, plans another 8.3 billion in taxes and another 3.5 billion in cuts for 2013.[18] Bailing banks and busting the state's balance sheet is an expensive business, even with real export-led growth. Continuing austerity will, as usual, only make things worse.

Iceland, in many ways, was Ireland on crack. Its bank assets to GDP ratio in 2007 was nearly 1000 percent. So when Iceland got into trouble, it was going to be the mother of all banking crises. But there was one important difference. Where Ireland followed the mantra of austerity, slashed spending, and bailed its banks, Iceland let its banks go bankrupt, devalued its currency, put up capital controls, and bolstered welfare measures. A comparison of the two is as close to a natural experiment of the effects of austerity and bailouts as you are likely to find.

Iceland's transformation from a protectionist social democracy to a laissez faire center of international finance was fast and furious. By 2007, average yearly incomes had soared to the equivalent of almost USD 70,000. The value of the stocks of the fifteen firms listed on the Icelandic Stock Exchange increased sevenfold between 2002 and 2007, and the local real estate market more than doubled in value.[19] The three Icelandic banks—Glitnir, Landsbanki, and Kaupthing—were behind this bubble. Their financial structure made Anglo-Irish look like a paragon of good management. Between 2004 and 2008, lending increased on average by nearly 50 percent a year. The banks self-funded on the basis of these loans and then invested heavily in their own stocks. When cross-financing between these three banks is added to the picture, self-investment was 70 percent of these banks' capital base.[20] If you are thinking of the great investment trusts from the era of the Wall Street Crash of 1929, you are not far off. On the back of this credit pump, private consumption increased and the Icelandic currency rapidly appreciated. By 2005, Iceland had become the most privately indebted country in the world.

By 2006, Iceland had begun to raise eyebrows abroad.[21] In February of that year Fitch Ratings issued a report stating that the Icelandic credit boom was a matter of concern, accurately predicting that even a slight global downturn would put the Icelandic banks underwater.[22] More seriously, the Icelandic banks were running out of liquidity. They began swapping their debt securities among themselves and then using them as collateral to borrow from the central bank. By the end of 2008, the central bank had lent the banks ISK 500 billion.[23]

By 2008, the Icelandic central bank found itself running out of liquidity when Glitnir, which had been struggling to refinance itself since the beginning of the year, found it couldn't access funding markets. The central bank offered it a loan equivalent to 25 percent of its reserves in exchange for 75 percent ownership, a de facto nationalization, which rather shocked the markets into action. The fallout from Glitnir immediately hit the other banks' funding sources such that private interbank credit was shut off as depositors withdrew their money. Meanwhile, the central bank was in no position to continue to act as a lender of last resort having already given away huge chunks of its reserves.

Iceland had crossed the Rubicon without realizing it. It was now in no position to bail out its banks even if it wanted to, and it wasn't in the euro so the ECB had no obligation to help. On October 6, 2009, the government passed emergency legislation that gave them the power to overtake troubled financial institutions, bypassing the central bank.[24] Any plans the central bank harbored to bail the banks were now dead. The banks were to be allowed to go bankrupt and be taken into receivership. Their debts were not socialized; instead bondholders and foreign creditors bore the brunt of adjustment.[25] The IMF was called in.

Significantly, the road ahead was not austerity. The immediate focus of the IMF program was to prevent the exchange rate from deteriorating to the point where it would cause hyperinflation in such a heavily import dependent economy. Breaking with IMF orthodoxy, capital controls were introduced, locking investors in. Three new banks were set up to take over the management of domestic accounts and performing assets. Nonperforming assets were left in the old, bankrupt banks. Creditors were free to claim those assets, but not the assets transferred to the new banks. In other words, the government decided to let institutional creditors shoulder the cost of the collapse rather than the taxpayers.

Allowing the banks to fail meant that they were less of a financial drain on the state. Their recapitalization cost close to 20 percent of Iceland's GDP[26]—a massive sum for such a small country, but an awful lot less than the still-growing Irish bailout via NAMA. Iceland's debt-to-GDP ratio in 2012 stood at 99 percent, a figure that would have been much higher had the banks been bailed out.[27] Instead of austerity, the government pursued an expansionary policy behind these capital controls for the first year, followed by an evenly distributed fiscal consolidation. Everyone tightened their belts as the cuts were accompanied by a shift to a more progressive tax code that included substantial tax hikes for top earners and measures to help low- and middle-income families.

In terms of growth Iceland has fared better than anyone would have dared hope. The IMF projected a contraction of 10 percent in 2009 that turned out to be 6.5 percent. Apparently—note to John Cochrane—fiscal multipliers do exist after all. In 2010, the economy contracted by 3.5 percent, and in 2011 growth returned at 3 percent, based in part upon real exports of goods and services.[28] Growth at a similar rate has continued into 2012, placing Iceland near the top of OECD growth performance.[29] With higher marginal rates of taxation, returning growth, capital control, and equal fiscal tightening, Iceland is on target to eliminate its budget deficit in 2014 and have a budget surplus of 5 percent in 2016.[30]

Unlike Ireland, employment growth in Iceland has been strong. Unemployment increased drastically after the crisis, going from a pre-crisis low of just over 2 percent to a high of 9 percent in 2009. Even at its height, however, unemployment in Iceland was lower than the European average and well below the levels of other crisis-ridden countries.[31] Unemployment stands at just under 6 percent in October

2012. To put that into perspective, only Norway, Switzerland, Austria, the Netherlands, and Germany—none of which experienced a serious crisis—boast lower rates of unemployment.[32]

Finally, consider this bonus to the Icelandic experience of not bailing their banks. After initially falling quite rapidly, real wages have been rising at a brisk pace.[33] This has helped reverse the trend of growing inequality witnessed between 1995 and 2007, when the after-tax Gini coefficient rose from 0.21 to 0.43, mostly because of the high incomes of top earners—a phenomenon seen in all highly financialized societies. By 2010, when capital income had collapsed and the tax code was reformed, the Gini coefficient was pushed back down to 0.245.[34]

Can we generalize from Iceland to elsewhere? After all, we previously argued that we should not generalize from the experience of the REBLLs to the much larger states of Southern Europe. So what's different here? Although Iceland is the definition of tiny, what matters in this case is not the size of the country, or its population, but the size of the banks relative to the size of the economy, its bank-assets-to-GDP ratio. In Iceland, that ratio was nearly ten to one at the time of the bust. In the United States that ratio was just over one to one. Iceland had ten times the bust of the United States' worst-case-ever scenario, and it not only survived, it prospered.

Iceland not only survived letting its banks go bust, it became a healthier and more equal society in doing so. Although Ireland is a small country, and Iceland is literally the size of a city, and a small one at that, perhaps there are still, in the comparison of these states, two key lessons for the natural history of austerity. First, when you do the exact opposite of the austerity playbook, you not only survive, you prosper. Second, above all, don't bail your banks.[35]

Taxing Times Ahead

So if Iceland gives us a positive lesson, where do we go from here? As it's usually set up, the options going forward in highly indebted societies are limited and uniformly bad: inflation (bad for capital and creditors), deflation (bad for workers and debtors), devaluation (bad for workers in the longer term and impossible in the euro), and default (everyone loses.) Debt forgiveness is a particular form default, which Iceland made a part of its strategy for cleaning up its mortgage market. The United States could really do with some of that, but unless you let the banks fail, creditors will always resist forgiveness. So, what does that leave us with? More austerity in the short to medium term to be sure. But the lessons of the 1920s suggest that this will come to an end by prompting one of the other options: devaluation, inflation, or default. Is there a more stable alternative future path? Yes, there are two, and neither is great, but they are, as Churchill said about democracy, the worst options except for the alternatives.

The first path is usually known by the pejorative sobriquet of *financial repression*. Carmen Reinhart and M. Belen Sbrancia recently discussed this possible path.[36] They concluded, by examining episodes of past high indebtedness, that states restructure their financial systems in periods of crisis in such a way as to allow them to create "captive audiences." Banks, pension funds, and other long-term debt holders are "encouraged" through capital controls, interest-rate ceilings, and other devices to hold a large amount of government bonds. The government then pays a low nominal interest rate on the bond while running a near-balanced budget with a positive but small rate of inflation. This creates an effective negative real interest rate on the bond such that the value of the debt shrinks over time.

Financial repression is basically a tax on captive bondholders and it works best when you have banks over a proverbial barrel—such as when they are losing money and are dependent upon state funding, just like today. Policies such as this "played an instrumental role in reducing or liquidating the massive stocks of debt accumulated during world war two."[37] Reinhart and Sbrancia find that the "liquidation tax" generated from financial repression amounted to, in the cases of the United States and United Kingdom after World War II, the equivalent of 3 to 4 percent of GDP a year.[38] Raising such funds would facilitate a significant debt reduction over time, and it would obviate the need for a corresponding period of extended austerity—austerity that wouldn't work anyway since it would cause the debt to get bigger, not smaller.

So we are talking taxes, which no one likes. But since I found out that in 2010 I paid more taxes than the General Electric Corporation—

really, I did, and so did you—I'm willing to give financial repression a chance.[39] Yes, it will greatly limit my opportunities to buy and trade exotic derivatives and engage in international financial arbitrage games, but you know what? I'm willing to give it up. After thirty years of all the gains and all the tax cuts going to the people who brought us the bubble, payback is coming. Not because of Occupy Wall Street and not because of my personal preferences, but because it's so much easier and more effective to do than it is to enforce self-defeating austerity that it's bound to happen.

Speaking of taxes, it's not just going to be sophisticated qua-si-hidden liquidation and/or so-called Tobin taxes on financial transactions that are levied, either. Personal taxes have room to grow, too—especially in the United States. A recent analysis from the Congressional Research Service, which gives us an idea of what Congress might be thinking, noted that top marginal rate of income tax in the United States in the 1940s an 1950s, the heyday of US power, "was typically above 90%" while "the top capital gains tax was 25%." Meanwhile "the share of income accruing to the top 0.1% of US families increased from 4.2% in 1945 to 12.3% in 2007."[40] This is an interesting juxtaposition of observations, to say the least. The justification for such reductions and gains is, of course, the supply side argument that more cash at the top leads to more investment and growth. Interestingly, the report concludes that "the result of the analysis suggests that changes over the past 65 years in the top marginal tax rate and the top capital gains tax do not appear correlated with economic growth."[41] But they do appear to be "associated with the increasing concentration of income."[42] Given that the US federal state spends 25 percent of GDP while only raising 18 percent, a cynic might conclude that the fact that all this income is concentrated in so few hands might make it a good target to reduce that budget deficit.

Pushing us further in this direction, several very serious and very mainstream economists are beginning to say things that a few years ago would have been heard only in the drunken bar huddling of disgruntled lefties. For example, tax economists on both sides of the Atlantic are beginning to argue that higher taxes on top earners can pay for debt reduction. Apparently, there is no need for austerity, after all. And since the upper-income brackets benefited the most from the last three decades of tax cuts, it would seem only too fair to increase the tax burden on them just a little. President Bush's former economic advisor Glenn Hubbard thinks that raising top taxes will never raise enough revenue to make a dent in the debt.[43] Moreover, 2012 presidential candidate Mitt Romney found such redistribution to be "un-American," showing an astonishing ignorance of the policies of Dwight Eisenhower (Republican).[44] But there is plenty of room to tax at the top *because of the bailouts*. It's the gift that keeps on giving. After the 1929 crash income inequality and financial-sector pay declined sharply relative to ordinary earnings, but this time they did not, so taxing now is simply taking the bailout back to the taxpayer. This idea does not just resonate with progressive circles in the United States.

A team of German economists recently calculated that a one-time capital levy of 10 percent on personal net wealth exceeding Euro 250,000 per taxpayer could raise revenue by 9 percent of GDP. This tax would fall on the wealthiest 8 percent of Germans, which as a group owns close to two-thirds of national wealth. At Euro 500,000 (2.3 percent of taxpayers) and Euro 1 million (0.6 percent of taxpayers), the levy would still raise the equivalent of 6.8 percent and 5.6 percent of GDP. Being one-time levies because of the "debt emergency," even if you factor in "expectations effects," such policies should not lead to dramatic changes in investment behavior or capital flight provided that the state credibly commits to keeping them as a one-off tax.[45] And just as in the United States, the space for more taxation in Europe at the top end of the distribution seems to be quite ample, as top marginal incomes are estimated to be no less than 20 percentage points below those that would maximize tax revenue to the government.[46]

Peter Diamond of the Massachusetts Institute of Technology and Emanuel Saez of the University of California, Berkeley, go further, arguing that taxing the top 1 percent at over 80 percent would raise, not lower, revenue.[47] They argue explicitly that "very high earners should be subject to high and rising marginal tax rates."[48] According to their calculations, raising the average income tax for the top income percentile to 43.5 percent from 22.4 percent, the level of 2007, would raise revenue by 3 percent of GDP, which is enough to close the US structural deficit while still leaving very high earners with more after-tax income than they would have had under Nixon.[49]

Finally, there are pots of gold offshore too. With all that money going to the top of the income distribution over the past thirty years an entire industry sprang up to hide it. Unfortunately, they hid it in plain sight in a handful of tax havens such as the Cayman Islands and Switzerland. If big, powerful states want to go after it, they know exactly where to look, which is what they have been doing of late.[50] Indeed, a new study by James Henry of the Tax Justice Network estimates that there is as much as 32 *trillion dollars*, which is over twice the entire US national debt, hidden away offshore not paying taxes, which makes for a very tempting target indeed.[51]

Think about this for a moment. Austerity has been tried and will keep being tried, at least in the Eurozone, until it's either abandoned or voted out. It doesn't work. In fact, as we have repeatedly seen, it makes the debt bigger and not smaller. So the debt is there and it needs to be paid off, or forgiven. Given that forgiveness outside the confessional is unlikely, and the other options, inflation and default, are even worse, it is pretty much inevitable that over the next few years financial repression and higher taxes on top earners will become a part of the landscape. The ongoing (at time of writing) negotiations over increasing taxes as part of the resolution of the 2013 US fiscal cliff debacle is simply the beginning. This is how we are going to deal with our debts—through taxes and not through austerity. Not because austerity is unfair, which it is, not because there are more debtors than creditors, which there are, and not because democracy has an inflationary bias, which it doesn't, but because austerity simply doesn't work.

POSTSCRIPT 2014: WHEN YOU FIND YOURSELF GOING THROUGH HELL, LOOK FOR AN EXIT [1]

Austerity Revisited

Just as one swallow does not make a summer, so a year and a half of more data doesn't change my assessment of austerity. It's still a dangerous idea and it still doesn't work. Yet the past 18 months has been hailed, especially in Europe, as a vindication of austerity policies because Europe is supposedly now in recovery. As can be seen in the chart below, it is true that the Eurozone economies as a whole stopped contracting in the last two quarters of 2013, while the UK has gone from laggard to leader in the growth stakes. Yet some issues need to stand scrutiny for the claim that austerity is producing what little growth we see in Europe to bear weight even if we discount the most recent figures, which augur a triple dip recession.[2]

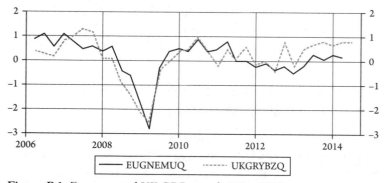

Figure P.1 Eurozone and UK GDP growth 2006–2014
Source: tradingeconomics.com

The first is the claim to recovery itself as a result of austerity policies, which once again deliberately confuses cause and correlation. As an analogy, imagine someone has a form of stomach cancer that leads doctors to have different diagnoses of what to do. The patient is encouraged not to undergo chemotherapy but to try an alternative therapy of acidic enemas and a crash diet of 800 calories a day. The doctors and the patient persist with this therapy and the condition worsens. Eventually the same doctors intervene and apply chemotherapy. The patient recovers, but she is now so much weaker than she should be from the experience that her prognosis is now much more uncertain. Nonetheless, the doctors proclaim that while the chemotherapy was important, it was the enemas and the crash diet that really saved her. This is precisely what has happened in the Eurozone, with austerity as the alternative treatment and ECB liquidity provision in 2011 and 2012 as chemo. It's quack medicine being hailed as a wonder drug despite the evidence.

But even if we accept that growth has returned despite austerity, it's hard to see the emergence of a sustained rate of growth in the recent figures sufficient to reduce the huge pile of debt that austerity has generated. Remember, government debts got bigger, not smaller, under austerity. Countries saw their underlying GDP shrink—and their debts get reciprocally bigger, the more that they cut—the so-called "denominator" effect. In fact, if one looks at gross debt figures, Portugal has doubled, Spain has nearly tripled, and Ireland has nearly quintupled their respective debts. Second, if as *Austerity* maintains, what is at the heart of all this is a banking crisis nested within a set of dysfunctional institutions and not a public spending crisis, then one must ask how austerity, fiscal tightening, budget cuts, and all the rest can possibly restore growth. The wrong diagnosis, and the wrong medicine, is still unlikely to lead to a satisfactory recovery.

Budget Cuts Still Can't Solve a Banking Crisis—But a New Central Bank Chief Can Buy You Time

This book was published in April 2013, nearly one and a half years ago at the time of writing this postscript. I finished the actual writing of *Austerity* in October 2012, just as the full effects of the "Draghi put" were beginning to be felt in European bond markets. The "Draghi put" was the Long Term Refinancing Operations (LTRO) of the European Central Bank (ECB) of December 2011 and February 2012, combined with new ECB President Mario Draghi's promise of July 26, 2012, that he would do "whatever it takes" to save the Euro. That is, if he had to, he would buy sovereign bonds directly to keep yields down through a program called Outright Monetary Transactions (OMT).

Never has so much effect been gained by doing so little. Words alone, it seemed, calmed the markets because OMT was not actually used. Its promise, plus a trillion and more in liquidity, sufficed. From January 2012 through August 2014, Italian ten-year yields fell from 7.1 to 2.73 percent. Spanish ten-year bonds went from a peak of 7.36 percent in July 2012 to 2.4 percent today. Meanwhile, Greece's ten-year bond went from a post-bondholder haircut of 29.89 percent in May 2012 to a comparatively mild 6.2 percent today despite enduring a collapse of a nearly a third of GDP and seventeen straight months of deflation.[3] So the yields went down, which is good. But what does a central bank liquidity-put designed to back-stop financial markets that are running out of funding (the purpose of the LTROs and OMT) have to do with cutting the state's budget? Recall that austerity is defined in this book as:

> A form of voluntary deflation where the economy adjusts through the reduction of wages, prices, and public spending to restore competitiveness, which is (supposedly) best achieved by cutting the state's budget, debts, and deficits. Doing so, its advocates believe, will inspire "business confidence" since the government will neither be "crowding-out" the market for investment by sucking up all the available capital through the issuance of debt, nor adding to the nation's already "too big" debt.[4]

Given such a definition, the answer is, nothing at all. Budget cuts can't triage a banking problem, but that hasn't stopped its advocates pretending that it can. To see why this is the case, let's recap what's actually still going on in Europe.

The crisis in Europe had two phases. The first phase we can call "the break-up that never happened," which began in May 2009 when then ECB president Jean Claude Trichet told the markets that "we are not at all embarking on quantitative easing."[5] In saying this Trichet effectively told the markets that the ECB was not going to backstop the system such that holders of Euro-denominated sovereign debt could not swap bonds for cash on demand.[6] The diverse set of national bonds whose yields had tracked German bunds for seven years started to move rapidly apart from them. This was amplified by a change in government in Germany from a left to a right coalition, which led to damaging equivocation over the backstopping of Greece. Greece's own admission of dodgy deficit numbers plus the dozen or more "Merkozy" summits that followed, where Germany and the ECB played "pass the parcel" over who was going to stop the rot, added still more uncertainty to the mix. The end result was that by mid-2011 periphery bond yields had split apart from German bunds and yields rose to unprecedented levels.

These yield spikes were not however driven by market concerns over the ability of the Spanish, or any other state, with the possible exception of Greece, to pay its pensions to retired teachers. The markets were instead pricing in the risk that the Eurozone would break up. Specifically, they were pricing in the possibility that the Euro-denominated assets that market agents held lots of would rapidly devalue in the event of a break-up of the Euro since neither the central bank (the ECB) nor the most solvent state (Germany) seemed prepared to backstop them. Dithering for nearly two years over the meaning of treaty articles and inconclusive policy responses from multiple summits made the situation worse.[7] The state of the public purse was simply not driving events.[8] The perception of assets going to zero without insurance was.

The second phase of the Eurozone crisis might be called the "US crisis redux." It ran from April to November 2011 and it made an already bad situation critical. In this latter phase of the crisis large European banks saw their funding sources dry up in an almost perfect re-run of the US crisis of 2007-8.[9] As chapter 3 of *Austerity* details, both London-based Repo markets and US money market funds stopped lending to

European banks when the collateral they pledged in such transactions, European sovereign debt, lost value.[10] As liquidity drained from the system yields spiked across the board from already high levels as markets began to worry about default-risk among European banks ricocheting back to their sovereign hosts. Even Germany's famously dull Bunds spiked in the first half of 2011 as break-up risk and default risk combined to compel the ECB into action, the result of which was an initial trillion and a half Euros of basically free money being funneled into European banks under the guise of the LTRO and ELA (Emergency Liquidity Assistance) programs. But the public bailout of the European banking sector did not stop there.

As Oliver Wyman, the banking industry's key consultant group noted in October 2013, of the €700 billion that European banks have raised since 2007, "€350 billion has come from the public sector....In fact, total state support approved for the EU financial sector totals more than €5 trillion, equivalent to 40 percent of [Eurozone] GDP."[11] Of capital injected into banks to keep them afloat, "only about 10 percent of the original capital injected has been repaid."[12] Returns on equity have collapsed to around 4 percent while cost bases have risen, all of which implies without official support these banks would be bankrupt. Again, as Oliver Wyman put it bluntly, "otherwise insolvent banks have been recapitalized and the monetary policies of the ECB and national central banks have allowed banks to fund themselves at low cost."[13]

So to return to the first point, what does any of this—Draghi and friends dumping five trillion Euros into the banking system to save it—have to do with cutting state budgets? The answer is still nothing. Central bank policy, not public sector cuts, brought down yields and stabilized European sovereign debt markets. And so long as the markets believe that Draghi's promise to use Outright Monetary Transactions (OMT)—direct bond buying by the ECB if yields spike again—is credible, then those yields will stay down. Bad central bank policy, intergovernmental fudging, incomplete institutions, and a slow-motion bank run through the wholesale markets for interbank funding in Europe caused the crisis.[14] Five trillion Euros of taxpayer-backed money, better central bank policy, and a move toward completing the institutions of a proper banking union to compliment the monetary union have stabilized the crisis. But it has not solved the crisis, despite appearances. This is a critical issue that we return to below.

Debts, Yields, and Austerity

This "liquidity-not-austerity" effect is seen most clearly in the relationship between government debt and bond yields. The pro-austerity camp argues that yields were spiking because the markets cared about the "out of control government spending and debt" rather than break-up or liquidity risk, and so spending had to be cut. If so, central bank policy should have been ineffective since yields and debts should be *positively* correlated. As the debt goes up so should the yield as default risk is priced in. No amount of central bank liquidity should reduce yields on government debt if the markets care about the absolute volume and/or the rate of growth of the debt. In fact, backstops to bond markets should make austerity-hungry markets more nervous rather than less since it would imply official support for supposedly unsupportable debt loads. Yet if this is true, then to take two examples, Ireland and Italy's numbers on debt loads relative to their ten-year bond yield since 2012 look really odd.

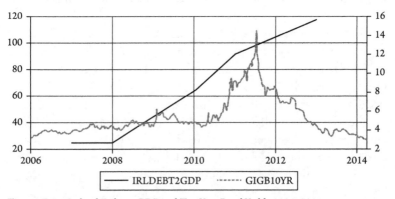

Figure P.2a Ireland Debt to GDP and Ten-Year Bond Yields 2006–2014

Source: tradingeconomics.com.

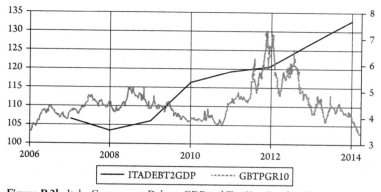

Figure P.2b Italy: Government Debt to GDP and Ten-Year Bond Yields 2006–2014
Source: tradingeconomics.com.

You don't have to estimate a fancy statistical model here to note that since the "Draghi-put" yields and debt-loads have been *negatively* correlated in a rather large and obvious way, and this is true of every bond issuer in Europe. Government debts have continued to go up as austerity bites while the yields have continued to go down, the exact opposite of the austerity case, which strongly suggests that central bank policy was what counted, and liquidity, not austerity, calmed the markets. And if the lower yields now enjoyed by sovereigns means that the affected governments have a bit less interest to repay, then they can have a less restrictive fiscal stance, and yes, Europe can grow, a little. But let's be clear that growth is coming from central bank policy pulling down yields, not austerity. Austerity continues to harm, not help.

The comparison with the US, which triaged and delevered its banks 2008–09 could not be clearer. The US, despite its historically slow recovery, has much lower unemployment rates while the Eurozone as a whole hovers around 12 percent. Europe's periphery sits in near perma-depression conditions, with Greece and Spain bearing 27 and 24 percent unemployment respectively. Even the success cases, according to the European Commission at least, of Portugal and Ireland have 15 and 11.5 percent unemployment respectively, and that factors out the depressing effects (in both senses of the word) of immigration on these numbers. But even the brute averages across these two areas tell a simple story.

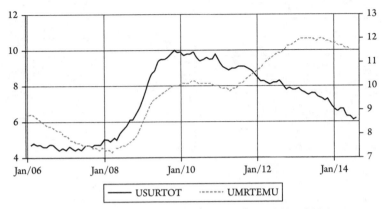

Figure P.3 US and Eurozone Unemployment Rates 2006–2014

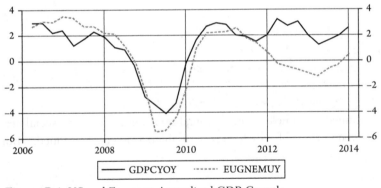

Figure P.4 US and Eurozone Annualized GDP Growth
Source: tradingeconomics.com.

At least as far as Europe is concerned, if this is a recovery, then it is some definition of the word recovery I have hitherto been unaware of. Unemployment is stuck at level once deemed not just politically unacceptable but economically impossible. Similarly, when annualized, European GDP growth is barely positive and yet the Eurozone recovery is being heralded from the rooftops at every possible opportunity. Sadly, it seems that facts still don't get in the way of a good ideology, which means harmful policies are still the only game in town.

Austerity after 2013—Performing Recovery Despite the Evidence

When one digs into the country cases the story does not get any better for those still arguing for austerity. The UK has seen a dramatic return to growth despite its cuts. But does this vindicate austerity policies as Chancellor George Osborne and his "booster-in-chief" Chris Giles at the *Financial Times* seem to argue? The answer is once again no. To see why one must first recall the rather mild telling-off the IMF gave the UK for excessive austerity when they did their country report in May 2013.[15] The IMF advocated that infrastructure spending be brought forward to offset the contractionary effects of austerity policies. Little did they know that the UK had already done just that.

As Simon Wren Lewis and Jonathan Portes both noted, UK austerity was effectively put on hold in late 2011 and the beginning of 2012 when the UK government began to notice that a contractionary policy was not expansionary after all.[16] Specifically, real government consumption went from -0.1 percent in 2011 to +2.6 percent in 2012. This boost to consumption, right where it matters in terms of consumptive bang-for-the-pound, effectively put austerity "on-hold" in the UK before the IMF even issued its warnings. The rhetoric of austerity continued nonetheless, and the reality of budget cuts on social services, one third of which targets disabled workers, continued.[17] But with the chokehold off the economy could breathe. What let the UK economy spring from the trap, however, was the same thing that landed the UK in such trouble in the first place.

While housing is not single-handedly driving the UK recovery, it is integral to it. The boost to growth that easing up on austerity provided in 2012 was given a further boost by an unexpected fall in the UK savings rate later that same year.[18] This fall in savings, plus the UK government's decision to put the UK financial sector back together again with bigger airbags, combined with the ease-off on austerity to pump up a new housing bubble, centered once again in London.[19] The result has been the restart of mortgage lending via a scheme that gets 80 percent loan to value (LTV) loans to 95 percent at the expense of the public purse, basically giving everyone who qualifies their own Fannie and Freddie guarantee. The result has been a dramatic surge in house prices in London and a new consumption spurt due to this wealth effect.[20]

In other words, it's the same old growth model put back together again, and this time around even the Bank of England is growing concerned.[21]

Indeed, it is a remarkable commentary on the state of the hollowed-out finance-monocrop that is the UK economy that even such modest growth is met with a massive flood of imports, with the UK posting the worst balance of payments figures since 1955.[22] Growth may be there, but it is primarily benefitting Chinese and other exporters—not the British worker. It also tells a sorry story about who is buying all that property when British real wages have fallen eight percent since the crisis, with increasing evidence of international money laundering on a massive scale increasingly coming to light.[23]

Finally, if the UK really were still being as austere as the government pretends, then the confidence effects of the cuts would be seen in UK business confidence surveys as early as 2010 when the cuts were announced, as per the "expansionary-contraction" thesis detailed in chapter 5. Instead, we see UK business confidence plummeting from April 2010, reaching its nadir in January 2012, before bouncing off bottom just when the aforementioned factors all came into play.[24] We should have also seen a pick-up in business borrowing levels earlier if such confidence effects were in play. Yet the Bank of England's "Trends in Lending" series saw consistent falls in business lending from January 2010 through to January 2013, which only began to creep up once these stimulus factors came into play.[25]

This is perhaps of little surprise when one considers that the government's own 2013 review of its "ward of state" bank—the Royal Bank of Scotland Group—concluded that RBS had significantly overshot in its reduction of lending to business such that "a perception has risen among some small and medium sized enterprises (SMEs) that RBS is unwilling to lend. A recent customer survey showed that 30% of SMEs disagreed with the statement that RBS was "open for lending.""[26] This result was typical of UK bank financing of SME's with three out of four applications being rejected in 2013. After all, if the bank that is 81 percent owned by the state will not lend to business, why should anyone else?[27]

That the UK's opposition Labour party has now embraced the need to continue the cuts even if they win the next election speaks to the sorry state of the revenue side of the UK budget more than it does to any logic of expansionary fiscal contraction.[28] Put simply, UK public spending was made possible by over-reliance on a financial sector that is now under pressure to lend more while building capital and reducing risk, so tax revenues have slumped. That, plus a politically unsustainable tax-put on the middle of the income distribution for revenue that neither the government nor the opposition wants to take the blame for, means cuts rather than revenue increases are on the cards for both parties if they want to win the next election.[29] As such, continuing cuts in the UK make sense more as political insurance for both parties to stay in power than as any sensible economic strategy.[30]

Ireland exited its bailouts to great applause in December 2013 and is now able to float ten-year bonds at a little over 3 percent. That they are able to do so has once again everything to do with the "Draghi put" lowering bond yields and bank funding costs and very little to do with Ireland's extraordinary austere budgetary stance over the past several years where it "consolidated almost 20 percent of GDP over an 8 year period, with no significant industrial or social upheaval."[31]

Although a recent European Parliament–sponsored account of austerity programs in the periphery conducted by the think tank Brugel argued that, in the Irish case, "fiscal consolidation was done in a balanced way…which contributed to restored trust in Irish public finances,"[32] it is hard to square this with the fact that Ireland's gross debt to GDP now stands at 123 percent and may rise to 140 before stabilizing, while its budget deficits are still in the range of 6 to 8 percent, even if they are projected to come down further. So the key point remains—was it budgetary consolidation that restored trust or was it the knowledge that Irish and other Euro denominated bonds could be swapped for cash that lowered the yields? The evidence for the former position seems to be more asserted than demonstrated.

Consider that in Ireland, while all that ECB liquidity has lowered yields, it has also allowed Irish banks to play an indefinite game of "extend and pretend" with the non-performing loans (NPLs) that constitute, according to the IMF, nearly a quarter of all loans on their books.[33] One way or another those losses will have to be recognized, and when they are there is, according to Morgan Kelly, a very high probability of a very large knock on effect to the small and medium-sized enterprise sector as the banks call in whatever loans they can to cover these losses, which will have a major and deleterious effect on employment.[34]

But even if one allows for all this, the lessons of the Irish experience are simply not applicable to other states. Again as the Brugel report notes, Ireland's "tremendous success in the export sector…substantially reduced the impact of the fiscal adjustment on the economy."[35] However, that trick is not available to anyone else since "much of the [Irish] export base can be considered exogenous to the economy," such that Ireland was able to "engineer a deflation…while leaving exports untouched."[36]

As *Austerity* details, the majority of Ireland's exports are "boxes in boxes out" tax arbitrage and transfer pricing games that are possible only because of its unique role as a gateway to Europe for foreign multinationals due to its super-low corporation tax rate. This export story is neither sustainable if growth falters in third-country markets, nor is it repeatable elsewhere since, by definition, not everyone can be a tax-arbitrage hub.[37] And none of the relatively rosy projections for post-bailout Ireland that ignore these facts bother to factor in that Ireland has lost 50,000 graduates a year to immigration for the past five years. They are Ireland's future tax base that the government needs to pay back that massive pile of debt they accumulated by bailing their banks and then applying austerity. Sadly, they don't seem to be coming home any time soon.

The other periphery states of the Eurozone, even the larger and less peripheral ones, have fared little better one year on. Portugal may be next to exit its bailout programs, but unemployment stands at 15.3 percent and it is estimated to rise again to 17.7 percent in 2014.[38] Public debt has risen to 124 percent of GDP and, while its growth profile picked up in 2013, there is no evidence that this is due to the confidence effects of austerity finally kicking in. After all, their debt is still rising because of the severity of the cuts. Rather, like France in mid-2013, Portugal's recent growth spurt is due to the fact that both countries missed their deficit targets in 2013 such that when their deficits increased the economy's automatic stabilizers (taxes down, transfers up) actually kicked in and provided a fiscal boost.

Portugal grew fastest in the second quarter of 2013 and growth slowed the more it tightened in later that year. France grew most rapidly that same quarter to great applause—and then growth fell to zero the next quarter as they tightened again. Growth happened because both countries *stopped doing austerity*, briefly, not because they were doing it. And while Portugal has across many indices been one of the best pupils in the austerity class, but despite all their efforts, and the effect of the "Draghi put" on bond yields, investment has fallen sharply over the past two and a half years. This hardly bodes well for future growth to pay back all that debt, debt built up because of the austere crisis response, and not prior to the crisis.[39]

Spain and Italy have hobbled along with insolvent banks and insolvent governments respectively, with "extend and pretend" being the name of the game in politics and economics in both countries. Spain recorded marginal positive growth in the latter half of 2013, but its annualized growth rate remained negative while unemployment remained stuck at 26 percent. Italian unemployment performance in 2013 was much better than Spain, coming in at half the Spanish rate, but annualized growth remained negative throughout 2013, as its debt to GDP ballooned to 132 percent. Meanwhile, continued political instability in Italy suggests that the road forward for more austerity and technocratic structural reform is limited at best.

Greece, the poster child for both profligacy and austerity, suffered the harshest austerity regime and has fared worse of all. Even the European Parliament-sponsored Brugel review admits as much with a wry degree of understatement. As they put it in their assessment of how Greece has responded to austerity, "the first and most striking finding is that reality proved the initial program assumptions largely wrong."[40] Those initial assumptions, concerning projected paths of GDP, domestic demand, and unemployment under austerity that structured both Greek programs' outcome expectations were off by twenty, twenty-four, and seventeen percentage points respectively versus that reality.[41]

In fact, Greece lost nearly a third of GDP in a five-year period while generating unemployment of over 25 percent. And while their debt load fell to 157.2 in 2013, it has risen again to 175.1 by August 2014. The notion that this debt load is ever going to be repaid is pure fantasy. But it is fantasy with a cost since it is in Greece where the human cost of austerity comes to the fore. To take just one set of public health examples, since the beginning of the crisis austerity, cuts in Greece have resulted in a 25 percent cut in hospital and primary care funding, which in turn resulted in a 32-*fold increase* in HIV infections between 2009 and 2013. Suicides have increased by 45 percent and infant mortality has increased by 43 percent over the same period. And in 2013, Greece had its first domestic cases of malaria since 1974.[42]

So Why Does It Continue? Welcome to the Class-Specific Put-Option

So if it's still not working, another year on, why does it continue? In *Austerity*, the answer I gave was that it was part of the "Greatest Bait and Switch in Human History," where the private debts of the banking systems of the developed world were bailed and recapitalized via the public sector balance sheet. The result was that private debt was turned into public debt such that the benefits went to the insiders and the costs went to taxpayers. After another 12 months of thinking about this, I came to a more pointed description of this process in a column I wrote for *The Guardian* newspaper in 2013.[43] That is, while austerity is still the "Greatest Bait and Switch in Human History," it is perhaps more appropriately thought of as a "class specific put option" written on the majority of asset-poor OECD citizens. To see why this is the case, we have to remember what a put-option is and how banks actually work.

A put-option is a contract where the writer of the contract has the obligation to pay for X asset at Y time, the right to which the buyer can exercise as "the option." On this definition, the so-called "Greenspan put" in global markets prior to the crisis was a put-option in the sense that once US asset values fell to a specific level, the US Federal Reserve (the writer of the contract) cut interest rates to compensate for those losses. The more recent "Draghi put" was a put-option insofar as the ECB wrote an option to cover the risk of break-up and liquidity risk in the Eurozone via the LTRO programs. Austerity is then a "class-specific put-option" in the following sense.

We hear a lot today about the increasing concentration of wealth and income in countries across the OECD, especially concerning the increasing share of income held by the top one percent, which peaked at 24 percent in the US just before the crisis and may have surpassed that figure in 2013.[44] But if one expands that set a little to include the top ten percent of the income distribution, one finds that they take home over 50 percent of all income. Although the figures are not as easily available, it's probably then reasonable to say then that the top

30 percent of the income distribution of these societies earns the vast majority of income and owns most of the assets of these countries.

Now, given that assumption, let's think about how banks actually work, since things are seldom what they seem. When you "save," you don't actually save anything. When you deposit money in a bank in an act of saving, you are actually giving—at least in many European countries—an un-secured loan to a highly levered derivatives trading firm on the hope that you will get it back with interest later on.[45] Similarly, when a bank gives you a loan to buy an asset, a house for example, that asset is the bank's liability. Their asset is instead the loan, which is your liability, aka the mortgage. So like exports and imports in the global economy, bank/borrower assets and liabilities are symmetrical and sum to zero.

Given this, when you bail out a bank or a banking system, you are not just bailing the bankers. You are bailing the savers, the pensions, the mortgages, the derivatives written on these loans and annuities, and all the rest that constitute the bank's assets, which are your liabilities and vice versa. So when governments bail banks they are simultaneously bailing the assets and incomes of the top 30 percent of the income distribution.

So think of bailouts as a put option exercisable by the top 30 percent on the bottom 70 percent of the income distribution. When the top 30 percent, people like me and (possibly) you, get our assets bailed and public debt balloons as a consequence; the cost of exercising the put-option is paid for by people who don't have many such assets and rely on government spending and public goods, but that's what gets cut. The poorest segment of society is forced to pay out on an insurance policy that they never agreed to guarantee, and for which they never received a single insurance premium from the holders of the bailed (i.e. insured) assets. This is why austerity is best thought of as a class-specific put-option. It's free asset insurance for the top end of the income distribution, those who also just happen to be the people that vote most and fund elections. That in the long run this individually rational action will prove collectively disastrous for the top end too is a cost not internalized in the option's price. But it is one that we all have to pay the longer austerity continues. One can only help but wonder if the May 2014 elections to the European parliament, which saw large gains for nationalists, populists, and non-mainstream left parties is the first sign of the 70 percent waking up to the reality of the put?[46]

The New Institutions of Austerity: The Good, the Bad, and the Pointless

Despite all this, some interesting institutional engineering has occurred in the Eurozone over the past 12 months. Some of it is good, some of it is pointless, and some of it is downright dangerous. In the first category, we can put the EU banking union proposal that found its final form in March 2014. The banking union is a critical part of the institutions that should have been built at the time of the monetary union but were not.[47] That is, when you have a bunch of national level banks all borrowing in a foreign currency, which is what the Euro is to each of them *de facto*, and many of them have become bigger than the sovereign underwriting their risks, then you had better have some pan-European institutions for bank supervision, bank regulation, and common deposit insurance. Sadly, since the EU seemed to think, and still thinks, that the only institutions worth building were those that restricted the actions of sovereigns rather than banks, that didn't happen, the result of which is the banking mess described above. Yet as of early 2014, the banking union finally found its feet, which is good. But once again, a closer inspection suggests that it's not quite the set of institutions it pretends to be.

First of all, while any banking union is better than no banking union, this one still has several key pieces missing.[48] To be credible, the banking union needs, as Paul De Grauwe put it, "an authority with financial clout. They don't have it so we don't have a banking union."[49] De Grauwe's problem is that while the agreed-upon single supervisory mechanism that places the ECB in charge of the solvency of banks above national regulators is a good idea, and a common resolution mechanism that gives those regulators the power and money to shut down failing institutions is better still, the entire set-up is cash limited at $55 billion Euros. That's not a lot of cash when one considers that Hypo Real Estate, a German mortgager that got into trouble in 2008, needed over 100 billion Euro in state guarantees to stay afloat.[50]

Second, the fund itself will be built up over an eight-year period, which is a bit of a prayer that nothing much happens between now and 2022, while its recapitalization if it's ever used will be limited by the fact that there is no mutualization behind it.[51] And perhaps most crucially, even if we get eight years down the line without a hiccup, this set up does nothing for what are euphemistically known as "legacy assets"—the between 1.2 and 1.5 trillion Euro in NPLs cluttering up the balance sheets of European banks right now.[52] As Wolfgang Munchau has repeatedly argued, this set up may work for the next crisis, but it does nothing for the current one.[53]

Third, while the Single Supervisory Mechanism (SSM) and Single Resolution Mechanism (SRM) are much needed new institutions, banking unions are stabilized by deposit insurance more than any other factor. And while the banking union agreement guarantees normal deposits of up to 100,000 Euros across the union, there is no central fund to back this up. It all falls on the national authorities, which is the problem that banking union was supposed to solve in the first instance. The other "big-bag-o'-Euros" out there, the European Stability Mechanism (ESM), the successor to the European Financial Stability Fund (EFSF) that bails out states cannot be used to either refund the SRM, nor can it pay out over deposit insurance shortfalls. In short, the banking union that Europe needs, one that would allow today's legacy assets, mainly the bad loans stuck in the Spanish and related banking sectors to either be asset-swapped out or recorded as losses without triggering a systemic implosion, needs something more than this to be effective. It needs some form of common deposit insurance fund, an ECB special purpose financing vehicle to act to take the NPLs off the banks' books, or an extension of the ESM to work properly, none of which seems to be on the cards.

It does however signal the winding down of official support for the European banking sector, which may have several unintended consequences. One, the possible future implosion of the Irish SME sector, was noted already. The other is the further downgrading of European banks rather than their stabilization, which is what the ratings agency Fitch did to 18 EU banks right after the banking union deal was signed.[54] As Fitch put it, "the likelihood of a downgrade or downward revision is based on further progress being made in implementing the legislative and practical aspects of enabling effective bank resolution frameworks, which is likely to reduce implicit sovereign support for banks in the EU."[55] For some banks then at least, the banking union may be more bad news than good, which is bad news for Europe as a whole.

While the new institutions of the banking union might be a qualified good, some others such as the ESM and its policy arm, Outright Monetary Transactions (OMT), might be considered a tad pointless.[56] After all, these institutions are a bit like the old doctrine of Mutually Assured Destruction (MAD) from the cold war. It works only because it isn't used. If the doctrine were ever tested, the results would be disastrous for both sides.[57] If Spain, for example, applied to the ESM for a loan and OMT is activated to relieve its bond yield strains, it would be tantamount to a full admission of sovereign insolvency, which would start the very bank run through the bond markets that these institutions are designed to avoid. At that point, as bond dealer Bill Blain put it, these new institutions would be "enough to cover the first 20 seconds of the next European financial crisis when the NPLs are in the region of 1.5 trillion."[58]

Some of the other new institutions, such as the Treaty on Stability, Coordination and Governance (renamed the intergovernmental Fiscal Compact) that came into effect in March 2012 are however downright dangerous.[59] This new treaty calls for national budgets to be "balanced or in surplus" in the medium term with enforcement of this rule guaranteed by stricter monitoring and "preferably constitutional" provisions in national legal frameworks. Countries that have "significant observed deviations" from the new fiscal limits enshrined in the treaty will have automatic sanctions placed upon them. In addition, signatory states agree that, "all major policy reforms that they plan to undertake will be discussed *ex ante* and, if appropriate, coordinated among themselves" (Article 11).[60] As if the limits on actions by states to compensate for exogenous economic shocks were not already binding enough, the EU just set them tighter—but to what end?

The specifics of this treaty strain basic logic. For example, the macroeconomic imbalances procedure (MIP) at the heart of the treaty, which sets the "scorecard" for how well countries are doing, allows countries to have a maximum current account deficit of four percent or a surplus of six percent.[61] Given that imports and exports sum to zero, that surplus of +2 percent must be offset somehow. But as *Austerity* and a host of other analyses have pointed out, we can't all run a surplus at once. Someone has to buy the exports, and if the treaty disallows corresponding deficits inside the Eurozone then they must be dumped outside. But with the US consumer cash-strapped and the

Asian economies also running on exports, it's far from clear who that can be. Deficits and surpluses may sum to zero, but in the EU, only one side of the equation is up for punishment. When it was reported that Germany actually ran a 7.3 percent current account surplus in early 2014 and the European Commission referred to this as a structural imbalance, Germany publically refused to take the criticism.[62]

The treaty is also riddled with such distributional and power imbalances. The MIP set unemployment as "excessive" at only 10 percent or above, while public debt is "excessive" once it gets over 60 percent. Sustained high unemployment is then tolerable, moderately high public debt is not, and budget deficits above 3 percent are still deemed quite unacceptable. Add this all together, and then recall the Treaty article where all major policy reforms must be discussed *ex ante* among signatories, and you might just get the feeling that the EU is trying to make fiscal policy illegal.

Regardless of whether one is a Keynesian or not, such a fiscal stance is building fragility into the system since even the most liberal OECD states still tax and spend at least 30 percent of GDP. Tying the state's hands *ex ante* to this extent while completely ignoring the level of internal demand or the possibility of serious external shocks shows that Eurozone governance hasn't moved very far in its thinking over the few years. The project is still all about trying to make the entire Eurozone into a giant Germany via wage reductions that will result, in theory, in a perma-surplus against the rest of the world. That can never work on its own terms, and it certainly cannot work if the underlying problem is still a banking crisis that is being at best half-addressed by a set of incomplete institutions.

In short, Europe is not and still cannot be made into a single economy. It is constituted by different varieties of capitalism that work on orthogonal principles.[63] The current path of recovery via structural reform (more on this shortly) and new treaty commitments ignores this fact, trying to make very different sets of national institutional complementarities into one set of complimentary trans-national institutions. Economies are historically specific complexes of institutions and ideas. The current attempt to turn the whole of Europe into a net exporter in the German image cannot work once one recognizes this. Just as designing one set of flawed banking institutions to cover the continent risks ending badly, we risk doubling-down on our downside odds with a flawed one-size fits all fiscal reform agenda. There have indeed been some positive institutional reforms in the past year, but as is usually the case, they are nested in some severe accidents-waiting-to-happen. We have a whole new set of stringent rules to stop the public sector doing things while the new rules on the private sector, where the problems still lie, are at best half-hearted measures.

Between the ECB's Stealth Bailout and the Goldilocks' Dilemma

Partial, positive, and pathological institutional reforms apart, what we are left with on a day-to-day basis is the ECB's on-going stealth bail-out of the European banking system. What is keeping the proverbial wheels on the wagon is still central bank liquidity support, but that may be running into its own limits. What the LTRO program incentiv-ized periphery banks to do is best summarized in a ditty told to me by a Spanish bond trader:[64] "You borrow at 1 (percent) and buy (a local bond) at 10 (percent). You use the spread to bury the dead (non-per-forming loans (NPLs) on your balance sheet). You bank it at four (the bond) and Repo more (use the lower yielding and higher rated bond to borrow more money–again), then you hit-up the Germans (the ECB) for more (*pace*–five trillion Euros in total support)."

In other words the LTRO program is not just backdoor quantita-tive easing that uses local bank balance sheets as a surrogate for the ECB's balance sheet. It is a stealth resolution mechanism for all of the NPL's that clutter up the balance sheets of European banks and that continue to block the credit channels to the real economy. This is why European growth is so sclerotic. Not because public debts are too high–US debt is higher and yet growth is faster there because the US delevered and recapitalized its banking system. The Eurozone has not yet done that.[65] What Draghi has done to date is to flush the system with liquidity. More needs to be done.

Partly because of the fear of what a fundamental restructuring of the banking system will do to the real economy, and partly because in the Eurozone, 80 percent of intermediation activities are done by banks and not by capital markets, there is nowhere else to park the dodgy assets that need to come off these banks' balance sheets except the ECB, and they don't want the job. The LTRO and related programs have bought time—but they have not brought solvency to the sector. The ECB recently announced a set of targeted LTROs and negative deposit rates to encourage more lending to the real economy and bring down the Euro to boost exports.[66] The results to date have been weak. Deflation seems to be taking hold throughout the Eurozone and growth remains sclerotic.[67] Moreover, the "success" of the LTRO program in bringing down yields may built a kind of "Goldilocks' Dilemma" into Eurozone policy that makes this situation all the tougher.

As I argued in a piece in *Foreign Policy* magazine in July 2014, imagine that the Eurozone abandons austerity tomorrow and growth accelerates.[68] As a result, interest rates will have to rise. At that moment, the periphery banks holding all the local bonds that they bought with free LTRO cash will see their asset base shrink in value as yields go up, bond prices go down, and their balance sheets implode. Given this, growth can't get "too hot." The ECB needs an environment of slow but positive growth for this stealth resolution mechanism to work itself out. However, not only is such a process painfully slow, if growth is "too cold," these policies can't work, since only higher rates of growth will allow the banks to repair their balance sheets as new loans replace their NPLs. Given this constraint, where growth can't be either too hot or too cold, any loosening up on austerity risks undermining the policies that have brought yields down and re-liquidated the banks.

The ECB seems to be pinning its hopes on negotiating this dilemma on a new set of stress tests called the Asset Quality Review (AQR).[69] The AQR potentially provides the ECB with a way to triage the worst offenders of the banking system without setting off a general panic. By admitting a few bad apples without suggesting that the whole barrel is rotten, "bad bank" solutions, such as Ireland's National Asset Management Agency (NAMA) and the proposed (at the time of writing) triaging of Portugal's Banco Espirito Santo (BES), may become the preferred model for other states' financial sector restructuring, which could have a positive effect on the needed downsizing and recapitalization of the European financial sector, despite the Goldilocks' constraint.

Yet even here the problems are much larger than are commonly acknowledged. Price Waterhouse Cooper's European Portfolio Advisory Group calculated in July 2014 that outstanding European NPLs stand at 1.22 trillion Euros, which means NPLs have increased 2.5 times since 2008. So despite raising 350 billion Euro in new capital and getting 350 billion more from public sources—and around 50 from the issuance of complex securities called "contingent capital (co-co's)"—the entire sector still needs a capital raise of around 300 billion. Doing this in the context of a "one NPL at a time" bail-out via backdoor QE in a Goldilocks' constraint is hard enough. But doing it in the context of self-harming, and ultimately pointless austerity policies and attendant growth destroying institutions makes it much harder still.[70]

The Persistence of—and Resistance to—Austere Ideas

Ideas move at a different speed from policy. Having an idea is costless while admitting one's ideas are wrong is costly. Implementing new ideas into policy is therefore both costly and slow. This is why governing ideas change more slowly than policy. And yet the past year has seen more than a few dramatic shifts in the topography of ideas on austerity, but not where it matters most.

The first place to look for any change in ideas is the least likely place to find it. That would be in the policy stances and research documents of the Troika (the European Commission, the ECB, and the IMF) whose analyses framed austerity policy in Europe. Given how large the forecast errors were in the policy estimates of the Troika, as noted above, one would think that some new thinking might have occurred in response to these errors, and indeed, as we shall see that has indeed happened with one third of the troika, the IMF. With the other two thirds however, we see a shift in emphasis, but the underlying ideas remain the same, despite the evidence.

The Brugel report on austerity commissioned by the European Parliament highlighted earlier usefully analyses the language of Troika documents over time and notes the shift from the use of terms such as "fiscal," "consolidation," and "reform," which dominated the initial reform documents to a greater emphasis on terms such as "growth" and "employment."[71] This is perhaps unsurprising given the lack of growth and high unemployment produced by the implementation of these policies.[72] Alongside this shift, however, is another shift, associated with terms such as "structural reform" and "privatization," which increase in use over this same period. This perhaps suggests that in highly stressed economies where confidence effects failed to show up, other revenue and growth strategies had to be found. But most tellingly, as far as admitting error is concerned, acknowledgement is in short supply. As the Brugel report notes, "since greater economic and social cohesion is a major EU objective…we study how often issues such as poverty, fairness and inequality are discussed in the documents," and they note that "except for Greece, the issue received practically no attention in the Commission program documents."[73] Taken together, such inter-temporal shifts hardly suggest a paradigm shift in thinking among two-thirds of the relevant policymakers.

The False Promise of Structural Reform

One could cite this shift from austerity to structural reform and privatization as evidence of new thinking in terms of a renewed emphasis on growth over austerity via structural reform. But it's really part of the same old set of ideas. First you consolidate, then you do structural reform, then you grow, in theory. This is a massive topic and I would be the last person to argue that the countries of Southern Europe do not need their share of reforms. Indeed, as I argued in *Austerity*, two of them in particular, Greece and Portugal, may need entirely new business models. But as the recent history of European and other structural reform efforts have shown, getting substantial economic reform in these countries is not going to happen if the method employed is top-down technocratic command and control. Moreover, if the reforms are based upon errant assumptions in the first place, then the chances of success diminish further.

First of all, attempting to reform labor and product markets in the middle of a depression is akin to repairing the roof when it's on fire. The oft-heard argument that this has to be done now because the Southern economies didn't do any reforms previously when the "good times" were here does not stand empirical scrutiny. As Peter Hall showed recently, on the OECD index for product market regulation, a reasonable index of flexibility, from 1998-2003 Italy and Spain outperformed Germany and the Netherlands.[74] Similarly, as Hall also notes, "measured in terms independent of wage costs, labor productivity increased in countries such as Portugal and Greece (although not in Spain and Italy) at rates commensurate with those in Northern Europe over the decade up to 2009."[75] Along these metrics at least, the notion that these countries haven't reformed at all is simply not true.

Take Italy and Spain, for example. Much is made of how so-called "insiders" (unionized workers) benefitted from the Euro as wage costs soared and competitiveness slumped. As a consequence, the Troika argues that wages for these workers, as a necessary part of the adjustment, need to fall to restore competitiveness. Yet as Jonathan Hopkin has demonstrated, Italian unionized industrial wages were pretty much flat throughout the 2000s.[76] Ironically, the folks that made out the best were those in the non-tradable sectors that formed part of the Berlusconi "pro-business" coalition. Given this, labor market reform in Italy has the wrong target in its sights.

In Spain, the sections of the labor market bearing most of the downward costs of adjustment and unemployment are young workers on temporary contracts. That is, those already working in the most flexible part of the labor market.[77] How making Spanish labor markets more flexible at this juncture will restore growth in Spain, or anywhere else, is therefore unclear. Ireland, for comparison, already has some of the most flexible labor markets in the world. It's not clear how abolishing Ireland's already low minimum wage will restore the balance sheet of Anglo-Irish Bank, or how, to take another comparative example, getting rid of the Greek taxi driver's monopoly in Athens will lead to a faster recovery in the Greek export sector.

Finally, as Pepper Culpepper's analysis of the Monti government's inability to get reforms through in Italy without the support of social partners spells out clearly, and the World Bank's 2004 report on a decade of structural adjustment programs (structural reform in the third world) previously admitted, countries need to own reforms for them to work.[78] Brussels can insist on reforms, but that doesn't mean states will persist with them, especially if the logic behind them is so flawed to begin with. Democracy is not a moral hazard problem to be overcome: it is the key to reform.

Indeed, the entire fascination with structural reform of labor markets as the key to growth is at best dubious since it's based upon a rather stunning misreading of Germany's economic turnaround in the mid-2000s.[79] Germany's 2000s turnaround is often attributed to the so-called Hartz reforms of that decade, which reduced welfare protections and increased labor market participation. Germany "took the bitter medicine," so the story goes, and so should everyone else. The problem is that the medicine can't work for two reasons. The first we have encountered already. The whole of the EU can't run a surplus against the rest of the world. Germany is only Germany because everyone else isn't Germany. An entire continent can't play the same trick when they are each other's major export markets.

Second, and more importantly from the point of view of structural reform, the idea that the Hartz reforms led to Germany's recent growth spurt turns out to be empirically false. Dustmann et al., have shown, using German data, that the reason wages fell in Germany was the reunification of the country a decade earlier plus the expansion of the German auto-sector abroad, both of which limited wage increases for a decade before the Hartz reforms. This plus lower input costs from Eastern European suppliers over that same period led to even more price-inelastic export goods that benefitted from the boom of the 2000s and continuing demand from outside the EU post crisis.[80] All the Hartz reforms actually did was create a very low-paid, sheltered, low-productivity service sector in Germany that has increased German inequality quite dramatically, to the point that Germany has just brought in a minimum wage for the first time.[81] If Dustmann et al are correct, then the ability of anyone else to pull this trick off is zero.

Given all this, why then do we see this shift in focus from the expansionary wonders of austerity to the necessity of structural reform? We see it because "structural reform" is where you move the goalposts to once the first set of goals turns out to be a mirage, as expansionary fiscal consolidation and debt reduction via austerity turned out to be. The only problem is that structural reform's proponents are going to have to move the goalposts again once these strategies also fail to produce positive results, as they have done so many times before, if they are not embedded in the societies that undertake them.

The IMF and Tensions in the Troika

The one part of the Troika that has substantially shifted their ideas is the IMF. As *Austerity* details, starting in 2008 under then Managing Director Dominique Strauss-Kahn, the IMF hewed to a much more expansionary line than it had done in previous crisis episodes. Cynics, like me, initially thought this was a case of "now that core country assets are at risk, we bail rather than fail," but the transformation has proven to be more than opportunism. As Cornel Ban details, the IMF's policy ideas have shifted substantially over the course of the crisis across multiple positions.[82]

The most well-known shift is the so-called "Battle of the Boxes" where the IMF estimated negative fiscal multipliers greater-than-one for the periphery countries of Europe, which meant that a one Euro cut in public expenditure led to a greater-than-one Euro cut in final consumption and GDP, with no offsetting confidence effects.[83] Negative multipliers also imply positive ones, as the reciprocal demands, and as such this challenge was not limited to the technical boxes of IMF reports. In putting this out there, the entire neoclassical edifice of the ECB and EC approach to the crisis was challenged from within the Troika itself.

Unsurprisingly, the EC hit back at the end of 2012 with its own version of multiplier estimates to counter the IMFs, arguing that, in essence, Troika policies were fine, and the multipliers would have been less than one such that contraction would have had a positive effect after all, had it not been for lot of people talking about the break-up of the Euro, which made things worse.[84] The IMF continued with this new line despite this attempted refutation by the EC, and also the ECB.[85] Indeed, the IMF's research thrust over the past five years has moved quite far from being the advocates of consolidation that they once were. Inequality as a constraint on growth, the need for higher taxes on top earners, the positive effects of public investment, environmental, and even wealth taxes now litter the IMF's research landscape.[86] And most recently the IMF just put the final nail in the coffin on Reinhart and Rogoff's pro-austerity "Growth in the Time of Debt" paper.[87] Indeed, the IMF has gone so far as to make the *Washington Post* publish under the headline that "Communists Have Seized the IMF!"[88] Perhaps hyperbolic, but when *this* IMF is in the same policy bed as the EC and the ECB, continued frictions are bound to result.

From Excelgate to the End of Austerity?

Speaking of Reinhart and Rogoff, perhaps the most dramatic turn-around in thinking in the past year has come from these two economists. Famous for their paper "growth in a Time of Debt" hat predicted a rapid fall in future growth rates if debt to GDP ratios went past

90 percent, a University of Massachusetts at Amherst economics graduate student asked Professor Reinhart for the excel file that their paper was based upon, got it, and picked it apart until nothing was left, all to great public *sturm und drang* in what became known as "Excelgate."[89] The robustness of the results notwithstanding, I have a degree of sympathy for Reinhart and Rogoff's position. As I argued in *Austerity*, given a choice between having more or less than 90 percent debt, and holding the method of debt reduction apart, who wouldn't want less rather than more? Not paying back lots of interest is probably a better thing than doing so, on balance.

What got these two economists into trouble was less what they said than the manner in which it was picked up by those Aditya Chakrabortty at *The Guardian* calls "Austerity Jihadists," who used the 90 percent meme to beat the drum for cuts everywhere regardless of the qualification and caveats of the original paper. Taking the authors down was therefore more about taking the wielders of the 90 percent meme down more than anything else. Battered and bruised from this affair, one might expect a doubling-down by Reinhart and Rogoff after these attacks. But they simply carried on with their work, letting the data take them where it will, and where it took them to today is quite remarkable.

In January 2014, Reinhart and Rogoff authored a new piece NBER working paper called "Recovery from Financial Crises: Evidence from 100 Episodes."[90] As well as extending prior work on the costs and duration of crises, this paper is remarkable for its core claim that the current downturn, especially in the Eurozone, has no comparison. This time, apparently, it really is different. Indeed, their conclusion is worth quoting at length:

> "The current phase of the official policy approach is predicated on the assumption that growth, financial stability and debt sustainability can be achieved through a mix of austerity and forbearance (and some reform). The claim is that advanced countries do not need to resort to the more eclectic policies of emerging markets, including debt restructurings and conversions, higher inflation, capital controls and other forms of financial repression. Now entering the sixth or seventh year (depending on the country) of crisis, output remains well

below its pre-crisis peak in ten of the twelve crisis countries. The gap with potential output is even greater. Delays in accepting that desperate times call for desperate measures keep raising the odds that, as documented here, this crisis may in the end surpass in severity the depression of the 1930s in a large number of countries."

When the two intellectual figures perhaps most synonymous with arguments *for* austerity, in the public mind at least, have come this far, it shows us how in some quarters there really has been a shift away from austerity thinking in a very short period, which is most welcome. Sadly, those quarters do not write policy for the Eurozone. That's done by the Troika and implemented by governments keenly aware that they are exercising the class specific put-option as described above, which is why, despite such ideational shifts, policy continues.

In closing this postscript, a special mention must be reserved for the pre-ideological thinking of François Hollande, President of France, for actually justifying French budget cutbacks in January 2014 by invoking Jean Baptiste Say's truism that supply creates its own demand.[92] I've talked long and hard about the bankruptcy of both European banks and European ideas, but it takes a lot to beat this as an example of the bankruptcy of a political class. When the putative socialist alternative to austerity thinking goes one better than the opposition citing naive supply-side ideas that are 211 years old for support, you know that austerity is going to keep going despite any and all evidence, because most of all, it remains a dangerous, but seductive, idea.

Mark Blyth
South Boston, Massachusetts
August 2014

NOTES

FM

1. Tony Judt's *Ill Fares the Land* (2010) is a must read in this regard.
2. Isabel Sawhill and John E. Morton, "Economic Mobility: Is the American Dream Alive and Well?" *Pew Charitable Trust*, 2009, Economic Mobility Project; Tom Hertz, "Understanding Mobility in America," Washington DC, Center for American Progress, April 26, 2006.

CHAPTER ONE

1. John Cochrane "Fiscal Stimulus, Fiscal Inflation, or Fiscal Fallacies?" Version 2.5, February 27, 2009, http://faculty.chicagobooth.edu/john.cochrane/research/Papers/fiscal2.htm.
2. For the premier academic treatment of the relationship between inequality and credit, see Raghuram G. Rajan, *Fault Lines: How Hidden Fractures Still Threaten the World Economy* (Princeton, NJ: Princeton University Press, 2010).
3. "United States of America Long-Term Rating Lowered to 'AA+' due to Political Risks, Rising Debt Burden; Outlook Negative." *Standard & Poor's*, August 5, 2011.
4. Oliver Blanchard, "2011 in Review: Four Hard Trutths," IMF Direct, December 21, 2011, http://blog-imfdirect.imf.org/2011/12/21/2011-in-review-four-hard-truths/.
5. Figures from the Trading Economics website, http://www.tradingeconomics.com/data-all-countries.aspx.
6. How the big banks of Europe fit into our story of why austerity has become the only game in town will concern us much in chapter 3.
7. A solvency problem is what happens when short-term liquidity problems become long term. Flooding the markets with cash stops short becoming long.
8. Deficits were supposed to cause inflation. It turns out that they did not.

9. For the outside, and more accurate figure, see Better Markets, "The Cost of the Wall-Street Caused Financial Collapse and Ongoing Economic Crisis Is More Than $12.8 Trillion." September 15, 2012, http://bettermarkets.com/sites/default/files/Cost%20Of%20The%20Crisis.pdf.

10. Aaron Kirchfeld, Elena Logutenkova, and Nicholas Comfort, "Deutsche Bank No.1 in Europe as Leverage Hits Valuation," *Bloomberg*, March 27, 2012, http://www.bloomberg.com/news/2012–03–26/deutsche-bank-no-1-in-europe-as-leverage-hits-market-valuation.html.

11. Tyler Durden, "Presenting Total Bank Assets as a Percentage of Host Country GDP," February 17, 2010, http://www.zerohedge.com/article/presenting-total-bank-assets-per-centage-host-countries-gdp.

12. Not only that, unilateral cutting worsens the ratio of debt to GDP, making existing debt more expensive at the same time that tax receipts fall.

13. For a wonderful example of this as pure propaganda, see the ECB-produced cartoon on the "inflation monster," http://vimeo.com/12324309.

14. This is why the emphasis put on the Greek government's ability to build a coalition for austerity policy in 2011 was at best half the answer. If all your trading partners are cutting too, then there is no external demand to make up for the collapse in domestic demand. All that does is shrink the economy and increase your debt relative to your GDP.

15. The second edition of Quiggin's brilliant *Zombie Economics* contains a chapter on austerity. John Quiggin, *Zombie Economics: How Dead Ideas Still Walk Among Us* (Princeton, NJ: Princeton University Press, 2010).

16. Leigh Phillips, "ECB Austerity Drive Raises Fears for Democratic Accountability in Europe," *The Guardian*, August 22, 2011; Mort Zuckerman, "America Has No Choice but to Enter Its Own Age of Austerity," *Financial Times*, July 14, 2011, "The A-List" Commentary; Alberto Alesina, Silvio Ardagna, Roberto Perotti, and Fabiano Schiantarelli (2002), "Fiscal Policy, Profits, and Investment," *American Economic Review*, 92(3): 571–589; Peter Coy, "What Good Are Economists Anyway?" *Bloomberg Business Week*, April 16, 2009, cover story.

17. Carmen Reinhardt and Kenneth Rogoff, *Growth in a Time of Debt*, National Bureau of Economic Research (hereafter, NBER) working paper 15639, Cambridge, MA, January 2010.

18. See, for example, John Irons and Josh Bivens, "Government Debt and Economic Growth: Overreaching Claims of Debt 'Threshold' Suffer from Theoretical and Empirical Flaws," Economic Policy Institute, Briefing Paper 271, Washington DC, July 16, 2010. Irons and Bivens take the 90 percent threshold idea to task on grounds of reverse causation. That is, slow growth causes debt buildup.

19. Simon Johnson and James Kwak, *White House Burning: Our Founding Fathers, Our National Debt, and Why It Matters to You* (New York: Pantheon Books 2012), 163.

20. Ibid.

21. Menzie D. Chin and Jeffry A. Frieden. *Lost Decades: The Making of America's Debt Crisis and the Long Recovery* (New York: W. W. Norton, 2011).

22. Paul Krugman. *End This Depression Now* (W. W. Norton, 2012), 141–143.

23. Eric Helleiner and Jonathan Kirshner, eds., *The Future of the Dollar* (Ithaca, NY: Cornell University Press, 2009).

24. They might turn out to be quite small, at least for anyone not in the financial sector. I return to the issue of financial repression in the conclusion.

25. For a typical example, see the two-page spread from the Peter G. Peterson Foundation, "For a Stronger Economy, Deal with the Debt," in *Bloomberg Businessweek*, August 27, 2012. It contains a linear projection out to 2040. By that time global oil supplies may have run out, and the last thing we may care about is sovereign debt.

26. "Budget of the United States Government, Fiscal Year 2002," Executive Office of the President of the United States, 224, table S. 2, http://www.gpo.gov/fdsys/pkg/BUDGET-2002-BUD/pdf/BUDGET-2002-BUD.pdf.

27. Alberto Alesina, "Tax Cuts vs. 'Stimulus': The Evidence Is In," *Wall Street Journal*, September 15, 2010, Opinion; Carmen M. Reinhart and Kenneth S. Rogoff "Growth in a Time of Debt," *American Economic Review*, 100, 2 (2010): 573–578.

28. Timothy Noah, "Introducing the Great Divergence," *Slate*, September 3, 2010, Part of a series entitled "The United States of Inequality," http://www.slate.com/articles/news_and_politics/the_great_divergence/features/2010/the_united_states_of_inequality/introducing_the_great_divergence.html.

29. See US Census Bureau website, http://www.census.gov/hhes/www/poverty/about/overview/index.html, accessed September 19, 2011.

30. Robert Wade in John Ravenhill (2010), *Global Political Economy*, 3rd ed. (New York: Oxford University Press), 396.

31. That is, while workers' money wages have increased, when adjusted for inflation, they have remained stagnant. See Lawrence Mishel and Heidi Schieroltz, "The Sad but True Story of Wages in America," Economic Policy Institute, Washington DC, March 15, 2011, http://www.epi.org/publication/the_sad_but_true_story_of_wages_in_america/. For a handy graphic of the same, see Zaid Jilani, "As Wages Stagnate, the Typical American Family is Working 26 Percent Longer than in 1975." Think Progress, July 11, 2011, http://thinkprogress.org/economy/2011/07/11/265311/graph-family-26-percent-wages/?mobile=nc.

32. For contrasting academic and popular renditions of this, see "Strategies for Fiscal Consolidation in the Post-Crisis World," IMF Working Paper, Fiscal Affairs Department. February 4, 2010, http://www.imf.org/external/np/pp/eng/2010/020410a.pdf. And Mort Zuckerman, "America Has No Choice but to Enter Its Own Age of Austerity," July 14, 2011, *Financial Times* A-List comment, http://blogs.ft.com/the-a-list/2011/07/14/america-has-no-choice-but-to-enter-its-own-age-of-austerity/#axzz2Es8OMDcs.

33. Smith, Adam (1776), *An Inquiry into the Nature and Causes of the Wealth of Nations*, ed., R. H. Campbell and A. S. Skinner (Indianapolis, IN: Liberty Fund, 1981), 341.

34. We note in particular how the crisis was at base a crisis of the "instruction sheet" of neoclassical economic theory. Indeed, the crisis itself can be considered a $13 trillion experiment on the robustness of these ideas, which begs a very important question. If these ideas were indeed falsified in the crisis, why are they still being used by financial and governmental elites to diagnose the crisis?

CHAPTER TWO

1. The same morality play is the British Government's explanation for the riots of August 2011 and the EU-IMF-Troika's lauding of the Baltic States as austerity champions in July 2012. Morality plays cover all contingencies.

2. Andrew Lo, "Reading about the Financial Crisis: A 21-Book Review," mimeo, prepared for the *Journal of Economic Literature*, October 24, 2011. Available at http://mitsloan.mit.edu/finance/pdf/Lo-20120109c.pdf.

3. Lo, "Reading about the Financial Crisis."

4. Raghuram Rajan, *Fault Lines: How Hidden Fractures Still Threaten the World Economy* (Princeton, NJ: Princeton University Press, 2010); James Barth, Gerard Caprio Jr., and Ross Levine, *Guardians of Finance: Making Regulators Work for Us* (Cambridge, MA: MIT Press, 2012); Simon Johnson and James Kwak, *Thirteen Bankers: The Wall Street Takeover and the Next Financial Meltdown* (New York: Pantheon Books, 2010).

5. Gary Gorton, *Slapped by the Invisible Hand: The Panic of 2007* (New York: Oxford University Press, 2010).

6. Greta R. Krippner, *Capitalizing on Crisis: The Political Origins of the Rise of Finance* (Cambridge, MA: Harvard University Press, 2011).

7. T-bills were in short supply because Asian governments were vacuuming up as many as they could to add to reserves and manage their exchange rates. See Martin Wolf, *Fixing Global Finance* (Baltimore, MD: Johns Hopkins University Press, 2008); and Eric Helleiner and Jonathan Kirshner, *The Future of the Dollar* (Ithaca, NY: Cornell University Press, 2009), chap. 3.

8. As we shall see later, this fear of contagion is what in part drives austerity in the Eurozone.

9. "Mark to market" accounting rules also contributed.

10. If anything, it's the absence of the state in the repo markets that's worth commenting upon, since the absence of the state's guarantee of insurance explains the system's vulnerability to a bank run.

11. Assets are tied to the economy and can be a win-win thing for both buyer and seller. Derivatives are a zero-sum game in which only the bank makes money on both sides of the trade since one person's payout is another's loss. I thank Bruce Chadwick for this succinct formulation.

12. Futures and forwards typically allow purchasers to hedge against future price movements; swaps typically allow the trading of risks; options confer the right to buy or sell something in the future.

13. A CDS is called a swap but is actually quite different from most swaps. It was called a swap mostly to avoid regulations that would kick in if it were named what it really is, an insurance contract. Insurance requires reserves to be set aside, but swaps don't, which was a huge part of their problem. Again, I thank Bruce Chadwick for this clarification and Bill Janeway for stressing the lack of an insurance reserve as a key structural weakness of CDS.

14. As we shall see shortly, the economic models used to price such risks told investors that this was the case.

15. Confusingly, the entity that collected the payments of the CDO was sometimes called a CDO (sometimes an SIV), but ignore that distinction for the purposes at hand.

16. A CDS is actually an insurance contract with an embedded option to generate an income stream.

17. As Bill Janeway notes, however, in the case of CDS "the protection seller is under no obligation to establish reserves...[and] need have no insurable interest in the referenced entity," with the result that a very large, liquid, and unbacked market in risk emerged in short order. That it was unbacked proved to be its main weakness. See Bill Janeway, *Doing Capitalism in the Innovation Economy* (Cambridge: Cambridge University Press, 2012), 163–164.

18. As per above, government bond purchases by Asian central banks cut the supply of T-bills, and this made CDOs even more attractive.

19. Peter S. Goodman, *Past Due: The End of Easy Money and the Renewal of the American Economy* (New York: Henry Holt, 2010), chap. 5.
20. Gillian Tett, *Fool's Gold* (New York: Free Press, 2009).
21. Or SPV (special purpose vehicle).
22. Diversification is more than "not putting all your eggs in one basket." Good diversification seeks to add assets that are uncorrelated or negatively correlated with other assets in a portfolio. Uncorrelated assets still must be expected to earn more than one would expect to get by depositing cash in a checking account, to be worth risking money and inclusion in a portfolio. Moreover, uncorrelated assets do not deliver those returns in a synchronized fashion: they do not have to rise and fall at the same moment in time.
23. There are, however, limits to both strategies. Specifically, if everyone tries to become fully diversified, then, paradoxically, they will end up buying more or less the same assets, and using the same hedges to cover their exposures, which is what had happened by 2006. Their individual portfolios may be diversified even if the sum of those portfolios is not diversified. This is why so-called systemic risk, which is in part the risk you cannot diversify, never really goes away. We shall encounter this shortly.
24. Peter T. Larsen, "Goldman Pays the Price of Being Big," *Financial Times*, August 13, 2007, quoted in Dowd et al., "How Unlucky Is 25-Sigma," University College Dublin, Centre for Financial Markets, working paper series WP-08-04 (2008): 1, http://irserver. ucd.ie/bitstream/handle/10197/1175/WP-08-04.pdf;jsessionid=0973D543CCE4C7590 E24E76120BDEC64?sequence=1.
25. Roger Lowenstein, *When Genius Failed* (New York: Random House, 2000), 126–127.
26. Dowd et al., "How Unlucky Is 25-Sigma," 5.
27. Andrew Haldane, "Why Banks Failed the Stress Test," (speech at the Marcus-Evans Conference on Stress-Testing, London, February 9–10, 2009).
28. Three recent books have done a great job of showing us how the ideas that constitute modern finance, its theoretical structure, were a huge part of what went wrong. Justin Fox's *The Myth of the Rational Market* (2009), John Cassidy's *How Markets Fail* (2009), and John Quiggin's *Zombie Economics* (2010) lay out in great detail how the economic theory of the past thirty years was constructed, what it presumed about the world, and why those ideas failed in the 2007–2008 crisis. In what follows, I draw on their work and on my own prior work on the subject. What I stress here, and add to their discussion, is the role that economic theory plays in providing stability, and promoting instability, in the financial system.
29. As the old joke has it, an economist is someone who sees something happen in the world and then asks if it's true in theory.
30. See Mark Blyth, *Great Transformations: Economic Ideas and Political Change in the Twentieth Century* (Cambridge: Cambridge University Press, 2002); and Blyth, "When Liberalisms Change: Comparing the Politics of Deflations and Inflations," in *Neoliberalism, National and Regional Experiments with Global Ideas*, ed. Arthur T. Denzau, Thomas C. Willett, and Ravi K. Roy (London and New York: Routledge, 2006), 71–97.
31. This was epitomized in the following quip attributed to Keynes. When a reporter asked, "If businessmen are as stupid as you think, how come they make a profit?" Keynes replied, "Easy. They compete against other businessmen."
32. This analysis was called the microfoundations critique and was initially proposed by such economists as Robert E. Lucas and Robert J. Barro.

33. Hence the still-manic finger-pointing at Fannie and Freddie, despite their ability to generate a global crisis being zero. There's only one Fannie and Freddie, and yet we have multiple states in crisis.

34. Which, as we shall see shortly, is the same thinking behind Eurozone austerity policies.

35. Which is a bit like saying those who want to hold public office are the most qualified to hold it.

36. As Andrew Haldane and Robert May have argued regarding this set of ideas, what they term "asset pricing theory" (APT) "is not a theory in the sense habitually used in the sciences, but rather a set of idealized assumptions on which financial engineering is based; that is, APT is part of the problem itself." Haldane and May, "Systemic Risk in Banking Ecosystem," *Nature* 469 (2011): 352.

37. In the end, the Lehman CDS contracts did clear, with the state standing behind every transaction. See "DTCC Completes Settlement of Lehman CDS Contracts Resulting in $5.2B in Net Fund Transfers," October 22, 2008. streetinsider.com, http://www.streetinsider.com/Trader+Talk/DTCC+Completes+Settlement+of+Lehman+CDS+Contracts+Resulting+In+$5.2B+In+Net+Fund+Transfers/4087312.html.

38. The $13 trillion figure comes from the Better Markets institute's estimate of the costs of the crisis to the US economy, which is arguably the most comprehensive to date. See Better Markets, "The Cost of the Wall Street-Caused Financial Collapse and Ongoing Economic Crisis Is More Than $12.8 Trillion," Better Markets report, September 15, 2012. http://bettermarkets.com/sites/default/files/Cost%20Of%20The%20Crisis.pdf.

39. A good source on the composition of the balance sheet of the US Federal Reserve is found at "Factors Affecting Reserve Balances," Board of Governors of the Federal Reserve System, http://www.federalreserve.gov/releases/h41/.

40. Better Markets, "The Cost of the Wall Street-Caused Financial Collapse."

41. IMF Fiscal Affairs Department, "The State of Public Finances Cross-Country Fiscal Monitor: November 2009," November 3, 2009, 37, http://www.imf.org/external/pubs/ft/spn/2009/spn0925.pdf.

42. As we shall see in the chapter 3, there are other, less obvious mechanisms at play, too.

43. IMF World Economic and Financial Surveys, Fiscal Monitor, Navagating the Challenges Ahead, 14–15. May 14, 2010. http://www.imf.org/external/pubs/ft/fm/2010/fm1001.pdf.

44. Ibid.

45. See "'Getting Paid in America' Survey Results," National Payroll Week 2010, http://www.nationalpayrollweek.com/documents/2010GettingPaidInAmericaSurveyResults_FINAL.pdf; Annamaria Lusardi, Daniel J. Schneider, and Peter Tufano, "Financially Fragile Households," National Bureau of Economic Research, NBER working paper no. 17072, Cambridge, MA, May 11, 2011 http://www.nber.org/papers/w17072; Lawrence Mishel and Heidi Schieroltz "The Sad but True Story of Wages in America," Economic Policy Institute, Washington DC, March 15, 2011. http://www.epi.org/publication/the_sad_but_true_story_of_wages_in_america/.

46. Number of guns taken from http://en.wikipedia.org/wiki/Gun_violence_in_the_United_States

47. All figures in this section come from bank financial filings. GDP figures come from Eurostat. Details are found in chapter 3.

48. Nassim N. Taleb, "The Great Bank Robbery," *Project Syndicate*, September 2, 2011. http://www.project-syndicate.org/commentary/the-great-bank-robbery.

CHAPTER THREE

1. Greek workers actually work longer hours than their German compatriots. See "Labor Productivity Level in Total Economy," OECD, search "labor forces statistics average hours worked," http://stats.oecd.org/.
2. Dagmar H. Lojsch, Marta Rodriguez-Vives, and Michal Slavik, "The Size and Composition of Government Debt in the Euro Area," European Central Bank, Occasional Paper Series 132, October (2011): 15, http://www.ecb.europa.eu/pub/pdf/scpops/ecbocp132.pdf.
3. Leon Mangasarian, "U.S. Losing Financial Superpower Status, Germany Says," *Bloomberg*, September 25, 2008, http://www.bloomberg.com/apps/news?pid=newsarc hive&sid=ahUuZ8Z5rkDA&refer=germany.
4. Angela Merkel quoted in Abraham Newman, "Flight from Risk: Unified Germany and the Role of Beliefs in the European Response to the Financial Crisis," *German Politics and Society* 28, 2 (Summer 2010): 158. Newman also quotes Steinbrück as saying that "so much money is being pumped into the market that capital markets could easily be overwhelmed, resulting in a global period of inflation," ibid.
5. "Economic Report of the President (2010)," U.S. Government Printing Office, (Washington DC: Government Printing Office, 2010), 87.
6. Center for European Economic Research (ZEW), "ZEW Indicator of Economic Sentiment:Optimism Returns," Center for European Economic Research. August 18, 2009, http://www.zew.de/en/press/1255/zew-indicator-of-economic-sentiment—optimism-returns.
7. Henry Farrell and John Quiggin, "Consensus, Dissensus and Economic Ideas: The Rise and Fall of Keynesianism during the Economic Crisis," unpublished manuscript (2011), 16.
8. Chris Giles and Gillian Tett, "IMF Head in Shock Fiscal Warning," *Financial Times*, January 27, 2008, http://www.ft.com/intl/cms/s/0/106230b0-cd29-11dc-9b2b-000077b07658. html#axzz22sXtZh8H; Olivier Blanchard, Giovanni Dell'Ariccia, and Paolo Mauro, "Rethinking Macroeconomic Policy," International Monetary Fund, IMF Staff Position Note (2010), http://www.imf.org/external/pubs/ft/spn/2010/spn1003.pdf.
9. Farrell and Quiggin, "Consensus, Dissensus and Economic," 22.
10. Robert Skidelsky, *Keynes: The Return of the Master* (New York: Public Affairs, 2009).
11. See Gerald Feldman, *The Great Disorder: Politics, Economics and Society 1914–1924* (New York: Oxford University Press, 1997) for the definitive account of the German inflation.
12. Adam Ferguson makes the case that the German hyperinflation was a case of deliberate monetary stimulus. I find Feldman's argument more convincing and I draw upon it here. See Adam Ferguson, *When Money Dies: The Nightmare of Deficit Spending, Hyperinflation and Devaluation in Weimar Germany* (New York: Public Affairs, 2010) for the alternative view.
13. On ordoliberalism, see Brigitte Young and Willi Semmler, "Germany's New Vision for the Eurozone: Rule-based Ordoliberalism?" unpublished manuscript (2011); and Steven J. Slivia, "Why Do German and U.S. Reactions to the Financial Crisis Differ?" *German Politics and Society*, 29, 4 (winter 2011): 68–77.
14. For a good overview of this period see Werner Abelhauser, Deutsche Wirtschaftsgeschichte seit 1945, C. H. Beck Verlag, Munich 2004, 69.

15. See Peter Katzenstein, *A World of Regions* (Ithaca, NY: Cornell University Press, 2005).

16. Alan Greenspan, "Inflation: The Real Threat to Sustained Recovery," *Financial Times*, June 25, 2009, http://www.ft.com/intl/cms/s/0/e1fbc4e6–6194–11de-9e03–00144feabdco.html#axzz1rw5D7xpm.

17. Jeffrey Sachs, "Time to Plan for Post-Keynesian Era," *Financial Times*, June 7, 2010, http://www.ft.com/intl/cms/s/0/e7909286-726b-11df-9f82-00144feabdco.html#axzz1rw5D7xpm.

18. Jean-Claude Trichet, "Stimulate No More-It Is Now Time for All to Tighten," *Financial Times*, July 22, 2010, http://www.ft.com/intl/cms/s/0/1b3ae97e-95c6-11df-b5ad-00144feab49a.html#axzz1rw5D7xpm.

19. Chris Giles, "G20: All Change on the Fiscal Front," *Financial Times*, June 5, 2010, http://blogs.ft.com/money-supply/2010/06/05/g20-all-change-on-the-fiscal-front/#axzz22zcCMeF9.

20. Wolfgang Schäuble, "Maligned Germany Is Right to Cut Spending," *Financial Times*, June 24, 2010, http://www.ft.com/intl/cms/s/0/9edd8434-7f33-11df-84a3-00144feabdco.html#axzz22sXtZh8H.

21. ECB, *Monthly Bulletin*, European Central Bank, June 2010, 83–85.

22. Stephen Kinsella, "Is Ireland Really the Role Model for Austerity?" *Cambridge Journal of Economics* 36 (January 2012): 232.

23. "Monthly Bulletin," European Central Bank, June 2010, 84.

24. Figures through 2010 from stats.oecd.org; for 2011 "Euro Area and EU27 Government Deficit at 4.1% and 4.5% of GDP respectively," Eurostat, http://epp.eurostat.ec.europa.eu/cache/ITY_PUBLIC/2-23042012-AP/EN/2-23042012-AP-EN.PDF.

25. Georgios P. Kouretas "The Greek Crisis: Causes and Implications" *Paneoeconomius* 57, 4 (December 2010): 391–404.

26. Or buy CDS protection on the bonds, or go short on them to make money on the downside, but eventually you want to get out.

27. See "Total Government Net Debt (% of GDP) Data for Year 2007, All Countries," Economy Watch, http://www.economywatch.com/economic-statistics/economic-indicators/General_Government_Net_Debt_Percentage_GDP/2007/.

28. As we shall detail in the conclusion, it's best to use GNP rather than GDP in the Irish case, since Ireland is a base for foreign multinationals that declare profits in Ireland for tax reasons. As such, Ireland's net income from foreign sources and its foreign obligations are outsized relative to other countries and its services exports are overstated.

29. Stephen Kinsella and Kevin O'Sullivan, "An Institutional Architecture for Meta-Risk Regulation in Irish Banking: Lessons from Anglo-Irish Banks Minsky Moment," forthcoming in *Journal of Banking Regulation* (2013), 6.

30. Ibid., 5.

31. Kinsella, "Is Ireland Really?" 224.

32. John Mauldin, *Endgame: The End of the Debt Supercycle and How It Changes Everything* (Hoboken, NJ: John Wiley & Sons, 2011), 223.

33. Francisco Carballo-Cruz, "Causes and Consequences of the Spanish Economic Crisis: Why the Recovery Is Taken So Long?," *Panoeconomicus* 58, 3 (2011): 314.

34. Robert Fishman, "Anomalies of Spain's Economy and Economic Policy-Making," *Contributions to Political Economy* 31 (2012): 67–76.

35. The Oliver Wyman report on expected losses in the Spanish banking sector of 59.3 billion euros has been challenged as flawed by some analysts who suggest much larger

losses. See Oliver Wyman, "Asset Quality Review and Bottom Up Stress Test Exercise," September 28, 2012, http://www.bde.es/f/webbde/SSICOM/20120928/informe_ow280912e.pdf. For a riposte, see Tyler Druden, "How Oliver Wyman Manipulated the Spanish Bank Bailout Analysis" Zerohedge, September 28, 2012, http://www.zerohedge.com/news/2012-09-28/how-oliver-wyman-manipulated-spanish-bank-bailout-analysis.

36. "The Uncertainty Society," *The Economist*, May 3, 2012, http://www.economist.com/node/21548977.

37. "Total Government Net Debt (% of GDP) Data for Year 2012, All Countries," Economy Watch, http://www.economywatch.com/economic-statistics/economic-indicators/General_Government_Net_Debt_Percentage_GDP/2012/.

38. "UK to Dodge Greek Fate with Tough Budget—Osborne," *Reuters*, June 20, 2010, http://uk.reuters.com/article/2010/06/20/uk-britain-osborne-budget-idUKTRE65J0UX20100620.

39. "UK Economy Faces Crisis," BBC News online, February 7, 2010, http://news.bbc.co.uk/2/hi/8503090.stm.

40. Niall Ferguson, "A Greek Crisis Is Coming to America," *Financial Times*, February 10, 2010, http://www.ft.com/intl/cms/s/0/f90bca10-1679-11df-bf44-00144feab49a.html#axzz1syduMdbA.

41. Tellingly, googling "US like Greece Spring 2010" gets nearly 73 million hits as of December 20, 2012.

42. Peter Wise, "Trichet Calms Fears of Debt Crisis Spread," *Financial Times*, May 6, 2010, http://www.ft.com/intl/cms/s/0/df61c58e-00f7-11df-a4cb-00144feabdco.html#axzz1syduMdbA; and Ralph Atkins, Kerin Hope, and David Oakley, "ECB Warning to Debt-Ridden Governments," *Financial Times*, January 14, 2010, http://www.ft.com/intl/cms/s/0/63b15724-5926-11df-adc3-00144feab49a.html#axzz1syduMdbA.

43. Carmen M. Reinhart and Kenneth S. Rogoff, "Banking Crises: An Equal Opportunity Menace," NBER Working Paper, Series 14587, Cambridge, MA, December 2008.

44. Moritz Schularik and Alan M. Taylor, "Credit Booms Gone Bust: Monetary Policy, Leverage Cycles and Financial Crises, 1870–2008," *American Economic Review* 102, 2 (April 2012): 1029–1062.

45. Even the Germans will find rapidly diminishing returns to the euro beginning to set in fast in 2013, as the Eurozone continues to slash itself to prosperity.

46. There was also a third, more "public" argument that a common currency would lead to a greater popular identification with Europe on the level of citizen's identities. Quite the opposite seems to be happening in Spain at the moment.

47. I owe this insight to a presentation entitled "Will the Euro Survive the Crisis?" given by Martin Wolf at Brown University, April 17, 2012.

48. I thank Simon Tilford for this insight.

49. Barry Eichengreen, *Golden Fetters: The Gold Standard and the Great Depression 1919–1939* (New York: Oxford University Press, 1996).

50. This was sometimes referred to as "the d'Artagnan Principle" after Alexandre Dumas's Musketeers' cry "all for one and one for all."

51. See Martin Feldstein, "EMU and International Conflict," *Foreign Affairs* (November/December 1997); and "The Euro and Economic Conditions" NBER working paper 17617, Cambridge, MA, November 2011.

52. Paul Krugman, *Peddling Prosperity: Sense and Nonsense in the Age of Diminished Expectations* (New York: W. W. Norton, 1994).

53. Daniela Gabor and Cornel Ban, "Fiscal Policy in (European) Hard Times: Financialization and Varieties of Capitalism," paper presented at the Understanding Crisis in Europe workshop, Bristol Business School, May 11, 2012.

54. The proposed EU-wide banking union of September 2012 seeks to address this problem by making the ECB the monitor for all systemically important banks in the Eurozone—some 6000 entities. The main problem with the proposal, apart from the fact that the UK will remain largely outside its jurisdiction, is that supervision alone does not solve a problem of solvency. Unless the ECB is willing to become the direct lender of last resort to individual banks across the Eurozone, then simply telling a national regulator that a bank with 20 percent of GDP on its books that it is about to blow up will do nothing to solve the problem if the national regulatory does not have the cash to deal with the problem. Bailing indirectly through the European Stability Mechanism (ESM), the position Spain hobbled toward in September 2012, is limited by the size of the ESM and the continued resistence of the German government. In short, you can't credibly commit to providing unlimited liquidity with an instrument that is cash limited. See the proposal at http://ec.europa.eu/internal_market/finances/docs/committees/reform/20120912-com-2012–510_En.pdf.

55. As of December 13, 2012, the EU has taken the first steps toward the creation of a banking union that recognizes the severity of these problems. The proposal allows the ECB to act as the common bank supervisor with authority over the Euro Area's largest banks—those with assets of over 20 percent of GDP or 30 billion euros. Although significant, as indicated in the previous note (53), supervision and monitoring when you don't have the cash to credibly bail are at best a step toward a banking union. They are not an institutional fix in and of themselves.

56. Aaron Kirchfeld, Elena Logutenkova, and Nicholas Comfort, "Deutsche Bank No.1 in Europe as Leverage Hits Valuation," Bloomberg, March 27, 2012, http://www.bloomberg.com/news/2012–03–26/deutsche-bank-no-3-in-europe-as-leverage-hits-market-valuation.html.

57. All figures here are calculated from bank filings in years 2008 and 2011. See the following websites: http://media.bnpparibas.com/invest/annual-reports/ra2008en/default.htm; http://www.credit-agricole.com/en/Finance-and-Shareholders/Financial-reporting/Credit-Agricole-S.A.-financial-results/2008; https://www.db.com/ir/en/content/sec_filings_2008.htm; https://www.commerzbank.com/en/hauptnavigation/aktionaere/service/archive/unternehmensberichterstattung/2009_8/u_berichte_09_01.html; http://www.ing.com/Our-Company/Investor-relations/Annual-Reports/Annual-Reports-Archive.htm; http://group.barclays.com/about-barclays/investor-relations/financial-results-and-publications/annual-reports; http://www.investors.rbs.com/report_subsidiary_results; http://www.lloydsbankinggroup.com/investors/financial_performance/company_results.asp#2008.

58. Jay Schambaugh, "The Euro's Three Crises," Brookings Papers on Economic Activity, Washington, DC, Spring 2012, 24. Available at http://www.brookings.edu/~/media/Files/Programs/ES/BPEA/2012_spring_bpea_papers/2012_spring_BPEA_shambaugh.pdf.

59. As Standard & Poor's put it, "We estimate that about 20 large systemically important European banks have cross border exposures to creditors in peripheral countries that far exceed their own tier one core capital." Standard & Poor's, "The Five Key Risks for European Banks," Ratings Direct: Global Credit Portal, April 11, 2012, 3, http://www.standardandpoors.com/spf/upload/Ratings_EMEA/TheFiveKeyRisksForEuropeanBanks_11April2012.pdf.

60. Simon Tilford and Philip Whyte, "Why Stricter Rules Threaten the Eurozone," Center for European Reform, London, November 2011, 5–6. As they further note, "The very countries that have insisted on wrenching economic adjustments in the debtor countries have often been the ones that have done the most to conceal the fragility of their own banks," ibid., 8.

61. LCH Clearnet in London was the venue of choice. According to its website LCH Clearnet handles $12 trillion of repo trades each month by notional value. See "Fixed Income," LCH Clearnet, http://www.lchclearnet.com/fixed_income/.

62. Hyun Song Shin, "The Global Banking Glut and Loan Risk Premium," paper presented at the Mundell-Fleming Lecture, 2011 IMF Annual Research Conference, November 10–11, 2011, 17. Available at http://www.princeton.edu/~hsshin/www/mundell_fleming_lecture.pdf.

63. Gabor and Ban, "Varieties of Capitalism for All Seasons: Fiscal Policy in the European Crisis," unpublished manuscript (Spring 2012), 9, figure 1.

64. Shin, "Global Banking Glut," 20.

65. Ibid., 21.

66. Gabor and Ban, "Varieties of Capitalism," 12.

67. Ibid., 14.

68. "Bank of International Settlements," *Quarterly Review* (June 2010): 19.

69. Paul De Grawue, "How Not to Be a Lender of Last Resort," CEPS Commentary, Center for European Policy Studies, Brussels, March 23, 2012, 2.

70. Schambaugh, "Euro's Three Crises,"

71. Another excellent overview is provided by Philip R. Lane, "The European Sovereign Debt Crisis," Journal of Economic Perspectives 26, 3 (Summer 2012): 49–68.

72. Eurozone countries still have their own central banks, but they are central banks in name only. They are really the payments processors for exchanges between Eurozone countries through a network called the Target Two system. Some economists are very worried that imbalances in this system threaten to bankrupt the German central bank. Others discount the possibility entirely. It is indicative of EU institutions that knowledgeable insiders cannot even agree on how these institutions actually operate. For a useful summary of the positions, see Silvia Merler and Jean Pisani-Ferry, "Sudden Stops in the Euro Area," *Breugel Policy Contribution* 6 (March 2012): 1–16, http://www.bruegel.org/publications/publication-detail/publication/718-sudden-stops-in-the-euro-area/.

73. Gillian Tett, "Beware Hidden Costs as Banks Eye 'Grexit,'" *Financial Times*, May 24, 2012, http://www.ft.com/intl/cms/s/0/73c76b8a-a5b4-11e1-a3b4-00144feabdco.html#axzz241THBegL.

74. Dani Rodrik, *One Economics, Many Recipes* (Princeton, NJ: Princeton University Press, 2007); David R. Cameron, "The Expansion of the Public Economy: A Comparative Analysis," *American Political Science Review* 72, 4 (December 1978): 1243–1261.

75. Friedrich Hayek, *The Road to Serfdom* (Chicago: University of Chicago Press, 1994).

76. Paul De Grauwe, "Fighting the Wrong Enemy," Vox, May 19 2010, http://new.voxeu.org/article/europe-s-private-versus-public-debt-problem-fighting-wrong-enemy.

INTRODUCTION TO CHAPTERS FOUR, FIVE, AND SIX

1. John Maynard Keynes, *The General Theory of Employment, Interest and Money* (Orlando: Harcourt Brace 1964), 3.
2. And even here, it is contentious. See Ha Joon Chang, *Kicking Away the Ladder: Development Strategy in Historical Perspective* (London: Anthem Press, 2002).
3. David Colander, personal communication, August 7, 2012.
4. As a leading light of the Scottish enlightenment, Sir James Steuart, put it concerning how markets undermine sovereign ambition, "The statesman looks about with amazement; he who was wont to consider himself as the first man in society...perceives himself eclipsed by...private wealth, which avoids his grasp when he attempts to seize it." Steuart in Albert Hirschman, *The Passions and The Interests: Political Arguments for Capitalism before its Triumph* (Princeton, NJ: Princeton University Press, 1977), 82.
5. Karl Polanyi, *The Great Transformation* (Boston: Beacon Press, 1984).
6. As Rousseau memorably put it "The first person who, having enclosed a plot of land, took it into his head to say 'this is mine' and found people simple enough to believe him, was the true found of civil society." Jean-Jacques Rousseau, *Basic Political Writings* (Indianapolis, IN: Hackett, 1996), 60.
7. Hirschman, *Passions and the Interests*.
8. Alexander Gerschenkron, *Economic Backwardness in Historical Perspective, a Book of Essays* (Cambridge, MA: Belknap Press of Harvard University Press 1962); Giovanni Arrighi, *Adam Smith in Beijing: Lineages of the Twenty-First Century* (New York: Verso Books, 2007); Dani Rodrik, *The Globalization Paradox* (New York: W. W. Norton, 2011).
9. Albert Hirschman, *The Rhetoric of Reaction: Perversity, Futility, Jeopardy,* (Cambridge, MA: Belknap Press, 1991).
10. Since this topic could occupy a whole book on its own, I discuss here what I see as the main contributions to this sensibility, extending from the seventeenth century to the present. The selection is based upon a class on the history of economic thought that I have been teaching since 1997, Classics of Political Economy. For two fabulous books on early economic thought from which this section draws, see Hirschman, *The Passions and the Interests* (1977) and Murphy, *The Genesis of Macroeconomics* (2009).
11. Keynes, *General Theory*; and Joseph A. Schumpeter, *Capitalism, Socialism and Democracy* (New York: Harper Torchbooks, 1942).
12. Blyth, *Great Transformations*.
13. Milton Friedman, *Capitalism and Freedom* (Chicago: University of Chicago Press, 1962), introduction, xiv.

CHAPTER FOUR

1. John Locke, *Second Treatise on Civil Government* (Indianapolis, IN: Hackett, 1996), v. 26.
2. Ibid., v. 27.
3. Ibid., v. 28, v. 33.
4. Ibid., v. 31.
5. Ibid., v. 46. As Locke put it, "and thus came in the use of money, some lasting thing that men might keep without spoiling," ibid., v. 47.

6. Ibid., v. 50.

7. The question as to whether this is active consent of the people or an indirect consent produced through their legislative delegates remains ambiguous in Locke. Regardless, those represented were holders of property. Locke was no mass suffrage democrat just as the United States is still a liberal "republic" as well as a democracy.

8. Locke, *Second Treatise*, v. 140.

9. Ibid., v. 222 and 227.

10. David Hume, "Of Public Credit" 1752. II ix 28, quoted in Antoin Murphy, *The Genesis of Macroeconomics* (New York: Oxford University Press, 2009), 111.

11. Murphy, "Genesis," 105.

12. Hume, "Essays, Moral, Political, and Literary," Library of Economics and Liberty, Of Money I, http://www.econlib.org/library/LFBooks/Hume/hmMPL32.html#Part II, Essay IX, OF PUBLIC CREDIT.

13. Steven G. Medema and Warren J. Samuels, *The History of Economic Thought: A Reader* (New York: Routledge), 142.

14. Ibid.

15. Ibid., 143.

16. Hume, "Essays, Moral, Political, and Literary," Of Public Credit, II.IX. 5. http://www.econlib.org/library/LFBooks/Hume/hmMPL32.html#Part II, Essay IX, OF PUBLIC CREDIT.

17. Ibid., II.IX 12.

18. Ibid., II.IX 14.

19. Ibid., II.IX 25 and 26.

20. "Germany Offers to Send Tax Men to Greece," *The Local: Germany's News in English*, February 25, 2012, http://www.thelocal.de/national/20120225–40979.html; and Chiara Vasarri, "Italy Tax Agents on Frontline of Anti-austerity backlash," Bloomberg, May 17, 2012, http://www.bloomberg.com/news/2012–05–16/italy-tax-agents-on-frontline-of-anti-austerity-backlash.html.

21. Dave Kansas, "Investors Won't Like Obama's Budget," *Wall Street Journal*, March 8, 2009, http://online.wsj.com/article/SB123646725826362641.html?KEYWORDS=obama+government+spending+crowding+out; Dave Kansas, "Obama Needs a Move to the Middle," *Wall Street Journal*, July 22 2009, http://online.wsj.com/article/SB10001424052970203946904574302332578189864.html?KEYWORDS=obama+government+spending+crowding+out.

22. Simon Johnson and James Kwak, *White House Burning: The Founding Fathers, Our National Debt, and Why It Matters to You* (New York: Random House, 2012); Carmen M. Reinhart and Kenneth S. Rogoff, *A Decade of Debt* (London: Center for Economic Policy Research, 2011).

23. "Monthly Statement of the Public Debt of the United States: January 31, 2011," United States Department of the Treasury, http://www.treasurydirect.gov/govt/reports/pd/mspd/2011/opds012011.pdf.

24. Adam Smith, *Wealth of Nations* (Buffalo, NY: Prometheus Books, 1991), 587.

25. See Murphy, "Genesis," 155–179, for a good overview of Smith's economics.

26. Albert Hirschman, *The Passions and The Interests: Political Arguments for Capitalism before Its Triumph* (Princeton, NJ: Princeton University Press, 1977).

27. Murphy, "Genesis." Although some commentators see Smith as being critical of banks, there are other parts of the *Wealth of Nations* in which he is positively enthusiastic about them.

28. Adam Smith, *An Inquiry into the Nature and Causes of the Wealth of Nations* (Indianapolis, IN: Hackett, 1996), 64.
29. It may lead to inflation, but that's another matter, and, oddly, it's one that didn't seem to preoccupy Smith all that much.
30. Smith, *Inquiry*, 64, 65.
31. Ibid., 66.
32. Ibid.
33. Ibid., 76.
34. Ibid., 66.
35. Ibid., 73.
36. Ibid., 74.
37. Ibid., 66.
38. Ibid., 77.
39. Ibid., Book V.
40. Ibid., 177.
41. Ibid., 181.
42. To which he adds that taxes should be certain, convenient, and low, Smith, *Wealth of Nations*, 498–499.
43. Smith finds the rents derived from lands to be arbitrary. Taxes drawn from the produce of the land to be a hidden tax on landlords. Similarly, taxes on the wages of labor are a disguised tax on the employer. See Smith, *Wealth of Nations*, 508–509, 535.
44. Smith, *Wealth of Nations*, 556.
45. Ibid., 556.
46. Ibid., 576.
47. Ibid., 579.
48. This is a theme we shall see reappearing in the work of Joseph Schumpeter.
49. Ibid., 581.
50. Ibid.
51. Ibid., 588, 588–589.
52. Ibid., 589.
53. Ibid., 590.
54. Carmen Reinhart and Kenneth S. Rogoff, *This Time Is Different: Eight Centuries of Financial Folly* (Princeton, NJ: Princeton University Press, 2009).
55. Murphy, "Genesis," 176–185.
56. Ibid., 43–71.
57. Ben S. Bernanke, "The Global Saving Glut and the U.S. Current Account Deficit," remarks by Governor Ben S. Bernanke at the Homer Jones Lecture, St. Louis, Missouri, April 14, 2005; Wolf, *Fixing Global Finance*, (Baltimore, MD: Johns Hopkins University Press, 2008).
58. See Philip Plickert, "Ungleichgewichte," *Frankfurter Allgemeine Zeitung*, August 13, 2012, http://www.faz.net/aktuell/wirtschaft/aussenhandel-ungleichgewichte-11854842.html.
59. Julia Collewe, "Angela Merkel's Austerity Postergirl, the Thrifty Swabian Housewife," *The Guardian*, September 17, 2012, http://www.guardian.co.uk/world/2012/sep/17/angela-merkel-austerity-swabian-housewives.
60. David Ricardo, *Principles of Political Economy and Taxation* (New York: Prometheus Books, 1996), 66.
61. Ibid., 73.

62. Ibid., 74.

63. Ernest Gellner, *Nations and Nationalism* (Ithaca, NY: Cornell University Press, 1983); Benedict Anderson, *Imagined Communities* (New York: Verso Books, 1983); John Breuilly, *Nationalism and the State* (Chicago: University of Chicago Press, 1994).

64. Polanyi, *Great Transformation*; Thomas Humphrey Marshall, *Citizinship and Social Class* (Cambridge: Cambridge University Press, 1950).

65. John Stuart Mill, *Principles of Political Economy*, Book V, chap. 7.

66. For an overview of New Liberal thought see John Allett, *New Liberalism. The Political Economy of J. A. Hobson* (Toronto: University of Toronto Press, 1978); David Weinstein, "The New Liberalism of L. T. Hobhouse and the Re-envisioning of Nineteenth Century Utilitarianism," *Journal of the History of Ideas* 57, 3 (1996): 487–507.

67. For an overview of this school of thought, see Peter J. Boettke, *The Elgar Companion to Austrian Economics* (Northampton: Edward Elgar Publishing Limited, 1994).

68. Keynes, *General Theory*, 383.

69. Herbert Hoover, *The Memoirs of Herbert Hoover: The Great Depression, 1929.1941* (New York: The Macmillan Company), 30.

70. Ibid.

71. Herbert Stein, *The Fiscal Revolution in America* (Chicago: University of Chicago Press, 1969), chap. 1.

72. Mark Blyth, *Great Transformations: Economic Ideas and Institutional Change in the Twentieth Century* (Cambridge: Cambridge University Press, 2002), 51–52.

73. Wesley C. Mitchell, "Business Cycles" in *Committee of the President's Conference on Unemployment, Business Cycles and Unemployment* (New York: McGraw-Hill 1923), 10, quoted in Dean L. May, *From New Deal to New Economics: The American Response to the Recession of 1937* (New York: Garland Press, 1981), 69.

74. Joseph Schumpeter in Douglass Brown, *The Economics of the Recovery Program* (New York: Whittlesey House, 1934); and J. Bradford DeLong, "'Liquidation' Cycles and the Great Depression," 1991, unpublished paper, available at http://econ161.berkeley.edu/pdf_files/liquidation_cycles.pdf.

75. Delong, "'Liquidation' Cycles," 8.

76. As Schumpeter put it, "Any revival that is merely due to artificial stimulus...leaves part of the work of depressions undone and adds to an undigested remnant of maladjustment." Schumpter (1934), 16, in DeLong, "'Liquidation' Cycles," 9.

77. Ibid., 9.

78. Blyth, *Great Transformations*, 72–75.

79. Peter J. Wallison, "Cause and Effect: Government Policies and the Financial Crisis," *Critical Review* 21 (2009): 365–377.

80. Jeffrey Friedman, "A Crisis of Politics, Not Economics: Complexity, Ignorance, and Policy Failure," in *Critical Review* 21 (2009): 127–185.

81. *Memoranda on Certain Proposals Relating to Unemployment*, presented by the Minister of Labour to Parliament, May 1929 (London: H.M. Stationery Office, 1929).

82. Karl Polanyi, *The Great Transformation* (Boston: Beacon Press, 1984), chaps. 1 and 2.

83. Rowena Crawford et al., "A Survey of Public Spending in the UK," Institute for Fiscal Studies Briefing Note 43, Institute for Fiscal Studies, London, September 2009, 5, table 2.2, http://www.ifs.org.uk/bns/bn43.pdf.

84. Joan Robinson, "The Second Crisis of Economic Theory," *American Economic Review* 62, 1/2 (March 1972): 2.

85. Stanley Baldwin, quoted in Keith Middlemas and John Barnes, *Baldwin: A Biography* (Oxford: Oxford University Press, 1972) quoted in George C. Peden "The 'Treasury View' on Public Works and Employment in the Interwar Period," *The Economic History Review* 37, 2 (May 1984): 169.

86. John Maynard Keynes, *The Collected Writings of John Maynard Keynes: Volume VIII* (Cambridge: Cambridge University Press), 19–23, quoted in Peden, "The 'Treasury View,'" 170.

87. John Quiggin, *Zombie Economics* (Princeton, NJ: Princeton University Press, 2012).

88. Robinson, "Second Crisis," 1.

89. Ibid., 4. In other words, if investors are unsure about the future and hold back on investment, then income and employment adjust downward.

90. Churchill budget speech, House of Commons 1929, quoted in Quiggin, *Zombie Economics*, 213.

91. George. C. Peden "Keynes, The Treasury and Unemployment in the 1930s," *Oxford Economic Papers* 32, 1 (March 1980): 6.

92. Peden, "The 'Treasury View,'" 173. Interestingly, this is the same argument given today by conservative historian Niall Ferguson for why stimulus policies don't work. See Niall Ferguson, "It Is the Stupid Economy," Joe Posner Fire Works and Co., op-video, http://www.joeposner.net/video/niall-ferguson-its-the-stupid-economy.

93. See the discussion of Henderson in Bill Janeway, *Doing Cpaitalism in the Innovation Economy* (New York: Cambridge University Press, 2012), 246–247.

94. Janeway, *Doing Capitalism*, 248.

95. See Hopkins's view in Peden, "The 'Treasury View,'" 175, 176.

96. Peden, "The 'Treasury View,'" 176.

97. Ibid.

98. Ibid., 177.

99. Peden, "Keynes, The Treasury," 9.

100. Eichengreen, *Golden Fetters: The Gold Standard and the Great Depression 1919–1939* (New York: Oxford University Press, 1996).

101. Blyth, *Great Transformations*.

102. Ibid.

103. Although some authors portray the Depression in the UK as being effectively over by 1934, the recovery was primarily centered in and London. The rest of the country languished with high unemployment for the remainder of the decade. See Nicolas Crafts and Peter Fearon, "Lessons from the 1930s Great Depression," *Oxford Review of Economic Policy*, 26, 3 (2010): 285–317.

104. Keynes, *General Theory*.

105. Robinson, "Second Crisis," 8.

106. Keynes, *General Theory*, 4–22, 46–51.

107. Ibid., 147–174.

108. For an argument as to why Keynes's General Theory was just that based upon the epistemology of statistics, see Nicholas Werle, "More Than a Sum of Its Parts: A Keynesian Epistemology of Statistics," *Journal of Philosophical Economics* 4, 2 (2011): 65–92.

109. Keynes, *General Theory*, 104.

110. Joseph A. Schumpeter, *Capitalism, Socialism and Democracy* (New York: Harper Torchbooks, 1942), 392, 294.

111. I concentrate on Schumpeter's 1942 volume rather than his 1939 two-volume set, *Business Cycles: A Theoretical, Historical, and Statistical Analysis of the Capitalist Process* (London: McGraw Hill, 1939) because *Business Cycles* is much more a restatement of his earlier work than a reaction to contemporary developments. That is, except for one line, where he states that "there seems in fact to be an element of truth in the popular opinion that there must be help from outside of the business organism, from government action or some favorable chance or event for instance, if there is to be a recovery at all." It remains, however, one line. Schumpeter, *Business Cycles*, 1:154. I thank Bill Janeway for drawing my attention to this aspect of *Business Cycles*.
112. Ibid. 132.
113. Ibid., 32.
114. Ibid.., 83.
115. Ibid., 106.
116. Ibid., 124.
117. Ibid., 127, 133.
118. Ibid., 137, 134.
119. Ibid., 145, 152–153.
120. Ibid., 160.
121. Ibid., 161.

CHAPTER FIVE

1. *Erst Sparen, Dann Kaufen!* (first save, then go shopping) is the very ordoliberal/Austrian slogan emblazoned on a German postcard from 1952 that is stuck to the door of my fridge at home.
2. Joseph Schumpeter, *Capitalism Socialism and Democracy* (New York: Harper Torch Books, 1942), 82.
3. Peter A. Hall and David Soskice, *Varieties of Capitalism: The Institutional Foundations of Competitive Advantage* (Cambridge: Cambridge University Press 2001), 1–55.
4. Mark Thompson, "The Survival of 'Asian Values' as 'Zivilisationskritik,'" *Theory and Society* 29, 5 (2000): 651–686.
5. The classic exposition of this thesis remains Barrington Moore's *Social Origins of Dictatorship and Democracy* (Boston: Beacon Press, 1966) and Alexander Gerschenkron, *Economic Backwardness in Historical Perspective* (Cambridge, MA: Harvard Belknap Press, 1962).
6. Woo Cummings, ed., *The Developmental State* (Ithaca, NY: Cornell University Press 1999); but also Wolfgang Streek and Yamamura, *The Origins of Non-Liberal Capitalism* (Cambridge: Cambridge University Press 2002).
7. Gerschenkron, *Economic Backwardness*; and Leonard Seabrooke, *The Social Sources of Financial Power* (Ithaca, NY: Cornell University Press, 2006).
8. The world's first welfare state was founded in Germany, in the nineteenth century, by Otto von Bismark.
9. David J. Gerber, "Constitutionalizing the Economy: German Neoliberalism, Competition Law and the 'New' Europe." *American Journal of Comparative Law* 42 (1994): 30.
10. Ibid., 42
11. Ibid., 44. Note again the concern with private as well as public power.
12. Walter Eucken, *Grundsätze der Wirtschaftspolitik*, (Tübingen: J. C. B. Mohr, 1952), 334, 336, quoted in Josef Hein, "Competing Ideas: The Evolution of the German and

Italian Welfare States and Their Religious Foundations," unpublished PhD diss., European University Institute, Florence, November 2012, 223.

13. Böhm, quoted in Gerber, "Constitutionalizing the Economy."

14. Eucken, cited in Sally Razeen, "Ordoliberalism and the Social Market: Classical Political Economy from Germany," *New Political Economy* 1, 2 (1996): 233–257, quoted in Volker Berghahn and Brigitte Young, "Reflections on Werner Bonefeld's "Freedom and the Strong State: On German Ordoliberalism" and the Continuing Importance of the Ideas of Ordoliberalism to Understand Germany's (Contested) Role in the Resolving the Eurozone Crisis," forthcoming in *New Political Economy*, p. 12 of manuscript version.

15. Gerber, "Constitutionalizing the Economy," 45.

16. Berghahn and Young, "Reflections," passim.

17. Ralf Ptak, "Neoliberalism in Germany: Revisiting the Ordoliberal Foundations of the Social Market Economy" in *The Road From Mont Pelerin: The Making of the Neoliberal Thought Collective*, ed. Philip Mirowski and Dieter Plehwe (Cambridge, MA: Harvard University Press, 2009), 102.

18. Gerber, "Constitutionalizing the Economy," 48–49.

19. If you detect echoes of the Eurozone debacle here, you should.

20. Crudely, supply creates its own demand.

21. Carl J. Freidrich, "The Political Thought of Neo-Liberalism" *American Political Science Review* 49, 2 (1955): 511. A contemporary example of achievement versus impediment competition is to compare the competition on products that occurs between BMW and Mercedes. This competition betters both products such that both firms sell more cars. Now, compare this to the patent battles between Apple and Samsung, which is impediment competition. It is designed to keep the other firm out of the marketplace regardless of the quality of the product.

22. Christian Watrin, "The Principles of the Social Market Economy: Its Origins and Early History," *Journal of Institutional and Theoretical Economics*, Bd. 135 (H3) (1979): 413. Or, as leading ordoliberal Wilhelm Rokpe argued, "A genuine, equitable and smoothly functioning competitive system can not in fact survive without a judicious moral and legal framework and without regular supervision of the conditions under which competition can take place." Ropke quoted in Christopher S. Allen, "The Underdevelopment of Keynesianism in the Federal Republic of Germany" in *The Political Power of Economic Ideas: Keynesianism Across Nations*, ed. Peter A. Hall (Princeton, NJ: Princeton University Press 1989), 281.

23. Watrin, "Principles," 416.

24. Ptak, "Neoliberalism in Germany," 104.

25. As Garber notes, ordoliberals had over half the seats on the advisory council in 1947 formed to give advice to the government. Garber, "Constitutionalizing the Economy," 59. Also, the West German employers association Die Waage spent over 11 million deutsche marks between 1952 and 1965 on publicity campaigns supporting ordoliberal ideas. Ptak, "Neoliberalism," 122.

26. Allen, "Underdevelopment," in Hall, *Political Power*, passim.

27. One of the less noticed consequences of partition in 1945 was that two-thirds of Germany's Protestants vanished into the German Democratic Republic. German Catholics suddenly became a much more sizable minority. I thank Joseph Hien for this observation.

28. Graber, "Constitutionalizing," 61–62. Ptak describes Erhard as "an avid participant in the ordoliberal mainstream," Ptak, "Neoliberalism," 115. Friedrich describes him as

"the spokesman for the creed of the neo-liberals in German and European politics." Freidrich, *American Political Science Review 49*, 2 (1955): 510.

29. I thank Josef Hien for the details on this important transition period.

30. See the description of the Wirtschaftwunder at http://en.wikipedia.org/wiki/ Wirtschaftswunder.

31. Allen, "Underdevelopment," 271. The fact that all of this was made possible by an astonishingly favorable macroeconomic context—the Bretton Woods international monetary system and American acceptance of an undervalued Deutschmark given Germany's strategic position in the Cold War—should also be acknowledged. It seldom is, however, especially among German policy makers.

32. Allen, "Underdevelopment," 271 and 268.

33. Ibid., 277.

34. Ibid., 281.

35. Peter J. Katzenstein, ed., *Between Power and Plenty* (Ithaca, NY: Cornell University Press, 1976).

36. Kate McNamara, *The Currency of Ideas: Monetary Politics in the European Union* (Ithaca, NY: Cornell University Press, 1998); Nicolas Jabko, *In the Name of the Market* (Ithaca, NY: Cornell University Press, 2006).

37. Ha Joon Chang, *Kicking Away the Ladder: Deveopment Strategy in Historical Perspective* (London: Anthem Press 2002).

38. I thank Alex Gourevitch for this point.

39. Martin Wolf, *Fixing Global Finance* (Baltimore, MD: Johns Hopkins University Press, 2010),197.

40. Schumpeter was Austrian trained, Austrian by birth, and built his career around Austrian ideas. Despite this, he is not usually considered a member of the Austrian school. I consider him to be the de facto Austrian (school) ambassador in residence in the United States, at Harvard no less. As David Simpson has shown, the minor differences between Schumpeter and Austrians were technical, not substantive. David Simpson, "Joseph Schumpeter and the Austrian School of Economics," *Journal of Economic Studies 10*, 4 (1983): 18–28. http://www.emeraldinsight.com/journals. htm?articleid=1709331.

41. Robinson, "Second Crisis," 2.

42. Remember, in the Keynesian world, the point of spending money to stimulate the economy is not that money is causal per se. Rather, the point is to raise prices sufficiently to alter the expectations of investors, which in turn impacts employment and consumption.

43. Ben Bernanke, "The Great Moderation," remarks at the meetings of the Eastern Economic Association, Washington DC, February 20, 2004. http://www.federalreserve. gov/boarddocs/speeches/2004/20040220/default.htm.

44. The rate of interest on the loan is less than the rate of return on the asset given rising prices, but the more interest rates play catch up, the more the returns are squeezed.

45. Ludwig von Mises, "The Austrian Theory of the Trade Cycle," in *The Austrian Theory of the Trade Cycle and Other Essays*, ed. Richard M. Ebeling (Auburn, AL: Ludwig von Mises Institute, 1996), 30.

46. Ibid. 31.

47. There is also "financial repression"—we turn to this in the conclusion to this book.

48. Ludwig von Mises in Ebeling, *Austrian Theory*, 33.

49. Gottfried Haberler, "Money and the Business Cycle," in Ebeling, *Austrian Theory*, 37–65.
50. Murray N. Rothbard, "Economic Depressions: Their Cause and Cure," in Ebeling, *Austrian Theory*, 65–93.
51. Peter Boetke, "Is Austrian Economics Heterodox Economics?" The Austrian Economists website, http://austrianeconomists.typepad.com/weblog/2008/05/is-austrian-eco.html.
52. See many of the pro-Austrian sentiments on the hedge-fund news site www.zerohedge.com.
53. John Maynard Keynes, *The General Theory of Employmemt, Interest and Money* (New York: Harcourt Brace, 1963), 3.
54. United States Bureau of Labor Statistics, News Release, "Union Members Summary," January 27, 2012, http://www.bls.gov/news.release/union2.nro.htm.
55. Irving Fisher, "The Debt Deflation Theory of Great Depressions," *Econometrica*, 1, 4 (1933): 337–357.
56. John Quiggin "Austrian Economics: A Response to Boettke" posted on Johnquiggin. com, March 18, 2009, http://johnquiggin.com/2009/03/18/austrian-economics-a-response-to-boettke/.
57. Good luck with that. Somalia is a shining example of such zero-state political economies.
58. For a more detailed account see Blyth, *Great Transformations*, chaps. 5 and 6.
59. Milton Friedman, "The Role of Monetary Policy," *American Economic Review* 58, 1 (March 1968): 1–17.
60. Milton Friedman and Anna Schwartz, *A Monetary History of the United States 1867–1960* (Princeton, NJ: Princeton University Press, 1971).
61. A. W. Phillips, "The Relation between Unemployment and the Rate of Change of Money Wages in the United Kingdom, 1861–1957," *Economica* 25, 100 (November 1958): 283–299.
62. Michael Bleaney, *The Rise and Fall of Keynesian Macroeconomics* (London: Macmillan, 1985), 140, author's italics.
63. Public choice theory is often called the Virginia school of political economy.
64. Buchanan and Wagner, *Democracy in Deficit: The Economic Consequences of Lord Keynes* (Indianapolis, IN: Liberty Fund 1977), quote located in online version of text, http://www.econlib.org/library/Buchanan/buchCv8c5.html#8.5.25.
65. Milton Friedman, "Inflation and Unemployment: The New Dimensions of Politics," in Milton Friedman, *Monetarist Economics* (London: Institute of Economic Affairs, 1991), 105.
66. Finn Kydland and Edward Prescott, "Rules Rather Than Discretion: The Inconsistency of Optimal Plans," *Journal of Political Economy* 85, 2 (1977): 473–490.
67. For a good introduction to the politics behind central bank independence, see Adam Posen, "Central Bank Independence and Disinflationary Credibility: A Missing Link," *Oxford Economic Papers* 50, 3 (1998): 335–359; Ilene Grabel, "Ideology, Power, and the Rise of Independent Monetary Institutions in Emerging Economies," in *Monetary Orders: Ambiguous Economics, Ubiquitous Politics*, ed. Jonathan Kirshner (Ithaca, NY: Cornell University Press, 2003); Sheri Berman and Kathellen McNamara, "Bank on Democracy," *Foreign Affairs* 78, 2 (April/May 1999): 1–12.
68. Posen, "Central Bank Independence."
69. Brian Barry, "Does Democracy Cause Inflation? Political Ideas of Some Economists," in *The Politics of Inflation and Economic Stagnation*, ed. Leon N. Lindberg and Charles S. Meyer (Wasington DC: Brookings Institute Press, 1985): 280–315.

70. Mark Blyth, "Paradigms and Paradox: The Politics of Economics Ideas in Two Moments of Crisis," *Governance: An International Journal of Policy, Administraton and Institutions* 26, 4 (December 2012): 1–19.

71. Berman and McNamara, "Bank on Democracy."

72. Paul Krugman, "The Structural Obsession," The Conscience of a Liberal, blog, June 8, 2012, http://krugman.blogs.nytimes.com/2012/06/08/the-structural-obsession/.

73. Steven Schulman, "The Natural Rate of Unemployment: Concept and Critique," Journal of Post-Keynesian Economics 11, 4 (Summer 1989): 509–521.

74. Daniel C. Dennett, *Darwin's Dangerous Idea: Evolution and the Meanings of Life* (New York: Simon and Schuster 1996)

75. Blyth, *Great Transformations*, 147–151; Posen, "Central Bank Independence."

76. John Williamson, "A Short History of the Washington Consensus," paper commissioned by Fundación CIDOB for the conference "From the Washington Consensus towards a New Global Governance," Barcelona, September 24–25, 2004, quote from p. 1.

77. Ibid., 1, my italics.

78. Williamson, "A Short History," 2. The fact that fiscal discipline is *primus inter pares* on the list is telling.

79. Korea joined the OECD in 1986. Elsewhere Williamson moves from claiming that these ideas constitute the actual practices of the OECD to claiming that they are "drawn from that body of robust empirical generalizations that forms the core of economics." John Williamson, "Democracy and the Washington Consensus," *World Development* 21, 8 (August 1993): 1113.

80. Katherine Weaver, *The Hypocrisy Trap: The World Bank and the Poverty of Reform* (Princeton, NJ: Princeton University Press, 2008).

81. On the history of the March of Dimes, see http://www.marchofdimes.com/mission/history.html.

82. Louis Pauly, *Who Elected the Bankers? Surveilence and Control in the World Economy* (Ithaca, NY: Cornel University Press. 1998).

83. Dani Rodrik, "Goodbye Washington Consensus, Hello Washington Confusion?" *Journal of Economic Literature* 44, 4 (December 2006): 973.

84. World Bank, *Economic Growth in the 1990s: Learning from a Decade of Reform.* (Washington, DC: World Bank 2005), quoted in Rodrik "Goodbye Washington," 976.

85. Barbara Stallings and Peres Wilson, "Is Economic Reform Dead in Latin America? Rhetoric and Reality since the 2000s" *Journal of Latin American Studies* 43, 4 (2011): 755–786.

86. Rawi Abdelal *Capital Rules: The Construction of Global Finance* (Ithaca, NY: Cornell University Press, 2006).

87. Rodrik, "Goodbye Washington," 975.

88. Studies have shown that economic growth is more likely to drop during an IMF program and after its completion, while social inequality increases. Faced with this reality leftist governments in countries such as Brazil abandoned IMF conditionality and adopted much more heterodox policy mixes. See, for example, Cornel Ban, "New Paradigm or Edited Orthodoxy: Brazil's Liberal Neo-Developmentalism" *Review of International Political Economy*, 1–34. First online publication, http://www.tandfonline.com/doi/pdf/10.1080/09692290.2012.660183.

89. Jacques J. Polak, "The IMF Monetary Model: A Hardy Perennial," Finance and Development, December (1997): 16–19; "The IMF Monetary Model at Forty," IMF Working Paper 97/49, IMF: Wasgington DC, April (1997): 1–20, http://www.imf.org/external/pubs/ft/wp/wp9749.pdf.

90. Polak, "IMF Monetary Model," 17, my italics.
91. Polak, "IMF Monetary Model," 18.
92. According to the IMF's official historian, the anti-inflationary drive of the Polak model came from Polak's mentor, Jan Tinbergen, an official of the central bank of the Netherlands during the pre-Keynesian interwar years. See Margaret Garritsen de Vries, "Balance of Payments Adjustment 1945–1986: The IMF Experience," Washington DC, IMF, 1987, 29–30.
93. A superior study of the early years of the IMF is Sarah Babb, "Embeddedness, Inflation, and International Regimes: The IMF in the Early Postwar Period," *American Journal of Sociology 113* (2007): 128–164.
94. World Bank, *Economic Growth in the 1990s*.
95. Karl Polanyi, *Great Transformation* (Boston: Beacon Press, 1944): 143.
96. James M. Buchanan, "'La scienza delle finanze': The Italian Tradition in Fiscal Theory," in *Fiscal Theory and Political Economy*, ed. James M. Buchanan (Chapel Hill: University of North Carolina Press, 1960), 23–76.
97. Angelo Santagostino, "The Contribution of Italian Liberal Thought to the European Union: Einaudi and His Heritage from Leoni to Alesina," *Atlantic Economic Journal*, August 2012. Published online at http://link.springer.com/content/pdf/10.1007%2 Fs11293-012-9336-0.
98. Francenso Forte and Roberto Marchionatti, "Luigi Einaudi's Economics of Liberalism," University of Torino, Department of Economics Working Paper 02/2010, 9, http://www.cesmep.unito.it/WP/2010/2_WP_Cesmep.pdf.
99. Cited in Forte and Marchionatti "Luigi Einaudi's Economics," 24.
100. Quoted in Santagostino, "Contribution," 6.
101. One should also note that the influence of Bocconi graduates extends far beyond the academy. For example, Mario Monti, the current EU-imposed prime minister of Italy was the former president/rector of the Bocconi School. Corrado Passera, the current minister of economic development of Italy is a Bocconi graduate, as is Vittorio Grilli, the Italian minister of economy and finance. I thank Lorenzo Moretti for this insight.
102. Alberto Alesina and Guido Tabbellini, "A Positive Theory of Fiscal Deficits and Government Debt in a Democracy," NBER working paper 2308, Cambridge, MA, July 1987, published as "A Positive Theory of Fiscal Deficits and Government Debt." *Review of Economic Studies* (1990) 57: 403–414.
103. For a great overview of this area, see Bruce Bartlett, "Starve the Beast: Origins and Development of a Budgetary Metaphor," *Independent Review 12*, 1 (Summer 2007): 5–26.
104. Alesina and Tabellini, "Positive Theory," 2.
105. Torsten Persson and Lars E. O. Svensson, "Why a Stubborn Conservative Would Run a Deficit: Policy with Time Inconsistent Preferences." *Quarterly Journal of Economics* (May 1989): 325–345.
106. Ibid., 326.
107. There is a rather large flaw in this model. If the conservative incumbents spent enough, they might just engineer a boom that could get them reelected, which would leave them on the hook for all that debt they just generated. One could invoke voters with rational expectations to solve the problem. But if one did that, then one would have to presume that these same rational voters would know what the conservatives were doing before they did it, and the whole process would never get off the ground.
108. Persson and Svensson, "Why a Stubborn Conservative," 337.

109. Francesco Giavazzi and Marco Pagano, "Can Severe Fiscal Contractions Be Expansionary? Tales of Two Small European Countries," NBER Macroeconomics Annual 1990, Cambridge, MA, 75–122. Incidentally, the former is a professor at the Bocconi School while the latter is the president of the Einaudi Institute for Economics and Finance (EIEF).

110. Sachverstandigenrat zur Begutachtung der Gesamtwirtschaftlichen Entwicklung 1981. Vor kurskorrekturen-Zur finanzpolitischen und waehrungspolitischen situation im sommer 1981, July 4, 1981, available at http://www.sachverstaendigenrat-wirtschaft.de/fileadmin/dateiablage/download/gutachten/0901061.pdf.

111. M. Hellwig and M. J. M. Neumann, "Economic Policy in Germany: Was There a Turn Around?" Economic Policy 5 (October 1987): 137–138.

112. Giavazzi and Pagano, "Severe Fiscal Contraction," 80.

113. Ibid., 81.

114. Ibid.

115. Ibid., 82.

116. Ibid., 103.

117. Ibid.

118. Ibid., 105.

119. Alberto Alesina and Roberto Perotti, "Fiscal Expansions and Fiscal Adjustments in OECD Countries," NBER working paper 5214, Cambridge, MA, August 1995.

120. Ibid., 4

121. Ibid., 17.

122. Ibid., 17–18.

123. Ibid., 18.

124. Ibid., 22 and 23.

125. Ibid., 24.

126. Alberto Alesina and Silvia Ardanga, "Tales of Fiscal Adjustment" NBER Macroeconomics Annual 1998 and Economic Policy 13, 27 (1998): 489–545.

127. Ibid., 490.

128. Ibid., 491.

129. Ibid., 492. Economic "Shock Therapy" from Russia, military "shock and awe" from the Iraq war, and similar failed doctrines spring to mind here.

130. The structural deficit is the deficit that would exist if the economy was producing at its potential. The difference between the actual deficit and the structural deficit is then attributed to cyclical factors, which result in the economy producing below potential. I thank Stephen Kinsella for this definition.

131. Alesina and Ardanga, "Tales of Fiscal Adjustment," 498, quote from p. 499.

132. Recall that for Giavazzi and Pagano Denmark was the positive case and Ireland was mixed, Alesina and Ardanga, "Tales of Fiscal Adjustment," ibid., 514.

133. Ibid., 514.

134. Ibid., 514–515.

135. Ibid., 516. As the authors conclude, "A large fiscal adjustment that is expenditure based and is accompanied by wage moderation and devaluation is expansionary," (my italics).

136. The ECOFIN meetings perform the same coordinative function among European finance ministers as does the G20 finance ministers discussed in chapter three.

137. Peter Coy, "Keynes vs. Alesina: Alesina Who?" Bloomberg Businessweek Magazine, June 29, 2012, http://www.businessweek.com/stories/2010-06-29/keynes-vs-dot-alesina-dot-alesina-who.

138. Alberto Alesina and Silvia Ardanga, "Large Changes in Fiscal Policy: Taxes Versus Spending," NBER working paper 15434, Cambridge, MA, October 2009.

139. Milton Friedman and Rose Friedman (1962), *Capitalism and Freedom* (Chicago: University of Chicago Press, 1982), vii.

140. Alesina and Ardanga, "Large Changes," 15.

141. Ibid., 3.

142. Ibid., 4.

143. Ibid., 5.

144. Ibid., 9.

145. Ibid., 12.

146. Ibid.

147. Ibid., 13.

148. Ibid. It was, I think, Robert Solow who once remarked, Why is it in such models that when the government buys a typewriter it's a dead loss, yet when the worst author buys one, so long as he resides in the private sector, it leads to growth?

149. Alberto Alesina, "Fiscal Adjustment: Lesson From History." Paper prepared for the Ecofin meeting in Madrid, April 15, 2010, available from http://www.economics.harvard.edu/files/faculty/2_Fiscal%20Adjustments_lessons.pdf.

150. Ibid., 4.

151. Ibid., 7.

152. Ibid., 10.

153. Ibid.

154. Anis Chowdhury, "Revisiting the Evidence on Expansionary Austerity: Alesina's Hour." VoxEU, February 28, 2012, http://www.voxeu.org/debates/commentaries/revisiting-evidence-expansionary-fiscal-austerity-alesina-s-hour.

155. Keynes, *General Theory*, 3.

156. Ibid.

CHAPTER SIX

1. Note that for the purposes at hand I am not trying to show that the Keynesians or anyone else was "correct" and that reflationary policies saved the day. All I need to do here is to show that austerity did not, as the British say, do what it says it does on the tin. Proving Keynes right is not necessary to prove austerity wrong. My target here is more limited. For what it's worth, he was right, but that's in another book. See Blyth, *Great Transformations*.

2. Ralph Benko, "Signs of the Gold Standard Are Emerging from Germany," *Forbes*, September 24, 2012, http://www.forbes.com/sites/ralphbenko/2012/09/24/signs-of-the-gold-standard-are-emerging-from-germany/; and Robin Harding and Anna Fifield, "Republicans Eye Return to Gold Standard," *Financial Time*, August 23, 2012, http://www.cnbc.com/id/48770752/Republicans_Eye_Return_to_Gold_Standard.

3. Liaquat Ahamed, *Lords of Finance* (New York: Penguin Books, 2009); Fred L. Block, *The Origins of the International Economic Disorder* (Berkeley: University of California Press, 1977); Karl Polanyi, *The Great Transformation* (Boston: Beacon Press, 1984); Barry Eichengreen, *Golden Fetters: The Gold Standard and the Great Depression 1919–1939* (New York: Oxford University Press, 1992).

4. Because you can print it by fiat (by command) of government.

5. "Conventional" meaning you think it's valuable because other people think its it's valuable—it's a convention.

6. More specifically, if holders of foreign cash want money that they can spend locally, they can take that foreign paper to their local bank and exchange it for a discount (think buying and selling currency after a trip abroad), or they can take it back to the home country and exchange it there "at par" for gold and buy their own currency at par at home with the gold received. As such, you can hold it, and it will hold its value.

7. Think of the famous Cross of Gold speech by William Jennings Bryant as the agricultural equivalent of the industrial workers' demands for unions to control wages.

8. Five, including the special case of financial repression. See conclusion.

9. Again, if you are thinking Eurozone here, you are not wrong.

10. Eichengreen, *Golden Fetters*, 9.

11. Miguel Almunia et al., "From Great Depression to Great Credit Crisis," NBER Working Paper 15524, Cambridge, MA, November 2009.

12. Fred Block, *The Origins of the International Economic Disorder* (Berkeley: University of California Press, 1977).

13. Block, *Origins*, 20.

14. Also at play here was the "seniority swap" that occurred when the 1929 Young Plan for reparations payments reversed the credit-default seniority of commercial claims over reparations claims that were present in the previous Dawes plan arrangements. Once this credit-protection clause was removed in 1929, commercial (i.e., American) capital evacuated Germany. For a discussion of this phenomena, see Albrecht Ritschl, "The German Transfer Problem, 1920–1933: A Sovereign Debt Perspective," London School of Economics, Center for Economic Performance, Discussion Paper No. 1155, July 2012, http://cep.lse.ac.uk/pubs/download/dp1155.pdf.

15. Eichengreen, *Golden Fetters*, 226.

16. The cases in question are the contractions undertaken by German and the new Eastern European states in the period 1920–1921. The United States is sometimes cited as a case of expansionary austerity in this period too. For why this is not the case, see Daniel Kuehn, "A Note on America's 1920–21 Depression as an Argument for Austerity," *Cambridge Journal of Economics*, 36 (2012): 155–160.

17. Eichengreen, *Golden Fetters*, 123.

18. Herbert Stein, *The Fiscal Revolution in America: Policy in Pursuit of Reality* (Washington DC: AEI Press, 1996), 14.

19. Ibid., 20.

20. Stein, "Fiscal Revolution," 26.

21. Ibid., 31.

22. Herbert Hoover, State Papers, vol. 2, 105, quoted in Dean L. May, *From New Deal to New Economics: the American Liberal Response to the Recession of 1937* (New York: Garland Press, 1981), 33.

23. United States Bureau of the Census, Historical Statistics, Colonial Times to 1957, Washington DC, 1960, 70.

24. Although if you are interested, see Mark Blyth, "Beyond the Usual Suspects: Ideas, Uncertainty and Building Institutional Orders," *International Studies Quarterly 51*, 4 (December 2007): 747–759.

25. Blyth, *Great Transformations*, 74–77.

26. Franklin D. Roosevelt, *The Public Papers and Addresses of Franklin D. Roosevelt*, vol. 7 (New York: Macmillan, 1938), 236–247.

27. Block, *Origins*; Charles P. Kindleberger, *The World in Depression, 1929–1939* (Berkeley: University of California Press, 1986).

28. N. F. R. Crafts, "Long Term Unemployment in Britain in the 1930s," *Economic History Review 40*, 3 (1987): 427.
29. Eichengreen, *Golden Fetters*, 283.
30. IMF World Economic Outlook, "The Good the Bad and the Ugly," in *Coping with High Debt and Sluggish Growth*, chap. 3, October 2012, 110. http://www.imf.org/external/pubs/ft/weo/2012/02/pdf/text.pdf.
31. Ibid., 111.
32. Erik Lundberg, "The Rise and Fall of the Swedish Model," *Journal of Economic Literature* 23 (March 1985): 5.
33. Ibid.
34. Gustav Cassel quoted in Villy Bergstrom, "Party Program and Economic Policy: The Social Democrats in Government," in *Creating Social Democracy: A Century of the Social Democratic Labor Party in Sweden*, ed. Klaus Misgeld et al. (University Park: Pennsylvania State University Press, 2000), 136.
35. Sheri Berman, *The Social Democratic Moment: Ideas and Politics in the Making of Interwar Europe* (Cambridge, MA: Harvard University Press, 1998), 154.
36. Bergstrom "Party Program," 138.
37. Blyth, *Great Transformations*, 113–115.
38. Benny Carlson, "The Long Retreat: Gustav Cassel and Eli Heckscher on the 'New Economics' of the 1930s," in *Swedish Economic Thought: Explorations and Advances*, ed. Lars Jonung (London: Routledge, 1987), p. 181.
39. Sven Steinmo, "Political Institutions and Tax Policy in the United States, Sweden, and Britain," *World Politics 41*, 4 (July 1989): 500–535.
40. Blyth, *Great Transformations*, 119–123.
41. Rudolph Meidner, "Our Concept of the Third Way: Some Remarks on the Sociopolitical Tenets of the Swedish Labor Movement." *Economic and Industrial Democracy 1*, 3 (August 1980): 349.
42. Mancur Olson, "How Bright are the Northern Lights? Some Questions about Sweden," Institute of Economic Research, Lund University, 1991.
43. Eichengreen, *Golden Fetters*, 128.
44. Ritschl, "The German Transfer Problem," 7.
45. Schact (1927), 76, in Eichengreen, *Golden Fetters*, 136.
46. Eichengreen, *Golden Fetters*, 139.
47. Berman, *Social Democratic Moment*, 178.
48. And the Young Plan's subordination of commerical debt. See Ritschl, "German Transfer Problem," 8–13.
49. Eichengreen, *Golden Fetters*, x.
50. Wilhelm Dittman quoted in Berman, *Social Democratic Moment*, 189.
51. Ibid.
52. Hilferding quoted in Berman, *Social Democratic Moment*, 192.
53. Fritz Naphtali, quoted in Berman, *Social Democratic Moment*, 193.
54. Wirtschaftliches Sofortprogramm der N.S.D.A.P. (Munich: Eher Verlag, 1932). Available at http://www.calvin.edu/academic/cas/gpa/sofortprogramm.htm.
55. Adam Tooze, *The Wages of Destruction: The Making and Breaking of the Nazi Economy* (New York: Penguin Books, 2006).
56. John Maynard Keynes, "The United States and the Keynes Plan," *New Republic*, July 29, 1940, quoted in Bill Janeway, *Doing Capitalism in the Innovation Economy* (Cambridge: Cambridge University Press, 2012), 254.

57. "From Those Wonderful Folks That Brought You Pearl Harbor" is the title of a book that inspired the TV show *Mad Men*. See http://en.wikipedia.org/wiki/Jerry_Della_Femina. I use it here not to be funny but because it's fundamentally accurate. Austerity empowered the Japanese military, and so it brought the world Pearl Harbor.

58. Jonathan Kirshner, *Appeasing the Bankers: Financial Caution on the Road to War* (Princeton, NJ: Princeton University Press 2007), 62.

59. Yuji Kuronuma, "Showa Depression: A Prescription for 'Once in a Century' Crisis." Japan Center for Economic Research, Research Paper, April 2009, 2.

60. Koichi Hamada and Asahi Noguchi, "The Role of Preconceived Ideas in Macroeconomic Policy: Japan's Experiences in Two Deflationary Episodes." Economic Growth Center, Yale University, Discussion Paper Number 908, New Haven, CT, March 2005, http://www.econ.yale.edu/growth_pdf/cdp908.pdf.

61. Kirshner, *Appeasing the Bankers*, 62–63.

62. Quoted in Hamada and Noguchi, "Role of Preconceived Ideas," 20.

63. Ibid.

64. Ibid.

65. Hamada and Noguchi, "Role of Preconceived Ideas," 16–17.

66. Ibid., 17.

67. Junnosuke Inoue, "The Repeal of the Gold Embargo: An Appeal to All the Nation," quoted in Hamada and Noguchi, "Role of Preconceived Ideas," 17.

68. Kirshner, *Appeasing the Bankers*, 71–72.

69. Kuronuma, "Showa Depression," 2.

70. Kirshner, *Appeasing the Bankers*, 72.

71. Ibid., 68.

72. Ibid., 69.

73. Ibid., 72.

74. Kuronuma, "Showa Depression," 3.

75. Ibid., 3; Kirshner, *Appeasing the Bankers*, 78.

76. Kuronuma, "Showa Depression," 3.

77. Kirshner, *Appeasing the Bankers*, 83.

78. Eichengreen, *Golden Fetters*, xx.

79. Ibid., 173.

80. Ibid., 174.

81. Ibid.

82. Stephen Schuker, "France and the Remilitarization of the Rhineland, 1936," *French Historical Studies 14*, 3 (1986): 332.

83. "These powerful oligarchs appointed the fifteen regents and three auditors who, along with the governor and assistant governors, managed the affairs of the bank," Kirshner, *Appeasing the Bankers*, 96.

84. Ibid., 97.

85. Ibid., 98–99.

86. Ibid., 100–104.

87. As Kirshner puts it, "While it is true that finance did not actually push Flandin overboard, it did lean him over the railing, life preserver in hand, and shout questions about how cold the water was," ibid., 103.

88. Eichengreen, *Golden Fetters*, 371.

89. Ibid., 376.

90. Kirshner, *Appeasing the Bankers*; and Stephen Schuker, "France and the Remilitarization of the Rhineland, 1936," *French Historical Studies 14*, 3 (1986): 299–338.

91. Kirshner, *Appeasing the Bankers*, 108.

92. Ibid., 121.

93. Schuker, "France and the Remilitarization," 330–331.

94. James Thomas Emmerson, *The Rhineland Crisis: A Study in Multilateral Diplomacy*, (Ames: Iowa State University Press, 1977), 80.

95. Francesco Giavazzi and Marco Pagano, "Can Severe Fiscal Contractions Be Expansionary? Tales of Two Small European Countries," NBER Working Paper 3372, May 1990, http://www.nber.org/papers/w3372.

96. Ibid., 12.

97. Alberto Alesina and Roberto Perotti, "Fiscal Expansions and Adjustments in OECD Economies," *Economic Policy 21* (1995): 207–247.

98. Ibid., 514. Recall that for Giavazzi and Pagano Denmark was the positive case and Ireland was mixed.

99. Alberto Alesina and Silvia Ardagna, "Tales of Fiscal Adjustment," *Economic Policy 13*, 27 (1998): 516.

100. Alberto Alesina and Silvia Ardanga, "Large Changes in Fiscal Policy: Taxes Versus Spending," National Bureau of Economic Research, Working Paper 15438, 2009, 12.

101. Alesina and Ardanga, "Tales," 528.

102. Roberto Perotti, "The 'Austerity Myth': Pain Without Gain," unpublished manuscript, June 16, 2011. Published as Bank of International Settlements Working Paper 362, December 2011, http://www.bis.org/publ/work362.htm.

103. Michael Ulf Bergman and Michael Hutchinson, "Expansionary Fiscal Contractions: Re-Evaluating the Danish Case," *International Economic Journal 24*, 1 (2010): 71–93.

104. See Jamie Guajardo, Daniel Leigh, and Andrea Pescatori, "Expansionary Austerity: New International Evidence" IMF Working Paper 11/158, July 2011, 33. Available at http://www.imf.org/external/pubs/ft/wp/2011/wp11158.pdf.

105. Alesina and Ardanga, "Tales," 534–535.

106. Ibid., 516.

107. Stephen Kinsella, "Is Ireland Really the Role Model for Austerity?" *Cambridge Journal of Economics 36*, 1, (2012): 223–235.

108. Ibid., 233.

109. John Considine and James Duffy, "Tales of Expansionary Fiscal Contractions in Two European Countries: Hindsight and Foresight," Department of Economics, National University of Ireland, Galway, working paper series 120, July 2007, 11.

110. Roberto Perotti, "The 'Austerity Myth': Pain without Gain," unpublished manuscript, June 16, 2011. Quote from p. 5. Published as Bank of International Settlements Working Paper 362, December 2011.

111. Ibid., 234.

112. Ibid.

113. Ibid.

114. Roberto Perotti also notes that the Irish expansion is "much less remarkable than previously thought." See Perotti, "The 'Austerity Myth,'" 4.

115. John Quiggin, "Expansionary Austerity: Some Shoddy Scholarship," available at http://crookedtimber.org/2011/10/24/expansionary-austerity-some-shoddy-scholarship/.

116. Ibid.

117. Ibid.
118. Franceso Giavazzi and Marco Pagano, "Non-Keynesian Effects of Fiscal Policy Changes: International Evidence and the Swedish Experience." NBER working paper 5322, Cambridge, MA, November 1995.
119. Ibid., 3.
120. Ibid., 19.
121. Ibid., 20.
122. Ibid., 21.
123. Ibid., 21–22.
124. Ibid., 23.
125. Ibid., 24.
126. Ibid., 29. The word "laxitude" is theirs.
127. Peter Englund, "The Swedish Banking Crisis: Roots and Consequences" Oxford Review of Economic Policy 15, 3 (1999): 89.
128. Ibid., 94.
129. Richard Koo, "The World in Balance Sheet Recession," Real-World Economics Review 58 (2011): 19–37.
130. Roberto Perotti's discussion of Sweden in "The 'Austerity Myth'" is a vastly superior account of the Swedish experience that concludes that what made the difference wasn't expectations—it was exports. See especially, 37–41.
131. Arjun Jayadev and Mike Konczal, "The Boom Not the Slump: The Right Time for Austerity." The Roosevelt Institute, August 23, 2010. Available at http://www.rooseveltinstitute.org/sites/all/files/not_the_time_for_austerity.pdf
132. Ibid., 1.
133. Ibid., 2.
134. See Daniel Leigh (team leader), Pete Devries, Charles Freedman, Jaime Guajardo, Douglas Laxton, and Andrea Pescatori, "Will It Hurt? Macroeconomic Effects of Fiscal Consolidation" IMF World Economic Outlook, October 2010, http://www.imf.org/external/pubs/ft/weo/2010/02/pdf/3sum.pdf, and http://www.imf.org/external/pubs/ft/weo/2010/02/pdf/c3.pdf.
135. Ibid., 94.
136. Specifically, the authors argue that a 1-percent of GDP budget cut leads to a half a percent reduction in GDP and a third of a percent increase in unemployment over two years, ibid.
137. Ibid.
138. Ibid.
139. Ibid.
140. For the Republicans' pick-up see http://www.frumforum.com/gops-new-line-budget-cuts-bring-boom-times/. For the CRS study, see Jane G. Gravelle and Thomas L. Hungerford "Can Contractionary Fiscal Policy be Expansionary?" Congressional Research Service 7–5700 R41849, June 6, 2011.
141. Ibid., 12.
142. Ibid., 15.
143. Perotti, "'Austerity Myth.'"
144. Ibid., 6.
145. Jamie Guajardo, Daniel Leigh, and Andrea Pescatori, "Expansionary Austerity: New International Evidence" IMF Working Paper 11/158, July 2011, 5. Available at http://www.imf.org/external/pubs/ft/wp/2011/wp11158.pdf.

146. Ibid., 29.

147. Nicoletta Batini, Giovanni Callegari, and Giovanni Melina, "Successful Austerity in the United States, Europe and Japan," IMF Working Paper 12/190, July 2012. Available at http://www.imf.org/external/pubs/ft/wp/2012/wp12190.pdf.

148. Ibid., 7. My italics.

149. Ibid., 8.

150. IMF World Economic and Financial Surveys, World Economic Outlook, "Coping with High Debt and Sluggish Growth," October 2012. www.imf.org/pubs/ft/weo/2012/02/index.htm.

151. Christine Lagarde, "Latvia and the Baltics: A Story of Recovery," Riga, June 5, 2012. http://www.imf.org/external/np/speeches/2012/060512.htm; International Monetary Fund, A Conference on "Lessons From the Recovery in the Baltics," Riga, The Great Guild, June 5, 2012, http://www.imf.org/external/np/seminars/eng/2012/latvia/index.htm.

152. Jörg Asmussen, Member of the Executive Board of the ECB, introductory remarks to panel "Lessons from Latvia and the Baltics," Riga, June 5, 2012, http://www.ecb.int/press/key/date/2012/html/sp120605.en.html.

153. Deutsche Welle, "IMF Hails Latvia's Austerity Drive as Eurozone Model," http://www.dw.de/dw/article/0,,15999966,00.html.

154. Olivier Blanchard, "Lessons from Latvia," IMF Direct, http://blog-imfdirect.imf.org/2012/06/11/lessons-from-latvia/.

155. Neil Buckley, "Myths and Truths of the Baltic Austerity Model" *Financial Times*, June 28, 2012, http://blogs.ft.com/the-world/2012/06/myths-and-truths-of-the-baltic-austerity-model/.

156. The role of all the REBLL countries, including Romania and Bulgaria, in defending the cause of fiscal austerity was acknowledged by Chancellor Angela Merkel in a historical speech before the German Parliament in December 2011, "Merkel Outlines Euro Crisis Stance before Summit," http://www.reuters.com/article/2011/12/02/eurzone-merkel-highlights-idUSL5E7N21JP20111202.

157. Romania was a partial exception insofar as its exports tripled in value over the 2000s, but even that was not enough to close its ballooning current account deficit. I thank Cornel Ban for this correction.

158. Stijn Claessens and Neeltje van Horen "Foreign Banks: Trends, Impact and Financial Stability," International Monetary Fund Working Paper, January 2012, http://www.imf.org/external/pubs/ft/wp/2012/wp1210.pdf.

159. Daniela Gabor, *Central Banks and Financialization: A Romanian Account of How Eastern Europe Became Sub-Prime* (Basingstoke: Palgrave Macmillan, 2010).

160. For house price growth in the new member states and its connection with the forex credit bubble, see Ray Barrell, Phillip Davis, Tatiana Fic, and Ali Orgazani, "Housegold Debt and Foreign Currency Borrowing in the New Member States of the EU," Working Paper no. 09–23, Brunel University, West London, 6–8.

161. Ralph De Haas, Yevgeniya Korniyenko, Elena Loukoianova, and Alexander Pivovarsky, "The Vienna Initiative and Financial Stability in Emerging Europe," VoxEU, April 4, 2012, http://www.voxeu.org/article/financial-stability-emerging-europe-vienna-initiative.

162. The Vienna Initiative was triggered by written letters sent to the European Commission by a number of West European Banks that had heavy exposures in Eastern Europe. See R. De Haas, Y. Korniyenko, E. Loukoianova, and A. Pivovarsky, "Foreign

Banks and the Vienna Initiative: Turning Sinners into Saints," EBRD Working Paper No. 143, London, 2012. Wolfgang Nitsche, "The Vienna Initiative/European Bank Coordination Initiative: Assessment and Outlook," Austrian Ministry of Finance, Working Paper 4/2010, 1–20. http://www.bmf.gv.at/Publikationen/Downloads/WorkingPapers/WP_4_2010_The_Vienna_Initiative.pdf.

163. Based on data presented in Gabriele Giudice, Ingrid Toming, Francesco di Comite, and Julia Lendvai "Fiscal Consolidation in the Midst of Crisis," European Commission, D.G. ECFIN, March 1, 2012, http://ec.europa.eu/economy_finance/events/2012/2012–03–01-lv_semminar/pdf/fiscal_consolidation_inthe_en.pdf.

164. Statement by Dominique Strauss Kahn on French channel Canal 6, May 20, 2010, file available at http://media.hotnews.ro/media_server1/audio-2010–05–21–7300052–0-dominique-strauss-kahn.mp3. For an analysis of the context, see Cornel Ban, "Crunch Time in Romania's Austerity Plans," *Osservatorio Balcani e Caucaso*, May 28, 2010.

165. Victoria Stoiciu, "Austerity and Structural Reforms in Romania," International Policy Analysis Series, Friedrich Ebert Stiftung, Berlin, August 2012. http://library.fes.de/pdf-files/id-moe/09310.pdf.

166. Neil Buckley, "Latvia Weighs Human Costs of Its Austerity Programme," *Financial Times*, November 6, 2011, http://www.ft.com/intl/cms/s/0/6fb57f46–0717–11e1–90de-00144feabdc0.html#axzz28AyZGXsw; Iyantul Islam, "Latvia: Why We Need to Go beyond the "Success" of Fiscal Austerity" *Social Europe Journal*, June 18, 2012, http://www.social-europe.eu/2012/06/latvia-why-we-need-to-go-beyond-the-success-of-fiscal-austerity/.

167. Eurobarometer (2009) National Report, Executive Summary, Latvia, No.72, European Commission, available at http://ec.europa.eu/public_opinion/archives/eb/eb72/eb72_lv_en_exec.pdf; [22] Eurobarometer (2011) First Results, No.76, European Commission, available at http://ec.europa.eu/public_opinion/archives/eb/eb76/eb76_first_en.pdf.

168. Iyanatul Islam and Anis Chowdhury "Latvia: Going Beyond the Fiscal Austerity Debate" VoxEU, June 27, 2012, http://www.voxeu.org/debates/commentaries/latvia-going-beyond-fiscal-austerity-debate-1; International Monetary Fund, Republic of Latvia: Article IV and Second Post-Program Monitoring Discussions, Concluding Statement of IMF Mission, November 26, 2012, http://www.imf.org/external/np/ms/2012/112612.htm.

169. European Commission, "European Economic Forecast: Spring 2012."

170. Islam and Chowdhury, "Latvia: Going Beyond," 2012.

171. Mark Weisbrot and Rebecca Ray, Center for Economic and Policy Research, "Latvia's Internal Devaluation: A Success Story?" December 2011, 9.

172. Zsolt Darvas, "Internal Adjustment of the Real Exchange Rate: Does It Work?" VoxEU, July 6, 2012. http://www.voxeu.org/article/internal-adjustment-real-exchange-rate-does-it-work

173. Latvia's public debt went up from 10 percent of GDP in 2008 to 40 percent of GDP in 2012.

174. Michael Hudson and Jeffrey Sommers, "Latvia Is No Model for an Austerity Drive," *Financial Times*, June 21, 2012, http://www.ft.com/intl/cms/s/0/73314cbe- baee-11-e1–81e0–00144feabdc0.html#axzz27yGkORAr. Ethnic politics were less prominent in Estonia, where the driving forces of austerity were the strength of economic neoliberalism among elites, weak state institutions, and prior experiences with austerity.

See Ringa Raudla and Rainer Kattel, "Why Did Estonia Choose Fiscal Retrenchment after the 2008 Crisis?" *Journal of Public Policy 31*, 2 (2011): 163–186.

175. Ironically, the ethnic card was played by Romanian dictator Nicolae Ceausescu in an earlier austerity binge during the 1980s that ultimately contributed to his regime's violent demise. See Cornel Ban, "Sovereign Debt, Austerity and Regime Change: The Case of Nicolae Ceausescu's Romania," *East European Politics and Societies* (forthcoming, 2013).

CHAPTER SEVEN

1. Al Jazeera, Prostitution on the Rise in Crisis Hit Spain, video, posted August 4, 2012, http://www.aljazeera.com/video/europe/2012/08/20128474948466393.html; Liz Alderman, "Amid Cutbacks, Greek Doctors offer Message to Poor: You are Not Alone," *New York Times*, October 24, 2012, http://www.nytimes.com/2012/10/25/world/europe/greek-unemployed-cut-off-from-medical-treatment.html?pagewanted=all&_r=0.

2. Barry Eichengreen, *Golden Fetters: The Gold Standard and the Great Depression 1919–1939* (New York: Oxford University Press, 1996).

3. Eric Helleiner, *States and the Reemergence of Global Finance: From Breton Woods to the 1990s* (Ithaca, NY: Cornell University Press, 1994).

4. See Emily Cadman, Steve Bernard, and Tom Braithwaite, "Investment Banking by Numbers," *Financial Times*, October 1, 2012, see http://www.ft.com/intl/cms/s/0/6dafe58e-0972–11e2-a5a9–00144feabdco.html#axzz28A9VDZXo for some data.

5. Gillian Tett, "Banking May Lose Its Allure for the Best and Brightest: The Really Stark Relative Shrinkage of Finance Might Lie Ahead," *Financial Times*, October 31, 2012, http://www.ft.com/intl/cms/s/0/de219c48–235f-11e2-a66b-00144feabdco.html#axzz2FKXtAl2V; Brett Philbin, "Wall Street Could Shrink, Pay Smaller Bonuses," Marketwatch, October 9, 2012, http://www.marketwatch.com/story/wall-street-could-shrink-pay-smaller-bonuses-2012–10–09.

6. Alex Preston, "£1 million Isn't Rich Any More: The Rise and Fall of Investment Banking," *New Statesman*, October 3, 2012, http://www.newstatesman.com/business/business/2012/10/1m-isnt-rich-anymore-rise-and-fall-of-investment-banking.

7. Ian Guider and Louisa Nesbitt, "Ireland Bails Out Stricken Banks with $7.7 Billion." *Bloomberg*, December 22, 2008, http://www.bloomberg.com/apps/news?pid=newsarchive&sid=aMeWECsf8.oU; John Murray-Brown and Neil Dennis, "Ireland Guarantees Six Banks' Deposits." *Financial Times*, September 30, 2008, http://www.ft.com/intl/cms/s/.

8. Fintan O'Toole, "Let's End Charade before EU Chiefs Get More Power," *Irish Times*, November 29, 2011, http://www.irishtimes.com/newspaper/opinion/2011/1129/1224308280035.html.

9. "NAMA Won't Be Part of National Debt," *RTE.ie*. http://www.rte.ie/news/2009/1020/nama-business.html; "Government Fights to Keep NAMA Debt Off Its Books," http://www.independent.ie/business/irish/government-fights-to-keep-nama-debt-off-its-books-3078860.html.

10. Jean Claude Trichet, quoted in Stephen Kinsella "Is Ireland Really the Role Model for Austerity?" *Cambridge Journal of Economics* 36 (2012): 223.

11. Liz Alderman, "In Ireland, Austerity Is Praised, but Painful," *New York Times*, December 5, 2011, http://www.nytimes.com/2011/12/06/business/global/despite-praise-for-its-austerity-ireland-and-its-people-are-being-battered.html?_r=2&hpw&.

12. Alderman, "In Ireland."
13. Enterprise Ireland, "Start a Business in Ireland," government website, http://www. enterprise-ireland.com/en/Start-a-Business-in-Ireland/Startups-from-Outside-Ireland/ Why-Locate-in-Ireland-/Start-Up-friendly-environment.html; http://www.doingbusi- ness.org/rankings.
14. "OECD Tax Database," http://www.oecd.org/tax/taxpolicyanalysis/oecdtaxdatabase. htm#vat.
15. Office of Central Statistics, "Measuring Ireland's Progress 2010," http://www.cso.ie/ en/newsandevents/pressreleases/2011pressreleases/measuringirelandsprogress2010/.
16. World Bank, "Exports of goods and services (% of GDP)." http://data.worldbank.org/ indicator/NE.EXP.GNFS.ZS.
17. Martin Malone, Mint Partners, client analysis, July 2012. Personal Communication.
18. O'Toole, "Let's End Charade."
19. Robert Wade, "Iceland as Icarus," *Challenge* 52, 3 (May/June 2009): 5–33; Robert Wade and Sigurbjörg Sigurgeirsdóttir. "Iceland's Rise, Fall, Stabilisation and Beyond," *Cambridge Journal of Economics* 36 (2012): 127–144.
20. Report of the Special Investigation Commission (SIC) on the Causes of the Icelandic Banking Crisis, April 12, 2010, http://sic.althingi.is/pdf/RNAvefKafli2Enska.pdf.
21. The IMF sounded an early alarm in its 2006 Article IV Consultation. IMF, Iceland, 2006 Article IV consultation concluding statement, May 15, 2006, http://www.imf.org/ external/np/ms/2006/051506.htm.
22. "Republic of Iceland—Fitch Report November 2006." http://www.bonds.is/ news-analysisrating/credit-rating-news/sovereign-credit-rating/nanar/6565/ republic-of-iceland-fitch-report-november-2006.
23. The banks also set up online deposit accounts in Britain, Holland, and elsewhere to pump money into the country. This was the birth of the Icesave, which later became a source of serious diplomatic contention among Iceland, Britain, and Holland. Then the crisis hit.
24. Act No. 125/2008: On the Authority for Treasury Disbursements due to Unusual Financial Market Circumstances, etc. http://www.tryggingarsjodur.is/modules/files/ file_group_26/fréttir/Act_No125-2008.pdf.
25. Report of the Special Investigation Commission (SIC) on the Causes of the Icelandic Banking Crisis, vol. 7, 84–85.
26. Thorolfur Matthiasson and Sigrun Davidsdottir, "State Costs of the 2008 Icelandic Financial Collapse," *Economonitor*, December 5, 2012, http://www.economonitor. com/blog/2012/12/state-costs-of-the-2008-icelandic-financial.
27. "Iceland Debt to GDP," http://www.tradingeconomics.com/iceland/government- debt-to-gdp.
28. Statistics Iceland, http://www.statice.is/.
29. "Iceland—2012 Article IV Consultation Concluding Statement of the IMF Mission," http://www.imf.org/external/np/ms/2012/030212.htm.
30. "Iceland—2012 Article IV Consultation."
31. Stefán Ólafsson and Arnaldur Sölvi Kristjánsson, "Income Inequality in a Bubble Economy: The Case of Iceland 1992–2008," conference paper for Luxembourg Income Study Conference, June 2010, http://www.lisproject.org/conference/papers/ olafsson-kristjansson.pdf.
32. Statistics Iceland, http://www.statice.is/.
33. Statistics Iceland, http://www.statice.is/.

34. Ólafsson and Kristjánsson, "Risk of poverty and income distribution 2011," Iceland Statistics, March 26, 2012, http://www.statice.is/.

35. Bill Janeway objects to this parable of Ireland and Iceland for two reasons (personal communication, November 4, 2012). First, it underplays the systemic risk generated by failing banks in larger economies. Second, as well as bail or fail, there is a third option, which can be thought of as "bail, reform, and then send to jail." Both objections are valid. But, as to the first, while the costs of austerity are massive, real, and lasting, the costs of systemic risk are, if there is always a bailout, hypothetical. To assume that the disease is always worse than the cure gives banks a license to extort taxpayers. As to the second objection, while the possibility of "jail for bail" remains theoretically attractive, the actuality of banks repeatedly paying fines for misdeeds suggests that this particular reform path may be more closed than we like to admit.

36. Carmen Reinhart and M. Belen Sbrancia, "The Liquidation of Government Debt" National Bureau of Economic Research Working Paper 16893, March 2011.

37. Ibid., 3.

38. Ibid., 5.

39. Jake Tapper, "General Electric Paid no Taxes in 2010," ABC News, March 25, 2011, http://abcnews.go.com/Politics/general-electric-paid-federal-taxes-2010/story?id=13224558#.UHb2avl26mk.

40. Thomas L. Hungerford, "Taxes and the Economy: An Analysis of the Top Tax Rates Since 1945," Congressional Research Service R42729, September 14, 2012, 1.

41. Ibid., 16.

42. Ibid.

43. Glenn Hubbard, "Forget the Debt Ceiling and Focus on Debt," Financial Times, May 26, 2011, http://www.ft.com/intl/cms/s/0/87607668–878e-11e0-af98–00144feabdc0.html#axzz28v5uYiL5.

44. "Mitt Romney Says 'Redistribution' Has 'Never Been a Characteristic of America.'" PolitiFact, accessed December 14, 2012, http://www.politifact.com/truth-o-meter/statements/2012/sep/20/mitt-romney/mitt-romney-says-redistribution-has-never-been-cha/.

45. Stefan Bach and Gert Wagner, "Capital Levies for Debt Redemption" VoxEU, 15, August 2012, http://www.voxeu.org/article/eurozone-crisis-time-tax-rich.

46. Stefan Bach, Giacomo Corneo, and Viktor Steiner, "Optimal taxation of top incomes in Germany," VoxEU, June 29, 2011, http://www.voxeu.org/article/taxing-rich-case-germany.

47. Thomas Pikkety and Emmanuel Saez, "Taxing the 1%: Why the Top Tax Rate Could Be Over 80%," VoxEU, December 8, 2011, http://www.voxeu.org/article/taxing-7-why-top-tax-rate-could-be-over-80.

48. Peter Diamond and Emmanuel Saez, "The Case for a Progressive Tax: From Basic Research to Policy Recommendations," Journal of Economic Perspectives 25, 4: 165.

49. Ibid., 167.

50. David Jolly, "US and Switzerland Reach Deal in Sharing of Financial Account Data," New York Times, June 21, 2012, http://www.nytimes.com/2012/06/22/business/global/22iht-tax22.html.

51. James S. Henry, "The Price of Offshore Revisited: New Estimates for 'Missing' Global Private Wealth, Income, Inequality and Lost Taxes." Tax Justice Network, July 2012, 5, http://www.taxjustice.net/cms/upload/pdf/Price_of_Offshore_Revisited_120722.pdf.

POSTSCRIPT

1. With all due apologies to Winston Churchill. Original quote: "when you find yourself going through hell, keep going." Nice line, but very bad policy advice if the policy one persists with is fundamentally flawed.

2. See Richard Portes, "Drahgi has to do, as well as say, whatever it takes." *Financial Times*, August 21, 2014. http://www.ft.com/intl/cms/s/0/9f01f282-285e-11e4-9ea9-00144feabdc0.html#axzz3B3Usbmbx.

3. All figures in this postscript are taken from either Bloomberg.com or tradingeconomics.com unless otherwise indicated.

4. Mark Blyth, *Austerity: The History of a Dangerous Idea* (New York: Oxford University Press, 2013), 2.

5. Jean Claude Trichet, "Introductory Comments with Q and A," European Central Bank, Press Conference, May 7, 2009. http://www.ecb.europa.eu/press/pressconf/2009/html/is090507.en.html.

6. See Eric Lonergan, *Money*, 2nd ed. (London: Acumen Publishers, 2014), 165–166.

7. As the Brussels based think tank Brugel put it recently in a report that they prepared for the European Parliament, "European policy indecision…[and]…the unclear stance on debt restructuring in general…left many investors in a high state of uncertainty. This uncertainty weighed on sentiment and investment decisions." Directorate General for Internal Policies, Economic Governance Support Unit (EGOV), Committee Study on "The Troika and Financial Assistance in the Euro Area: Successes and Failures," (February 2014): 26. Available at http://www.bruegel.org/publications/publication-detail/publication/815-the-troika-and-financial-assistance-in-the-euro-area-successes-and-failures/.

8. See Paul DeGrauwe and Yuemei Ji, "Panic Driven Austerity in the Eurozone," available at http://www.voxeu.org/article/panic-driven-austerity-eurozone-and-its-implications.

9. Note the timing of this phase relative to Mario Drahgi's decisive intervention one month later.

10. Blyth, *Austerity*…84–87.

11. Oliver Wyman, "The Shape of Things to Come: What Recent History Tells US About the Future of European Banking," Oliver Wyman Consulting Group, August 2013, 14, available at http://www.oliverwyman.com/insights/publications/2013/oct/the-shape-of-things-to-come.html#.Uztu_K1dUxM.

12. Ibid.

13. Ibid., 3

14. See Matthias Matthijs and Mark Blyth (eds.) *The Future of the Euro* (New York: Oxford University Press, 2015),

15. See Ainsley Thompson and Paul Hannon, "IMF Sounds Warning on UK Austerity," available at http://online.wsj.com/news/articles/SB10001424127887324659404578498573982221716.

16. See Jonathan Portes, "What Osborne won't admit: growth has increased because of slower cuts," *New Statesman*, September 10, 2013, available at http://www.newstatesman.com/politics/2013/09/what-osborne-wont-admit-growth-has-increased-because-slower-cuts, and Simon Wren Lewis, "Osborne's Plan B," available at http://mainlymacro.blogspot.co.uk/2013/12/osbornes-plan-b.html.

17. For an excellent analysis of the disproportionate effect of UK budget cuts on low-income and disabled persons see Mary O'Hara, *Austerity Bites: A Journey to the Sharp End of the Cuts,* (Policy Press: Bristol, 2014).

18. See Simon Wren-Lewis, "Some Notes on the UK Recovery," available at http://mainlymacro.blogspot.co.uk/2013/12/some-notes-on-uk-recovery.html.

19. For typical reports see http://www.standard.co.uk/news/london/london-living-through-biggest-house-price-bubble-ever-9221297.html and http://www.ft.com/intl/cms/s/0/1f02ede2-8a8f-11e3-ba54-00144feab7de.html?siteedition=intl#axzz2xHDgYfaC.

20. "Affordable home ownership schemes," *GOV.UK*, 2014, https://www.gov.uk/affordable-home-ownership-schemes/help-to-buy-equity-loans.

21. Larry Elliott, "Bank of England poised to act over house price momentum," *The Guardian*, March 27, 2014, http://www.theguardian.com/business/2014/mar/27/bank-of-england-house-prices.

22. See *Trading Economics*, "United Kingdom Current Account," 2014, http://www.tradingeconomics.com/united-kingdom/current-account.

23. See Cynthia O'Murchu, "Tax Haven Buyers Set off Property Alarms in England and Wales," *Financial Times*, July 31, 2014, available at http://www.ft.com/intl/cms/s/0/6cb11114-18aa-11e4-a51a-00144feabdc0.html#axzz39YIQrTmo and Mark Blyth and Jonathan Hopkin, "Londongrad Calling," *Foreign Affairs*, April 21, 2014, available at, http://www.foreignaffairs.com/articles/141350/jonathan-hopkin-and-mark-blyth/londongrad-calling.

24. See *Trading Economics*, "United Kingdom Business Confidence," 2014, http://www.tradingeconomics.com/united-kingdom/business-confidence.

25. See *Bank of England*, "Trends in Lending," 2014, http://www.bankofengland.co.uk/publications/Pages/other/monetary/trendsinlending.aspx.

26. See *Independent Lending Review*, 2013, http://www.independentlendingreview.co.uk/index.htm.

27. See James Quinn, "Osborne to Tell Banks: Increase SME lending," *The Daily Telegraph*, May 24, 2014, available at http://www.telegraph.co.uk/finance/newsbysector/banksandfinance/10854724/Osborne-to-tell-banks-increase-SME-lending.html.

28. See Blyth, *Austerity* ... chapters five and six, for a discussion of this idea.

29. On the UK's tax put see "Higher Rate Tax Payers Pay Heaviest Burden" *Financial Times*, March 12, 2014, available at http://www.ft.com/intl/cms/s/0/2c5553b8-aa10-11e3-8497-00144feab7de.html#axzz2xHDgYfaC.

30. For an analysis of this dynamic see Mark Blyth and Richard Katz, "From Catch all Politics to Cartelization: The Political Economy of the Cartel Party," *Western European Politics*, vol. 28 (1), January 2005, 34-61, available at http://www.markblyth.com/wp-content/uploads/2013/08/Blythkatz.pdf.

31. Stephen Kinsella, "Post-Bailout Ireland as the Poster Child for Austerity," *Ireland's Recovery from Crisis*, (forthcoming, 2014), 2. The eight-year figure includes austerity budgets through 2016.

32. "The Troika and Financial Assistance in the Euro Area..." 36.

33. IMF financial soundness indicators cited in *Ibid.*, 38. See also https://www.centralbank.ie/publications/Documents/Macro-Financial%20Review%202013.2.pdf.

34. See lecture "Whatever Happened to Ireland?" by Professor Kelley available at https://www.youtube.com/watch?v=8LCofepdUzE&list=PLHKVjBSDqMB7OF1pdtOW6eRR5DUgBzuUU.

35. "The Troika and Financial Assistance in the Euro Area..." 36.

36. Kinsella, "Post-Bailout Ireland..." 5.
37. Although it doesn't stop everyone trying. David Cameron's support of the Loch Earn declaration on the need to tax global corporations being swiftly followed with a cut in UK corporation tax being a classic example.
38. See www.tradingeconomics.com/Portugal and "The Troika and Financial Assistance in the Euro Area..." 40.
39. "The Troika and Financial Assistance in the Euro Area..." 42.
40. "The Troika and Financial Assistance in the Euro Area..." 23
41. Ibid. from IMF data, figures 14 and 15, 24.
42. See "Greek Austerity Tragedy Shows Where not to Make Cuts," *New Scientist*, February 26, 2014, available at http://www.newscientist.com/article/dn25125-greek-austerity-tragedy-shows-where-not-to-make-cuts.html#.UztWtq1dWOx.
43. Mark Blyth, "Eternal Austerity Makes Sense: If You are Rich," available at http://www.theguardian.com/commentisfree/2013/nov/15/eternal-austerity-makes-sense-if-rich-david-cameron
44. For the definitive work, and numbers, on this topic see Thomas Piketty, *Capital in the 21st Century*, (Cambridge: Harvard Belknap Press, 2014).
45. I thank Eric Lonergan for this formulation.
46. See "European Parliament / Results of the 2014 European elections," http://www.results-elections2014.eu/en/election-results-2014.html.
47. Erik Jones, "The Forgotten Financial Union," in Matthijs and Blyth (eds.) *The Future of the Euro...* (forthcoming, 2015).
48. For a good overview of the banking union see http://europa.eu/rapid/press-release_MEMO-14-57_en.htm?locale=en.
49. Paul De Grauwe, quoted in "Europe Strikes Deal to Complete Banking Union," *Reuters*, March 20, 2014, available at http://www.reuters.com/article/2014/03/20/us-eu-bankingunion-idUSBREA2J0ZJ20140320.
50. See Thomas Huertas and María J. Nieto, "How much is enough? The case of the Resolution Fund in Europe," available at http://www.voxeu.org/article/ensuring-european-resolution-fund-large-enough.
51. That is, sovereigns could pool risk to raise capital for it more cheaply, but that would be debt mutualization and is thus beyond the pale.
52. The most comprehensive publicly available estimate of outstanding European NPLs comes from the consultancy Price Waterhouse Cooper. They estimate the total at 1.22 Trillion Euros. See Price Waterhouse Cooper, "European Portfolio Advisory Group: Market Update," July 2014, table one, 3, available at https://www.pwc.com/et_EE/EE/publications/assets/pub/euro_npls.pdf.
53. See for one example of why, Wolfgang Munchau, "This is not the Banking Union Europe is Looking for," available at http://www.ft.com/intl/cms/s/0/92bbb0a6-6330-11e3-886f-00144feabdc0.html#axzz2xZpym4NP.
54. See "Fitch Revises Outlooks on 18 EU State-sponsored Banks to Negative on Weakening Support," *Reuters*, March 26, 2014, http://www.reuters.com/article/2014/03/26/fitch-revises-outlooks-on-18-eu-state-sp-idUSFit69388220140326.
55. Ibid.
56. For an overview see http://www.ecb.europa.eu/press/pr/date/2012/html/pr120906_1.en.html.
57. I thank Bill Blain for this analogy.
58. Bill Blain, Personal Communication, December 11, 2013.

59. Available at http://european-council.europa.eu/media/639235/stootscg26_en12.pdf.
60. Fiscal Compact quoted in, Nicolas Jabko, "The Crisis of EU Institutions and the Weakness of Economic Governance," in Matthijs and Blyth (eds.) *The Future of the Euro*...(forthcoming, 2015), manuscript version, 16-17.
61. See http://ec.europa.eu/economy_finance/economic_governance/macroeconomic_imbalance_procedure/mip_scoreboard/.
62. See http://mobile.reuters.com/article/idUSBREA0D0MU20140114?irpc=932 and http://europa.eu/rapid/press-release_IP-14-216_en.htm and http://www.bloomberg.com/news/2014-01-15/germany-snubs-export-critics-as-surplus-outstrips-that-of-china.html.
63. Peter Hall, "Varieties of Capitalism and the Euro Crisis," presented at the International Conference of Europeanists, Washington DC, March 15, 2014.
64. Read the bits outside of the brackets first and then re-read the whole thing.
65. See Wolfgang Münchau, "Don't Kid Yourself that the Eurozone is Recovering," *Financial Times*, September 29, 2013, available at http://www.ft.com/intl/cms/s/0/99394460-26aa-11e3-bbeb-00144feab7de.html#axzz2xZpym4NP.
66. See Mamta Badkar, "The Era of Negative Interest Rates Has Begun," *Business Insider*, June 5, 2014, http://www.businessinsider.com/june-ecb-decision-2014-6.
67. See Claire Jones, "Eurozone Inflation Falls to a Fresh Low of 0.4 percent," http://www.ft.com/intl/cms/s/0/e8eabd1a-1892-11e4-a51a-00144feabdc0.html?siteedition=intl#axzz394degk4M.
68. Mark Blyth, "Europe's Goldilocks Dilemma," available at http://www.foreignpolicy.com/articles/2014/07/14/europe_goldilocks_dilemma_austerity_growth.
69. See Claire Jones and Sam Fleming, "EU Regulators Unveil Stress Tests for Banks," http://www.ft.com/intl/cms/s/0/bcc23a90-cf74-11e3-bec6-00144feabdco.html#axzz36nXwwv6s.
70. This is the reason why Oli Rhen, EU Commissioner for Economic and Monetary Affairs, said in an interview in El Pais 23rd January 2014 that "it will take another ten years to fix the Spanish crisis,"http://elpais.com/elpais/2014/01/23/inenglish/1390468961_868224.html.
71. "The Troika and Financial Assistance in the Euro Area..." 17–23.
72. "The Troika and Financial Assistance in the Euro Area..." 19–21.
73. Ibid.,. 22.
74. Hall, "Varieties of Capitalism and the Eurocrisis," table one, 9.
75. Ibid., 10.
76. Jonathan Hopkin, "The Troubled South: The Euro Crisis in Italy and Spain," in Matthijs and Blyth (eds.) *The Future of the Euro*...(forthcoming, 2015), manuscript version, 6.
77. Ibid., 6–7.
78. Pepper Culpepper, "The Political Economy of Unmediated Democracy: Italian Austerity Under Mario Monti," prepared for the International Conference of Europeanists, Washington DC, March 15, 2014, and Dani Rodrik, "Goodbye Washington Consensus, Hello Washington Confusion," *Journal of Economic Literature*, 44, 4, December 2006.
79. Ironically, just as the risk of inflation in a recession that haunts the Eurozone today is based upon a prior misreading of German history of the 1920s. See Blyth, *Austerity*... 56–57.

80. Christian Dustmann, Bernd Fitzenberger, Uta Schoenberg, and Alexandra Spitz-Oener, "From Sick Man of Europe to Economic Superstar: Germany's Resurgent Economy," *Journal of Economic Perspectives*, 28, 1, (Winter 2014), 167–188.

81. See http://inequalitywatch.eu/spip.php?article114

82. Cornel Ban, "Austerity versus Stimulus? Understanding Fiscal Policy Change at the International Monetary Fund Since the Great Recession," forthcoming in *Governance*, 2014.

83. For a summary see OECD http://www.oecd.org/eco/outlook/OECD-Forecast-post-mortem-policy-note.pdf.

84. See "Autumn economic forecast: sailing through rough waters," *European Commission*, http://ec.europa.eu/economy_finance/eu/forecasts/2012_autumn_forecast_en.htm#documents

85. See http://www.ecb.europa.eu/pub/pdf/mobu/mb201212en.pdf, box 6, 82–85.

86. Ban provides a useful mapping exercise of this shift in ideas in the fund. See Ban, "Austerity versus Stimulus?"

87. Andrea Pescatori, Damiano Sandri, and John Simon, "Debt and Growth: Is There a Magic Threshold?" IMF Working Paper, February 2014.

88. Howard Shneider, "Communists have seized the IMF," *Washington Post*, February 26, 2014, http://www.washingtonpost.com/blogs/wonkblog/wp/2014/02/26/communists-have-seized-the-imf/.

89. For an overview see http://en.wikipedia.org/wiki/Growth_in_a_Time_of_Debt.

90. Carmen Reinhardt and Kenneth Rogoff, "Recovery from Financial Crises: Evidence from 100 Episodes," NBER Working Paper 19823, January 2014.

91. Ibid., 10–11.

92. See Wolfgang Munchau, "The Real Scandal Is France's Stagnant Economic Thinking," available at http://www.ft.com/intl/cms/s/0/0a469808-7f6e-11e3-b6a7-00144feabdco.html#axzz2xZpym4NP.

INDEX

322 | INDEX